"A marvelous synthesis of Spain's history and culture, engagingly told and attractively illustrated."

Paul Smith, Professor Emeritus,
Department of Spanish and Portuguese, U.C.L.A.

"For a readable and thorough but not over-long account of Spanish history, *The Story of Spain* by Mark Williams is hard to beat."

Lonely Planet Guide to Spain

"Written in a style that clearly allows the reader to grasp the intricacies of Spain's historical elements."

Spain 21 Magazine

"The book features sixteen pages of splendid color illustrations."

Hispania

"The dramatic historical pageant of Spain is clearly presented in a sustained synthesis that engages the reader from first page to last."

Midwest Book Review

The Story of

The Dramatic History of Europe's
Most Fascinating Country

Mark R. Williams

GOLDEN ERA BOOKS

Library of Congress Cataloging in Publication data:
Williams, Mark R. 1949-
    The Story of Spain : the dramatic history of Europe's most
    fascinating country/Mark R. Williams. –2nd American ed.–
    San Mateo, CA : Golden Era Books, c2009.
            p. ; cm.
            ISBN: 978-0-9706969-3-9 ; 0-9706969-3-0
            Previous edition: 2004
            Includes bibliographical references and index.

        1. Spain–History 2. Historic sites–Spain–
        Guidebooks. I. Title.

DP66 .W55 2009   2009901403
946–dc22   0908

Cover designed by Einar Vinje, Walnut Creek, California

To Eleonore, once again,
and for Chico, who was there
in the beginning

About the Author

Acknowledgments

Mark R. Williams is a freelance writer living near San Francisco, California. He received his M.A. degree in History from the University of California (Santa Barbara) and did further studies at the University of Madrid.

Williams was Senior Contributor for *Lookout Magazine* (Spain) and Chief Editor of *Chevron USA/Odyssey* magazine. He has written for the *International Herald Tribune, El País, Washington Post, Los Angeles Times, San Francisco Chronicle, Diario 16* and many other newspapers and magazines. His books include *Northern California: Off the Beaten Path* (Seventh Edition, 2006) and *In Search of Lemuria* (2001).

For their guidance and influence during my graduate studies in history at the University of California (Santa Barbara), I would like to thank Harold Kirker, Joachim Remak, and Philip Powell. For his assistance during my studies at the University of Madrid and later suggestions for this book, I thank Richard Herr of the University of California (Berkeley). I must also thank Ken Welsh, who taught me how to persist, and Mark Little, a great editor and fine person who left us too soon. For their assistance with the design and production of this new edition, hats off to Vinje Design and Malloy, Inc. Finally, a word of appreciation to Ken and Arlene Brown, formerly of Lookout and Santana Books in Spain, for their generosity and gentility.

Contents

A Word About Names

The name "Iberia" is used mainly as a geographical term for the entire peninsula, including modern Spain, Portugal, and Andorra. With place names the Spanish spelling is retained except in special cases that would seem awkward. Thus Spain and the Canary Islands (not *España* and *Las Islas Canarias*), but Sevilla, Zaragoza, and Mallorca rather than the English variations. Specific places (found in the Sights & Sites section at the end of each chapter) are treated differently. The generic name is left in English and the actual place name in Spanish; hence the Church of Santa María rather than St. Mary's Church or *La Iglesia de Santa María*.

Regarding the names of individuals, throughout antiquity and the early Middle Ages the anglicized versions are used (Theodosius instead of Teodosio and St. Isidore, not San Isidro). Later, however, Spanish spelling seems more appropriate in most cases—Pedro rather than Peter, Teresa instead of Theresa.

For the sake of consistency even the Spanish monarchs, whose names are normally anglicized, remain as Fernando, Felipe, Isabel and Juan Carlos (King John Charles I for the current monarch would be ridiculous). A few exceptions include historical figures who were not Spanish: hence Christopher Columbus rather than the Cristobal Colón and Joseph (not José) Bonaparte.

Furthermore, Spaniards have *at least* two family names, those of the father *and* mother in that order. Normally, we use the first surname (rather than the second or both); Francisco Franco Bahamonde is just Francisco Franco. But there are exceptions, especially if the father's name is a common one. Pablo Ruiz Picasso called himself Picasso and Federico García Lorca is often referred to as Lorca or as García Lorca, but never as García.

Throughout the book the metric system has been retained so that distances are given in kilometers rather than miles, which will make it easier for travelers visiting the sites.

The Spanish Stage

The Iberian Peninsula forms a bridge between two continents and two seas. Thrusting out from one corner of Europe like a clenched fist, Iberia's pivotal location made it a focus for migrants, traders, colonizers, and conquerors throughout antiquity. The ancient Greek geographer Strabo compared the peninsula's shape to a tautly stretched ox hide, lying out in the sun to dry. The southern coast lies only a ferry ride away from North Africa, so throughout history the threat of invasion was always present. Control of at least one side of the narrow Mediterranean gateway became crucial.

With roughly 492,000 square kilometers, Spain occupies about eighty-five percent of the peninsula, making it the third largest European nation after Russia and France. (Spain's islands comprise another 15,000 sq. kms.) Its area is roughly twice that of the British Isles or the same size as California plus about one-third of Nevada. Spain's topography has been likened to a castle, its courtyard occupied by a lofty plateau called the *meseta* and its walls formed by mountain ranges. Most prominent of the mountains are the Pyrenees, which stretch in a largely unbroken natural barrier from the Mediterranean to the Bay of Biscay.

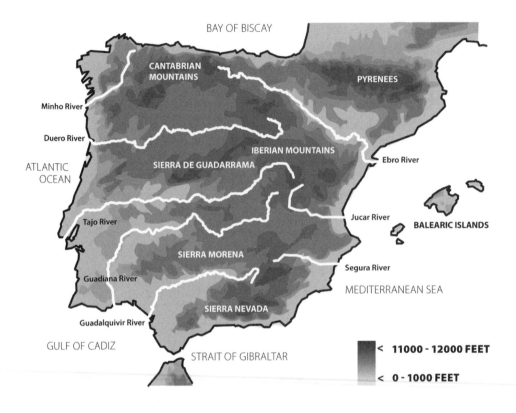

BAY OF BISCAY

CANTABRIAN
MOUNTAINS

PYRENEES

Minho River

Duero River

IBERIAN MOUNTAINS

ATLANTIC
OCEAN

SIERRA DE GUADARRAMA

Ebro River

Jucar River

BALEARIC ISLANDS

Tajo River

SIERRA MORENA

Segura River

Guadiana River

MEDITERRANEAN SEA

SIERRA NEVADA

Guadalquivir River

GULF OF CADIZ

STRAIT OF GIBRALTAR

< 11000 - 12000 FEET

< 0 - 1000 FEET

Topography of the Iberian Peninsula

Unlike the relatively uniform land forms of France or Italy, Spain offers a bewildering variety of physical conditions and rock types, which make it a geologist's dream. And more plant varieties grow here than in any other country in Europe. As the proud Spaniard says: *"Quien dice España dice todo."* (Whoever speaks of Spain says it all.)

The Spanish plain (*la meseta*) encompasses two major regions—Castilla and Extremadura—and is bounded on the northwest by the Cantabrian Mountains. This mountain barrier partially explains the separate development of Galicia, Asturias, and the Basque region. On the *meseta's* north and east lie the Iberian Mountains, which help define the regions of Navarra, Aragón, Cataluña, and Valencia. And on the south, the Sierra Morena range separates the central tablelands from Andalucía. To the west, the descent from the Spanish "castle" is a gradual series of steps down to the Atlantic coastal plain on which Portugal resides. The central plain itself consists of two plateaus separated by more mountains. Old Castilla and the Duero River lie to the north; the much larger region of La Mancha, together with Extremadura, spread southward. From this stark land would spring the conquistadors of the Spanish Empire.

Amost half the Spanish soil is unproductive and mineral resources are nearly exhausted. Few rivers are navigable, and the lakes are not significant. Extremes in climate add to the harsh picture: the region of Galicia, for instance, enjoys year-round rainfall—far too much in fact—while in desiccated Almería province rain is an occasion for wild rejoicing. Aridity and civil war have been called Spain's twin curses. In terms of rainfall, the country can be split into "wet Spain" (taking in most of the far north from Cataluña to rainy Galicia) and "dry Spain," about three-fourths of the country receiving less than fifty centimeters of rain annually.

Rugged terrain and nasty weather are often stressed to explain Spain's intense regionalism, its poverty, and other national traits. But the country also has rich pasturelands in the north and carefully irrigated farms near Valencia that yield up to four harvests per year. The *vegas* of Andalucía grow every sort of fruit and vegetable—grapes, olives, figs, almonds, lemons, oranges, avocados. So it's no wonder that today many Arabs still long for their "vanished gardens of Córdoba" in this earthly paradise called Spain.

The Spanish Map

The seventeen regions of Spain, as defined by the constitution, reflect political and cultural realities that date back centuries. Each region enjoys significant autonomy and is distinctive in landscape, climate, population and customs. These essential differences have given rise to the perennial question: Where is the *real* Spain?

Introduction

Alexandre Dumas wrote that Africa began at the Pyrenees. Even though the author meant to praise Spain's romantically rustic, hence "African" qualities in the mid-nineteenth century, the phrase stuck. And stung, especially coming from a Frenchman. It also touched a central theme of Spanish history: the peninsula's uncertain relationship with the rest of Europe.

Spaniards have historically looked beyond the Pyrenees with mixed emotions—admiring their neighbors, but fearing the loss of their own identity should the European influence gain the upper hand. Spain is obviously a part of Europe both geographically and culturally. But it is a highly distinctive part, with the ability to confound even those foreigners who think they know it well. The Duke of Wellington remarked, "In Spain, two times two does not always equal four." More recently, noted British anthropologist Julian Pitt-Rivers added, "Every country and society is different, but Spain is a bit *more* different." It is this difference that makes the Story of Spain so intriguing.

During most of antiquity Iberia lay directly in the path of classical ancient civilizations, much more a part of the glories that were Phoenicia, Carthage, Greece, and Rome than most of its northern neighbors. Another distinctive event of seminal importance occurred in the year AD 711, when the Moors crossed the strait from North Africa and began several centuries of occupation. Moorish culture would reach dizzying heights and profoundly affect Spain's history. It can even be argued that for centuries civilization *ended* at the Pyrenees, that is, all the "barbarians" lived to the north.

Equally important to Spain's difference was the Reconquest (*La Reconquista*), which created a militant brand of Christianity to deal with the Moorish infidels as well as a sense of "manifest destiny" that would carry over into the New World. Spain began to go its own way, paying only grudging notice to such fundamental European developments as feudalism and the Renaissance. Under monarchs such as Fernando and Isabel, Carlos I, and Felipe II, the newly united nation had other concerns, namely launching the greatest colonial venture yet seen—the Spanish Empire.

That first voyage of Columbus in the year 1492 marked the birth of a new world and a "new man," but it also helped push a somewhat bewildered young nation, just recently united, to the pinnacle of power. In a few decades Spain emerged from behind the Pyrenees like a colossus to loom over the European stage for more than a century. It would conquer and colonize most of the Americas, bringing its distinctive language and culture to untold generations. A unique Spanish genius would fully blossom during the breathtaking Golden Century with Cervantes, Velázquez, and other cultural giants.

Yet within 150 years after 1492 Spain was already in an advanced state of decay. Political and economic greatness were long gone, and the last embers of the Golden Century were growing cool. Each stunning triumph had been followed by an equally dramatic catastrophe, and in most forms of endeavor, Spain's present seemed forever dwarfed by its past. This sudden rise and equally rapid decline have puzzled historians ever since. Many Spaniards have concluded that the original achievements were more illusion than reality, and many historians now support this view. For others, the period from Fernando and Isabel to Felipe II represents an era to which they will forever aspire to return.

This decline (and the centuries of floundering that appeared to follow) is the central enigma of Spain's modern history. When faced with other major European movements—the Protestant Reformation, the Enlightenment, the French Revolution, Liberalism—Spain's unshakable role was to stand fast against all change. This posture inevitably pushed it ever further into a kind of intellectual, political, and economic backwater from which it could never seem to emerge. Spain is prominent by its absence from Europe's intellectual and scientific advances.

Most Spaniards would prefer to forget much of their violent modern history, but no nation can ever really escape the dark shadows of its past. The philosopher George Santayana, born in Ávila, Spain, but raised in the United States (where he became an eminent Harvard scholar), once remarked: "Those who cannot remember the past are condemned to repeat it." If there is one place where history really *does* repeat itself, it is Spain.

Indeed "Spain is Different" (as tourist posters used to proclaim), and its story at times seems to lie beyond the European mainstream. Yet Dumas had it wrong: Africa does *not* begin at the Pyrenees, but the unique land called Spain most certainly does.

Chapter 1

In the Beginning Was Iberia

Spain's story began one day in the confused muddle we call pre-history, when the first eccentric innovator picked up a piece of charcoal from the cold ashes and scratched a few lines on the wall of a cave. With a little practice the rough outline of a bird, fish, or horse appeared. Then, as generations passed and aspiring artists perfected their primitive techniques, charcoal was replaced by crude mixtures of ochre, blood, and animal fat. Even certain styles developed and gained acceptance. Cave painting had been born, and with it Art.

In 1879, a Spanish marquis and his daughter were poking around in a recently discovered cave near Santillana del Mar (Santander province). From deep inside the 275-meter-long cavern the little girl called out "Bulls! Bulls!" and her father went to investigate. The bulls were really bison, just two of about 150 animals painted on the walls and ceiling of what came to be called "The Sistine Chapel of prehistoric art."

The paintings were prehistoric, but hardly primitive. Those fortunate enough to visit Altamira Cave are astounded that our remote ancestors, stretching back in history more than six hundred generations, could create art that seems almost contemporary in style and technique. These are not childish scrawls by grunting cavemen, but thoughtful creations that have somehow managed to survive for more than fifteen thousand years.

The Altamira paintings are vivid and realistic: bellowing bison stand proudly, wild boars cavort, horses gallop. In order to depict the swelling muscles of stampeding animals, artists used the irregular relief of the cave's rocky surface. The strokes are confident, the colors bold—reds, yellows, browns, shades of violet and black from mixtures of ochre, animal fats and blood, minerals, and charcoal. The artists employed flint tools to incise outlines on the rock face, then added color using brushes made of twigs, feathers, tufts of hair or fur, and clumps of moss. Working with artificial light, they painted in awkward positions, often lying on their backs like Stone Age Michelangelos in places where the roof and floor were just a few meters apart. Even more amazing than the technique is the sophistication in terms of perspective and the artists' ability to capture innate qualities of the animals depicted.

Indeed, the discovery seemed so incredible that it met with widespread skepticism until similar paintings were later discovered in France. It was— and still is—hard to believe that people so removed from us in time could seem so close in spirit. The paintings span that seemingly infinite void concealing the dark and murky origins of life on the peninsula. Preserved by some remarkable act of serendipity, this cave art is a tiny but treasured piece of the story of Spain.

In geological terms the story began many eons ago, when the Strait of Gibraltar formed between the European and African continents as water from the Atlantic poured into the Mediterranean. This became *the* basic fact of all Spanish history: despite the Pyrenees, the Iberian Peninsula was inextricably linked to Europe, not Africa. It was the beginning of a long and stormy affair.

Spain has perhaps the world's most important archaeological site at Gran Dolina in the Sierra de Atapuerca, an area of low limestone hills near Burgos. A century ago railroad workers uncovered the first of many caverns here that have since yielded a remarkable collection of human fossils dating back at least 800,000 years. This is the earliest evidence by far of hominids in Europe, and they were deemed a new species, *Homo antecessor*, by Spanish archaeologists. These creatures were quite different from later, more primitive species such as Heidelberg men and Neanderthals, and the skull of one child is remarkably "modern" in appearance. *Homo antecessor* may have been a distant ancestor to *Homo sapiens* who ended up following some evolutionary dead end. Nearby lies the Sima de Huesos (Pit of Bones) site, which is filled with much younger fossils (a mere 300,000 years or so) that represent an estimated *three-fourths* of all known human remains worldwide from the mid-Pleistocene period (ca. 125,000 to 780,000 years ago). They are generally classified as *Homo heidelbergensis*, previously considered Europe's oldest race and ancestral to the Neanderthals.

Other early remains on the peninsula have been dubbed "the Gibraltar Woman," from the same period (ca. 35,000 BC) and race as the Neanderthal man, her more famous cousin unearthed in Germany about the same time. These legendary lowbrows, who fashioned the first spears and observed primitive funeral cults, probably came from beyond the Pyrenees; an African origin is unlikely because Neanderthals did not have boats to cross the strait in large numbers. Fossil evidence indicates that Gibraltar may well have been their last home after being driven from the rest of Europe by more advanced people.

Cro-Magnons were precursors of modern man in physical appearance and could boast flint tools, rituals, and art. Because theirs was a colder time, they tended to live in caves and used rough (rather than polished) stone implements, and hunted mammoth, bison, and reindeer. They also had quaint customs like covering corpses with red ochre and fashioning drinking cups from human skulls. Among the many caves thought to have sheltered this race is one at Nerja (Málaga) famous for its stalactites and stalagmites.

After about 40,000 BC or so something profound was happening to human culture, not only in things like tool making but the probable invention of language, which allowed cultural transmission on an unprecedented scale. There were some signs of that intangible thing called consciousness, a level of self-awareness above the world of animal instincts and the ultimate source of creativity.

The pinnacle of Upper Paleolithic (Old Stone Age) life on the peninsula came with the Magdalenian culture, which stretched across southern France and the Cantabrian range in Iberia over a period of some ten thousand years. These were the cultural innovators who painted Altamira and hundreds of other caves in the region. The "capital" of Magdalenian Spain was the area around present-day Santander, but one outpost may have been at Benaoján near Ronda (Málaga), site of La Pileta Cave and its magnificent wall paintings. However, there is some debate about the origins of this marvel of troglodyte art as the drawings depict a giant fish and an archer, rare subjects in the Magdalenian world.

Equally mysterious are the origins of the extinct Guanche culture of the Canary Islands, which still existed when the first Europeans of the modern era arrived around AD 1400. Although some romantics believe the Guanches were survivors from the "Lost Continent" of Atlantis, archaeological evidence suggests that these tall, fair people arrived from North Africa during the Cro-Magnon era. The Guanches left hundreds of cave sites (three hundred in one mountain alone) and an alphabet, which has never been deciphered.

The end of the last Ice Age (about 8000 BC) ushered in a long transitional period before the arrival of Neolithic (New Stone Age) cultures from the eastern Mediterranean five millennia later. With gradual warming of the climate, the nomadic life of hunters melted away with the glaciers, as reindeer and other game migrated northward. One theory holds that with the climatic changes Magdalenians departed en masse for parts unknown, leaving behind isolated pockets of stay-at-home types. Hence the possible origin of the Basques, who speak a language thought to be unrelated to any other.

Evidence suggests that new races, probably coming from North Africa, entered the peninsula during the next fifty centuries or so. They have been called Iberians, proto-Berbers, or even refugees from Atlantis for lack of more concrete evidence. Whoever they were, they brought their own form of art: "rock-shelter" paintings that have survived along Spain's eastern coast. These are quite distinct from earlier cave drawings and resemble African and even Anatolian art. They were done out-of-doors for all to see and depicted hunting and dancing scenes entirely different from the brooding introspection of Altamira's art. On one hand rock-shelter painting showed progress by using human forms to tell stories. On the other hand, this new art took a distinct dip from earlier standards; the images are often just red or black stick men. But it is fascinating nonetheless.

Neolithic is the name given to the period marking the dawn of civilization in Mesopotamia and Egypt about the year 5000 BC. With the arrival of many remarkable changes—farming with the plow, livestock and wheat raising, use of polished stone implements, basket and pottery making, permanent villages and fortifications, communal burial rites, boat building, weaving of cloth, rudimentary work with copper—one could finally speak of *civilized* man. In contrast to the painfully slow development of the Old Stone Age, the innovations of the new era arrived at breakneck speed—within the span of three millennia, the blink of an eye in prehistoric time. The shortage of excavated finds means lots of guesswork, but it appears that the "new age" reached Iberia by 3000 BC and spread slowly during many centuries. Most likely the new culture came from the eastern Mediterranean area via the Danube Valley, from Egypt along the North African coast, or possibly by sea.

This new influence explains the rise of what is called the Culture of Almería, a Neolithic society in southeastern Spain dating from about 2500 BC. Theories abound regarding the roots of this culture, which is considered one of the ethnic cornerstones of the Spanish people. One school traces the Almerians to the Hammites, descendants of the biblical Ham. Another claims that the newcomers were dark migrants seeking refuge from the choking aridity then transforming much of North Africa into a desert, a people possibly related to the founders of Indus Valley civilization and the Dravidian-speakers of southern India. A second phase at Almería is called the culture of Los Millares, and the faint ruins of its capital now stand on a bare, eroded hill that four thousand years ago yielded rich harvests. This emerging bronze culture revolved around local copper deposits and may have had links with the Aegean area, perhaps Crete.

One intriguing chapter of Iberian pre-history emanating from the Almería beachhead was the "era of megaliths." These striking stone burial chambers, often called dolmens, are found throughout Europe, but appear in abundance on the peninsula. The origins of the megalith-building culture are obscure, but probably go back once again to the eastern Mediterranean. The great barrow grave at Newgrange in Ireland dates from about the same time, and legend has it that "missionaries" of the megalith came from the south to build it. Stonehenge, dated about a thousand years later, may also have felt the influence of this culture.

With the spread of these great prehistoric stone cathedrals, Iberia achieved its first "golden age" of architecture. The best examples of megalithic dolmens are found near Antequera north of Málaga. Entering the Menga Chamber for the first time is a humbling experience; about thirty cyclopean boulders (weighing up to 130,000 kilos each) were somehow carried from the nearby mountains to build a table-like tomb, and the massive roof is supported by a row of gigantic pillars. The renowned modern architect Le Corbusier was so impressed by this stunning architectural feat that he signed the guest book: "to my predecessors."

One thing is certain: even the ancients had their version of "The Two Spains." Throughout most of the peninsula's lengthy history, nearly every advanced culture has inhabited the "periphery," the hospitable eastern coast and southern Andalucía. Both the *meseta* and the rainy north were shunned by civilized men and reserved for barbarians. Hence, the central plateau and its indigenous nomads were little touched by the megalith builders.

At the dawn of the second millennium before Christ, the Millares culture of Almería was already in decline and may have gone down in a blaze of strife and anarchy. The times were changing: megalithic practices of burning the dead were giving way to individual burials in cists. True bronze technology (mixing copper and tin in the correct proportions) began to appear on the peninsula, with ore-rich Almería at the vanguard.

The Bronze Age—in which metal replaced stone, wood, and bone for tools and weapons—lasted until the introduction of iron many centuries later. Metal workers made everything from bronze jewelry to shields (the same level of technology Spaniards encountered in Mexico 3,500 years later). Center of this technology was El Argar near Almería, spreading north and west over the next few centuries. Many historians like to call this Bronze Age people the first Iberians (archaeologists use the term in a stricter sense). In any case, settlers from El Argar colonized Menorca and built huge cone-shaped stone piles called *talayots* that were part defensive tower and part sepulcher.

A small Iberian plaque from El Cabecico del Tesoro de Verdolay

By 1500 BC the cultural center of gravity was shifting from the Almería area to the valley of the Guadalquivir River, which was like a smaller version of Mesopotamia in its role in the rise of an advanced civilization. Here agriculture thrived, and the nearby Sierra Morena mountains held important deposits of copper and silver. These metals became the linchpins of the fabulous lost civilization of Tartessos, the most intriguing riddle of ancient Iberia.

History, said Bacon, is like the planks of a shipwreck: more of the past is lost than has been saved. So it is with Tartessos, forgotten until an intrepid German archaeologist named Adolf Schulten rekindled interest by publishing a book on the subject in the 1920s. Using time-battered evidence and vague clues, he pieced together a flawed mosaic of the past. A major find appeared during routine dredging off a pier at the Tharsis Copper Company near the mouth of the Rio Tinto. An ancient wreck yielded more than four hundred bronze weapons, plus needles, buttons, and other artifacts. Caches of jewelry were also found throughout Andalucía, adding to the mystery. Professor Schulten spent the rest of his life in a futile search for the famed Tartessian capital, which he believed lay somewhere between Cádiz and Huelva.

Evidence about Tartessos' actual location has remained more literary than archaeological, references such as "the boundless silver-rooted springs of the Tartessus River" (Strabo). Perhaps it was Scheria, the land at the end of the world described by Homer in *The Odyssey*, which was a wealthy sea power boasting a capital with a solid-bronze palace. In Greek mythology, the tenth task assigned to Hercules was to travel to a land in the west and capture the magnificent oxen of Geryon, a three-headed king. Someone by the same name appears in Tartessian mythology, as reported by Greek historian Hesiod. Geryon was the dynasty's founder and a kind of early cattle baron.

Then there is the biblical reference about Jonah who, before being swallowed by the whale, was traveling by ship to a place called Tarshish: "And from Tarshish came ships bringing gold and silver, ivory, apes, and peacocks." Were Tarshish and Tartessos the same place? The reference suggests a well-developed empire, whose ships may have reached Britain and the African coast in search of tin.

Despite all the allusions we know few facts about Tartessos. The most fanciful notion is, once again, that the kingdom was a colony of refugees from Atlantis. It *is* curious that Plato, our main source on Atlantis, dated the disaster at around 1500 BC, just about the time Tartessos began its rise, and that he placed the "lost civilization" somewhere near the Pillars of Hercules, as the Strait of Gibraltar was known during antiquity. Today most historians believe Tartessian civilization sprang from native roots rather than outside influences. Its origins might stretch back to Los Millares and be linked to the dolmens of Antequera and elsewhere. This would make Tartessos the peninsula's first fully developed indigenous culture and the legitimate historical ancestor of all later Iberians.

Greek historians said the kingdom encompassed all of southern Iberia, and included some two hundred towns and villages. (Spanish place names with Tartessian origins end in -ippo, -uba, -igi, -ucci, and -urgi.) Later, the geographer Strabo described an extensive network of canals near the mouth of the river we call the Guadalquivir. He added that Tartessians claimed to have ancient books six thousand years old and laws written in verse. Unfortunately, except for a handful of undeciphered inscriptions these writings vanished long ago.

The chief task for researchers is to find the location of the sumptuous capital, if indeed one existed. Greeks used the name Tartessos for the river and the territory, but never for a city. Nevertheless, Schulten and others placed it at the mouth of the Guadalquivir, perhaps buried under tons of silt deposited over centuries. (Most of Las Marismas swamps were formed over the past three thousand years.) A more likely site is the mouth of the Rio Tinto, which has run red since antiquity from copper deposits in the interior. Yet despite the many puzzle pieces, Tartessos continues to elude us.

The name "Iberian" can be used to describe the people and culture of Spain at the dawn of history. However, a narrower definition is applied specifically to cultures of the southern and eastern peninsula, which stretched along the seaboard as far as the Rhone in southern France. (Place names with Iberian roots often carry the endings -ili, -ilti, -ilu, -iltu, and -urris.) These Iberians included a confusing medley of tribes speaking languages from one common origin. The Cerretani, Andosini, Arenosi, Ausetani, Indicetes, Laietani, and Cvossetani lived in the area that later became Cataluña.

Iberians were a dark people with long skulls and lived in easily defended hilltop settlements. Using various sources, we can piece together a common character sketch of the typical Iberian: he was stoical, quarrelsome, devoted to bulls and horses, suspicious of strangers, superstitious in religion, and respectful of his elders. Above all, he was individualistic and disliked organization. In short, much like Spaniards throughout history.

Some historians have detected links between Iberian languages and Basque and even proposed that this enigmatic race is a surviving pocket of the original Iberians. They spoke at least two languages that, like Basque, were not Indo-European or related to Celtic. There is also a curious correlation between some words:

Iberian	Basque
egiar	*egin* (to do)
salir	*zillar* (silver)
saltu	*saldi* (horse)
nescato	*neskato* (young girl)

Nevertheless, attempts to use modern Basque lexicons to translate 2,300-year-old Iberian texts have failed, and most scholars have dismissed the link. But questions about both races persist, and the Basques, who remain very much on the modern scene, continue to defy ethnic or linguistic classification.

One theory holds that they are survivors of a Stone Age culture like the Magdalenians and are totally unrelated to coastal Iberians, to the Berbers (as some have suggested), or to any other modern race. Other linguists claim vague similarities between Basque and Finnish, Hungarian, Turkish, Dravidian and even some American Indian tongues. Some romantics have even proposed it was the language spoken by Adam and Eve in the Garden of Eden! In any case, the Basque language is exceptionally difficult and complex. (It's said that the devil, as a punishment for his outrageous offenses, was condemned by God to learn Basque.) It was once spoken in most of the western and central Pyrenees and parts of the Cantabrian range. Words of Basque origin in Spanish are few: *izquierda* (left), *barro* (mud), and *perro* (dog), for example.

By about the year 1000 BC the Basques were already surrounded by Celtic peoples, who in turn present their own historical puzzle. This fair, round-headed race from middle Europe began moving into the peninsula about 900 BC and was long considered, along with the Iberians, as a key component of the Spanish race. Today some skeptics doubt they were even in Spain. Yet the reliable Greek historian Herodotus referred specifically to Celts on the peninsula by the fifth century before Christ, if not earlier. The problem seems to lie in distinguishing Celtic from purely indigenous remnants that pre-dated the invasions. The Celtic practice of burning their dead has hampered investigation because archaeologists rely heavily on burial sites for evidence. Among the few existing remnants of Celtic culture are the sculpted stone bulls, *los toros de Guisando* in Ávila province.

"Vase of the Birds" from Azaila, Teruel

Nevertheless, a few basic facts are generally accepted. Celtic penetration across the Pyrenees flowed and ebbed during several centuries and spread over about two-thirds of the peninsula. Although nothing like an empire ever existed, they did occupy the entire *meseta* and most of the north and west. (Place names with a Celtic connection often end in -briga.)

The Celts brought iron metallurgy and the short broad sword with them at about the same time the Phoenicians were introducing this key innovation along the coast. Celts were mostly pastoral by nature, lived in the interior, drank fermented wheat beer (*cerveza* is a Celtic word), and cooked with lard. They also introduced the custom of wearing trousers. Robed Iberians resided along the coast as farmers, fishermen, or merchants, ate more fish than meat, used olive oil and preferred wine mixed with honey. One strange Celtic practice involved placing the infirm alongside roads and paths with the hope that someone passing might have suffered the same illness and be able to help.

The Celtic racial influence has been diluted almost beyond recognition over the centuries, although Spaniards claim that a definite blond or red-haired type, lyrical and melancholic, comes from Galicia in the northwest. It is curious too that both Galician and Irish legends support the idea that Eire's first people came from Iberia. In Galicia, tradition holds that King Breogan and his sons sailed north and encountered an island. One son severed his own right hand and threw it ashore dramatically so that he should be remembered as the first person to touch the unknown land.

About the same time Celts were entering Iberia from the north, Phoenician traders were gaining a toehold in the south. They were the first colonizers from an identifiable civilization: Phoenicia was a commercially oriented empire of Semitic peoples based in what is today Lebanon and northern Israel. Phoenicians were dark, with wide foreheads, high cheekbones, and hooked noses according to art from the period. Their most important legacy is the alphabet we use (in slightly modified form) today. Though never a great military power, Phoenicia grew strong as a trading partner to mightier empires and essentially controlled Mediterranean commerce by 1000 BC. Expansion was chiefly triggered by the need to find raw materials, chiefly metals, for the manufacture of luxury goods for the neighboring (and often threatening) Assyrians and Babylonians.

According to legend, one Phoenician king was following an oracle when he ordered an expedition from Tyre to found a city near the Pillars of Hercules. The old cliché about the ancients believing this spot marked the end of the world, the beginning of a "sea of darkness," is only partly true. In fact, the Phoenicians went far beyond the Pillars in search of tin and other wealth, north and south along Atlantic shores as far as Britain and western Africa. Phoenician sailors called the peninsula *i-schephan-im,* translated as either "remote" or "filled with rabbits." The name was later altered to *Spania* and to *Hispania* during centuries of Roman rule. Still later, it became España.

The founding of Gadir by Phoenicians around the year 1100 BC would make today's city of Cádiz the oldest in Europe. The chronology comes from a Roman historian writing much later, who dated the founding eighty years after the fall of Troy. But archaeological evidence and the first literary references suggest a later date. In either case, Gadir was still very old, older in fact than Rome. The name means "fortress" in Phoenician, and the town occupied the strongest part of a small archipelago near the mouth of the Guadalete River. (Today the islands are joined by landfill, and the existence of modern Cádiz prevents excavation of the site.)

Other colonies sprouted along the entire southern coast: at Malaca (Málaga), Sexi (Almuñécar), and Abdera (Adra), where both climate and natives were hospitable. The Phoenicians were seeking copper and silver, both abundant in Andalucía, and hoped to exchange manufactured goods in return. However, they underestimated hostility from nearby Tartessos, which monopolized this mineral wealth. A naval battle to decide the issue ended in the burning of the once-mighty Tartessian fleet, according to one report. Henceforth, the Phoenicians not only exploited the mines, but also took over their rival's old Atlantic trading routes.

Fishing was second to mining in economic importance (tunny fish appear on Phoenician coins). During ancient times vast schools of enormous blue-fin tuna migrated through the Strait of Gibraltar and were caught, salted, and shipped throughout the known world. Gadir became a thriving seaport that served a substantial merchant fleet, and the streets teemed with Phoenicians, Tartessians, Greeks, and Celts.

The city's most important religious temple was devoted to *Moloch*, the fire-god to whom children were sacrificed. It sat on the same spot today occupied by the Cádiz cathedral. Another temple of note, boasting a pair of solid bronze columns, was dedicated to *Melkart*, the protective god of the city and its trade. It was famous throughout the ancient world (supposedly visited by Julius Caesar), but was razed by the Moors when they conquered the peninsula centuries later.

Phoenician towns followed a certain pattern, with sheltered anchorage, fresh water, arable land, and an elevated site for defense. Almuñécar (Sexi) is a perfect example of the ideal site, atop an isolated promontory jutting into the sea. The cemetery here has yielded some outstanding Phoenician artifacts,

About t
Carthaginian
capital was t:
ram, and "di
Thereafter, C
Carthage wa:
secretive con
decades, hist
beyond the I

I
(from the Al
remarkably l
above all else
right conque
first and serv
plored the w
Iberia's
Ibiza, where
hillside. Altl
have survive
their own te:
bols of imm
artifacts hav
In tim
change of str
First Punic
from the La
and bankru
Hamilcar B
Hannibal, d
south. Here
Turdetanos,
By thi
very "well-d
dals into b:
Hamilcar h

including alabaster jars bearing the names of Egyptian pharaohs and decorated ostrich eggs filled with red ochre, which was used as a cosmetic.

With the arrival of the Phoenicians, Iberians came into direct contact with an advanced Mediterranean civilization for the first time. They readily adopted new ways to form a fairly uniform society, making it easier for later colonizers to take over. Tribes of the interior (like the Castilians much later) fought this "opening up" of Iberia for several more centuries. Meanwhile, they lived in flea-infested squalor and brushed their teeth with urine, while coastal Iberians became part of a larger Mediterranean culture—building towns, mining silver, working iron and bronze, and drinking wine.

The Iberian language took on written form by adopting the Phoenician alphabet, and imported gods crept into the local pantheon. Carvings and figurines even reveal an acquired taste for the sumptuous burials favored by Phoenicians. The tomb of Pozo Moro in Albacete province has proved very rich, yielding sculpture of the fierce god Reshef, a giant marine monster, a boar fighting monsters, and ancient erotica. This tomb has been reconstructed at the National Archaeological Museum in Madrid.

When Phoenicia was defeated at home by Assyria and again by Babylonia, the stage was set for the rise of its most important colony—Carthage. Phoenicia's decline likewise encouraged Greeks to establish trading posts in Spain. Since time immemorial this land to the west fascinated the Greeks. In mythology, Hercules reached the limits of the Mediterranean and raised two enormous columns called the Pillars of Hercules, the twin mountains of Gibraltar and Mt. Acho in Ceuta. (As an interesting footnote, the legend said that the hero engraved an S-shaped legend around the pillars that read: "Do not go beyond here." This S shape crossed by two lines somehow evolved into the dollar sign.) Hercules then proceeded on his quest for the golden apples of the Hesperides and the cattle of Geryon in the mysterious land beyond. The Greeks gave us the name Iberia, possibly a word for "river." They also used *Hesperia*, meaning "land of the setting sun," which appears in Hercules' mythological quest for the golden apples of Hesperides.

According to Herodotus, the first Greek in Iberia was the adventurer Kolaios of Samos, who was blown off course and landed at Tartessos during the reign of Arganthonius. His reception was a warm one, and he returned to Greece with a cargo of 1,500 kilos of silver from the king, whose name itself meant "he of the silver land." It is more likely that the voyage of Kolaios,

about
Tarte:

600 I
the n
Catal
they s
small
Hem

the p
legac)
de Elo
is clea
This
ago r
Baza,
(Ano

heger
same
last P
busir
Num
that
rifice

and r
that
Iberi
end
inde

pot.
slam
"Bey
. . .

counterattack, but his young son Hannibal managed to escape. His son-in-law, Hasdrubal Barca, took a softer approach and tried to win over the Iberians. Tradition credits him with founding Barca (Barcelona) and a capital at Cartago Nova (Cartagena), where he built a palace. A prosperous town grew up there, based on silver mining, and all went well until an Iberian slave, seeking revenge for the crucifixion of a native leader, assassinated Hasdrubal.

With this act a man of true destiny entered the scene, as power passed to Hannibal Barca, considered one of history's great military geniuses by the age of twenty-five. Hannibal married a native princess and carried the conquest into the interior as far as present-day Salamanca. And from the growing concern over his victories sprang the Carthaginians' greatest contribution to Iberia: they brought the Romans.

Sights & Sites

Alicante: Castle of Santa Barbara, original site of Carthaginian fortress overlooking town and harbor.

Ampurias (Gerona): Ruins of Emporion, largest Greek settlement in Iberia.

Antequera (Málaga): Menga and Viera chambers and Romeral dolmen; El Torcal (16 kms. south) was the possible source of giant stones used in construction.

Ávila province: Los Toros de Guisando, stone figures believed to be Celtic.

Barcelona: Archaeological Museum is especially good on the megalithic civilization; also Greek and Roman collections from Ampurias and a scale model of Emporion.

Benaojan (Málaga): La Pileta Cave has excellent cave art.

Canary Islands: Canaries Museum in Las Palmas de Gran Canaria features Guanche ethnography; at Cuatro Puertas on Gran Canaria is a mountain honeycombed with burial caves; Los Verdes Cave on Lanzarote, at the foot of Corona Volcano, has underground galleries where Guanches took refuge from pirates.

Elche (Alicante): Palm Grove where the Dama de Elche was found, originally planted by Phoenicians; museum at Alcudia contains early Iberian pieces.

Ibiza (Balearic Islands): Large Punic necropolis at Puig des Molins has about two thousand tombs; Archaeology Museum features ancient ceramics.

The Bulls of Guisando, pre-Roman stone carvings near Avila

Madrid: National Archaeological Museum spans entire ancient period and includes outstanding displays such as the hunters of Torralba and Dama de Elche.

Menorca (Balearic Islands): More than two hundred megalithic monuments called talayots; sites include Trepuco near airport and Els Tudons near Ciudadela.

Nerja (Málaga): Nerja Cave chronicles many epochs of prehistory.

Puente Viesgo (Cantabria): El Castillo Cave, with the very first Iberian images—outlines of human hands which pre-date Altamira.

Ribadesella (Asturias): Tito Bustillo Cave is another good site for cave art.

Santanilla del Mar (Santander): Site of Altamira Cave, the "Sistine Chapel" of prehistoric art.

Chapter 2

The Romans Were Here

Segovia's magnificent aqueduct captures the spirit of Spain's Roman heritage. Standing on the Plaza del Azoguejo, it is an aesthetic and engineering triumph and an inspiring sight that has awed observers for the past two thousand years.

Sometime during the first century after Christ, white granite boulders weighing several tons each were carted down from the nearby Guadarrama Mountains. Here they were cut and chiseled into building blocks so perfect that no mortar was needed to join them. The aqueduct is about 800-meters long and contains 118 stone arches, which provide its strength and simple beauty. It still carries water down a cleavage in the hilly terrain from seventeen kilometers away.

There are no other remnants here—no theater, forum, or arena as in most Roman towns—for one simple reason. Segovia was a military post to keep conquered tribes at bay. The Romans had a genius for civil engineering, but their aqueduct at Segovia did not serve solely to transport water. Just as today we stand in awe before it, so too did the semi-barbaric Celts and Iberians, surely intimidated by the glories of Roman civilization.

Rome . . . the name itself resounds like the ring of a bronze bell or the clang of an iron sword against a heavy shield. Although Romans destroyed their foes mercilessly and violence became the national sport, they also brought peace and culture to the Mediterranean world. Romans built roads, bridges, and aqueducts; towns and commerce flourished; and law prevailed over the whims of the few. Even today, Roman ruins in the most desolate corners of North Africa are the only sign that civilization has passed that way.

Rome ruled the Iberian Peninsula, which they called Hispania, for more than six centuries (218 BC to AD 409). During this decisive period, the country was transformed to such a degree as to make previous history seem irrelevant. In their cultural baggage Romans brought the language that forms the base of all peninsular tongues (except Basque), an advanced legal system, and architectural and engineering principles still used today. Later, Romans also brought a new religion called Christianity, which further served to unite disparate ethnic and linguistic groups. Indeed, some have argued that under Rome Spain enjoyed real political and cultural unity for the first and *last* time. The larger Hispanic identity emerged in place of localism, and the notion of Spain itself can be considered a Roman creation. Therefore Spanish history as such did not really begin until this time.

From Hispania Rome received much in return. Vast mineral and agricultural wealth financed imperial projects, and three emperors and some of the great names in Latin literature were born here. Hispania was the pride of the empire, the most Roman of all its provinces. But reaching such an exalted status required two centuries of horrific struggle.

Before Hannibal disembarked with his father at Gadir, he had sworn an oath of eternal hatred for Rome, and he lived his life with the dream of its destruction. When he finally took charge sixteen years later, Hannibal was famed for an incredible tolerance for physical suffering, and he enjoyed the fanatical loyalty of his men. Soon he was leading Carthage's army to new victories on the peninsula. Hannibal's success on the battlefield caused alarms to sound throughout Rome. An earlier treaty between the rival powers had sliced the peninsula into two zones—everything north of the Ebro River fell under Roman control, while lands to the south belonged to Carthage. There was one exception, a Greek/Iberian town on the east coast named Saguntum that looked to Rome for special protection.

Hannibal saw in Saguntum a chance to provoke his sworn enemies. After a bitter eight-month siege, the town fell and Rome was forced to respond.

Iberia was suddenly thrust into center stage of the greatest military encounter of ancient history: the Second Punic War (218-201 BC). In this struggle between the titans of antiquity the stakes were high and the fighting savage. (Hannibal was known to routinely kill Iberian hostages.) Carthage was larger and wealthier, but Rome superior in manpower and enthusiasm. And, of course, it had destiny on its side.

Two Roman legions (about five thousand men each) landed at Emporion, but Hannibal had already left the peninsula with an army of fifty thousand foot soldiers, nine thousand cavalry, and three-dozen elephants. The most famous trek in military history would take them across the Alps and into Italy where, at Cannae, they annihilated a Roman army. Dozens of would-be spectators, including eighty members of the senate, also perished. Then, in one of history's most debated military decisions, Hannibal decided to rest his army for the winter rather than pressing on to victory. After the lull he never managed to finish off his enemy.

Meanwhile, Rome had opened a second front in Hispania. Roman legions pinned down an army under Hannibal's brother, Hasdrubal, rendering it incapable of lending a hand in Italy. (When they finally did arrive, the Carthaginians were badly beaten, and Hasdrubal's severed head was thrown into his brother's camp.) A member of an illustrious Roman family, the dashing Publius Cornelius Scipio, arrived in Hispania to assume command. The new general captured Cartagena in a surprise attack, then followed up with a series of victories that climaxed with the fall of Gadir. Scipio went on to defeat Hannibal and end the war at Zama in North Africa. Carthage's power was at an end, but Punic cultural influence survived for centuries. To celebrate his Iberian victory, Scipio decided to settle wounded and retired soldiers at a spot he called Itálica, whose ruins lie near present-day Sevilla. It became Rome's first colony in southern Spain and later a monumental city and birthplace of two future emperors.

The war's cost to Rome was frightening, but only the beginning of the bloodshed; it would take two centuries and more than 150,000 lives to subdue the peninsula. Over the past several centuries Celts and Iberians had intermingled, especially in the Ebro Basin, and created a hearty race feared for its courage and tenacity. Not that the blending was complete. One Roman historian noted that Iberian soldiers wore purple linens while Celts preferred sheepskin and black woolens. These "Celtiberians" soon realized that the defeat of Carthage was only an interlude and that the victors were not liberators.

The Romans were baffled by the native people: warlike by nature, they were a tough and wiry race with unkempt hair and a "harsh" way of speaking. Their system of justice was likewise severe—criminals were thrown off cliffs— and they were wildly superstitious, reading the entrails of slain enemies to predict the future. Celtiberians were heroic and loyal, loved liberty but lacked discipline, and could endure terrible hardships. They carried the leaves of poisonous plants into battle rather than be captured alive. Even today, Spaniards refer to a stubborn person as "very Iberian." The collective-minded Romans found this Hispanic individualism disconcerting. One historian noted that tribal pride prevented the Celtiberians from uniting into a defensive confederation, adding that they never learned to hold their shields together (Roman style) in battle. Though they fought bravely, it was always "each man for himself." This lack of cohesion cut both ways, however. Because Celtiberians never united, they could not be decisively defeated. War thus became a neverending affair that brought neither submission nor peace.

Savage guerrilla tactics suited to the rugged terrain proved so exasperating that legionnaires dreaded peninsular service to the point of mutiny. In battle, Celtiberian warriors would charge shouting war cries, shaking their long locks, and leaping around as if dancing to frighten the welldisciplined Romans, who could only wonder what cruel twist of fate had brought them there. These *hispani* enjoyed superior numbers and, surprisingly, better weapons. The Celts in particular had fearsome cavalry and a short iron sword that the Romans quickly adopted. Iberians used an infamous saber that "cut off arms at the root of the shoulder, severed heads from bodies with a chopping blow, exposed entrails, and caused horrible wounds," according to one chronicle. The *hispani* never learned to hold their shields together, but they did something no other colony could—hold out for two hundred years against Rome. By contrast, Gaul (France) succumbed to Caesar in a mere ten years.

After the Punic War and arrival of Roman culture, Iberians were forced to undergo profound changes. Areas along the coast, long-exposed to colonial powers, readily accepted the Roman presence, but there was strong resistance in the interior. The Lusitanians, a fierce tribe living in present day Portugal and Extremadura, led revolts in the west. In 150 BC a massacre of eight thousand unarmed Lusitanians sparked an eight-year revolt led by Viriathus, a shepherd who had escaped the slaughter. This charismatic figure, claimed by both Spain and Portugal as their first national hero, abandoned his flocks for a life of banditry and brilliant soldiering. He soon outwitted the Roman army in the west, and at one time controlled most of central Spain. In the end only treachery could defeat Viriathus: Romans bribed three of his aides to murder him in his tent. At a spectacular funeral, his corpse was burned on an elevated pyre, while warriors danced in a frenzy around it.

The death of Viriathus smothered the Lusitanian revolt, but around the same time several tribes on the *meseta* rose up. The Celtiberian War lasted twenty years and broke the back of two Roman armies before another Scipio, the grandson of Hannibal's nemesis, arrived to crush the revolt. The town of Numantia (near present-day Soria) emerged as the immortal Spanish symbol of resistance as six thousand souls faced the cream of the Roman army. Ringed by barren peaks, Numantia sits above the Duero River on a dry, stony plateau. Here, it was said, the wind was so strong it could knock down a legionnaire carrying a heavy pack. It was a fitting site for the harsh drama to come. Although this was classic guerrilla country, the Numantians chose to make a stand in their heavily walled town. Repeated attacks were thrown back, and a force of twenty thousand Romans retreated in disgrace. Outraged, the Roman senate was forced to send its finest general and an army of sixty thousand men to starve out a wretched Celtiberian village.

Scipio the Younger was an interesting type: intelligent, cultured, a patron of the arts, and the person credited with introducing the Greek custom of shaving to bearded Romans. Yet in war he was a ruthless commander who gave no quarter. Upon arriving at Numantia, the general launched a get-tough campaign on the demoralized legionnaires, forbidding hot baths and making them eat breakfast standing up among other measures. The Romans established a seamless blockade around the town, hoping to starve the defenders into submission, and after nine months the Numantians wavered. But when Scipio insisted on unconditional surrender, they dug in for a last hopeless stand. Finally, in an ultimate gesture of Iberian defiance, the last survivors got drunk on beer, set fire to their town, and perished in the flames rather than surrender. (Cervantes later immortalized the events in his play *The Siege of Numantia*.) For his efforts the conquering general became known as Scipio Numantinus, but Rome had paid a harrowing price. The job was still not finished, however, for in the wild Cantabrian Mountains hardened defenders would resist the invaders for another century.

Romanization began about 200 BC and continued for six centuries. The process was complete in areas such as the coast and river valleys, where contact was greatest, but proceeded slowly in remote areas like Asturias. There many of the old pre-Roman ways remained in place. Romanization took many forms and was embraced or resisted in a myriad of ways. Roads, bridges, aqueducts and other structures were the first visible signs of the new order. Romans were ancient history's greatest builders, and eventually thirty-four different major roads covering 21,000 kilometers linked the far-flung corners of Hispania. Among the earliest was the Via Herculea, a coastal road from the Pyrenees to Gades (Cádiz), and the Via Augusta running through the heart of the country. Some historians say these were probably Spain's best roads until at least the 1920s.

The peninsula was divided into two provinces—Hispania Citerior and Hispania Ulterior—with Cartago Nova (Cartagena) and Corduba (Córdoba) the respective capitals. Romans soon recognized that Hispania was a vital component of their power, a place where civil wars could be decided and vast fortunes made. Above all its precious metals were enticing, just as the mines of Mexico and Peru attracted Spaniards centuries later. Existing works at Rio Tinto were greatly expanded, and it was said that at Cartagena forty thousand slaves worked the silver mines. The other economic pillar was agriculture: especially olive oil, wheat, and wine. Romans introduced irrigation and the *latifundia* system, huge land grants to men of power. The salting of fish became an important industry in the south; even more so was the production of *garum*, a kind of fish paste that Romans craved around cocktail time.

Towns and cities became key components of the Roman way. Urban life lured *hispani* with pleasures and privileges, and later with the ultimate prize of citizenship. Little by little the new towns exerted influence on the countryside, and cities such as Itálica and Mérida represented the triumph of urban civilization. The first area urbanized was Baetica, a province named for the Baetis River (today the Guadalquivir) that corresponded roughly to Andalucía. Roman writers made note of the "clusters of small dwellings of whitened adobe," Iberian forerunners of the classic whitewashed *pueblos* of today. Urban life also flourished along the eastern seaboard.

Rome's ultimate legacies were its language and laws. Latin was crucial in cementing Roman control, and the vulgar language spoken by soldiers—quite different from literary Latin—began to evolve, ever so slowly, into the various

Romance tongues spoken on the peninsula. You can see firsthand the meaning of Roman law in the Charter of Urso, on display at Madrid's National Archaeological Museum. Inscribed on these bronze tablets are the fundamentals of citizenship and law, just two of the rewards Rome promised in return for submission. There are provisions for due process under the law and guarantees of essential public works, along with clauses forbidding burials within the city walls and other practical matters.

Local customs in religion and burial practices were deeply rooted and gave way slowly over centuries. Romans tolerated traditional gods (numbering in the hundreds) except in extreme cases, such as a cult of human sacrifice they stamped out at Gades. Gradually Roman gods—Jupiter, Juno, Minerva, Mars—replaced local ones with similar identities. For example, the old Phoenician god Melkart became Hercules. Roman burial customs could be quite elaborate; at Carmona (near Sevilla) a huge necropolis of nine hundred tombs contains several large enough to include banqueting rooms and other extra touches for the wealthy.

Roman society was highly structured, but life for the average person was probably tolerable. The conquered became tributes more often than slaves, and later *hispani* were the first people outside Italy to enjoy Roman citizenship. At the bottom of the social scale were slaves, essential to an economy based on large-scale mining and agriculture. Above them came free peasants and urban artisans, who sold their goods and services in the open market. Next came full citizens, often from the professional classes, and finally elite members of the "orders," the gentry and aristocracy. The *equites*, for example, had enough money to own and equip a horse, while foot soldiers came from the poorer classes.

In Hispania, the fall of Numantia ushered in fifty years of peace, but the province would soon find itself riding a whirlwind. Concern over social inequalities led to a century of civil war that would sink the Roman Republic. The first upheaval involved a struggle between the aristocratic supporters of Sulla and the so-called popular party of Marius. Neither leader was a likable character: Lucius Cornelius Sulla was a moody patrician who could order an execution as easily as read a poem; Gaius Marius was the son of a farmer and passionately hated aristocrats. By all accounts he was a grim figure, a ruthless fighter involved in several slaughters.

One of Marius's biggest supporters, and therefore on the patrician hit list, was named Quintus Sertorius. After Sulla's victory he was exiled to

Hispania, where he organized a small army to lead a rebellion against patrician-controlled Rome. The western colony soon became a hotbed of populist support, and many *hispani* gladly joined in the fracas. Sertorius was a swashbuckling character puzzling to historians, who debate whether he was a Republican hero or an ambitious traitor who wanted to set up his own kingdom. At first defeated, he fled to Mauritania (Morocco) and helped locals battle the ruler of Tingis (Tangier), then led an expedition to the Canary Islands. A year later, he returned to Hispania at the head of a new rebellion.

The Roman emperor Julius Caesar defeated Pompey's army in Spain.

Fighting for Sulla's faction was Gnaeus Pompeius, the future Pompey the Great, then only twenty-three. Pompey was a brilliant cavalry officer, but when strategy alone would not suffice he bribed some underlings to murder Sertorius in his sleep. From his demeanor a word was coined; in typically *pompous* fashion, Pompey returned to Rome to boast that he had conquered 876 Hispanic towns.

The next round of civil conflict involved the familiar story of Pompey and Julius Caesar. Caesar had built his military reputation in Hispania and Gaul and was described as a man "furious for war." The poet Lucan recounted that the morning after one particularly bloody battle, Caesar ordered breakfast served amid a field of corpses so that he could contemplate their faces. Sulla once dismissed the future dictator by remarking, "he wears his girdle too loosely," a poke at his manhood. But Caesar was handsome and a notorious womanizer, deemed one of the "great fornicators" of antiquity by historians.

Armies in the provinces tended to grow independent of Rome and were faithful to their commanders. When Caesar crossed the Rubicon River and entered Italy (49 BC) to unleash a civil war, he had six loyal legions in Hispania while Pompey could count seven. Eventually Caesar met forces loyal to Pompey at Llerda (Lérida), and fought a brilliant battle. One final engagement occurred in at Munda, a site near Osuna that has never been pinned down conclusively. Here, Caesar's army met thirty thousand men led by Pompey's two sons and nearly tasted defeat himself. With his forces retreating and on the verge of panic, Caesar desperately grabbed sword and shield and rushed into the maelstrom shouting, "Are you going to let your general be delivered up to the enemy?" Inspired legionnaires lunged forward and carried the day. Caesar remarked, "On other occasions I fought for victory, but today I fought for my life." It was his last battle. After Munda, Caesar was joined by his eighteen-year-old grand nephew, Gaius Octavius (Octavian), and the pair traveled together by carriage throughout Hispania for several months (Mark Antony claimed they were lovers). At last Caesar returned to Rome to meet his day of reckoning, and Octavian went on to become Rome's first emperor.

Long after the fall of Numantia, mountain-dwelling tribes from wild Cantabria continued to resist. Nevertheless, in 38 BC Hispania was officially declared a part of Rome and a general tax introduced. (In Castilla, for the next fourteen centuries years were counted from this date.) The Cantabrians and Basques were not impressed by the Roman declaration, however, and believed liberty was worth more than Latin. To Rome's embarrassment, another round of revolts erupted and lasted a decade. Fighting was savage, and the rebels so tenacious that several legions mutinied rather than return to the front. The Cantabrians always seemed to have the last word: they sang and shouted victory slogans while being crucified, and mothers killed their own children rather than let them be taken captive. It is interesting that Cantabria-Asturias was the same region that stood alone against the Moors seven centuries later. And though they were defeated, the neighboring Basques were never Romanized.

Finally Octavian—by then known as Augustus—intervened personally, but was forced to remain several years before achieving final victory. During the campaign he contracted a serious illness and lived for a time at the future provincial capital of Tarraco (Tarragona). Today, you can wander through some of Spain's best preserved Roman ruins and see remains of the tower where he stayed and a temple built in his honor. (In another historical footnote, the infamous Pontius Pilate was born in Tarraco.)

Augustus Caesar was not an imposing figure: he limped, was frequently ill, and wore thick-soled shoes to disguise his shortness. Yet by the time of his death Rome enjoyed imperial grandeur and the first years of the Pax Romana, two centuries of unparalleled peace and prosperity. Hispania too entered the longest period of calm in its entire history, during which the last traces of Iberians and Celts ceased to exist as identifiable races. By the time of Augustus,

Roman Iberia

By the first century AD, the peninsula was divided into three large provinces. Under Augustus the inhabitants of fifty Hispanic towns had Roman citizenship, a privilege not lightly granted. Among the most important *civitas* were Emerita Augusta (Mérida), Corduba (Córdoba), Tarraco (Tarragona), Caesar-Augusta (Zaragoza), Cartago Nova (Cartagena), Emporion (Ampurias) and Gades (Cádiz).

Baetica (Andalucía) was considered the most Roman area outside Italy, with all the trappings of civilization, including an excellent postal system. Bridges, aqueducts, baths, theaters, and arenas sprang up everywhere.

Hispania's greatest city lay at Emerita Augusta (Mérida), the capital of Lusitania province (roughly Portugal and Extremadura). During the Pax Romana, Mérida ranked ninth in size in the entire empire and boasted a 25,000 seat *circus maximus* for chariot races. One famous charioteer named Diocles retired here after 1,462 victories. (Contrary to popular, Hollywood-induced mythology, Romans never used chariots in warfare, only for sport.) The theater survives as the most impressive reminder of Mérida's former glories. Sitting today in this architectural gem, it is hard to believe that the theater lay buried under rubble for sixteen centuries before being excavated. Other important ruins include a large arena (amphitheater) for gladiatorial events that could be flooded for simulated naval encounters; a bridge over the Guadiana River with 64 arches; and an aqueduct with three levels of elegant arches.

Mérida lay in the heart of a huge cereal-producing region, just one piece in the mosaic of Hispania's thriving economy. Especially productive was the highly cultivated river valley in the heart of Baetica, source of wine and olive oil. Other Hispanic exports included knives and swords from Toletum (Toledo) and minerals such as lead, iron, copper, silver and gold. Spain, the future world colonizer, lived through centuries as a colony itself, and much of the wealth ended up in Roman coffers.

Gades had a reputation as a wealthy and wicked town with its provocative dancers called *puellae gaditanae*. These "girls from wanton Gades with endless prurience swinging lascivious loins in practiced writhings" (as one writer put it) were in great demand at parties given by wealthy merchants. There are even references to hand clapping and castanet clicking and to a peculiar form of singing described as deep and emotional. Upon these descriptions Cádiz bases its claim as the birthplace of flamenco.

One of the most significant events in Spain's entire history is the disappearance of its forests. Ancient Iberia, even the now treeless *meseta*, was once thickly wooded over almost half its surface with oaks, junipers, and evergreens. The long process of deforestation started about this time, as trees were cut down for both fuel and timber. Later, other activities contributed to the consequent erosion of the topsoil. We know that the entire Ebro Delta, about three hundred square kilometers, has been formed by eroded deposits over the past two millennia.

Major gold mines lay in the northwest, especially at Las Medulas de Caruseco, where Romans left pyramids of slag fifty meters high. Asturcia (Astorga) became a kind of early-day gold rush town, swarming with both free and slave workers. Slave labor was vital to the empire, and slaves formed a sizable part of Hispania's population. They had an average life expectancy of about thirty years, while free workers could live to the ripe old age of forty.

Over the centuries the one Roman institution that changed the least was the family. The father demanded and received absolute and unquestioning obedience from his wife and children, and family unity formed the bedrock of Hispanic society, just as it does today. The emperor in turn regarded his subjects as children, and the state granted privileges and protection only to the well behaved. Rulers supplied "bread and circuses" to keep the masses content, and the system worked remarkably well.

Hispano-Romans considered religion as an excuse for communal gaiety, and enjoyed great processions and games in honor of the gods. There were so many holidays, in fact, that critics charged they were seriously interfering with normal affairs. The festive calendar opened in March, with the re-dedication of the vestal flame and clanging of sacred shields at the temple of Mars. The month also witnessed the festival of Liberalia, a time of unrestrained merriment. April was crowded with activities, climaxing in a festival to honor the goddess Flora, during which both men and women donned flower-adorned garb. December was another month of wine-filled festivities.

Gladiatorial contests were the most popular diversion. Under the emperor Domitian, women battled dwarfs to the death and spectators thrilled at seeing people being torn apart by wild animals. The fights followed an established ritual; according to accepted custom, the loser of an encounter was always stabbed in the throat, and even the way he stuck out his neck for the thrust was taught at gladiatorial school. Later, an attendant used a hot poker to make sure he was dead. However, contrary to legend the crowd did not point thumbs down to demand the loser's execution; scholars say that gesture meant "throw down your sword," which saved the defeated fighter from death.

The theater provided less brutal entertainment, but it had suffered a decline in status since the Greeks. Playwrights and actors were no longer held in high regard; indeed, an acting company was known as a *grex*, the same word used for a flock of sheep. Performances were given in vulgar Latin, the common language that was quite unlike the literary Latin of Cicero or Virgil.

One Spanish-born master of the language was Seneca the Elder, a famed instructor of rhetoric. His son, Lucius Seneca, was born in Corduba, a center of intellectual life as it would be under the Moors. The young Seneca moved to Rome, where he served as Nero's private tutor and a kind of imperial ghost-writer composing speeches for the emperor. But no man could survive so close to Nero, and trumped-up charges of treason led to an order that Seneca slash his wrists and bleed to death in aristocratic style.

Seneca the Younger was a brilliant philosopher and writer who expounded the ideas of Stoicism, by which an individual sought to transcend the restraints of pain and pleasure, happiness and woe, in order to free the spirit.

He was known for his pithy remarks, such as "Spain was Christian perhaps before Christ." His own views about such matters as slavery were remarkably liberal, and it has been suggested that he was secretly a Christian.

Other writers born in Hispania during the first century helped create Spain's "Silver Age" of literature. Seneca's nephew Lucan was an erudite historian who wrote an epic poem about the war between Caesar and Pompey. It seemed to defend the Republic, which got him into hot water with Nero, and he suffered the same fate as his uncle. The poet Martial was born near Caesar Augusta (Zaragoza), but left Hispania for sophisticated Rome. He is remembered for his satiric epigrams about the licentious life of Roman high society. Martial returned to his native land to retire in peace, and his later poems reflect country life during the idyllic days of the Pax Romana. He penned an adage for all ages: "Live today, for tomorrow may be too late." This attitude became a way of life in Spain.

During the Roman Empire's first century came an event of monumental significance: the introduction of Christianity to Iberia. Popular legend says that Saint James the Greater (Santiago), believed to be the brother of St. John, brought Christianity to the peninsula around AD 40. Reaching Zaragoza, he built a temple to the holy virgin, who had appeared to him above a marble pillar. (The *virgen de pilar* became the source for naming countless Spanish girls "Pilar.") According to tradition, James spent seven years spreading the faith, then returned to Palestine where he perished during a wave of persecutions. Later, followers supposedly brought his remains to Campus Stellae in the far northwest of Hispania, today called Santiago de Compostela. Although no historical evidence confirms any of this, the story forms an important chapter in Spain's national heritage. It is more likely that St. Paul visited, but most historians think that Christianity really arrived, ironically enough, via North Africa. Whatever the source, its seeds fell on fertile soil thirsty for mystical qualities so lacking in Roman religion.

However, it would be a mistake to think that Christianity spread quickly; the process lasted two centuries, with urban workers first to convert, followed slowly by the country folk. The very word "pagan" derives from Latin and means "peasant," that is, one who lives in a *pagus* (village). As late as the seventh century, many country districts remained stubbornly pagan. The eternally hardheaded Basques were the last to convert, but soon became the most fervid believers.

Tales of martyrdom have been exaggerated; at first the new church was too insignificant to receive much attention. Some notable exceptions include St. Vincent, who taunted his tormentors as they stretched him on the rack, and St. Engracia, who had her breasts ripped off and her liver cut out and fed to birds. St. Eulalia was only thirteen when she arrived at Mérida eager for martyrdom. She burst into the governor's chambers and shouted "The old gods are worthless and the emperor himself is nothing." For this the young girl was tortured to death, but according to legend she continued to sing triumphantly until the end. For circus-loving crowds, Christian martyrs were a new sort of athlete, "running on hot coals as if on roses, plunging into fires as if into streams of cool water, and garlanding themselves with tortures as if they were spring flowers," in the words of St. John Chrysostom.

The official Roman religion provided no doctrine or moral code, no promise of an afterlife, and no mystical aspects. Thus it is not surprising that Christianity found converts in Hispania and elsewhere. But for centuries it had to compete with other religions from the east, among them Mithraism from Persia. Mithras was a divine figure representing the sun. He was depicted as a young man stabbing a bull, and initiation rites involved a sacrificial killing. Women were excluded from the religion, which became immensely popular with soldiers. The spot on which Mérida's bullring stands today was once a temple to Mithras. Here, legionnaires were anointed with the steaming blood of slaughtered bulls in order to make them invincible in battle.

Another eastern cult eagerly adopted by Hispano-Romans revolved around Bacchus, god of wine, and the rites often became drunken orgies. Equally sensational was the cult of Cybele, the great mother-goddess. A complex pageantry swirled around her, such as processions of the faithful accompanied by drums, flutes, and cymbals. There were scenes of self-flagellation, and on the "day of blood" novice priests performed their own castration. The finale was a literal bloodbath, when devotees sat in holes and were showered with the blood of a slaughtered bull lying on the grating above.

Christianity and its rivals borrowed liberally from one another. The priests of Cybele celebrated the vernal equinox to compete with Easter, and the bull sacrifice took on aspects of the slaughter of the Christian lamb. The followers of Mithras celebrated December 25 as marking the sun's rebirth and beginning of the end to winter. Even today, it seems at times that Spaniards never really gave up their pagan heritage, but welded old rituals to their own version of Christianity. Hence the dazzling Easter processions of virgin queens and hooded penitents whipping themselves, and wild, wine-sodden parties mobbed by hysterical devotees, as in the procession of the virgin at El Rocio (near Huelva). Many religious celebrations end with a *corrida*, when bulls are killed in an elaborate ritual that the word "bullfight" does not adequately describe.

Romanization was not a one-way affair, and before long Hispania began to influence Rome itself. Born in Itálica, Trajan (Marcus Ulpius Traianus) became the first Roman emperor from the provinces. Under Trajan Rome reached its greatest extent, an area about the same as the United States with a population of more than 100 million and 300,000 kilometers of roads. And every inch of the Mediterranean shoreline belonged to Rome.

Trajan became emperor in AD 99 and ruled for eighteen years. He was broad shouldered and intelligent looking, brows furrowed as if he was deep in thought. Trajan was an artist who loved the arts, and he oversaw magnificent public works and monuments like Trajan's Column in Rome. But as a successful general, he believed Rome was getting soft for the lack of good enemies, and he vowed to revive military virtues. He personally led expeditions of conquest and was the first emperor to navigate the Persian Gulf.

On his deathbed Trajan adopted Hadrian, another Hispano-Roman, as his son and heir. Also from Itálica, Hadrian was married to Sabina, the emperor's niece. He was fair-skinned and wore a beard—the first emperor to do so. But his moderate temperament and feeble health made him very different from the frenetic Trajan. It was said that Hadrian's curious accent, typical of southern Spain at the time, caused laughter in the senate. While other emperors might have lopped off a few heads, the proud "Spaniard" studied Latin intensively and became a great orator. Under Hadrian the empire flourished as never before; conquests had ceased and defense was largely unnecessary. Notable exceptions were construction of Hadrian's Wall in Britain (to hold back warlike Scots) and the brutal suppression of a revolt in Palestine, which marked the end of the Jewish state for almost two millennia. Jews were scattered throughout the Roman world, and thousands of families chose Hispania. This was truly Rome's Golden Age in Hispania, climaxing with such stunning achievements as the Alcántara Bridge over the Tajo River, in the high country near Cáceres, and a twenty-four-kilometer-long aqueduct serving Tarraco.

The Romans built to impress, and they succeeded. Builders were so successful due to the versatility and strength of the arch and the fact that their mortar did not buckle under stress. They used a particularly effective blend of sandy earth called *pozzolana* and lime (with a dash of pork fat and the milk of figs) to create quicklime unsurpassed for centuries. With these twin strengths they could build major structures like the amphitheater at Itálica, which seated thirty thousand spectators.

Just as Mérida is a town of the Augustan age, so Itálica embodies the Hadrianic. It lay next to an important port until the Baetis River changed its course and trade moved to nearby Hispalis, site of modern Sevilla. Itálica was transformed by its native son into a showcase of Roman architecture, and its ruins reflect the city as Hadrian rebuilt it around the year AD 125. In its heyday Itálica boasted wide streets, rows of mansions (one with forty rooms), public baths, and the fourth largest amphitheater in the Roman world. You can still peer down into the arena and visit the chambers where Christians and other prisoners huddled in fear

Roman bridge at Cordoba, one of many still standing in Spain after two millennia

before being tossed out with the lions.(The word arena comes from the Latin word for "sand," which was used to dry up the blood that flowed profusely.)

There was a dark side of the Pax Romana, when power and cruelty became perversely equated, and the axe and rods (the *fasces* resurrected much later by Italian fascists) were the symbols of authority. Those not in lock-step with the Roman way might be flogged, crucified, burned or buried alive, hurled from a cliff, drowned in a sack, fed to wild beasts, or worse.

Although thousands of Christians perished in Spanish arenas, even Romans could not kill the new religion. It was a force to be reckoned with by the end of the second century. Finally legalized by Constantine, himself a convert, it later became the empire's official religion. Christianity had come a long way since the crucifixion of a carpenter's son three centuries earlier.

The year AD 248 was the 1000th anniversary of Rome's founding; it also marked the beginning of a long twilight period before Rome's decline and eventual fall. Chinks in the imperial armor were beginning to appear, signs that the Pax Romana, like all things, must have an end as well as a beginning. To shore up the crumbling empire, Constantine later moved his capital east to the Bosphorus and the ancient city of Byzantium (renamed Constantinople and later Istanbul), far from Hispania.

Archaeologists tell us that by the third century Spanish towns were already building massive walls to discourage attackers. The Roman walls in Barcelona's old quarter, for instance, went up in response to waves of Franks and Alemanni raiding toward the end of the century, long before the main barbarian invasions came. And not all of Hispania's troubles came from the outside: there were peasant revolts and demands for regional autonomy; the provincial administration was hopelessly corrupt; and the slave system, hence the entire economy, was breaking down under the influence of Christianity. The once rebellious religion eventually became the unifying principle of the empire and finally a force of repression as Christians began to root out heresies with a passion. The most serious was Arianism, which denied the concept of the Trinity. Bishop Hosius from Córdoba led the battle against it and emerged as one of the fathers of the Nicene Creed (325), the cornerstone of Roman Catholicism.

Priscillian, the bishop of Ávila, expounded a uniquely Spanish heresy. He claimed that the world had been created by the devil and was ruled by him, and that life was a punishment for sinful souls. Even though its founder was decapitated, this heresy survived for three centuries. Priscillianism allowed dancing in the church ritual, a practice that survives in the "dance of the Seises" held each year during Corpus Christi at the Sevilla Cathedral.

At the end of the Roman era another Spanish-born emperor, Flavius Theodosius, completed the circle by banning all forms of paganism, outlawing the Olympic Games, squelching heresy, burning temples, and behaving in a quite un-Christian manner. By then, Rome's power was just a memory. On his deathbed in 395, Theodosius divided the once-invincible empire into sections ruled by his two sons, one in Constantinople and the other in Rome. Just fourteen years later, Hispania would fall to rampaging barbarians from the north, which slammed shut the book on six centuries of Roman rule.

The eastern incarnation survived until a generation before Columbus, who arrived on the scene to launch the logical successor to the glory that was Rome—the Spanish Empire. Indeed, Rome's two most important legacies—language and religion—form the core of *hispanidad* (Spanish civilization and culture), which encompasses most of *Latin* America down to this day.

Sights & Sites

Alcántara (Cáceres): Arched bridge 194 meters long and 70 high (highest in the Roman world) over the Tajo River.

Ampurias (Gerona): Costa Brava's major historical attraction with ruins of old houses; traces of plaza and amphitheater.

Baelo-Bolonia (Cádiz): Near Tarifa, remnants of a large fish-salting enterprise; temples dedicated to Juno, Jupiter, and Minerva.

Barcelona: Archaeological Museum has many artifacts from Roman Ampurias; defensive wall in the Barrio Gótico is partially Roman.

Carmona (Sevilla): Main attraction is a huge necropolis of 800 tombs, some no more than delicate urns filled with ashes.

Itálica (Sevilla): Excellent museum; ruins of one of the largest arena outside Rome; network of streets.

Mallorca (Balearic Islands): Ruins of theater at Alcudia near Cabo Formentor; artifacts from Pollentia at Bellver Castle in Palma.

Mérida (Badajoz): Temples, theater, two aqueducts, arches, Guadiana bridge, and museum of Roman art.

Sagunto (Valencia): Site of ancient Saguntum features a variety of ruins.

Salamanca: Called Salamantica by Romans; well-preserved bridge over the Tormes River.

Segovia: The world-famous aqueduct is an inspiring sight.

Roman ruins at Italica outside Sevilla, where two future emperors were born

Sevilla: Archaeological Museum with pieces from Itálica, including Mercury with winged sandals and a bust of the emperor Trajan.

Soria: Museum of Numantia dedicated to the famous last stand.

Tarragona: Ruins of walls and amphitheater; museum includes superb mosaic, head of Medusa; outside town are triumphal Arch of Bera, the Tower of the Escipiones (a two-tiered aqueduct), and the Mausoleum of Centcelles.

Chapter 3

Medieval Spain

The view of Toledo from the far bank of the Tajo River stirs images of savage sieges and heroic defenders. A deep gorge nearly encircles the granite rock on which the city stands, and the sheer cliffs make other defenses unnecessary on three sides. It is not surprising that this imposing site was an important Celtiberian and Roman stronghold. Nor that the next peninsular power, the Visigoths, chose it as their capital. What *is* surprising, however, is the almost total absence of Visigothic remnants in Toledo and in Spain generally. A rough-hewn country church, a few pieces of jewelry or a regal crown sitting in a museum, an obscure law code: these are the legacies of *three centuries* of Gothic Spain.

In Toledo, guides will point to the spot where King Roderick deflowered the lovely daughter of a count whose vengeance would bring the Moors to Spain. But the place and even the story itself are highly suspect. The Visigoths (or West Goths) seem destined to inhabit a murky region sandwiched between the Romans and Moors, the Spanish version of the Dark Ages. And yet, there is something oddly fascinating about this Germanic race so ill at ease in Latin Spain. Take its peculiar kings with strange names—Witteric,

Wamba, Wittiza, and Chindasuinth—who wore purple slippers and ermine robes and let their hair and beards grow long.

Of thirty-four Visigoth kings only fifteen died of natural causes. Atawulf, the first in a dismal line of succession, was killed at the urging of Sigeric, who reigned for just one week before he in turn fell at the hands of Walia. The path to the throne bounced from elective to hereditary and back again, but the issue often became moot as regicide came like clockwork. Between the years 531 and 555 alone, four successive kings were murdered. Among them was one notoriously amorous monarch, who was dining one evening when the lights suddenly dimmed and sword thrusts from a dozen outraged husbands and fathers ended his life.

Despite the chaos and confusion, the Visigoths for a time boasted the largest and strongest kingdom in Western Europe. The shaky unity they finally achieved was Spain's first attempt to become a unified nation. Yet Gothic accomplishments in Spain proved inconsequential: the large-scale herding of animals; the horseshoe arch; and a few dozen surviving words are their legacy. Among the Germanic words that entered both English and Spanish: *werra* (war/*guerra*), *raubon* (to rob/*robar*), *helm* (helmet/*yelmo*), and *harpa* (harp/*arpa*.) Their greatest impact, perhaps, was choosing a capital on the *meseta* at Roman Toletum (Toledo). For the first time the more advanced coastal regions looked to the interior as the source of political power.

The Goths' apparent lack of significance is misleading, however. Ortega y Gasset, one of Spain's foremost modern thinkers, went so far as to blame most of his country's later political ills on them. They were barbarians, he said, but even worse they were *weak* barbarians, who never achieved any unity or stability and never introduced the feudal institutions found elsewhere in Europe. Spain was being "different" for the first time.

The Gothic chapter opened in 409 with the first arrival of the legendary blond barbarians from the north, trying to grab slices of the splintering Roman Empire. The Suevi (Swabians) from the upper Danube and the infamous Vandals from the Vistula River area swarmed across the Pyrenees. According to one story, these tribes were invited by a Roman general making a personal bid for power, but (as barbarians will do) they soon got out of hand. Within a short time they had overrun the peninsula with virtually no opposition, not even in Cantabria, which had frustrated the Romans for two centuries. The Suevi headed for Galicia and the Vandals landed in the south, which they named *Vandalucía* according to one story.

Meanwhile, Rome itself was sacked in 410 by another barbarian horde of Teutonic persuasion, the Visigoths. These flaxen-haired warriors dressed in skins had moved down slowly from the Baltic region (perhaps Gotland) and settled in Transylvania and the Danube basin. From there they began to nibble away at the crumbling empire, and under Alaric they violated Rome itself, the first time in eight centuries that a hostile army entered the eternal city.

The emperor was spared, however, and soon allied his tottering dominions with these Goths, the most "civilized" of all the barbarians. Rome's last-ditch defensive plan involved pitting one tribe against another, and the Goths under Atawulf were signed on to rid Hispania of other invaders. In return, they would receive lands in southern France and become senior partners in a Roman confederation. The plan seemed to work: after scattering Rome's enemies in short order, they returned north of the Pyrenees and formed a Gothic nation with its capital at Toulouse.

While the defeated Vandals were busy licking their wounds, an invitation arrived from yet another rebellious Roman general asking them to fight for him in North Africa. After crossing the sea in Roman ships, about eighty thousand Vandals settled in what are today Morocco and Algeria. Meanwhile, the Suevi planted a kingdom in the northwest, which would survive for another 180 years.

Goths continued to trickle slowly into the peninsula, but the floodgates really opened when the last remnants of the empire at Rome fell in 476. Gothic king Euric and his son Alaric suddenly found themselves ruling over the largest political unit in Western Europe, stretching from the Loire River to the Pillars of Hercules. Shortly after, however, the upstart Franks pushed the Goths out of Gaul, and Hispania became their tenuous new power base. Goths numbered only about 200,000—mostly in the rural interior—compared with several million Hispano-Romans. At no point were they ever more than a small minority of the population. Like oil and water, they would not mix, and during most of the period the two races lived apart, both legally and socially.

Nevertheless, Gothic rule was not despotic, and their laws did not try to subjugate the *hispani* other than with an onerous tax system. Indeed, these most Romanized of barbarians seemed awed and intimidated by the legacy of their predecessors. Euric's law was written in Latin and drafted by Roman lawyers; Goths used Roman coins; even their gravestones were inscribed in

Latin. They lived in Roman cities because there were no Gothic ones, and *hispani* kept their own governors and town councils organized in the old Roman framework.

A major difference between the two peoples was religion. Goths had adopted the Arian view of Christianity (which denied the Trinity) and came to think of it as their own, while Hispanics practiced the "Roman religion," later to be called Catholic. Feelings ran high, and when one king failed to convert his new bride, a Frankish princess, he ordered that cow dung be poured over her on her way to church. While Catholics and Arians feuded, pagan practices survived in the countryside. Priests fought in vain to stamp out the dances and bawdy songs of pagan crowds on saint's days, and many so-called Christians still considered Thursday to be Jupiter's Day and refused to work.

Hispano-Romans looked with disdain on their overlords. To these urbane people the Goths, with their long locks and gaudy jewelry, seemed illiterate, primitive, and warlike, country bumpkins with odd customs and harsh laws. For example, tampering with public documents brought two hundred lashes, a shaved head, and amputation of the right thumb; conviction of homosexuality meant castration while rapists were punished with public circumcision. Another curious legal custom was the "ordeal of hot water," by which those accused of theft were questioned while being submerged in boiling water. Confessions were fast and frequent. Capital punishment fell on magicians, makers of spells, anyone invoking storms to damage the grape harvest or demons to make men mad, and on those who inquired into the future or offered sacrifices by night. Such laws did not go down well among free-spirited coastal residents, who looked to Rome and Byzantium, certainly not Toledo, as models of civilization.

This spirit of independence did not bode well for Gothic hopes of controlling the peninsula, and by the middle of the sixth century Byzantine armies were threatening to retake Spain for the new Roman Empire based in Constantinople. In an effort to restore lands of ancient Rome, Justinian led a series of successful forays against the Vandals of North Africa, climaxing with the conquest of *Septum* (Ceuta) at a key position on the Strait of Gibraltar.

A few years later Byzantines landed in southern Spain, where they allied with a myriad of factions—anyone opposing the current king, Roman Catholics, and the bulk of coastal residents who traditionally resented the Goths. The invaders established important posts at Málaga and Cartagena to serve as bridgeheads for the re-conquest of Spain. This "second coming" materialized, and they seized most of the southeastern coast and the Balearic Islands to create a new Byzantine province called *Spania*. This little-known occupation lasted about seventy-five years and brought Greek and eastern Mediterranean culture to Spain. Many priests went to Constantinople to study Greek, once again the literary language of the educated. Indeed, there was more cultural contact between Spain and the imperial capital than with France, which was wallowing in medieval squalor at the time. Yet little remains of the Byzantine period, other than some scattered artwork and the ruins of a few churches.

Gothic control of the peninsula was also compromised by the Basques, who were never conquered and at one point even invaded the Gothic domain, sweeping down the Ebro Valley to the Mediterranean before retiring. The Suevi had a sizable kingdom in the northwest, but were finally conquered during the reign of King Leovigild. He is considered the greatest of all Visigothic rulers despite his rabid persecution of Catholics (including his own martyr son, St. Hermenegild). Among other things, he established a truly regal court at Toledo, annulled the ban on marriage between Goths and Hispano-Romans (it had been a capital crime), and crushed a rebellion in Cantabria.

Leovigild tried to make the monarchy hereditary (rather than elective) by passing the crown to his son Reccared, who became a crucial figure in his own right. With great flourish he converted to Catholicism, burned all Arian books he could find, and united the kingdom under one religion in around 590. This concept of national unity stemming from religious unity later became fundamental to Spanish political thought. Toledo was the religious (as well as political) capital of Spain, an honor it retains to this day, and a crucial alliance formed between the monarchy and the church against the nobility. The clergy thereafter wielded substantial political power and were given control of education.

The trend toward unification spilled over into the cultural arena as well, as Gothic and Hispanic styles and customs became less rigidly defined. Goths felt threatened and insisted on keeping both their language and their distance from the natives, but inevitably fell under the power of a stronger Roman-Latin culture. Although archaeological evidence is slim, it appears they adopted Roman and Byzantine styles with gusto, as seen in artifacts such as the treasure of Guarrazar or the magnificent crown of Reccesuinth.

The Goths had their own smiths and potters, but could not boast architects, sculptors, or painters. It is ironic that the word "gothic" came to describe the splendid architectural style seen in churches built hundreds of years later, a style *unknown* to the Goths. The word itself had come to mean "barbaric and uncouth," and Renaissance architects, enamored with the classical style, sneered at the late-medieval cathedrals as crude and ugly, in other words gothic. The name stuck.

The cultural intermingling is embodied in St. Isidore (560-636), the era's leading intellectual figure. He is known for a history of the Goths (one of the precious few in existence) as well as theological writings, but his father was governor of Cartagena and may well have been a Byzantine. Isidore expounded the glories of Roman civilization as preserved through Christianity and compiled a renowned encyclopedia that could be found in nearly every European monastery. Unfortunately, he also wrote the first anti-Jewish treatise in the West, and one of his pupils, King Sisebut, decreed that Jews must accept conversion or leave—another common refrain throughout Spanish history. A large Jewish population, perhaps larger than the Goths themselves, had resided on the peninsula for centuries and deeply resented the persecutions. Those who refused to convert moved to North Africa. It's said that at the time of the Moorish invasion a hundred years later, their descendants had not forgotten what the Goths did and took appropriate revenge.

After decades of skirmishes the Byzantines were finally pushed out in 624, and at long last Goths ruled the *entire* peninsula with the exception of the Basque lands. The peninsula was united under one ruler, something that did not occur again until the reign of Felipe (Philip) II almost a thousand years later. Finally the Goths could replace the old Roman system of provincial government with their own. But these advances were only straws in the wind; the seventh century witnessed a progressive collapse of the social order that would climax in the crucial year of 711, when the Moors changed Spain forever.

In essence, very few people felt any allegiance to the crown. The monarchy faced chronic revolts by generals and bishops, popular local uprisings, and economic disruption and chaos. In addition, massive numbers of escaped slaves were roaming the kingdom. (The Catholic Church was the largest slaveholder.) When the monarchy attributed its troubles to a "Jewish conspiracy," savage anti-Semitic riots broke out, leading to hundreds of deaths. To make matters worse, a *real* invasion plot hatched between Jews and Moors was discovered. Tales of conspiracy had fulfilled themselves and repression was turned up a notch.

To understand the times, it must be remembered that throughout history Spaniards have lived in fear of invasion and piracy from North Africa. The Goths were no exception and had very good reasons for concern. In 675, the Moors made a half-hearted attempt to invade the peninsula, but were turned back before they could disembark.

But who were these Moors, the people who would rewrite Spanish history so profoundly? The word derives from the Latin *mauri*, a name for the Berber tribes living in Roman *Mauretania* (roughly modern Algeria and Morocco). Although the name Moors has no real ethnographic meaning, it can be used to refer to all Muslims—whether Berber or Arab—who conquered the Iberian Peninsula. Islam had recently swept across North Africa, and within a generation of Mohammed's death (632) it reached the far west at Tingis (Tangier). Here the Arab vanguard encountered Byzantine colonies and native Berbers, that mysterious race that resisted from their mountain strongholds until an Arab general named Musa finally triumphed.

In response to the failed Moorish invasion of 675, Gothic king Wamba made the mistake of calling up priests for military service. His reign came to an abrupt end when the clergy joined a band of hostile nobles led by Ervigius. Wamba was drugged and dressed as a monk by the rebels, who also shaved his head. When the king awoke he was so embarrassed he did not even dispute the naked power grab, and Ervigius became king. The final crisis of Gothic Spain erupted a few years later, when King Wittiza tried to pass on the throne to his son Achila. The nobles elected their own man, Roderick by name, and thrust the peninsula into a civil war that ended with the interloper seated on the throne.

That same year (710) Musa sent four hundred Moors under Tarif to reconnoiter the soft Iberian underbelly. They landed at the spot closest to Africa, today site of Tarifa, and returned with both information and booty, including "women of rare beauty." But Musa still had doubts about a full-scale invasion that involved crossing the sea. Arab commanders felt far more comfortable in the desert, "an ocean in which no oar is dipped," according to the Muslim Koran.

From the very beginning Moorish Spain is cloaked in myths and legends, a kind of rosy romantic haze akin to "A Thousand and One Nights." Thus we hear the story of lovely Florinda, a patrician girl at the royal court whose feminine charms nearly drove Roderick to madness. The stricken king would hide in the bushes while Florinda bathed in the Tajo, and one day he was finally overcome with desire and took the beautiful maiden right on the river bank. But Roderick would reap the proverbial whirlwind. Florinda's father was Count Julian, the Byzantine governor of Septum (Ceuta) on the African side of the strait. Julian came to fetch his daughter, and the king, unaware that his crime was known, asked Julian to send him a certain breed of African hawk. The count promised to send hawks such as the king never dreamed of. According to the story, Julian then approached the Moors with an invasion plan. There may be some truth to this yarn, but the real count, whose name was probably Olian Olban, may merely have made a pragmatic deal with Musa to save his own skin. Some evidence also points to supporters of the ousted Prince Achila as the culprits in inviting the Moors into Spain. They believed that after deposing Roderick and taking some booty, the invaders would leave.

Whatever the truth, Musa ordered Tariq ibn-Ziyad (the prefix *ibn* means "son of"), governor of Tangier, to mount another reconnaissance mission. This time about ten thousand men made the trip, but the Moors were still not thinking of staying. Only later did they realize that no riper plum awaited plucking than Gothic Spain.

"You must know how the Grecian maidens, as handsome as houris, their necks glittering with innumerable pearls and jewels, their bodies clothed with tunics of costly silks and sprinkled with gold, are awaiting your arrival, reclining on soft couches in the sumptuous palaces of crowned lords and princes." With these words the Arab Tariq intoned his mostly Berber troops on the eve of their departure for Spain. In April of 711 they landed at ancient Calpe, the limestone mass they called *jabal-tariq* (Tariq's rock), which is the origin of the name Gibraltar.

The attack caught Roderick off guard, but he rushed from the far north with an army of questionable loyalty to do battle with the Moors. In July, the two forces met somewhere near the Guadalete River in southwestern Andalucía in a confused encounter in which followers of Achila, including the bishop of Sevilla, fought alongside the Moors. Roderick's army was annihilated after a large number of his troops changed sides in mid-battle, and the king himself vanished. As the dust cleared, all that could be found was his white charger with its gilded saddle adorned with rubies and emeralds, his golden mantle embroidered with pearls, and one silver boot. According to another legend, Roderick escaped and was rescued by an old hermit. The dying king gave his last confession and was absolved on the condition that he would be entombed with a serpent until his soul departed. Roderick agreed and was last heard uttering faintly, "Now he is gnawing, gnawing me in the part where I have most sinned."

Thus commenced the Moorish chapter of Spanish history, several centuries during which most of the peninsula developed quite differently from the rest of Europe. It was a traumatic period in which a new religion, language, and culture were stamped on the land. This culture became so imbedded in the Hispanic mentality that it ceased to be alien; in fact, many natives willingly became Muslims. Spain was being "different" again. Two centuries after the conquest, *Al-Andalus* (as the Moors called Spain) was Europe's cultural capital, glittering in a medieval sky with few stars. But the Moors also destroyed the burgeoning, albeit feeble, Gothic unity and left a legacy of separatism and strife that poisoned Spain for centuries. If it was the best of times in some cultural areas, the worst has too easily been forgotten.

After his victory, Tariq gave orders that a group of prisoners be cut to pieces and their flesh boiled in cauldrons. The rest of the captured Goths were released and told to spread the word of Moorish methods. The tactic worked, and token resistance melted away. Tariq spent the winter of 711 in Toledo, the old Visigoth capital.

Perhaps a bit jealous at his underling's remarkable success, Musa himself led another wave across the strait the following summer, mostly Arabs this time. The Goths made their last desperate stand at Mérida, and remnants of their broken army fled to Asturias, where they joined tough local defenders to form the nucleus of the Christian Reconquest. But that was yet to come. In just a few years the Moors swept over most of the peninsula and into southern France, only to be stopped by the Franks under Charles Martel at the Battle of Poitiers (732). But Hispania now belonged to the caliph at Damascus, then capital of the Muslim world.

The Moors' easy conquest has puzzled historians, especially Spaniards suckled on stories of Viriathus and Numantia. The answer seems to lie in the basic weakness of the Visigoth state and the lingering hostility among Hispano-Romans toward their Germanic rulers. "Old Spaniards" naively believed that the Moors would fill their sacks with loot and be gone. Oppressed classes such as Jews and serfs had reason to celebrate the Goths' demise and to welcome the invaders. Jews in particular aided the Moors, and memories of this collaboration (Count Julian himself was possibly Jewish) cropped up throughout the Reconquest.

Al-Andalus encompassed the entire peninsula except for the extreme northwest. As this territory shrank over the centuries the name was retained, and the last area of Moorish occupation became Andalucía. The word's origin is not clear, but Berbers called this the "land of the Vandals," *Tamurt Wandalus*, and Al-Andalus is possibly a corruption. According to Muslim legend, when Allah was creating the earth and dealing out good and bad, each place was given five wishes. The land of Al-Andalus asked for a clear sky, a beautiful sea full of fishes, ripe fruit, and fair women. All these were granted, but a fifth wish—for good government—was refused because that would have created paradise on earth.

A Moorish tower in Toledo

The first Moorish descriptions reveal astonishment and admiration for the new land: the luxury of its kings, the wealth and monuments of its cities, especially Sevilla. General Musa traveled to Damascus with an entourage of captured Spanish women and told the caliph tales of thirty thousand captured virgins and phenomenal treasures such as Solomon's Table, made of solid gold studded with hundreds of rubies. He also remarked that the most striking thing about the Goths was the "effeminacy of the princes." (Three decades later, St. Boniface blamed the Goths' quick fall on their "moral degeneracy," code words for homosexuality.)

Musa arrived at the wrong time, however, and became immersed in a power struggle following the caliph's death. He was arrested by the new caliph and spent his last days in a filthy Arab prison dreaming of Al-Andalus. Back in Spain, his son took King Roderick's widow as his wife (as was Muslim custom) and named himself governor of the conquered lands. But he too was swept away by events and decapitated in Sevilla; his head was sent to Damascus to remind others of the pitfalls of ambition.

From the very outset the Moors became entangled in seemingly endless internal squabbles between rival Arab tribes and between the elitist Arab leaders and their Berber henchmen, who were treated as inferiors. The two leading Arab factions, the Yemenites and Kaishites, crushed a Berber revolt then turned on themselves in an orgy of massacres and assassinations. This civil strife helps explain why the Moors did not conquer the entire peninsula in those first years. If they had done so, the Reconquest might never have developed and Spain would be a Muslim nation today. Instead, a shadowy figure named Pelayo led a band of Asturian mountaineers and surviving Goths to the first Christian victory. It was a *crucial* turning point in Spanish history.

Moorish historians relate how, after years of fighting, only thirty men remained of Pelayo's army, living like wild beasts on honey in the mountains. Finally the weary Moors retired and declared, "What harm can thirty savage asses do to us?" But from the cave of Covadonga (where a shrine stands today), Pelayo organized resistance that culminated with the battle of Covadonga in about 720. According to Christian reports, 400,000 Muslims were miraculously killed when all the weapons they hurled flew back at them. In reality, Pelayo defeated a small marauding band in a skirmish. Nonetheless, the seeds of the Reconquest were planted.

The "savage ass" named Pelayo also helped create a great dynasty when his daughter married a local chieftain named Alfonso, founder of the kingdom of Asturias. Alfonso I reigned for eighteen years and won back extensive territory; by his death (757) the Christians occupied about one-quarter of the peninsula. Toward the end of the century Asturias united with Galicia in the far northwest. This small fortress-kingdom with its back to the coast welcomed refugees from the south and assumed the role of defender of Christian civilization. (For reasons of simplicity, we often refer to the confusing kaleidoscope of kingdoms as "the Christians.") To honor this role as cradle of the nation, the heir to the Spanish throne is called Prince of Asturias, the equivalent of Britain's Prince of Wales.

It is far from the truth to imagine Moorish Spain as ruled and inhabited by Arabs. Although many Arabs, mostly Syrians, occupied high positions, the bulk of the Muslims were Berbers. Later, converted Christians called *muwallads*, together with the offspring of the first waves of invaders, formed the nucleus of Moorish Spain. (The invaders brought no women, hence the second generation of Moors was already half Hispanic.)

Another misconception about Moorish Spain is that the Muslims vigorously tried to convert Christians and other "infidels," by sword point if need be. In truth many converted by choice and even adopted Arabic as their language. Moreover, Muslims allowed both Christians and Jews, as "people of the Book," to practice their religions if they submitted to Moorish rule. Those who resisted naturally met a harsher fate. Every non-Muslim had to pay a special tax, which provided another good reason for tolerance. This attitude lasted until the arrival of fanatical sects from North Africa three centuries later when intolerance became the norm. Forced conversions, pogroms, and deportations are as much the legacy of Christian Spain as Moorish.

After the first forty volatile years following 711, Al-Andalus cried out for order and unity. It arrived in the person of Abd-er-Rahman, called "the Wanderer," who would transform this mere province of Damascus into an independent state that would become the cultural light of Europe. This Syrian prince and future emir was one of those rare individuals who crop up every few generations. He was tall, fair-haired (almost red-headed), and considered handsome despite having only one eye.

When he was nineteen, the Umaiyad dynasty to which he belonged was overthrown and massacred by the Abbasids, descendants of the Prophet's cousin. Abd-er-Rahman escaped miraculously and made his way across North Africa, driven by a sense of destiny. This was based on a prophecy that Al-Andalus would be conquered by one who had (as he did) two curls of hair falling across his forehead. His mother had been a Berber slave in the caliph's harem, and he settled with her tribe upon reaching Morocco. Then, after encouragement from a pro-Umaiyad faction across the strait, he landed at Almuñécar south of Granada and rallied his supporters. Within a year he had crushed the opposition and was proclaimed Emir (commander) of Al-Andalus.

Abd-er-Rahman I ruled for thirty-two years. To protect his power he created an army of forty thousand Berbers and slaves from southern Europe. Threats from insurgents were soon smothered; the leaders' severed heads were filled with salt and myrrh, packed in boxes, covered with the Abbasid flag, and sent to Damascus. When they arrived, the caliph supposedly exclaimed, "Allah be praised, that the sea divides us from this devil."

In the year 777, the caliph in Damascus bribed Frankish king Charlemagne into invading Spain, and an army led by his nephew Roland unsuccessfully attacked Zaragoza. Deprived of plunder, the Franks sacked Pamplona as they retreated through Roncesvalles Pass in the Pyrenees.

"High are the hills, valleys dark and deep,
Grisly the rocks, and wondrous grim the steeps."

The pass is so described in the famous French epic poem *The Song of Roland*, which chronicles an attack on the retreating Franks. But contrary to the poem's version of history, the attack came not from the Moors, but from Basques outraged over the sacking of Pamplona. The entire episode clearly shows that the struggle between two religions often disguised questions of power and money. After all, Charlemagne's army was fighting the Moors on behalf of the caliph of Damascus, not Christianity.

The dynasty started by Abd-er-Rahman would last almost three centuries. Many brutal rulers followed, but there were good ones too. The emir's son was a virtual saint, who dressed in simple clothes and personally visited the poor and infirm. Unfortunately, during the emirate's entire history (756-929) scarcely a generation passed without a major revolt or external attack. Under Hakam I an uprising on the outskirts of Córdoba led to fierce repression, which included the crucifixion of three hundred rebels along the banks of the Guadalquivir. (To this day the site is called "the field of truth.") Those not killed were expelled, creating the nucleus of the Andalucían Quarter of Fez, Morocco. Hakam also ordered the infamous Day of the Foss at Toledo. All local leaders suspected of disloyalty were tricked into entering the governor's castle, where they were beheaded one by one and their bodies thrown into a trench. Hakam told his son: "Like the tailor who uses his needle to sew together pieces of cloth, so I used my sword to unite my divided provinces, for I have taken care that no rebel will disturb your slumbers." The son, Abd-er-Rahman II, was so nauseated by the bloodletting that he developed a nervous tic that caused him to blink his eyes constantly.

There were also threats from abroad. In 844, Norsemen (Vikings) suddenly appeared in "long ships" and started attacking ports along Iberia's Atlantic coast. From Galicia and Lisbon they crept south to the mouth of the Guadalquivir, then up-river to Sevilla, where they went on a weeklong binge of murder and pillage. Shortly after, the blue-eyed intruders were defeated and limped back to sea with less than half their ships.

Reports of such battles are the stuff that remains as history, not the years or decades of peace between them. But clanging sabers are only part of the story. By the reign of Abd-er-Rahman II (822-852), the emirate was well established and the country prosperous. Al-Andalus was among the richest Mediterranean states, with flourishing farms, commerce, and culture. The emir himself was living proof of fecundity, having fathered forty-five sons and forty-two daughters, if we can believe Moorish chroniclers. His prized possession was the famous jeweled belt called *al-thu'ban* (the snake), which enjoyed a fascinating history down through the Middle Ages. Among its later owners were El Cid and Queen Isabel, who finally used it to help pay for the conquest of Granada.

Abd-er-Rahman II patronized artists and philosophers like Ziryab, a gifted musician and maker of royal tastes in ninth-century Córdoba. Ziryab introduced Persian music to the court, and some scholars believe that its piercing falsetto singing accompanied by arabesques played on a lute may have been a key component in the birth of flamenco. (Centuries later, Gypsies introduced its more formal elements.)

As everywhere in the Arab world, eunuchs played a vital role in regal affairs and often rose to high government posts. One reason was that castrated males at court and in the harem were considered safe and trustworthy. The Koran pro-

The death of Roland at the Battle of Roncesvalles

hibited castration, but Moors got around the rules by buying the "finished product" from Jews and Christians. Eunuchs came from throughout Europe via the south of France, where they were castrated. Others lost their "manhood" after arriving, especially at Lucena (south of Córdoba), where there was a thriving trade in eunuchs.

Harems were large and well stocked with beautiful women of mind-dazzling variety. Moorish rulers favored fair women from the north, especially Galician blondes, and so the region's dialect was spoken widely at court. During periods of Moorish dominance, rulers of the small Christian kingdoms would often pay an annual tribute of young virgins, even their own daughters. The resulting interbreeding of Christian and Moor produced a race of leaders in which Arab blood became insignificant. Even so, rulers were proud of their Arab ancestry and would dye their hair black in an attempt to look the part. Harem women could experience remarkable social mobility if they numbered among the "favorites." The same held true for eunuchs, who stood ready to serve the royal pleasure.

During the first three centuries the emir resided at Córdoba, the undisputed capital of Moorish Spain. Although we must be skeptical of claims made by Arab historians, the city may well have been the most civilized in Europe at the time, when most towns were squalid medieval mazes. Córdoba attained its lofty status in the tenth century, when its patios, gardens, fountains, and palaces bedazzled visitors from abroad. Its population reached several hundred thousand, and the city boasted hundreds of mosques and public baths, libraries, paved and lighted streets, and even indoor plumbing.

The Great Mosque, arguably the Moors' greatest legacy, was built on the site of St. Vincent's Church, itself sitting atop the foundations of a Roman temple. When the Moors arrived, they used half the church themselves and allowed Christians to remain in the other half. The emir actually *purchased* the Christian section and tore down the structure to start a new mosque. The Great Mosque was embellished over two centuries and became the second most important place of worship, after Mecca, in the Muslim world. Architects blended a number of Mediterranean styles and used materials left over from Roman and Byzantine buildings. The structural challenge presented by the huge roof was solved with about eight hundred pillars and rows of double arches, inspired by Roman aqueducts. Surfaced with alternating red and white stone, these candy-striped marvels seem to intertwine like branches in an endless forest of jasper pillars. The mosque's interior is the best place in Spain to get a feel for the vanished world of the Spanish Moors, when the muezzin's shrill call summoned the faithful to prayer. This lingering mood is remarkable, given the fact that Christians re-taking Córdoba centuries later sealed most of the entrances, closed off the central courtyard, and built their own church right in the middle of the mosque. It was an architectural outrage, but probably saved Córdoba's Great Mosque from being razed later during the Reconquest.

For Moors cleanliness was next to godliness; there were hundreds of public baths in Córdoba, many not used since Roman days. Indeed, an interesting social history of Spain could be written using soap and water as the central metaphor. The Goths (not known for their personal hygiene) closed or destroyed most of the old Roman baths, but under the Moors they returned as an important social phenomenon. Later, Christian soldiers began to associate their own dirtiness with goodness, and bathing took on heathen or heretical connotations. For Spanish monks, physical dirt became the test of moral purity and faith, and they wore the same unwashed clothes for years. One Moorish saying summed it up: "Christians were sprinkled with water at birth and thus relieved from washing for the rest of their lives."

In addition to its public buildings, Córdoba soon acquired fame for its leather and metalwork, silk weaving, and other skilled trades. The Moors also introduced fine glasswork to the peninsula, as well as the beautiful glazed tiles

Iberia in 910

By the tenth century the peninsula remained under the firm control of Muslim rulers. Although standing in awe of the vibrant civilization to the south, Christians were starting to assert themselves.

called *azulejos* still popular today. Moorish houses had no windows or external adornment, keeping their inner charms veiled, like Muslim women, from public view. Flower-filled patios opening onto the street, so typical of Córdoba today, only became popular centuries later.

While the Christian kingdoms remained pastoral and backward, Al-Andalus had thriving urban centers with lively souks crammed along tortuous streets, a panorama not unlike contemporary Morocco. In fact, the best way to picture what Spain would be like today without the Reconquest is to visit the medinas of Tetuan, Chechaouen, and Fez, historic refuges of Andalucían Muslims. Here, descendants of the Spanish Moors still huddle in tiny cubicles working metal, wool, leather, and wood.

A babel of languages rose up from Moorish markets: Berber, Arabic, Hebrew, and Romance, which was the ever-evolving form of vulgarized Latin.

But language per se was less important than social and religious orientation; there were many devout Muslims who could not speak Arabic and Christians who could. Those who remained Christians in belief but Muslim in culture and language were called *Mozárabes* ("almost Arabs"). They developed a distinctive culture that included architecture (such as the church of San Miguel de Escalada near León) and the Mozarabic rite for the mass.

For centuries Spanish society was divided into three castes based on religion: Muslim, Christian, and Jew. There was a fair amount of toleration, and each caste had its accepted economic and social roles. Tailors, barbers, muleteers, masons, architects, and shoemakers were usually Moors, while Jews invariably became the physicians, pharmacists, interpreters, and money-changers. Jews were less prone to conversion or intermarriage than Christians and lived in close-knit communities centered on the markets. Ironically, they were the greatest beneficiaries of Moorish rule, enjoying the most significant cultural flowering since being driven from Palestine by the Romans several centuries before.

The emergence of three distinct castes based on religion had a profound effect on Spanish history. For one thing, feudalism and its hierarchy of rights and duties did not develop as in the rest of Europe. This in turn meant the lack of a strong class of leaders, the "elite" of society. Also, the concept of social position based on religious faith became a fundamental component of Spanish thinking down to modern times. (General Franco once remarked, "In Spain you are Catholic or you are nothing.")

Even after control appeared stable, periodic revolts plagued the Moors. The most famous of these involved Umar ibn-Hafsun, a *muwallad* of Gothic ancestry who ruled a rebel kingdom at Bobastro in the Málaga Mountains for four decades. Today a few scattered stones remain of his impregnable fortress perched over a gorge of the Guadalhorce River, near El Chorro. The revolt continued under Umar's sons until squashed by Abd-er-Rahman III, who had the rebel's ten-year-old corpse exhumed and crucified beside his sons' in front of Córdoba's Mosque.

Abd-er-Rahman III had succeeded his grandfather, Emir Abdullah, whose death in 912 brought down the curtain on a disastrous reign in which none of his eleven sons survived. All were either beheaded or poisoned, victims of palace intrigue or their father's own suspicions. The new emir was more European than Moor, both his grandmother and mother having come from Navarra.

His eyes were blue and his hair so light he died it black out of embarrassment, yet he spoke Romance with friends and family.

Abd-er-Rahman III had a strong will and a violent temper. One time after a defeat, he became so outraged that he had dozens of officers crucified for cowardice. His reign was one of almost constant warfare, with annual raiding expeditions in the north. And yet it was under his long reign that Moorish Spain reached its zenith of power and cultural achievement. Seventeen years after becoming emir, he proclaimed himself caliph of an independent state encompassing both Al-Andalus and the Moghreb (western North Africa). The title comes from the Arabic *khalifa,* meaning "representative of the Prophet," and it carried with it absolute authority in religious as well as civil and military matters. The break with Damascus was complete.

The young caliph became Europe's most powerful and respected ruler, but the Christian kingdoms were growing ever stronger, and Moroccan Berbers were distant and questionable allies. Power depended on eunuchs and other slaves from Eastern Europe, nicknamed "the silent" because they could speak neither Arabic nor Romance. The army itself was mostly Berber and not entirely reliable. Thus the caliphs became increasingly cut off from the people they ruled, retreating into the refined and sensual world of the court.

Abd-er-Rahman III began the incredible palace of Medina Azahara outside Córdoba and expanded and embellished the Great Mosque to its current dimensions. These were the crowning glories of Moorish architecture during the first centuries; the Alhambra came much later. Córdoba became Europe's leading city, a cultural beacon amid medieval backwardness. Even so, the figures given by Moorish historians—a million residents, 3,000 mosques, and 300 public baths—appear to be wild exaggerations. There is no evidence suggesting a city larger than about 100,000 residents, and the claim that the caliph's library contained 400,000 volumes is laughable.

There is also reason to question the Moors' heralded accomplishments in such fields as agriculture. For example, rather than introducing irrigation they merely adopted and improved earlier Roman works, which had made Hispania the breadbasket of the empire. Nevertheless, under the caliphate new crops were introduced: the orange, lemon, peach, apricot, fig, and pomegranate, as well as saffron, sugar cane, cotton, silk, and rice. In short, many of Spain's most important products today. The Moors also brought Arabian horses, which developed into the famed Andalucían breed taken to America centuries later. Moorish goods were prized throughout Europe and the East:

Cordovan leather, fruit and wine from Málaga, arms and damascene gold work from Toledo, Valencia's glazed pottery, silk from Granada. From the mines at Rio Tinto came copper, and those at Almadén yielded most of the mercury supply used in medieval Europe. Peninsular commerce was controlled by Al-Andalus, its currency used in the primitive Christian economies.

The north was culturally impoverished as well. While the Moors produced a ten-volume history of the caliphate, the kingdom of León could only muster a pitiful fifteen pages to record the reign of Alfonso V. Before the Moors people were either Goths or Hispano-Romans. The concept of being "Spanish," with a God-given destiny to re-take the peninsula, took root very slowly. Even the word *español* (meaning Spaniard or Spanish) was imported from Provence much later. (A major Castilian dictionary did not include the word until 1967.) Residents of the north thought of themselves as Christians who belonged to a village or region or possibly to a small kingdom. The kaleidoscopic swirl of Christian kingdoms—forever merging, separating, and merging again—make Spain's medieval history the most complex in Europe. From this confusing labyrinth emerged an endless cavalcade of kings who occasionally achieved immortality through odd names like Sancho the Fat or Wilfred the Hairy. But distinctive patterns were starting to form.

Asturias, with its capital at Oviedo, was the first of these. Later, Asturians left their mountain strongholds to found a new capital at León. The kings of Asturias-León assumed the title of *imperator*, harkening back to the fleeting days of Visigothic unity. Among them was Sancho the Fat, who was repudiated by his barons for being too obese to ride a horse. The pathetic monarch waddled off to Córdoba, where he received treatment from the caliph's physician, then returned home to oust his rival, Ordoño the Bad.

At the peninsula's northeastern corner was the Spanish March *(Marca Hispanica)*, a Frankish buffer state founded by Charlemagne after the failure of his Zaragoza expedition. Wilfred "The Hairy" began an independent line of counts, but the region, with Barcelona as its capital, remained in Frankish hands for two centuries. It enjoyed limited autonomy and special privileges, the start of a tradition that lives to this day in Cataluña.

The area between Asturias-León and the Spanish March gave birth to the kingdoms of Castilla and Navarra. In 951 Castilla, whose name derives from the abundance of castles along its frontier, became independent. According to legend, count Fernan González appeared one day before the king of León with a beautiful horse and a hawk. The king insisted on buying them and promised to double the price for every day that payment was not forthcoming. After many years the money had still not been paid, and the sum was so large that he granted Castilla's independence as payment. The Basque heartland in the crook of the Bay of Biscay remained untouched after the Moors found "a people like beasts" and decided not to invade. The mountainous portion of this region developed into the kingdom of Navarra during the tenth century.

These early kingdoms were governed almost as family properties in which marital alliances were often the crux. At times the history of the period reads like a lurid record of family feuds, lust, and bloodshed, with the Córdoban caliph often acting as arbiter between warring Christians. Compared with family ties, religion played only a minor role in political alignments. Toda, queen mother of Navarra, for example, was Fernan González's mother-in-law, Abd-er-Rahman's great aunt, and Sancho the Fat's grandmother.

Nevertheless, the Moorish-Christian frontier was often mobilized or in a state of war. To match Koran-inspired fanaticism, Christians found their own inspiration in the cult of St. James (Santiago). The site of his burial was neglected until the ninth century when, according to the legend, a local hermit saw a bright star shining above an oak tree and heard strange celestial music. When the local bishop investigated, he found three graves and an altar and proclaimed a miracle. One of the corpses was decapitated, as James had been. Next, just before a major battle, Ramiro I of Galicia announced that the saint had appeared to him in a dream—mounted on a white charger and carrying a banner emblazoned with a red cross. And yes, he promised Christian victory. The next day Christian soldiers attacked while shouting "Santiago!" and the Moors fled. The simple disciple of Christ had become the "Moor slayer" and champion of the Reconquest. (Santiago remains Spain's patron saint today).

The first pilgrims to the shrine of Santiago at Compostela began arriving in the ninth century. This trickle would later become a torrent, but before that happened Christian Spain would receive a nearly mortal blow that came close to stopping the Reconquest in its tracks. The resurgence of northern Spain had not gone unnoticed in Córdoba. In the middle of the tenth century a young man from a noble Arab family, named Muhammad ibn-abi-Amir (later called Al-Mansur, "the Victorious") appeared on the scene.

He was charming and ruthless in equal doses—a deadly combination throughout history—and before long had insinuated himself at court.

One day Caliph Hakam asked suspiciously, "By what skills does this
clever young man attract all my women and win their hearts?" He had reason
to worry; Mansur soon became the lover of his favorite, a Basque beauty
named Aurora. Hakam's heir was the young and hopelessly weak Hisham II,
and before long Mansur became caliph in all but name. He played the part of
the pious believer, but reports of his cruelty persisted. Once he had an
astrologer's tongue cut out when he foretold defeat. Upon hearing that his
own son was part of a gang of plotters, Mansur had him whipped to death
during dinner; another son was decapitated. Indeed, cutting off heads was
one of Mansur's favorite diversions, and one time he made a giant pyramid of
the ghastly trophies and rode round it in glee. He then had them salted,
boxed, and sent around the caliphate to frighten his enemies.

Mansur was not the kind of enemy the resurgent Christians needed: he
led fifty-seven expeditions into their territory in about twenty years. Finally
the worst happened. In the year 997, Mansur and his army captured Santiago
de Compostela and destroyed its shrine. Only the tomb of the saint himself
was spared, when an old monk refusing to flee impressed Mansur with his
bravery. To add insult to injury, the basilica's doors and bells were carried off
to Córdoba and used to embellish the mosque. News of Mansur's campaign
struck like a thunderclap across Christian Spain. In one daring swoop, centuries of painstaking advance seemed shattered beyond repair.

Sights & Sites

Visigothic and early Christian:
Celanova (Orense): 26 kms. south of town lies Santa Comba de Bande, a small Visigoth church in the shape of a Greek cross.
Covadonga (Asturias): Grand setting surrounded by Picos de Europa; famous shrine commemorates spot where Pelayo held off the Moors; tombs of Pelayo and Alfonso I.
León: Parts of medieval town date from tenth century, when the king of Asturias founded a new capital.
Madrid: At National Archaeological Museum are the crowns of Visigoth kings, Romanesque tombs and capitals.
Oviedo (Asturias): Cathedral contains holy relics from the fall of Visigoths at Toledo. Pre-Romanesque churches Santa María del Naranco and San Miguel de Lillo from ninth century.
Palencia: 14 kms. from town is Baños De Cerrato, site of San Juan Bautista church, the oldest in Spain (661).
Roncesvalles (Navarra): Spot where Basques massacred rearguard of Charlemagne's army, described in *The Song of Roland.*
San Miguel de Escalada (León): 28 kms. from León is a Mozarabic church built by monks expelled from Córdoba.
Segovia: Vera Cruz Chapel, erected in the the 13th century either by the Templars or the Knights of the Holy Sepulchre.

The palace of Medina Azahara near Cordoba has been called the world's biggest jigsaw puzzle.

Tarrasa (Barcelona): Three churches on the Roman-Visigoth site of Egara.
Toledo: Church of San Roman contains Visigothic Museum with bronze jewelry and votive crowns; more remains at Santa Cruz Museum include carved tombstone.

Early Moorish:
Almería: Alcazaba fortress dates to the eighth century; badly damaged by earthquake, but walls still extant; extensive gardens and museum.
Córdoba: The Mosque with its forest of candy-striped pillars; Medina Azahara palace, undergoing reconstruction, lies 6 kms. from town.

Chapter 4

Moros y Cristianos

A few kilometers west of Córdoba sit the ruins of Medina Azahara, "city of the flower." Named to honor the caliph's favorite wife, this royal residence ranked among the most sumptuous in history. Shimmering white against the dark hills of the Sierra Morena, it was described by an Arab poet as "a concubine in the arms of a black eunuch." But, like the caliphate itself, Medina Azahara's glories were short-lived. Rampaging Berbers destroyed the palatial city in 1010, and it lay buried and forgotten for nine centuries.

Strolling around today, visitors need a vivid imagination to summon up images of former magnificence. Built during the reign of Abd-er-Rahman III, the project consumed about a third of the royal budget and employed ten thousand workmen. Only the finest materials were used: ivory, carved cedar, ebony, onyx, and alabaster, mosaic tiles and marble columns. The caliph's rooms alone numbered four hundred; among them was one with walls sheathed in gold and a pearl the size of a dove's egg hanging from the ceiling. Thousands lived in or around the palace: servants, pages, musicians, and four-thousand Slavic eunuchs. Women in the harem numbered six thousand—enough for any man.

Despite these amenities Al Mansur preferred his own residence, and Medina Azahara fell into disrepair. During the crisis in the years following his sudden death (1002), rebellious Berber mercenaries pulled down the palace. Fired by religious zeal, they even used hammers to smash large pieces into smaller bits. Today tens of thousands of stone and plaster pieces are laid out neatly on the floor as if awaiting re-assembly of the world's biggest jigsaw puzzle. Black burn marks clearly show where the intense heat of bonfires seared the marble floor.

The fires of anarchy and destruction consumed more than a palace. During the first three decades of the new millennium, Moorish Spain slipped from the pinnacle of wealth, culture, and military power—capped by Mansur's victorious march on Santiago—into a mire of bloody strife. Wrote the poet, "Weep for the splendor of Córdoba, for disaster has overtaken her, then bid her goodbye, and let her go in peace since depart she must."

The effete Caliph Hisham II, who customarily wore a veil and makeup, did not produce an heir. Instead, he named Mansur's son Sanchuelo, a drinking and debauching partner, to succeed to the throne. Revolt followed revolt and by 1031, the year the caliphate ceased to exist, six more caliphs had followed. With their failure, Al-Andalus fractured into about twenty small kingdoms known as *taifas* (from an Arabic word for "faction" or "party") as geographical and racial feuds (essentially Berbers battling Arabs) triumphed over unified rule. The Moors remained formidable, however, controlling about two-thirds of the peninsula. The most powerful *taifas* were Sevilla and Granada, followed by Córdoba, Almería, Zaragoza, Badajoz, and Toledo. But religion alone did not define the political map; as a matter of course the petty kingdoms often fought and betrayed one another, even if it meant forming an alliance with Christians.

One infamous Sevillan ruler was Motadid, who boasted a harem of eight hundred women and used human skulls for flowerpots around his palace. For amusement, he kept the heads of defeated rivals in leather cases, taking them out occasionally to admire like precious jewels. Motadid's son, on the other hand, had his virtues: when one wife from the north longed for the sight of snow, he planted thousands of almond trees on a nearby slope so that each winter she could enjoy a white sea of blossoms. Such were the Moors.

As often happens in times of political decline, these decades following caliphate's collapse witnessed a brief cultural flowering. Each king tried to surpass his neighbors in the number and quality of books in his library poets under his patronage. It became a point of royal honor to write in the most refined manner on the finest parchment, using rhymed verses and intricate metaphors to score literary points.

The earthly temptations of Andalucía were hard to resist, and Moorish poets wrote of wine and women (or boys), dancing and song. The ceaseless search for poetic extravagance could lead to abominably bad verse. One bard wrote: "Such was my kissing, such my sucking of his mouth, that he was almost made toothless." Pleasure-seeking became an end in itself, and the Moors' love of wine often degenerated into drunken orgies. These former sons of the desert began to lose their warrior virtues and employ mercenaries (even Christians) to do their fighting.

For centuries Moorish raiding parties had swept into Christian lands, cutting down trees, burning crops, sacking towns, and lopping off a few heads before returning south across a wide "no man's land." There was no serious effort to conquer or hold land beyond natural barriers such as the Duero and Ebro rivers. Nor did the Moors lust for unconquered parts of "Spain" because no such place existed. The frontier between Christian and Moor was far from being a well-defined and sealed border. It ebbed and flowed like the tide, depending on shady alliances and who was stronger or more able to pay bribes. You can trace some outposts of this centuries-long struggle in the names of border towns containing the words *de la frontera*, such as Arcos de la Frontera in Cádiz province.

While Al-Andalus was falling from omnipotence to impotence, the northern kingdoms underwent the opposite experience. As Christian-held territory expanded, kings encouraged resettlement by granting municipal rights called *fueros*, which led to a spirit of independence. Local liberties led to popular representation in Cortes (parliaments) a hundred years before anything similar in England. (1163 in Aragón and 1188 in León compared with 1295 in England.) These early rights and institutions offered more liberty than the feudal servitude found in most of Europe, but the *fueros* would come back to haunt Spain time and again throughout history.

The Moorish-Christian frontier was like an early-day version of the Wild West and attracted adventurous types from the peninsula and beyond, especially after the pope called for a crusade. Slowly Christians gained the spirit that created *La Reconquista* (the Reconquest), the most distinctive factor of medieval Spanish history. War was a fact of life, though armies of the day were tiny by modern standards and would often agree in advance on the time and place of a battle. Sieges were often painfully long, and the attackers would build their own town nearby and try to outlast the enemy.

Christian progress was slow for several reasons. The central *meseta*'s rugged topography and harsh climate, not to mention the threat of Moorish reprisals, discouraged settlers. In addition, every time a Christian king died he divided his domains among his sons, which led to the splintering of power built up over years of struggle. The Moors' tribute system was eagerly adopted by Christians and resulted in a northward flow of gold. Unlike developing areas of Italy or Flanders, where wealth sprang from industry and commerce, in Christian Spain it came from war or the threat of war. Compounding the problem, money was used to buy land or more weapons rather than for economic development.

A Spanish woodcut of El Cid Campeador

The kingdom of León championed the Reconquest until the blows struck by Al Mansur. Navarra then moved to the fore under Sancho III, called "the Great" (1005-1035). He married the sister of the Castilian ruler and, in the confusion following the murder of his brother-in-law, gained control of Castilla and placed his son in charge. Fernando (Ferdinand) I in turn occupied León and assumed the title "emperor of the Spains." Castilla had become a kingdom in its own right—and one destined for greatness.

Meanwhile other peninsular powers were forming; in the lands that became Aragón a strong tradition of limited monarchy developed. To the east, the future region of Cataluña had remained largely unoccupied by the Moors, and in the eleventh century Ramón Berenguer I, count of Barcelona, became the first ruler of a completely independent entity.

Fernando I of Castilla became a leading figure in the Reconquest, capturing territory from Valencia to Portugal. But when he died, this emerging Christian power was again partitioned among his own sons, and outright war soon erupted between Alfonso of León and Sancho of Castilla. At the time Sancho was served by a young knight who became one of the most exalted figures in Spanish history—Rodrigo Diaz de Vivar, better known as *El Cid Campeador*. (The name Cid comes from the Arabic *seyyid*, or lord, while *campeador* is from the Latin *campi ductor*, leader in the field.)

The amazing Cid achieved lasting fame through the first great epic poem of Spanish literature, *El Cantar del Mio Cid* (1140), as well as in countless biographies and a Hollywood epic. But historians have long struggled to separate legend from fact, and some believe the Cid may be a composite of at least two individuals. In the epic he is a grave but majestic figure, who can subdue lions at a glance and wears his beard in a net to prevent the dishonor of having it tweaked, a mortal insult at the time. (The Cid once yanked out a handful of a defeated rival's beard to add insult to injury.) From historical accounts, we know that he was exiled by Alfonso VI and fought in the service of the Moors. Indeed, El Cid embodies the confusion of loyalties between Christian and Moor at the time.

Nonetheless, Christian Spain adopted El Cid as a national hero, and historians now feel that the epic might be close to the truth. Rodrigo was born in Vivar, a backward village a few kilometers from Burgos. He learned the soldier's profession early and rose rapidly in the service of Sancho. In an event that became the stuff of legend, the Cid's lord was murdered by a treacherous aide one dark (and probably stormy) night, and his brother fell under suspicion. Rodrigo personally made Alfonso swear an oath that he had no part in the crime. In a famous ceremony at Burgos, the Cid repeated three times, "If you are lying, please God that a traitor and a vassal kills you." This did not endear him to Alfonso, ruler of a reunited Castilla and León, and following a quarrel a few years later, the king sent the Cid into exile. He proceeded to fight in the service of the potentate of Zaragoza, a Moorish city in vassalage to Alfonso, then slipped briefly from the scene.

Meanwhile Alfonso himself became a major military figure. His armies penetrated deep into Andalucía and even reached Gibraltar, where he rode into the Mediterranean and exclaimed: "Here is the uttermost limit of Spain. I have touched it." In addition, Alfonso is remembered for replacing the centuries-old Mozarabic rite for the Mass with the Latin rite of the Roman church. Today, the only place in the world to see a Mozarabic Mass is a tiny chapel in Toledo's cathedral, where it has survived in an odd time warp of the kind found only in Spain.

In 1085, Alfonso's army recaptured Toledo in the first crucial victory of the Reconquest. It was a huge strategic step as well as a boost to morale, bringing Christians to the old Visigoth capital and into the heart of the *meseta*, the part called New Castilla. Shock waves flashed through Al-Andalus at the news of Toledo's fall. A Moorish scribe wrote: "Take to your horses, men of

Andalucía! To remain is pure folly. Garments begin to unravel by fraying at the edges, but our kingdom has ripped down the center."

Yet Christian elation was premature; the Moors were not going to roll over just yet. The kingdom of Sevilla, heretofore a Christian vassal, issued calls for help to Muslim Africa. The Almoravids were dark-skinned nomads from the Sahara—ancestors of the modern Tauregs—who had converted to Islam and swept north to conquer Morocco. Yusuf ibn-Tashufin founded Marrakech and governed lands stretching from Senegal to Algeria. This war-like sect, whose name meant "vowed to God," consisted of religious fanatics sworn to root out anyone who slipped from Muslim orthodoxy. Alarmed by Alfonso's victories, Mutamid of Sevilla petitioned Yusuf for help, remarking "If I have to choose, I would rather tend camels for the Almoravids than pasture swine under the Christians." His words were prophetic; as so many others the invaders chose to stay. The party was soon over for the "party kings."

An Almoravid army landed at Algeciras and marched to meet Alfonso near Badajoz. The Christians were used to fighting man-to-man style, by which a collection of individual triumphs brought overall victory. In the invaders they faced a compact force of infantry supported by lines of archers, which moved to the command of thunderous drums. Muslim victory was assured when Yusuf called in his Negro guard, equipped with rapiers and shields of hippo hide, and after the battle carts laden with severed heads rumbled off for display as war trophies. Alfonso himself barely escaped, and panic reigned throughout Christian Spain. In Galicia, one group even tried to gain protection by transferring its sovereignty to William the Conqueror, who had completed his conquest of England twenty years before.

After this crushing defeat, Alfonso was forced to turn again to the Cid. The enigmatic hero had meanwhile gained control of Valencia, but despite his nominal loyalty to the king, he emerged as an independent ruler. The Muslims stood in awe of the Cid, who seemed to be fulfilling an old prophecy: "If a Roderick it was who lost Spain (a reference to the last Visigoth king), another Roderick (Rodrigo) will restore it." Unfortunately, the Cid died suddenly in 1099. According to the epic, his corpse was clad in armor, lashed to his charger, and led out in front of the Christian army, causing a panicked retreat by the Moors. In reality, his followers gamely held Valencia another three years, then surrendered. During the next few years, the Almoravids controlled most of southern Iberia from their capital at Marrakech.

Iberia in 1150

By the twelfth century the Christians were making significant advances. Among these Christian kingdoms Castilla-Leon overshadowed its neighbors because it was larger, more populous, and was to become standard-bearer of the Reconquest.

Almoravid Spain was very different from the tolerant society of the caliphate and *taifas*. Driven by strict religious fundamentalism, they began to persecute Christians and Jews, whom they regarded as hopelessly corrupt. Wrote one chronicler: "Muslim women must be forbidden to defile themselves by entering a Christian church, since the priests are libertines, fornicators, and sodomites."

The persecuted fled north. The Muslim revival in fact helped consolidate the main Christian kingdoms and goad them into joint action. Alfonso I of Aragón, "El Batallador" (the Fighter), led the counterattack by retaking Zaragoza (1118), thus providing the young kingdom with its historic capital. When he died without an heir his brother Ramiro, living quietly as a monk, was lured out of his cell long enough to sire a daughter, the *infanta* Petronilla. She in turn was married off to Count Ramón Berenguer IV of the Catalonian ruling family, thereby uniting Aragón and Cataluña (1137). Ramiro returned to his monastery, unaware that his brief escapade had created a union of monumental consequence for Spanish history.

The Kingdom of Aragón was a misnomer because real power lay in Cataluña and its capital city of Barcelona. During the twelfth and thirteenth centuries, this kingdom prospered as a wealthy trading power and emerged as a great late medieval city on a par with Genoa and Venice. "Not a fish dared show itself in the Mediterranean without having the bars of Aragón on its tail," wrote one historian.

Meanwhile, another major peninsular force was born in the west—the kingdom of Portugal. Alfonso VI had two daughters: one married Raymond of Burgundy and their son reigned as Alfonso VII of Castilla. The younger daughter married *Henry* of Burgundy and the couple ended up with the county of Portugal as part of the dowry. Their son founded an independent Portugal in 1139, and so it remained, with the exception of one eighty-year period under Spain centuries later. It has been said that Portugal just managed to gain independence while Cataluña, later united with Castilla, just failed.

During the crucial centuries when the Spanish identity and character were formed, the "land of castles" was the center of peninsular gravity. Wrote one historian: "Castilla was born to war and suckled on war, and it was in war that she forged her warrior temperament, her will to command, and her ambition to achieve a great destiny." Castilla's role as linchpin of a new nation spread far beyond mere military leadership. Called Romance in the Middle Ages, the Castilian language originated in the north around the town of Burgos. The oldest written example is a manuscript penned in 964 by the monks of San Millán de la Cogolla (La Rioja), now regarded as the "cradle of Castilian." That was nearly two centuries before the finely wrought poetry of Gonzalo de Berceo and the Cid epic. Castilian (known to the world as Spanish) would emerge as the dominant peninsular tongue despite the ongoing presence of Catalán, Basque, Galician, and Portuguese. And, as every English speaker knows, language is a potent weapon to have on your side.

Although Christian resentment against the Muslim intruders had smoldered since 711, the idealized concept of a "holy war" to eliminate them only took hold in this period. The Moors were henceforth considered usurpers of Spanish soil and enemies of the Catholic faith. Castilians in particular began to look upon themselves as God's chosen race. Their soldiers fought for all Christendom, not just for their own kingdom. A tradition arose about the coming of a Spanish messianic king and final world emperor known as *El Encubierto* (the Hidden One), who would defeat the enemy and then march on to Jerusalem. Moreover, crusaders from throughout Europe flocked to the peninsula as a more convenient alternative to the Holy Land.

Fundamental to Reconquest mythology was the legend of *Santiago El Matamoros*, St. James the Moor Slayer, and his shrine at Compostela. In the decades following Mansur's destruction of the old church, the faithful began to rebuild. The magnificent Romanesque cathedral of today was embellished over centuries, including the incredible *portico de la gloria* by Master Mateo, perhaps the finest example of medieval carving in existence. Christian pilgrims once again flocked to Santiago de Compostela along a famous route sprinkled with Benedictine monasteries. The faithful carried cockleshells—part of their penance involved swallowing a raw scallop—and camped out along the way or enjoyed the hospitality of monks. The Road to Compostela became the greatest pilgrimage of the Middle Ages (Chaucer's "Wife of Bath" made it), and the site began to rival Jerusalem and Rome for importance. There was even the occasional anti-pope from Compostela, often a local bishop who had decided that St. James ranked above St. Peter in church hierarchy.

Another Christian icon was the Holy Grail, a gold-and-sardonyx chalice reputedly used by Jesus at the Last Supper. According to legend, it was brought to Spain in the fourth century and later became the proudest possession of the Aragónese monarchy. (A cup which some claim is authentic can be seen in Valencia's cathedral.)

But religion was just one of many motives driving the war wagons of the Reconquest; gold and glory spurred on many a knight-errant. The fusion of faith and warfare is best seen in the armies of monastic knights, the famous orders of the Temple (Knights Templar), Calatrava, Alcántara, and Santiago, the romantic heroes of song and story. The knights of St. James (Santiago), for example, wore white mantles emblazoned with a red cross, swore perpetual war on the infidel, and devoted themselves to the service of "God and the ladies." For these Christian warriors, victory in battle meant more than the remission of sins. Nobles and the more successful knights received huge land grants in the conquered territories, which survived as the hated *latifundios*. Many of Spain's noble families trace their lineage to the Reconquest and the lands granted to their ancestors. At the top of the pyramid were the *grandes* and beneath them the lesser nobility or *hidalgos*, an arrangement corresponding roughly to English barons and knights. (The word *hidalgo* comes from *hijo de algo*, son of some substance.) *Hidalgos* lived by a strict code that glorified land ownership and discouraged business activities and manual labor.

When warfare waned, the-rank-and file tended vast herds of sheep and cattle. Spain became the original home of the cattle ranch, an institution later taken to the Americas, especially Argentina and Mexico. The mounted Spanish *vaqueros* were direct ancestors of the immortal cowboys of the American West, and likewise served as vanguard for an expanding society. For gentlemen, raising livestock was considered superior to digging in the earth, and large sections of Castilla and Andalucía became pastures. After the introduction of the merino breed of sheep a bit later, demand soared for Spanish wool, the mainstay of the economy for centuries. Wool that was exported to the burgeoning factories of *other* countries.

After the conquest of Toledo by Christian armies, the problem arose of how to incorporate two alien cultures that were superior in many ways. It came to be accepted that the proper order of society consisted of Christian herders, warriors and priests, Muslim cultivators and artisans, and Jewish technicians and traders. The extreme form of this attitude held that *all* physical work was for Muslims and Jews, while the proper Christian job was to rule.

While Christian Spain continued to evolve, the Moors chafed under the yoke of their Almoravid rulers and began to rebel. What really sealed the fate of the Almoravids, however, was the rise of another fanatical sect in Morocco, the Almohades. Around the year 1126 the son of a mosque lamplighter from the Atlas Mountains claimed inspiration from Allah and took the title of *mahdi*, the expected one. Berber followers rallied to calls for a holy war to stamp out Almoravid "heresy." Coming from the mountains and foothills, the Almohades (which means "unitarians") were natural enemies of the desert-dwelling Almoravids. First they conquered Marrakech and then invaded Iberia, encouraged by reports of local sympathy. Before long Al-Andalus was again united under one Muslim reign. The Almohades were as intolerant as they were bellicose. Abd al-Mumin ordered all churches and synagogues razed, and Christians and Jews swarmed across the northern frontier. Friction with the north stepped up a notch, culminating in a stunning Christian defeat at Alarcos (between Toledo and Córdoba) in 1195. The flower of young Spanish knights fell, and the Castilian king himself narrowly escaped capture.

Despite their fanaticism, the Almohades ushered in a period of great cultural achievement for Moorish Spain, the brightest era between the caliphate and the glories of Granada centuries later. Interest revived in philosophy, medicine, mathematics, and literature, and the proto-sciences of astrology and alchemy. Architecture flourished with construction of the soaring minaret of the Sevilla mosque, today called La Giralda. This splendid tower was built with a wide ramp inside so that the sultan could ride his horse to the top. It is just one of a nearly identical trio by the same architect; the others are the Koutoubia of Marrakech and Rabat's Hassan Tower. Another Almohad remnant in Sevilla is the Tower of Gold, once covered with gilded tiles.

Arab poetry too enjoyed a renascence of sorts during the twelfth century. Every ruler worth his salt composed verse, and even scientific works were embellished with the appropriate lyrical flourish. Yet much of the poetry is tired and jejune. Princes are always lions or suns; women are gazelles or doves; the lightning in the rainstorm is like "the fire of the poet's love amidst his tears." This poetry was crafted for recital and song, and its lyric forms inspired the first ballads of European troubadours and, quite possibly, the soul-stirring adagios of *cante jondo* flamenco. At the end of each stanza of a recitation, Moors cried out *wa-allah* (Oh God!), just as today the flamenco singer's refrain is greeted with shouts of "*Ole!*"

The philosopher Averroes, born at Córdoba in 1126, is often cited as the pinnacle of Moorish learning and influence. He translated into Arabic the works of Aristotle, which had been virtually forgotten in the West, and when his commentary appeared in Latin, it caused an intellectual upheaval among Christian theologians such as St. Thomas Aquinas. Another son of Córdoba was the Jew Maimonides (1135-1204), who left Al-Andalus under cloudy circumstances and spent his life wandering the Mediterranean world. He was a renowned doctor who served as personal physician to the sultan of Cairo, and he wrote many medical treatises, including one on sexuality. Maimonides' chief fame rests with his philosophical works such as *Guide to the Perplexed*, a summary of medieval religious thought. A body of traditional Jewish Mysticism called the *Cabala*, which developed from Hellenistic roots, was compiled in the text of *Sefer ha-Zohar* ("The Book of Splendor"). Cabalism has been compared to Christian mysticism such as Gnosticism and Neoplatonism, with elements of alchemy and even astrology.

During much of the early Reconquest, Christian rulers were more concerned with fighting each other than the Moors. But after the debacle at Alarcos, they decided to cooperate, especially when the pope called for a new crusade against the Almohades. In June of 1212—a year as famous in Spain as 1066 is in England—soldiers from throughout Spain and Europe gathered at Toledo and marched southward, bound for the Sierra Morena. There they were helped by a mysterious shepherd who led the army through a pass marked by a cow's skull. (The young man was called *cabeza de vaca*, and one descendant later became a famous explorer in the Americas.)

The Moors could have easily ambushed the Christian forces in the mountain passes, but they made a huge tactical error by awaiting them on the rolling plains of Las Navas de Tolosa. Here the Almohad forces were annihilated—sixty thousand killed compared to only fifty Christian deaths, according to chroniclers. After the battle hundreds of thousands of Moors fled to North Africa, and the defeated Moorish commander promptly drank himself to death. While these reports may be suspicious, the battle did mark the beginning of the end for Muslim Spain; the thirteenth century would bring many more Christian victories. Portugal was the first to follow up, expelling the Moors in 1249, and Aragón retook Valencia and the Balearic Islands. But once again Castilla gained the most after Las Navas, adding the lion's share of Andalucía to its rule. Fernando (Ferdinand) III, later proclaimed a saint for his martial skills, captured Córdoba and re-consecrated the Great Mosque

Moses Maimonides, the great Jewish philosopher of medieval Spain

as a cathedral. With poetic justice, he sent captured Muslims to Santiago with the same bells Al-Mansur had Christians lug to Córdoba two centuries earlier.

The writing was on the wall and the ruler of Granada, one Mohammed-ibn-Alhamar, saw it clearly. Turban in hand, he approached Fernando and proposed an alliance. The price for cooperation in the conquest of Muslim Sevilla was Granada's independence as a Castilian vassal. Fernando was startled by Mohammed's groveling performance, but agreed and took Sevilla with his help. Upon returning to Granada and shouts of victory, the embarrassed Moor uttered ironically, "There is no victor but Allah." The words were later inscribed a thousand times throughout the Alhambra palace. When Fernando died four years later, a hundred knights from Granada carried torches at his wake. With his passing the Reconquest seemed to die as well, though his son led a handful of mop-up victories. But Mohammed's deal endured; for another two centuries the kingdom of Granada remained a Castilian vassal and the Moors' final bastion.

At some point one must sum up the Moors' legacy in Spain. Even a cursory look at the dates reveals that "the Arabs" did *not*, as is commonly stated, rule Spain for eight hundred years. In actual fact, the mostly Berber-Hispanic Muslims inhabited two-thirds of the peninsula for 375 years, about half of it for another 160 years, and the tiny kingdom of Granada—present-day Málaga, Almería, and Granada provinces—for a final 244 years. Along with the faulty chronology comes a whirlwind of praise for the earthly paradise the Moors supposedly created, the rose-tinted version found in Washington Irving's *Tales of the Alhambra*. For many romantics Al-Andalus will always be the epitome of chivalry and culture. In truth, the Moors did have a profound effect on the peninsula for good and bad.

During their heyday they led Europe in many endeavors, such as alchemy and medicine. Surgeons at Córdoba dissected corpses and were familiar with anesthesia. Doctors even used music for the treatment of mental disorders. The Moors introduced an advanced system of specialized hospitals for lepers (who were burned in France), the insane, and wounded soldiers. Muslim scholarship also excelled in astronomy, botany, and geography. Al-Idrisi, who ranks as the greatest medieval geographer, insisted that the earth was round; and it's said that Columbus later got most of his ideas from Arabic translations of classical works. The Moors brought Arabic numerals, replacing the clumsy Roman system, as well as algebra and higher mathematics.

The word algebra itself is Arabic in origin, as are thousands of others in modern Spanish. Among them are *alcázar* (castle), *arroz* (rice), *aduana* (customs), *alcalde* (mayor), *naranja* (orange), *azucar* (sugar), and *limón* (lemon). Spanish-English cognates from the same Arabic source include alcohol, alchemy, alkali, camphor, elixir, syrup, talc, nadir, zenith, almanac, zero, coffee, jasmine, saffron, and sesame.

Building on Roman traditions, agriculture and irrigation were Moorish strengths, seen in the splendidly cultivated *vegas* of Andalucía and Valencia. The Moors are also credited with bringing technology for the manufacture of paper and gunpowder to Europe. They can also claim many things thought of as typically Spanish, such as the guitar (developed from their lute), certain aspects of flamenco music, the tiled patio with its gurgling fountain, and even *gazpacho*, a cold soup of raw vegetables.

Moorish art was a fusion of east and west, using materials and techniques from the Romans, Goths, and Byzantines. When the Moors conquered Spain, they were an uncultured, nomadic people, but came to be imitators and transmitters of more developed civilizations. To this they added their own light, unmistakable touch whose ultimate expression is the Alhambra. Moorish Spain survives most visibly in its buildings, in which we see those typical touches—the horseshoe arch, superb carving in wood and plaster, imaginative use of textiles and tiles. The Moors definitely had a weakness for florid detail, and it lives on in Spanish *artesania*.

But there is another side to the Moorish story. For every building they put up, they tore down another with equal fervor. When the Almoravids took Segovia, for example, they pointlessly destroyed thirty-six arches of the magnificent Roman aqueduct. No better metaphor is needed for the triumph of ignorant barbarism over civilization. The Moors profoundly changed the course of Spanish history. In 711, the peninsula was at least as developed as the rest of Europe and might have become a powerful, unified state. Instead, Iberia's destiny was to bear the brunt of the Muslim invasions and deflect its national energies at a critical time. The old Roman-Gothic quest for unity was overturned by the Muslim fondness for anarchy, disunion, and separatism. The struggle between these two polar tendencies has haunted Spanish history ever since. The Moors' obsession with warfare and bloodshed, their lust for booty and gold, their fondness for torture and cutting off heads—all these spilled over into Christian Spain. Their constant raiding, cutting down trees and burning vegetation, helped make a desert of La Mancha and other areas, which even today are desolate and under populated.

Many Muslim attitudes crept into Spanish thought as well. Among them was the treatment of women, whom the Moors jealously veiled and guarded. Similarly, for centuries Spaniards kept their women behind *rejas* (iron grating on the windows). Christian kings readily adopted the Arab custom of taking foreign concubines; Alfonso VI had five wives, including the daughter of Motamid, ruler of Sevilla.

Finally, there was the Reconquest itself. If the holy crusade brought *fueros*, it also meant an economy based on tribute, plunder, and sheep-herding, all-powerful military orders, and a strong, aggressive aristocracy and church.

This fusion of religious and military ideals became the driving force of society, and Christianity was equated with the good and the right. Even today, Spaniards often regard political issues as moral questions on which there is no possibility of concession or compromise. In a constant state of alert, Spaniards developed a siege mentality that degenerated into an almost paranoid fear of foreign doctrines and influences. In short the Moorish occupation was a mixed blessing.

One of the many paradoxes of medieval Spain became evident after the virtual fall of Andalucía around 1250. While Islam was the great enemy for Christians, it was also the source of a culture in many ways superior to their own. Typical of this cultural confusion is the tomb of Fernando III in Sevilla's Cathedral. Here, a massive silver casket sits beneath an altar flanked by perpetually burning candles; three times a year it is opened and the monarch-saint's eerily preserved body exposed to public view. But his epitaph is written in four languages: Latin, Castilian, Hebrew, *and* Arabic.

The fall of the Almohades after Las Navas de Tolosa did not, as might be imagined, unleash a reign of intolerance and reprisals against Moors. In fact, Spain seemed to return for a few remarkable decades to an open, tri-cultural society. Every town had its prosperous Jewish quarter (*juderia*). In Toledo, the Church of Santa María La Blanca was used for worship by all three religions: Muslims on Fridays, Jews on Saturdays, and Christians on Sundays.

Fernando was succeeded by one of the bright lights among Spain's innumerable monarchs—his son Alfonso X, called "The Learned." This scholar-king oversaw an epoch of enlightened tolerance for Jews and Moors (he called himself King of Three Religions), but also recognized the unifying cultural role of Christian Castilla. Alfonso was fertile in mind and body; he fathered eight children with his wife and at least four others on the sly, wrote bawdy love poems, and denounced his enemies in rhyme. He authored a history of Spain and a treatise on chess complete with diagrams. He also edited one of Spain's literary treasures, the *Cantigas de Santa María (Songs in Praise of the Virgin Mary)*. This compilation of music, poetry, and about 1,300 illustrations in miniature opens a fascinating window on medieval life.

Alfonso helped build a bridge between medieval Europe and antiquity. Arab and Hebrew scholarship had survived the Reconquest in Toledo, and the king realized the possibilities by expanding the existing school of translators. Persian literature, Greek philosophy, Arabic medicine, and other wisdom were cast into Latin here. By 1251, Aristotle was being taught at the university of Paris, a profound step in the history of philosophy. Another work that arrived via Toledo was the *Canon of Ibn Sina*, Europe's standard medical textbook for the next five centuries.

Long after the fall of Rome, Latin continued as the universal language of commerce, diplomacy, and the church. The peninsula's Romance languages developed slowly, almost imperceptibly. Alfonso had many translations made from the original into Castilian, not Latin, which was an astonishing departure from scholarly norms. It was another major step toward the evolution of the "Castilian mystique." Castilian swallowed up both the Leónese and Aragónese dialects early on, whereas Galician continued as both a spoken and literary language. But even the stubborn Basques adopted Castilian as their written language until modern times. Catalán was another case altogether, more akin to medieval Provençal than to Castilian. Linguists considered it as a separate Romance language. Valencian and Mallorcan are dialects of Catalán.

The growing prominence of Castilian led to an emerging national literature. Among the earliest forms were epics about the Reconquest, medieval legends comparable with the Arthurian stories of England. They often revealed much about the formation of national traits; in *Las Mocedades del Cid* Guillen de Castro writes:

> "Always endeavor to attain
> what is honorable and important;
> but if you have made a mistake
> defend it and don't correct it."

Another classic was *The Book of Good Love* (1335) by Juan Ruiz (the Archpriest of Hita), a surprisingly ribald gem comparable to *The Canterbury Tales*.

The then backwater island of Mallorca produced an outstanding mind in Ramón Llull (1235-1315), who wrote in Arabic and Latin as well as Catalán. In an age when a person could still know all there was to know, Llull was a poet, philosopher, and mystic, and he wrote on every conceivable subject. Tragically, Muslim fanatics stoned him to death in Tunis.

The two centuries following the reign of Alfonso X witnessed an architectural flowering. With the passing of the solid but stodgy Romanesque came the lofty, refined

Musicians in the court of Alfonso X

Gothic style, the splendid cathedrals of Toledo, Burgos, and León—all soaring spires, stained-glass windows, and flying buttresses. When *Sevillanos* met to plan their cathedral they remarked, "Let us put up a building so immense that the rest of the world will think us mad." Such was the spirit of the age.

The decline of the Moorish kingdoms left many areas of Spain—especially in Aragón, Valencia, and Andalucía—with Muslim majorities. These *mudéjares* (from the Arabic "permitted to remain") presented no real threat, because they were largely glad to be rid of their Moroccan overlords. They created an innovative architectural style known as *mudéjar*, based on traditional Moorish skills at working in plaster and wood, fabric and tile. Bare walls of no great consequence were transformed into works of art. The horseshoe arch, florid detail, and other Moorish motifs were adapted to Christian and secular buildings, such as Toledo's Church of Cristo de la Vega. Two other *mudéjar* masterpieces are the castles of Coca (Segovia) and Sevilla. *Mudéjar* remained in vogue until the Renaissance style took over late in the fifteenth century, at a time when anything Muslim was considered inferior. But its themes and techniques survived and later turned up in buildings both in Spain and Spanish America.

Throughout Castilla's history the pendulum has swung between short creative outpourings and succeeding stages of profound malaise, unrest, and the inability to achieve a stable society. Such was the case in the years following the glorious era of Alfonso the Learned. Political turmoil bubbled over between the monarchy and aristocracy, the latter's power being virtually unchecked by the kind of strong middle class found in Cataluña. Castilla's dark days began when the nobility forced Alfonso to abdicate to his son Sancho. When they turned on the young heir like a pack of wolves, only the queen, María de Molina, held the kingdom together. Sancho died prematurely some years later, and she stepped in again to save the throne for her infant grandson. In a rough and wild age dominated by men, this exemplary woman managed to defeat the crown's enemies and was later immortalized in a play by Tirso de Molina called *La Prudencia en la Mujer*.

As if there were not enough problems, the Almohades had been replaced in Morocco by another belligerent dynasty, the Marinids. Encouraged by the chaos in Castilla, they captured Gibraltar, Algeciras, and Tarifa with the treacherous aid of the king's own brother, Juan. The siege of Tarifa witnessed one of the more famous incidents in Spanish history, the defense of its castle by Pérez de Guzmán. When he refused to surrender, the attackers threatened to murder his son, but Guzmán, henceforth known as "*El Bueno*," replied in true Iberian fashion. He threw out his knife and shouted, "Here is the weapon to do it, but I will never surrender." (No one is quite sure what happened to the son.) The Marinids were crushed at the battle of Rio Salado (1340), in which artillery was used for the first time in Europe. Four years later Alfonso XI recaptured Algeciras.

While Castilla watched the Strait of Gibraltar, Aragón had set sail on a very different course by turning outward to the Mediterranean in the manner of the prosperous Italian republics of Genoa and Venice. This was the era of Cataluña's famous maritime code, *Llibre del Consulat de Mar*. With Cataluña ever leading, Aragón managed to annex Sardinia and Sicily into its loose-knit empire, and they would remain in Spanish hands for centuries. In the early 1300s the feared Catalonian army (the *almogavars*) was sent from Sicily to battle the Ottoman Turks. Somehow along the way they established a duchy in Athens, and Catalán became the official language for sixty years. The great figure of Aragón's medieval empire was king Pedro (Peter) IV, "The Ceremonious." During the century Barcelona was Spain's greatest city and the largest shipbuilder in the Mediterranean, and Catalonian sailors ranged freely from the Black Sea to the coast of Senegal.

Aragón's commercial class likewise enjoyed a good deal of political independence, based on the concept of a contract with the monarchy. The rights of the ruled were protected through a strong parliament and by a unique individual called the *justicia*, a kind of watchdog of the king. Compared with Castilla and its vast estates, the nobility was economically weak, but together with the middle class they were a feisty lot. Parliament's oath of allegiance to the king read: "We who are as good as you swear to you who are no better than we, to accept you as our king and sovereign lord, provided you accept all our liberties and laws; but if not, not." This was delivered by the seated *justicia* while he crowned the kneeling king. Later rulers, from Felipe II to Franco, would have to deal with this spirit.

One bizarre figure from this period was Pedro de Luna, cardinal of Aragón, who was elected as Pope Benedict XIII during the Great Schism that wracked Christianity at century's end. Pontificating from Avignon in France, he was branded an anti-pope in 1409, and he withdrew to the stronghold of Peñiscola north of Valencia. There he waited for a call to return that never came and died in obscurity.

While Aragón was creating a Mediterranean empire, Castilla had wet its own commercial feet by developing the ports of Cartagena and Sevilla. Merchants from Genoa made inroads into this virgin market and controlled Castilian commerce for two centuries. (Hence, it was entirely appropriate that Columbus came from Genoa.) But by the end of the middle ages, Castilians had developed a "sheepherder's mentality"; commerce and industry were considered "things of the Jews and Moors." Thanks to the powerful Mesta, an organization of wealthy livestock owners, the rights of herders took precedence and agriculture suffered accordingly. (There were three main sheep runs, each about seventy meters wide, between Old Castilla and Extremadura.) The crown, perennially in debt, took its cut of the wool profits.

Castilla's monarchs also turned for finance to the old Jewish moneylenders, long after a new breed of capitalist banks replaced them in Italy, France, and even Cataluña. Jews prevailed as royal financiers right down to the days of Fernando and Isabel (Ferdinand and Isabella), when they were summarily expelled. Cracks in Spain's traditional tolerance, the old society of three religions, began to appear after 1300. Muslims were required to wear certain clothes and hairstyles, and Jews were blamed for various troubles, especially economic crises, as they were in Visigothic days. Persecution increased proportionately with society's ills, though it must be said that Spain at the time was still less anti-Semitic than other countries. During the same years when Spanish Jews held positions of power and married freely into the aristocracy, their French and English co-religionists were having property confiscated and being expelled en masse.

But the Jews' plight in Spain worsened with time. By some form of twisted logic, they were commonly blamed for the outbreak of the Black Death in Europe in the 1340s. (The name came from the large black blotches on the skin of the afflicted.) The severity of the bubonic plague is often overlooked, but as much as one-third of the continent's population perished in a few years, causing the virtual breakdown of civilization in many areas. Parts of Iberia were hard hit, especially Aragón. Anti-Semitism heated up during the rule of Pedro (Peter) the Cruel (1350-69) after he surrounded himself with Jewish financial advisers and tax collectors. One of them was Samuel Ha-levi, best remembered as the builder of Toledo's El Tránsito Synagogue. Among the clergy and their flocks, Jews came to represent the hated regime itself.

The diabolical state of Castilian politics is summed up in the story of Pedro the Cruel. After he inherited the throne at age fifteen, the eldest of five illegitimate brothers, a ruthless struggle commenced. It is generally accepted that Pedro murdered an archbishop, several cousins, brothers, and friends, not to mention, in all probability, his own French queen. Pedro lived in his *alcázar* in Sevilla, and there he murdered the Red King of Granada with thirty-seven of his courtiers. According to the story, the Muslim ruler arrived wearing a priceless ruby in his turban that Peter immediately coveted. He invited the group for a banquet, and as soon as they were seated his guards leapt out and murdered them one by one.

Some historians claim these stories were invented later to excuse Pedro's own murder by his half-brother, Enrique (Henry) of Trastámara (also known as Henry the Bastard). In fact, Pedro's own followers never called him "The Cruel" (at least publicly), but used the accolade "The Dispenser of Justice." There may have been more than sibling rivalry involved. When Enrique tried to depose his brother, it was the climax of years of struggle between Pedro and the Castilian nobility. Not one to take things lying down, the king appealed for help to Edward, England's famous Black Prince. In response, France sent mercenary Bertrand du Guesclin, head of the White Companies to support Enrique. In this way Castile became another theater of operations in a prolonged European conflict known as the Hundred Years War.

Edward dealt the rebels a shattering defeat, and Enrique fled briefly to Aragón, leaving the humiliated Guesclin behind as prisoner. In gratitude, Pedro presented his famous stolen ruby to the wife of the Black Prince, who shortly after returned to England. (The gem now adorns the imperial crown in the Tower of London.) To finish the sordid story, there was a notorious fight between the two half-brothers, not on a glorious battlefield but in a wretched tent. Enrique stabbed the king with his own hand as he shouted "You Jew bastard!" He would soon be crowned Enrique II, bringing the House of Trastámara to power in Castilla (and later Aragón) until the coming of the Austrian Habsburgs in 1516.

The weak and cowardly Juan II ruled Castilla for nearly half a century (1406-1454). He soon fell under the influence of a court "favorite" named Álvaro de Luna, and before long the king's sole function was to sign whatever his minister put in front of him. After many years of enduring Álvaro, bitterly jealous courtiers accused him of some trumped-up charge and gained the king's ear. After a sham trial Álvaro was beheaded and his mutilated body put

Iberia in the Fifteenth Century

The fifteenth century opened with the peninsula's political map little changed since 1250. What transpired over the next few decades was by no means predestined. Individual decisions and pure chance would prove more decisive than historical forces in the creation of modern Spain.

on display. But the vacillating king came to regret his action and died wishing he "had been born son of a workman rather than king of Castilla."

Faced with ineffective kings until the coming of Fernando and Isabel, the Castilian nobility prospered as never before. Léonor de Albuquerque, for example, could travel the entire breadth of Castilla without setting foot outside her estates. Meanwhile, in Aragón, the death of Martín I brought an end to the dynasty begun with the marriage of Berenguer and Petronilla. Lacking other suitable candidates, Fernando (Ferdinand) of Antequera, from a junior branch of the Trastámaras, was awarded the crown. Even though Castilla and Aragón remained separate, they were brought immeasurably closer by this sharing of the same ruling house.

Aragón rather than Castilla strongly backed this Compromise of Caspe (1412) for reasons of political survival. These were hard years for Aragón:

reeling from a severe manpower shortage caused by the plague, the previously booming economy began to badly falter. The fall of Constantinople to the Ottoman Turks in 1453 was a severe blow to Catalonian shipping interests, and a dynastic struggle and civil war added to the woes.

Things were not much better in Castilla. Juan was succeeded by his son Enrique, physically repellent and morally perverted. Enrique IV was incompetent and impotent, a deadly combination in a monarch. Some claimed his youthful debaucheries had impaired his sexual vigor, but tongues also wagged about his Moorish guards and a court "full of Jews in bright shirts." Whatever the reason, when his second wife gave birth to a daughter, it was assumed she was the offspring of the queen's affair with the dashing Beltran de la Cueva. Juana, the dubious heiress, was dubbed *La Beltraneja*—roughly translated as "Beltran's bastard girl." However, many claim this was all just vicious propaganda invented by her rivals, namely Isabel, Enrique's younger half-sister.

Born in 1451 at Madrigal de las Altas Torres (Ávila), the future queen Isabel (Isabella) was plump, with a fair complexion, chestnut hair, greenish-blue eyes, and the round face of a peasant girl. In the right light she could be attractive, and Enrique tried to use his sister to cement marriage alliances favorable to Castilla. Isabel had many suitors, but soon the choice boiled down to King Alfonso V of Portugal and Fernando (Ferdinand), heir to the throne of Aragón. Enrique favored Alfonso, a man twice Isabel's age. Fernando, on the other hand, was handsome, athletic, and shrewd—what the Spanish call *listo*. Isabel's choice would decide if Castilla would unite with Portugal or Aragón. In other words, the very composition of modern Spain.

To the eternal delight of romantics everywhere, the princess chose Fernando, and envoys were sent to arrange the marriage. Her decision aroused so much opposition, however, that the Aragónese heir chose to travel incognito to Castilla. Disguised as a servant, he waited on the others in his group whenever they stopped en route. Upon reaching Valladolid, Fernando and Isabel finally met, and the attraction was mutual. Nevertheless, objections persisted in some quarters. For one thing, the couple was so closely related by blood (first cousins) that a papal dispensation was required. This was obtained in short order, but it later proved to be a forgery concocted by the king of Aragón, the archbishop of Toledo, and Fernando himself. But nothing could stop the marriage of nineteen-year-old Isabel and Fernando, a year younger. At a ceremony in the fairytale castle of Segovia, the bride was clad head to foot in white brocade and ermine; the groom wore a majestic golden robe lined with sable. On October 19, 1469, the two teenaged heirs were married.

But before Fernando and Isabel could make their rendezvous with immortality, they had other business to attend to. Their storybook marriage had brought no unity to the peninsula, legal or otherwise. King Enrique for one was irate at the prospect of a union with Aragón and declared that his daughter Juana, not Isabel, was his rightful successor. Adding insult, the pope excommunicated the couple when he found out about Fernando's forgery. To the church they would later champion, they were living in sin.

Enrique's death in 1474 launched a succession crisis that soon led to outright civil war in Castilla. Parliament proclaimed Isabel queen, and she was easily persuaded that her young niece was illegitimate and her supporters traitors. (Though the Duke of Alba reminded her, "If we are defeated, *we* shall be the traitors.") The previously spurned Alfonso of Portugal led supporters of Juana, and he announced his intention to use force to put her on the throne. This was another era, and Fernando challenged the Portuguese king to a duel. The aging Alfonso wisely declined, and two armies met instead at Toro, where Juana's supporters were routed. Alfonso returned to Portugal, and Juana *La Beltraneja* was packed off to a convent. The Treaty of Alcaçobaça (1479) confirmed Isabel's inheritance and with it Spain's future: Castilla was wedded to Aragón, not Portugal.

In that same year Fernando's father finally passed away, leaving him king. The two medieval giants united by the vows of marriage, if little else, but it was an interesting match of monarchs as well as kingdoms. Isabel could be painfully pious at times, certain she was right by virtue of divine guidance. Fernando survived more on personal charm than willpower or intelligence, yet he could be cool and crafty in diplomatic haggling. But he knew his limitations and was usually quite willing to follow his wife's lead. Wrote the royal secretary: "He was given to taking advice, especially that of the queen."

In the beginning Fernando intended to reign as an equal. By law his power in Castilla derived solely from his spouse, but he demanded joint exercise of royal authority. He succeeded in winning all the trappings of power: both names on royal appointments, seals, and coins, and a motto that read *Tanto Monta, monta tanto, Isabel como Fernando*, roughly "He counts for as much as she does; she counts for as much as he does." Later, in the spirit of unity, he resigned himself to a secondary role. Nevertheless, there was an endearing romantic quality about the marriage that speaks volumes. Royal propaganda displayed this mutual love with decorative motifs such as a yoke and arrows (weapons of love) or love knots, and pictures of the monarchs exchanging kisses illuminated royal decrees. It was said they were "two bodies, ruled by one spirit."

Yet there was no real fusion of the two crowns, and they remained rather strange bedfellows. Despite its wars, Castilla was stronger and more dynamic than Aragón, with five times the population. The center was growing and expanding while the east, notably Barcelona, had experienced a sharp decline since its halcyon days a century earlier. Even after the marriage, Catalans were treated as foreigners in Castilla, where their archenemies, the Genoese, had a grip on banking and commerce. Economically, Castilians looked north to market their wool, while Aragón traded with the Mediterranean.

The two kingdoms were quite different politically as well. The Castilian Cortes (parliament) was weak, and the crown kept the nobility at bay, although they had recently been flexing their aristocratic muscles. In Aragón, the nobles had triumphed in terms of real power, and Cataluña and Valencia each had its own parliament and rights. Despite the marriage of the century, Spain was still—to borrow a phrase—a mere "geographical expression."

Sights & Sites

Ávila: Medieval walls average 10 mts. in height, with 88 towers and 8 gates.

Barcelona: Gothic Quarter has many late medieval buildings; Museum of Catalan Art displays Romanesque and Gothic treasures.

Burgos: Cathedral started in 1221 and continued for three centuries; here lies El Cid beneath soaring transept.

Coca (Segovia): *alcázar* here is one of the best examples of *mudéjar* style.

Córdoba: The Juderia, the old Jewish quarter, contains a synagogue dating to fourteenth century.

Guadalupe (Cáceres): Monastery built after appearance of Virgin around 1300; important symbol of *hispanidad*.

Huesca: 36 kms. from town is Loarre Castle (1096) with vast panorama of Ebro Valley.

La Oliva Monastery (Navarra): One of the first built by French Cistercians.

León: Superb Cathedral, especially stained-glass windows.

Leyre Monastery (Navarra): Spiritual center of Navarra; pantheon of kings.

Málaga: Alcazaba; museum of Moorish art; Gibralfaro ramparts.

Montserrat (Barcelona): An important pilgrimage site.

Palma de Mallorca : Gothic Cathedral built 1230-1601.

Pedraza de la Sierra (Segovia): Village retains medieval atmosphere with castle and narrow streets.

Peñiscola (Castellón): Stone castle was refuge of anti-pope Benedict XIII.

Poblet Monastery (Tarragona): Founded by Ramón Berenguer IV.

San Juan de la Pena Monastery (Huesca): Served as pantheon of kings of Aragón-Navarra .

Sevilla's Giralda Tower in the heart of the Barrio de Santa Cruz

Santiago de Compostela (La Coruña): Cathedral is one of world's finest; famous "door of glory" is Romanesque masterpiece.

Sevilla: Cathedral is Spain's largest, with tomb of Alfonso X; Giralda and Torre de Oro built by Almohades; *mudéjar*-style Alcázar; Santa Cruz was former Jewish quarter.

Siguenza (Guadalajara): Fortress-like cathedral begun in twelfth century, but not finished until 1495.

Teruel: The entire town is a showcase of *mudéjar* architecture.

Toledo: Superb Gothic cathedral features choir stalls, Mozarabic chapel; El Transito Synagogue with Sephardic museum.

Zaragoza: Gothic Seo Cathedral has *mudéjar* decoration; the Aljaferia is a Moorish palace from *taifas* period.

Chapter 5

Birth of the Spanish World

Romantic writers such as Washington Irving have created a windmill of words describing the glories of Granada. Yet few of the millions of tourists who visit each year realize that one of history's most important towns lies nearby. Sleepy Santa Fe straddles the road to Málaga in the heart of a highly fertile *vega*, once watered with the blood of Christians and Moors. A signpost at the town's entrance reads *La Cuna de Hispanidad*, literally "the cradle of Spanishness."

Although its drab, heat-hazed streets evoke few images of bygone glory, this dusty market town was the birthplace of the Hispanic world. Here, the newly united kingdoms of Castilla and Aragón ended centuries of Moorish occupation, thereby edging closer to the modern nation of Spain. And here too the man we call Columbus received permission for his great voyage of discovery. A street called *Calle* Cristóbal Colón and a humble plaque are the sole reminders that at Santa Fe was born an empire that would far surpass the splendors of Moorish Granada.

Santa Fe ("holy faith") was built in 1491 as a base camp for the final assault on Granada; hence its dubious claim to be "the only place in Spain not contaminated by Muslim heresy." A plaque affixed to the south gate, one of four at each point of a cruciform layout, commemorates the founding, and inscriptions recall the roles of different Spanish towns in the Reconquest's final act. Underscoring Santa Fe's military origins, a sculpture of a Moor's severed head sits atop the main church. Here is a place to ponder time's cruel verdicts. In 1492 Santa Fe witnessed some of history's most important months in that most famous of years, but today it is just a forgotten curiosity.

Before facing the Moors of Granada, Fernando and Isabel needed to consolidate their own precarious power. They turned first to the Castilian nobility, which for years had been chipping away at royal authority. In a series of bold moves, they forced the aristocrats out of parliament, took control of the noble-infested military orders, and ordered the destruction of all castles not vital to national defense. The carrot to match this royal stick was the granting of conquered lands in Andalucía to crown supporters. To back up this royal power-grab, Fernando and Isabel gained control of the medieval *Hermandades*. These brotherhoods of towns had their own police, usually bands of crossbowmen who pursued and shot down suspects, vigilante-style. The new monarchs welded these forces into a feared national police called the *Santa Hermandad* (Holy Brotherhood) dedicated to serving royal interests.

The next target was the church. The archbishop of Toledo was second in power only to the monarchs, and many other bishops were aristocrats with their own castles and private armies. Corruption and immorality were rampant from Toledo down to the village priest. Concubinage, for example, was an accepted practice among the supposedly celibate clergy. The sons of a priest could even inherit his property. The monarchs appointed Hernando Talavera, Isabel's confessor and a converted Jew, to reform these abuses.

Perhaps the greatest source of burgeoning royal power was the infamous Inquisition. This papal institution originated in the thirteenth century to deal with the Albigensian heresy, chiefly in France, and had become virtually extinct. Isabel gained the pope's permission for a revamped version. From the outset the Spanish Inquisition's main business was finding and weeding out "false" Christians, particularly Jews who had converted but secretly maintained their rites and customs. Jews or Muslims who practiced their religions openly were not within its jurisdiction and were allowed—at least for a few years—to continue. But the so-called *conversos* were considered unreliable and dangerous to a monarchy obsessed with unity and uniformity.

The Inquisition was a product of the times, born amid Spain's shaky new identity and fears of Jewish-Moorish alliances. Religious persecution was

The Catholic Monarchs, Fernando of Aragón and Isabel of Castilla (Ferdinand and Isabella)

part of the age, in Spain as much as in the England of Henry VIII and Mary Tudor, and it served crown interests by shoring up royal power at the expense of the nobles and clergy. The Spanish Inquisition was the one institution, other than the crown itself, common to both Castilla and Aragón.

As we have seen, Jews had suffered persecution since the days of Pedro the Cruel, and things were not improving. Jewish converts suspected of reverting to old ways were called *marranos*, derived from the word for swine. But the Inquisition and Christians generally were not anti-Semitic in a racial or ethnic sense. There were Jewish *conversos* in all areas of power—Talavera and possibly even the feared Grand Inquisitor, Dominican prior Tomás de Torquemada. Two prominent Jews financed the crown's military ventures, and even king Fernando had Jewish blood from his maternal grandfather.

It can even be argued that the Inquisition helped protect Jews by rescuing them from the threat of mob violence. Nevertheless, it struck terror in the hearts of converted Jews because its methods virtually guaranteed the guilt of the accused. Those unfortunate enough to fall under suspicion were secretly arrested and thrown into solitary cells, where they might wait months before learning the charges. Their accuser could remain anonymous, and torture was used to extract confessions from anyone maintaining their innocence.

Punishment was dealt out at a public display called an *auto de fé* (act of faith) that included processions, sermons, confessions, and executions. At the first such event, held in Sevilla in 1481, six convicted heretics were solemnly burned at the stake. The Inquisition's early years were especially bloody, with about two thousand executions in the 1480s alone. (Of an estimated twelve thousand death sentences over three centuries, about half occurred between 1481 and 1516.)

Shortly after the civil war ended, Isabel asked the pope for crusading rights against the last bastion of non-Christian Spain—the kingdom of Granada. Ruled by the Nasrid dynasty, this remnant of the *taifas* stretched about 180 kilometers from east to west and 75 inland from the sea. Swelled by Muslim refugees, the capital had about sixty thousand inhabitants; other cities were Málaga, famed for its figs and sweet wine, and the prosperous port of Almería.

Washington Irving and his romantic cohorts have spun a web of gilded prose around Moorish Granada, "enclosed by two rivers like a necklace of pearls." Supreme embodiment of this vision is the Alhambra, a reddish fortress-palace perched on a hill overlooking the old Moorish quarter, the Albaicin. Part of the Alhambra's glory comes from its superb location, a perfect blending of site and structure. Part derives from its exquisitely carved rooms and lush courtyards filled with the sound of splashing water. It's said that the royal baths had three taps, from which flowed hot, cold, and perfumed water. Although begun much earlier, the "red castle" did not reach its splendor until the fourteenth century, just as Granada was sliding into decadence. Indeed, the last piece of Moorish architecture may well have been the Patio of the Lions, delicate arcades resting on 124 slender pillars.

The centuries of impasse between Christian and Moor had not been without incident. In 1410 Enrique, the future king of Aragón, captured Antequera (Málaga). Three decades later, more Christian victories led to a puppet ruler in the Alhambra who paid an annual tribute. Moreover, the fall of the Byzantine capital at Constantinople to the Ottoman Turks (1453) shocked all Christendom, and appeals rang out to stop the infidels. Fernando and Isabel soon realized that war with an outside foe was a perfect means to unify their kingdoms.

In 1476, Sultan Mulay Hassan replied to Castilla's demand for payment of the annual tribute by retorting, "The mints of Granada no longer coin gold, but steel." But the Christians were too busy to pick up the gauntlet until five years later, when the castle of Zahara near Ronda fell to the Moors. At last they prepared for war, and Christian armies marched under the new regal symbol of yoke and arrows. This final crusade would last ten years (1482-92).

The chronic instability of Moorish Spain sprang from the harem, which produced numerous sons by different mothers, any of which might vie for the throne. The Moors' last family feud contributed greatly to Christian victory. Granada was split between supporters of Mulay's wife Aixa and her son Boabdil (called "The Unfortunate One" since birth) on one side and a beautiful Christian concubine named Soraya on the other. The sultan had fallen for Soraya and forsaken Aixa and her son, and civil war inevitably followed.

This was the stuff of legend. Tour-guides at the Alhambra will point out the "blood stains" (probably rust) on the floor of the Hall of the Abencerrajes, where Mulay had thirty followers of Aixa beheaded. In another story, Boabdil escaped from a tower prison by using a rope made from silk sashes. After Aixa's faction gained the upper hand, Mulay was forced to flee Granada to the protection of his brother, Al-Zaghal, governor of Málaga. Fernando reveled in the spectacle and proclaimed, "I intend to pick this pomegranate seed by seed." (The word *granada* means pomegranate.)

But the Spanish army proceeded with some difficulty, mostly financial. On one occasion Fernando was obliged to cut silver chalices (used at Mass) into pieces in order to pay his men. The queen, who served as army quartermaster, took personal loans and even pawned the crown jewels to pay for the campaign. Yet in truth about three-fourths of the costs of the Granada wars were paid by church taxes granted by the papacy.

A year after the war commenced, Boabdil was captured at Loja and cut a secret deal with Fernando. To assure the defeat of his hated father and uncle, he agreed to surrender Granada once his rivals were vanquished. In 1487, Málaga fell after a four-month siege, and Al-Zaghal was exiled and died blind and impoverished in Morocco. Thousands of Moors also crossed the sea, founding the town of Chechaouen in the Rif Mountains. (Today it remains, except for the occasional tour-bus, a perfect slice of old Al-Andalus.)

Málaga's fate decided the war; henceforth the capital was cut off from any hope of aid from North Africa. But when Almería too was captured, Boabdil reneged on the secret bargain and refused to surrender Granada. The stage was set for the invasion of the *vega* and the founding of Santa Fe. Massive walls and towers protected Granada, and Fernando chose to throw up a blockade rather than attack. When the queen joined the army she vowed not to change her blouse until Granada fell (her husband soon dissuaded her, it's said). One night a fire swept through the tent camp, and in April 1491 combat ceased while a new town of brick and mortar went up. In the following months, the noose around Granada tightened, but aside from the occasional skirmish the war became a stalemate favoring the Christians.

Into this scene strode that dogged adventurer who changed the world—Cristobal Colón, Cristoforo de Colombo, Christopher Columbus, the Great Admiral himself. Speculation has swirled around Columbus's origins and nationality, not to mention his fascinating if confused life prior to arriving in Spain. One noted historian claimed his name was Colom, from a family of Mallorcan Jews that had immigrated to Genoa and changed their name to Colombo. Another, more improbable, theory holds that he was the illegitimate son of the Prince of Viana, Fernando's disinherited elder brother. Columbus himself threw a smokescreen over his origins, probably because he was indeed the son of a humble weaver from Genoa and was taking a giant step up in a very class-conscious society. But add to the mystery the fact that he never wrote in Italian, not even letters to his brother Bartolomew, and doubts refuse to go away.

The red-haired, blue-eyed boy went to sea at age fourteen and may have later become a pirate. In 1476, he escaped from a sinking ship and swam to the Portuguese shore, there to remain for years working as a sailor and map salesman. He somehow married into a well-to-do family and began to devise a plan to reach the Orient by crossing the Atlantic. His bride's father was governor of an island in the Madeiras, and Columbus may have been privy to important nautical information that might have lent credence to his theories. In any case, he finally managed to present his ideas to the Portuguese king. Portugal was then at the vanguard of pushing back the world's maritime frontiers. With hostile Turks blocking traditional land routes, there was an all-out effort to find a sea passage to oriental spice markets. In 1488, Bartholomew Diaz sailed along the African coast and reached the Cape of Good Hope.

Spaniards too were caught up in the spirit of the age, and a decade before Columbus they occupied the Canary Islands. Stubborn Guanches managed to hold out for a time on Tenerife, but their position was hopeless. Sailors spoke of the "remarkable beauty" of the women, and within decades the pure Guanche strain was hard to find. Spain's possession of the Canaries was confirmed by a treaty that also gave the Portuguese a free hand along Africa's western coast. With the islands as a base, sailors began looking toward the setting sun. The existence of land to the west was, contrary to myth, a matter of common speculation; only the most ignorant believed that the earth was flat or the ocean inhabited by sea serpents.

After years of futile negotiations in Lisbon, Columbus left in disgust and sailed with his young son for Spain. In the summer of 1485, they landed at Palos near Huelva and sought shelter at the Franciscan monastery of La Rábida. Here Columbus met Fray Juan Pérez, the queen's former confessor, who took an interest in the project and arranged an introduction at court. Columbus's luck seemed to be changing.

Meanwhile, however, the Catholic Monarchs were up to their necks in the Granada campaign and could not consider another costly endeavor. A special commission under Talavera was appointed to study the matter, and Columbus received an annual retainer of twelve thousand *maravedis*, the wage of a common seaman. For years he lived on this stipend, following the court and occasionally taking part in fighting. Talavera and other members of the Council of Salamanca regarded the Italian as a wild visionary, but they were not merely ignorant clerics. Not since ancient Greece had any educated person doubted that the earth was a sphere. (Before the birth of Christ Strabo wrote, "If the extent of the Atlantic Ocean were not an obstacle, we might easily pass by sea from Iberia to India.")

The debate centered on the size of the ocean and the feasibility of a voyage. Columbus maintained that the distance between the Canaries and China was about four thousand kilometers, while the council believed—correctly as it turned out—that it was much larger. Of course, neither had any idea that lying between Europe and Asia was an unexpected surprise. When Columbus continued to press his case, the council proclaimed his plan "vain, impracticable, and resting on grounds too weak to merit the support of the government."

Columbus returned briefly to Portugal for another go at the king, and his brother Bartholomew left for England to try to interest Henry VII in the project. Fortunately for Spain, Columbus was what you might call a hardhead, and he refused to give up on Isabel. Some have speculated that he was so obstinate because he possessed "inside" information, possibly from a sailor named Alfonso Sánchez, who may have reached the West Indies after a storm blew his ship off course. But we will never know for sure.

One interesting footnote: The "forgotten" man in this saga was Giovanni Caboto from Genoa, who moved to Valencia about 1490 and, calling himself Juan Caboto, tried to convince officials of the westward route. Finally giving up, he moved to England and received a royal commission for a later voyage. In 1497 the man history calls John Cabot discovered Newfoundland (Canada).

By the summer of 1491 even Columbus was losing patience, and he traveled to La Rábida to visit his son. The sympathetic Juan Pérez wrote a letter to the queen at Santa Fe, and she agreed to see the Italian again. But Isabel had more pressing matters.

After months of stalemate and secret negotiations, Boabdil surrendered Granada in exchange for generous terms, and an agreement was ratified in November. When this became known a riot broke out in the city, and the Christian army entered earlier than expected, on January 2, 1492. It was an auspicious start for that most famous of years; the last stronghold of the Moors had fallen. Soldiers carried banners of Santiago and sang hymns as they marched up the Hill of Martyrs to the Alhambra. Here they planted a silver cross and the flag of Castilla on the Vela Tower, which could be seen all the way to Santa Fe. On January 6 the Catholic Monarchs entered Granada and received homage from Boabdil inside the Alhambra. Looking out on the silent and secretive city, they prepared to spend their first night in the fabled Moorish palace.

As part of the settlement, Boabdil, the twentieth and last sultan of the Nasrid dynasty, was given thirty thousand gold coins and a slice of the Alpujarras region south of Granada. Leaving the city for the last time, he looked back and wept for his lost kingdom. As every tour-guide knows, his mother then uttered, "You do well to weep as a woman for that which you could not defend as a man." Because Granada was handed over without a fight, the Albaicin quarter retains its Moorish flavor today, its houses featuring inner courtyards and Arabic inscriptions. Other pre-Christian remnants include a few arcades from the old silk market, the *alcaiceria*, and the *corral del carbon*, a caravansary.

The Treaty of Granada contained fifty-five articles guaranteeing Moorish rights. The vanquished were offered transit to Morocco, as well as the return trip to Spain within three years if they were not happy. Talavera, named first archbishop of Granada favored these lenient terms, but within a very few years everything would change. The troubles were far from over for the Moors.

The end came sooner for the Jews: just three months after Granada's fall, an expulsion order was issued for any Jew refusing Christian baptism. Adherence to any belief other than Catholicism became tantamount to treason. All his is ironic in that loans from two Jewish financiers (named Seneor and Abravanel) paid for the Granada war. After the expulsion decree, this same pair offered 600,000 *reales* to Fernando and Isabel

Columbus departs from Huelva on his historic voyage of discovery.

to have it lifted. According to one story, just as the king wavered, Grand Inquisitor Torquemada burst into the room and demanded that the order be executed. And so it was.

The expulsion of the Jews was a curious action in many ways and has been much debated. Such things were not unknown in medieval Europe: England had expelled its Jews in 1290 and France in 1306. But what stung so much in Spain was the high status, both culturally and economically, that Jews had reached during the Middle Ages. (Remember, the king himself was part Jewish.)

But consider the background. Traditional anti-Semitism among the peasantry had been whipped up in recent years by some sordid incidents and rumors. There was the infamous case of Benito García, a Christian convert who was arrested with a consecrated wafer (used in the Mass) hidden in his knapsack. After six days of torture he confessed to the ritual murder by crucifixion of a Christian child and named five *converso* accomplices. All the accused, no doubt innocent, were burned alive at Ávila. Many Christians regarded Jews—whether baptized or not—as the Moors' natural allies and potential traitors. It was an interesting coincidence that the crown was bankrupt, and Jews were generally prosperous merchants. Before fleeing, many were forced to sell everything at huge losses—a house for a donkey, a vineyard for a suit of clothes—if they did not suffer outright expropriation. With this regrettable decision, Spain lost a vital part of its citizenry and most of the urban middle class.

The expulsion order gave Jews four months to pack up and leave. An estimated fifty thousand converted and took their chances with the Inquisition as "new Christians"; about two hundred thousand left Spain forever according to traditional sources. Another few thousand were killed for refusing to do either. Recently some historians have challenged the "so-called expulsion" by asserting that Jews remained prominent in all areas of life and revising the number of emigrants to about forty thousand. In any case, the majority of these Sephardic Jews (from the Hebrew word for Spain, *Sefaradh*) settled in North Africa, Italy, Greece, Turkey, and the Levant. In their cultural baggage they carried the medieval Castilian language, called *ladino*, along with hundreds of ancient ballads that still survive in isolated Sephardic communities around the Mediterranean. It's said that old keys to their Spanish homes, long-since demolished, are passed from one generation to the next. (A final footnote to this story occurred in 1982, when Spain invited Sephardic Jews to become Spaniards again after 490 years of exile.)

The famous 1492 was quite a year. Less than a month after the expulsion order, Columbus finally got the royal nod, but not without plenty of drama. Upon Granada's surrender, the intrepid Italian approached Fernando again, but the answer was still no. With an encouraging letter from the French king in hand, Columbus rode off to Palos, where Father Pérez persuaded him to wait. The old fray then hopped on a mule and rode to Santa Fe, where a tear-filled plea convinced the queen to see Columbus once more. Even then, the explorer shot himself in the foot again with his extravagant demands, and the royal couple balked. Columbus rode off a final time and only the eleventh hour heroics of a friend at court, Luis de Santangel, convinced the queen. A rider overtook Columbus a few kilometers from Granada, and on April 17, 1492, a pact was signed at Santa Fe. It raised the curtain on a new world beyond even the Grand Admiral's wildest dreams.

Isabel was motivated by the chance to gain souls as well as gold. By sailing west to the Orient, she reasoned, Christians could attack Islam from the rear and even regain the Holy Land. The Reconquest could go on and on until the last infidel perished. Let us not forget that the first title inscribed on her tomb in Granada's Cathedral reads: "Extirpator of the Muhammadan heresy." Of course, economics too played its part. In an age before refrigeration, Eastern spices were in great demand for preserving and flavoring meats.

Pepper fetched forty times its original cost and a single pound of cloves was worth two cows.

With the fall of Granada, Spain was faced with a decision of truly historic implications—whether to carry the struggle against Islam into North Africa. Melilla in Morocco was captured in 1497 (it remains Spanish today), but the African campaign was postponed for a crucial decade. When the idea resurfaced it was too late. Spain's failure to follow up in North Africa is one of history's great "missed opportunities." But there were other concerns: domestic stability and, of course, the discovery and eventual conquest of America.

On the morning of August 3, 1492, a fleet of three small ships with 120 men, many criminals under temporary amnesty, sailed off from Palos. They stopped for final provisions in the Canaries, then pressed on westward. After thirty-one days without sighting land, the crew grew restless and rebellious, urging Columbus to turn back. Certain of his calculations, he asked for just two more days and promised to give up if land was not reached. (This supports the "inside information" theory.) Finally, at about midnight on October 12, the thirty-second day, a faint shape appeared on the horizon, "something like a white sand cliff gleaming in the moonlight," according to his journal. The next morning an exploratory group landed on a small island that Columbus christened San Salvador, a date celebrated each year throughout the Hispanic world as *El Dia de la Hispanidad*. Within a century Spanish language and culture would be found in most of the Americas.

Columbus spent several months searching for the fabulous cities of Marco Polo, but found only a few primitive tribes and a smattering of wealth. From the timbers of the foundered *Santa María* he built a fortress and left forty men behind before sailing for Spain. Eight months after leaving Palos for the great unknown, Columbus strode into the royal court at Barcelona. With him were six natives he called "Indians," the greatest misnomer in history. In a carefully rehearsed speech, he spread a world of untold riches at the monarchs' feet. When he finished, everyone fell to their knees in thanksgiving while solemn strains of the *Te Deum* poured forth.

It can be argued that the discovery of America in 1492 was the greatest single event in the history of mankind (though clerics of all religions would argue this point in favor of their own messiah). With one stroke it put an end to the Middle Ages, opened the colonial era, and shifted the center of gravity from the Mediterranean to the Atlantic. Most important, the discovery altered forever the concept that a man's station in life was inextricably linked with the class into which he was born. Men who could get the job done became leaders rather than those of high social status. For "go-getters" everywhere, America became an inspiration, a hope for better things in both material and idealistic realms.

During the next few years, Columbus made three more voyages to the Indies. The second expedition, in September 1493, was quite different—1,500 men in seventeen vessels led by the triumphant Italian sailor. They carried seeds, plantings, livestock—everything for a proper colony. But troubled winds were already blowing, for when the group reached San Salvador, nothing was left of the Spanish fortress. The natives told of incredible avarice and lust that caused them to massacre the settlers just a month after Columbus left. The Conquest would not be peaceful, after all.

In one of history's most cruel tricks, the dreamed-for lands of India and China continued to elude the great explorer, and he never recognized his actual accomplishment. When Columbus reached Cuba, for example, he imagined himself in the kingdom of the great Khan, and sent two "ambassadors" with letters from the queen off into the jungle searching for the fabled capital. Columbus founded the city of Santo Domingo on the isle of Hispaniola (Haiti/ Dominican Republic), and he later explored Jamaica, Puerto Rico, and the coast of Honduras on the mainland. But a far better dreamer than administrator, he was charged with incompetence and shipped home in irons (he was later released).

Aside from a few trinkets there were no riches for Columbus, and on returning from his last voyage, he was not even invited to court. Still muttering about the *Cipango* (Japan) of Marco Polo, he died bedridden and bitterly disappointed in Valladolid in May 1506 at the age of fifty-five. His funeral was simple, and the official chronicle failed to note his passing. For another decade his discoveries would be shrugged off as essentially worthless. One final ignominy: the New World received its name from an Italian with a better gift for public relations named Amerigo Vespucci. Sailing under the Castilian flag, this adventurer charted the coastline of South America. Vespucci's widely read letters described "lascivious women healthy as fish" and "cannibals with smoked human legs hung from the rafters of their huts." These images captured Europe's imagination, and one German cartographer decided to call the new continent "America" after Amerigo. The name stuck.

Another event of 1492 was the election of a Spaniard from a famous Italian family, Rodrigo Borgia, as Pope Alexander VI—the most corrupt pontiff in history. He became a close ally of Fernando and Isabel and named them *Los Reyes Católicos* (The Catholic Kings or Monarchs). His famous "line of demarcation," 370 leagues west of the Cape Verde Islands, conferred virtually all the new lands on Castilla. (Portugal was allowed to conquer the eastern area that became Brazil.)

Throughout the period Spain retained an essentially antiquated social structure whose iniquities were questioned by few. The grandees were addressed as "cousins" by the king and allowed to keep their hats on in his presence. The *hidalgos* jealously guarded the appellation "*Don*" and their family coat of arms. In a world in which where heraldry was the key to status, vast time and effort were spent on finding or inventing aristocratic ancestors in the family tree. Landowners comprised about two percent of the population, but owned ninety-seven percent of the land, while the vast majority of Spaniards were landless peasants. The Duke of Infantado, for example, lorded over eight hundred villages and ninety thousand subjects. This concentration of landed wealth was exacerbated toward the end of the Reconquest, when huge tracts of Andalucía, the *latifundios*, were handed out to important nobles. Soldiers of the military orders received smaller parcels in Extremadura and La Mancha.

The economy remained medieval, each kingdom a world unto itself. Before the wealth of the Indies began to trickle into Castilla, sheep-raising was the chief source of income. Aragón's economy was equally weak, having suffered numerous setbacks since the glories of its medieval empire. On the bright side, commerce seemed to thrive at traditional fairs like at Medina del Campo (Valladolid). People flocked to these colorful markets for the luxuries of medieval life: woolens and silks, perfumes and cosmetics, spices and honey. Towns remained primitive in appearance, with garbage thrown into a ditch running down the middle of the street where pigs fed, and people squatting in the street for bodily functions. (One thing Spaniards in the New World noted was the cleanliness of Indian towns.)

The joint monarchy continued its efforts to reform the indolent and immoral clergy. They succeeded in gaining some royal control over church coffers and the appointment of bishops—essentially the same battle Henry

VIII waged in England. In these struggles they were aided by Cardinal Mendoza, chief royal adviser during the crucial dozen years after 1482.

Mendoza's successor was the even more remarkable Cardinal Gonzalo Jiménez de Cisneros, known to history as Cisneros. Although coming from a poor background, he was named to the pivotal position of confessor to the queen. (He knew all the secrets.) Isabel proceeded to get him appointed archbishop of Toledo, and he launched more clerical reforms such as enforcing the vows of celibacy. More than a thousand friars fled to Morocco with their mistresses rather than conform.

But Cisneros was much more than a bishop. Among other things, the soldier-cardinal oversaw the Inquisition, developed the core of the Spanish navy, and personally led armies against Oran and Tripoli. One of his less-admired roles was ruthless persecutor of the Moors. The previously lenient policy underwent an abrupt switch under Cisneros, who sponsored forced conversions and bonfires of Islamic books. These strong-arm tactics provoked a revolt in Granada, and fighting quickly spread to the Alpujarras and Ronda mountains. Spanish armies led by the king and Gonzalo de Córdoba quickly crushed the uprising.

In 1502, a decade after the Jewish expulsion, an order went out demanding conversion or exile for all practicing Muslims in Castilla. Unlike the Jews, only a few hundred Muslims chose to leave. The rest decided that "Spain was worth a Mass" and took part in huge communal baptisms, like one in Granada at which water was flung from a mop twirled above the crowd. An estimated 300,000 Muslims converted in one year and were henceforth known as Moriscos. Cisneros tried to erase centuries of Islamic culture by decree, and the last remnants of Moorish Spain were ground into the dirt. The Arabic language was outlawed, Moriscos forbidden to wear traditional dress, and their public baths closed. Bathing itself became suspect; a common phrase used by the Inquisition was "the accused was known to take baths." For Cisneros and Isabel, the only acceptable water was holy water.

Yet Cardinal Cisneros is a complex figure. For all his militant Christianity he also embodied the learned humanism of the Renaissance. He founded the University of Alcalá de Henares near Madrid and sponsored the Polyglot Bible, which included the text in Hebrew, Latin, and Greek for the first time. (The preface stated that the Latin version was like Jesus between the two thieves at the crucifixion.)

The reign of the Catholic Monarchs was an era of cultural exuberance as well as military glory. In 1492 Nebrija published the first grammar text of a modern language, *Gramatica del Castellano*. When the queen asked the purpose of such a book, one adviser remarked, "Your majesty, language is the perfect instrument of empire." Fifteenth-century literature witnessed the decline of lengthy epics in favor of short poems called *romances*, ballads that form one of the world's great bodies of folk poetry. They describe the Moorish wars, El Cid, the murder of Pedro the Cruel, and moving love stories. The equally popular novels of chivalry cast a further mist over peninsular life with their idealized landscapes of enchanted islands, jousts and magical swords, hulking giants, and long-bearded wizards.

These ballads and novels had a profound influence on Spanish-American popular literature. Later, romantics such as Lord Byron and Washington Irving felt Spain's spell and are largely responsible for the lingering rose-tinted images of the legendary land beyond the Pyrenees. Closer to the modern novel (called the first European novel by some) was a masterpiece entitled *La Celestina* (1499) by the *converso* Fernando de Rojas. Written in powerful Castilian as lean as the land itself, the story involves an old hag who sells her wisdom and love potions to encourage seduction and romance.

The period's exuberance in architecture created the *plateresque* style, a strange blend of Gothic and *mudéjar* with ostentatious flourishes that were foreign to Renaissance ideals. More in step with the times, but still unmistakably Spanish, are three Renaissance churches built early in the sixteenth century at Granada, Málaga, and Jaén.

Spain—Castilla and Aragón to be precise—was preparing to take its place in Europe. By choosing Fernando over other suitors, Isabel had fated the nation to a future of embroilment in Aragón's Italian affairs, with a corollary hostility to France. For the next two centuries, Spain's basic foreign policy would be to encircle its Gallic neighbor. Fearful of losing their Mediterranean influence, the French invaded Naples. However, in 1504 this important Italian kingdom was confirmed along with Sicily and Sardinia as part of a growing "Spanish lake."

The wily Fernando used his son and daughters to cement desired alliances. Princess Isabel was wed to Alonso, heir to the Portuguese throne. At a famous double wedding, Juan, the Spanish heir, married Habsburg princess Margaret, and his sister Juana took the vows with archduke Philip (Margaret's brother), the Habsburg heir. Another daughter was Catherine (Catalina) of Aragón, who married Henry VIII of England and gave birth to Mary Tudor, the future queen. When Henry renounced the marriage years later, Catherine refused to submit and was imprisoned until her death in 1536.

Fernando's matchmaking formed a clever plan, but a series of tragedies conspired to prevent any of the Catholic Monarchs' children from reaching the throne. Prince Juan died, in effect, from sexual excess. He deeply loved his passionate, red-haired wife so much that doctors encouraged the newlyweds to sleep apart temporarily. But Isabel replied, "I cannot separate those whom God has joined." Within a few weeks Juan collapsed and died, profoundly changing the course of Spanish history. (One writer called his sarcophagus in Ávila "the tomb of Spain.") Rather than look to its own affairs, the new nation would become hopelessly entangled with Europe's squabbles.

Juana became first in line to succeed Isabel. Her spouse, Philip (Felipe) "the Fair" of Burgundy, was a notorious womanizer, and she "who could boast few personal attractions" was plunged into deep despair during his trysts. Soon the royal heiress acquired the moniker Juana *la loca* (Joanna the Mad). When the queen died in 1504, the thirtieth year of her reign, it was with the bitter realization that Castilla would go to an unstable daughter and her play-boy husband. Fernando retained Aragón, and in her last testament Isabel appointed her husband as regent for Juana in the event of her incapacity to rule. The queen made clear the fragility of the much-heralded union of Castilla and Aragón by stating that "all those lands discovered and yet to be discovered, conquered or yet to be conquered, shall remain in possession of *my* kingdoms of Castilla and León."

In effect, the union between the two regions was temporarily dissolved because the dynastic link ended. Meanwhile Juana and her spouse resided in Burgundy and Fernando was ratified as regent. An indignant Philip threatened to assert his wife's claims, with force if necessary. Fernando wisely withdrew, and in Toledo heralds proclaimed the accession of Juana to the crown of Castilla. To complicate matters, Fernando soon married the beautiful Germaine de Foix, teenaged niece of the French king. He hoped to sire an heir who would inherit Aragón and put a permanent end to the union with Castilla.

Fortunately for everyone, except poor Juana, Philip died suddenly just two months later, leaving the six-year-old Charles of Ghent—Philip and Juana's son—as heir to Castilla. Upon hearing the news of her husband's death, Juana seemed to collapse mentally. Following the advice of a monk who claimed

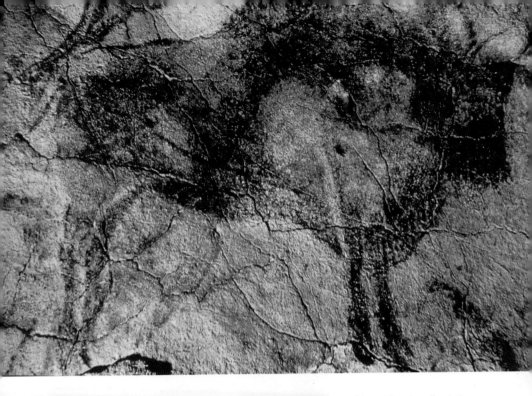

This prehistoric wall painting (above) is one of many discovered at Altamira Cave in northern Spain. The famous Dama de Elche statue (left), presumably of a goddess or queen, is a superb remnant of early Iberian culture.

Segovia's magnificent Roman aqueduct (above) is an inspiring sight that has awed observers for two millennia. The Roman mosaic (left) was discovered in the province of León. The Alhambra Palace in Granada (facing page) and the Great Mosque of Córdoba on the following spread (photographed by J.D. Dallet) are stunning examples of Moorish architecture in Spain.

The tomb of a young nobleman (above) in the
Cathedral of Sigüenza displays the medieval concept
of combining military prowess with cultural pursuits.
El Escorial (facing page), built outside Madrid by King
Philip II, features a royal library filled with thousands of
priceless volumes.

Velazquez painted the great Spanish victory at Breda (above) in the Low Countries. The renowned Emperor Charles V (Carlos I of Spain) appears in a portrait by Titian (left).

Philip was not really dead, she started touring the country with his body. This strange funeral cortege traveled by night for the next few months, the hearse drawn by eight black horses, followed by torchbearers, a train of attendants, and the queen. In another gruesome touch, Juana occasionally opened the casket to inspect the deteriorating corpse.

At last she relinquished the body for burial at Tordesillas and went into seclusion at a nearby palace. Here she would spend the next forty-six years, bouncing from periods of lucidity to deranged melancholy, as dead to the world as Philip's body lying in the monastery beside her. And through it all, until her death in 1555, she remained queen of Spain.

Cardinal Cisneros persuaded Fernando to return as regent. It's said that Machiavelli chose him as the model for a perfect prince in his famous political treatise, and Fernando lived up to the image by adroitly playing one foe off another to serve his ends. When the French king complained that the Spaniard had lied to him twice, he boasted, "I lied to him not twice but ten times." In 1512, Fernando annexed the independent kingdom of Navarra, completing the unification of the lands that today comprise Spain. The mighty Castilian army, modernized and led by Gonzalo Fernandez de Córdoba, was making its presence felt. It would not lose a pitched battle for more than a century. Around this same time soldiers began shouting "Santiago! España!" as they rushed headlong into battle.

This decade was also a fabulous one for the conquest of America, or *las Indias* as the new lands were called. During the first stage the only settlements were on Hispaniola and Cuba, but a generation after Columbus's landfall Spain had a mainland presence and the next twenty-five years witnessed a second wave pushing back the frontier. Searching for waters the Indians claimed had remarkable medicinal powers, "the fountain of youth," Ponce de León sailed west from Cuba and hit the mainland at a place he called Florida. A year later, Vasco Nuñez de Balboa and his expedition were hacking their way through the snake- and insect-infested jungle on the narrow isthmus linking North and South America.

Nuñez, or Balboa as he is commonly known, was an unsuccessful planter who evaded his creditors by hiding in a barrel on a ship bound for Panama. There his fortunes improved dramatically, and he was named to lead an expedition inland. In one of history's most dramatic moments, Balboa climbed to the top of a ridge, looked down, and sighted the "great southern ocean." Now there could be no doubt that Columbus had discovered a completely new continent. (One sad footnote: Balboa was later arrested by a jealous governor and beheaded as a common criminal.)

Contrary to legend, Balboa did not name his discovery. That honor belongs to the great Portuguese explorer Fernao de Magalhais (Ferdinand Magellan), who sailed for the crown of Castilla. In 1519, he left Sanlucár de Barrameda in Spain with five leaky vessels and 265 men to launch history's most daring voyage. After six months spent crossing the Atlantic and following the American coast southward, Magellan found the passage that today bears his name and rounded Cape Horn. Upon entering the calm waters of a huge ocean, he christened it *la Pacifica* (the peaceful). Three months and thousands of kilometers later, Magellan landed in the Philippines, where natives murdered him for reasons unknown. Command passed to his Basque pilot, Juan Sebastián del Cano, who carried on through the Indian Ocean and around Africa before returning with just one ship and eighteen men to an astonished nation. The expedition proved beyond any doubt that the earth was a sphere. Spain's later claims of the Pacific Ocean as a "Spanish sea" were largely meaningless given its size.

The great King Carlos I of Spain was also Holy Roman Emperor Charles V.

The Reconquest, with its crusading spirit and military values, was the perfect training ground for the conquest of America. For centuries Spaniards had been lured south by the promise of land and riches won at sword point. Most of the *conquistadores* came from dirt-poor frontier regions of Extremadura and Andalucía, and for such men the glories of war could not stop at Granada. Indeed, Spaniards would not halt until they had girdled the globe. While other nations had their explorers, the conquistadors were a unique Spanish archetype, a combination of reckless adventurer, daring idealist, and ruthless overlord. Most sprang from a hard and unforgiving part of Spain, which provided traits that helped them survive. The notorious Spanish tendency to improvise rather than plan also proved invaluable. The audacious exploration of the Amazon, for example, took place without the slightest preparation. Had the explorers insisted on guarantees of success, the project might never have been started. Spaniards needed only about fifty years to discover, explore, and at least partially subdue the lands and oceans of an entire hemisphere—an amazing feat. Even so, all was not "God, gold, and glory" to use the cliché of countless history textbooks. There were enormous administrative concerns involving the new lands, and the *Casa de la Contratación de las Indias* was set up in Sevilla to regulate commerce. For more than two centuries, this city on the Guadalquivir monopolized American trade and grew fat in the process. One important detail: because Columbus had received his commission solely from Isabel, Castilla insisted on all rights to the new lands; the Aragonese and Catalans were excluded.

There was also the question of what to do about the "Indians" once they were conquered. Early on, Columbus had sent slaves, properly baptized, back to Spain, but the clergy protested and slavery was curbed somewhat. However, it continued in practice for many decades, including the large-scale importation of slaves from Africa. Queen Isabel herself became involved in protecting the natives and helped set up the *encomienda* system, which legalized forced labor but included a wage for the Indians. Through this system the crown granted by contract with private companies most of the costs, duties and rights inherent in the colonial effort. In truth, the crown put up little money and few of the conquistadors were even soldiers.

Fernando died in 1516, and his remains were taken to Granada and deposited in the royal chapel beside Isabel. Together they left Spain on the threshold of world power and cultural glory. Ever since, many Spaniards have looked back at the reign of *Los Reyes Catolicos* as an era of innocent grandeur, before the burdens of empire came crashing down on a nation ill-prepared to face them. According to rumor, the medications Fernando took to increase his virility actually hastened his death. Moreover, the results were disappointing: his only son with Germaine de Foix died at birth. As fate would have it, both Castilla *and* Aragón would fall to the same heir, Charles of Ghent (son of Philip and Juana). Until his arrival, the irrepressible Cisneros took charge as regent, hoping to head off any attempts by the nobles to rally round mad Juana. When his authority to do so was questioned, he pointed to a row of cannons and bellowed, "There's my authority!"

Charles (known in Spanish history and henceforth in our story as Carlos) was born in Flanders in 1500. In his veins flowed the blood of most great European dynasties, and for four of them—Burgundian, Habsburg, Aragonese, and Castilian—he was the only heir. As a boy Carlos was left in the care of an aunt and received a French education proper for the heir to Burgundy. At fifteen he was given a rose of wrought-gold from Pope Leo X, sent "because he was soon to be the most important man in the whole of Europe." Spain too would soon find itself thrust into center stage.

In September of 1517 a fleet of forty ships anchored off Santander, and residents fearing attack fled into the hills. Carlos disembarked with a large entourage and marched south to find his mother and determine the extent of her madness. In an effort in impress the commoners thirty falconers led the stately procession, but all the pomp could not disguise the fact that Carlos cut a poor figure. As a youth he was clumsy and had the huge Habsburg jaw and a mouth that hung open, giving the impression he was stupid. Worst of all, he did not speak Spanish.

After visiting his mother at Tordesillas, Carlos became convinced of her madness and ordered her kept under house arrest. Although Juana was provided with everything befitting her position, including a staff of 155 servants, her internment created a perennial scandal for Carlos. Furthermore, the Castilian Cortes would only recognize him as co-ruler with his mother; on royal documents her name appeared first, followed by her son as "executor."

When the Habsburg emperor died, Carlos inherited the Austrian domains of his grandfather and became a leading candidate for the title of Holy Roman Emperor, still an elected position. His rivals included Francis I of France, and bribes to electors reached unprecedented levels. With the help of the Fugger banking house, Carlos was elected in 1519 as Emperor Charles V (he would be Carlos I in Spain).

At the age of nineteen this ungainly youth controlled the largest empire since Charlemagne and perhaps the most powerful since ancient Rome. It encompassed Castilla and Aragón, several Italian states, the Spanish Colonies in America, parts of France, the Low Countries (Belgium and the Netherlands), Luxembourg, Austria, Bohemia, and sections of Germany. Carlos' accession had an immediate impact on Spain and its neighbors, and for the first time Spaniards had to consider themselves part of Europe.

Unfortunately, warfare was part and parcel of having an empire. First Carlos had to worry about pacifying his Iberian kingdoms. Many Spaniards resented their foreign king and the influx of outsiders, mostly Flemish, to high posts. (The Flemish courtiers came to be identified with anything flashy, and left their name with Spain's traditional music and dance, *flamenco*.) When Carlos tried to extract money to pay for his election bribes, nobles erupted in the Revolt of the Comuneros. This full-scale civil war saw the razing of Medina del Campo, Castilla's medieval commercial center, and other atrocities. But the revolt petered out when it threatened to become a social movement and the nobles backed down. The rebels were crushed at the battle of Villalar (1521). Fortunately for Carlos, the Comuneros received no support in Aragón. However, an unrelated conflict called the Germania broke out in Valencia, led by the mysterious *rey encubierto*, supposedly an illegitimate grandson of Fernando. After this outbreak withered away, Spain could look forward to centuries of internal peace.

Just as well, because Carlos's forty-year reign, of which he spent only sixteen in Spain, involved an endless series of foreign conflicts. The self-proclaimed "defender of the faith," even made war on the pope, and all Europe was shocked when imperial troops went on a rampage and sacked Rome in 1527. One group of soldiers even camped out in the Vatican and built fires that damaged the Sistine Chapel.

This remarkable event sprang from Spain's ongoing problems with France, now worsened by an equally perennial rivalry between the Habsburg and Valois dynasties. Milan was the main object of contention; each side considered it vital to their interests. In a typically medieval gesture, Carlos challenged the French king to personal combat, but the battle of Pavia decided the conflict in 1525, on the Spanish king's birthday no less. Francis I was captured and briefly imprisoned in Madrid, where he remarked, "All is lost but honor." The sacking of Rome occurred later, after the pope created the Holy League of Cognac, an alliance concerned with the Habsburgs' awesome growth in power. But just three years later, Carlos dazzled all Europe when he was crowned Holy Roman Emperor by the pope at a lavish ceremony in Italy. The importance in all this for Spain was in solidifying its Italian territories and alliances, which for almost two centuries would be the ballast of imperial power, more than its sprawling American lands.

The second great front for Carlos was the struggle against Protestantism in northern Europe. The same year he stepped on Spanish soil for the first time, a renegade priest named Martin Luther had nailed his "ninety-five theses" to the door of the Wittenberg cathedral. Many German princes eagerly joined the Protestant revolt, for political as well as spiritual reasons. (Germany as such did not exist at the time, but a national identity was beginning to form.) If the empire hoped to maintain its control, it was vital to suppress Lutheranism. But the final showdown would have to wait.

After a settling-in period, Spaniards began to take a strong liking to Carlos and to enjoy their status as heart of the empire and defender of Catholicism against the hated Luther. Their king had survived adolescence and looked every inch a regal figure, with a high forehead, alert blue eyes, and an aquiline nose. We can see this imposing visage in several portraits done by Titian, in which Carlos appears clad in full armor beside his horse or in the thick of battle. Among his treasures was an immense collection of arms, including a 115-kilo jousting suit he once wore. (Much of the collection resides in Madrid at the Real Armería.)

The marriage of Carlos to Isabel, beautiful daughter of the Portuguese king, further endeared him with Spaniards. They would have three children, including future king Felipe (Philip) II. One of the king's infrequent extramarital affairs resulted in Don Juan of Austria, a great figure later in the story. Carlos also impressed his subjects when he learned Spanish and insisted on speaking it. One time, when he was interrupted by a French bishop, he retorted, "Do not expect to hear from me any language but Castilian."

Spain was ruled as part of a larger dynastic order in which each unit retained its own laws and customs. Apart from the Inquisition there was no unifying institution; Carlos was king of Castilla and king of Aragón, not king of Spain. Unfortunately, Castilla ended up footing the bill for the empire's endless wars and the emperor's personal extravagance and incessant travels. The money came from taxes and rapidly growing income from the Indies, which reached phenomenal figures by the 1540s. However, it was a delusion to base imperial power on Castilian resources alone. Other segments of the empire, notably Italy, were vital in financing Spanish aspirations.

The financial and human investment in war begun by Carlos continued for two centuries and became the major reason for Spain's ultimate decline. Another threat to Catholicism came from the Ottoman Turks and their allies along the Barbary Coast of North Africa, the old Muslim foes again. Throughout the century, the east and west Mediterranean were two political zones under two banners—Turkish and Spanish—and great battles occurred where they met.

Turkey was ruled by another larger-than-life figure named Suleiman the Magnificent, who took charge in 1520 and reigned for forty-six years, almost the identical period as Carlos. The struggle commenced when Turks swept up the Balkans to the gates of Vienna, seat of the Habsburg inheritance. Here they were halted in a heroic defense involving thousands of Spanish troops. The Turks were even more fearsome at sea, especially after linking up with Barbarossa, leader of the Barbary pirates. In 1529 he seized Algiers, and Tunis fell five years later. The Spanish coastline itself was under constant threat from the resurgent Muslims, compounded by the presence of Moriscos of questionable loyalty. Spain was paying the price for not carrying the Reconquest into North Africa.

Even today the Spanish coast, especially in Andalucía, is dotted with scores of hilltop watchtowers. Most date from this period to about 1600 and were designed to form a network of fire and smoke to warn coastal residents of attack. This explains why most of the original *pueblos* are lodged in the hills well away from immediate danger rather than along the coast.

Spain's battle-hardened army was Europe's best at the time, though it was small and depended greatly on foreign allies. The introduction of the *tercio*—infantry regiments of two or three thousand soldiers divided into pike men, swordsmen, and harquebusiers—was as significant for military history as the birth of the Roman legion. But the Spanish navy was relatively weak until the reign of Felipe II. Nevertheless, in 1535 Carlos assembled one of the century's greatest expeditions, involving four hundred ships and thirty thousand troops, to attack Tunis. The daring move was a resounding success, as Barbarossa fled and thousands of Christian slaves were freed of their shackles. It was the high water mark for Carlos.

Unfortunately, his follow-up assault on Algiers six years later ended in failure, with the loss of 150 ships and 12,000 men. It was the first resounding defeat for Carlos, a disaster in every sense, and became his last expedition against Islam. The western Mediterranean remained in the grip of the Barbary pirates, whose leadership passed to a ruthless leader named Dragut. Among those at the Algiers debacle was a man of some experience—Hernando Cortés, future conqueror of Mexico.

The first twenty-five years after 1492 were occupied with initial probings of the New World in which settlements remained along the coast. The next stage (until about 1540) saw the real conquest, when Spaniards pushed inland and created an empire in almost miraculous fashion. It was built largely on the ruins of two native empires: the Aztecs (or Mexicas) of Mexico and the Incas of Peru. From these bases Spaniards fanned out in all directions searching for the fabled land of gold called El Dorado.

In 1517, Hernández de Córdoba fought his way to Mexico's Yucatan Peninsula and found remnants of the once great Mayans. The news inspired Cortés. Born at Medellín in Extremadura, he came—like so many other conquistadors—from a family of poor *hidalgos*. Yet he was a dashing figure, suave and handsome. Leaving Spain at nineteen, he took part in the conquest of Cuba, married the governor's daughter, and was chosen to mount an expedition to Mexico. He remarked, "I came here to get rich, not to till the soil like a peasant."

Eleven ships crammed with seven hundred men and sixteen horses sailed in February of 1519. Upon landing at a spot he named Vera Cruz, Cortés ordered the ships destroyed so that his men would have no chance to retreat. The Spaniards quickly defeated the local tribe, and Cortés took an Indian mistress who served as translator. He learned of a great empire in the interior with its capital city of Tenochtitlán built in the middle of a lake. Soon an envoy from Montezuma, the Aztec ruler, appeared and seemed friendly. By an incredible stroke of luck, Aztec legends spoke of the god *Quetzalcoatl*, who had instructed them in agriculture and other things before departing to the east with a promise to return one day. He had been tall, with white skin and a beard, and to the natives it seemed that Cortés could be this god returned. When they discovered their mistake it was too late.

The Indians of Mexico had never seen horses, and the sight of the Spaniards' cavalry, not to mention war-dogs, muskets, and artillery, filled them with awe and terror. Leaving a small garrison behind, Cortés and his force made their famous advance on the capital and, backed up by Indian allies who hated the Aztecs, entered without opposition. Obtaining native allies continued as a key to Spanish military ventures throughout the era. Montezuma welcomed the Spaniards, who marveled at the palaces, exotic gardens, and pillars of solid gold. But problems soon arose, and Cortés and his men had to fight their way out of the capital amid horrific bloodshed. Many drowned under the weight of the gold they tried to carry away.

Eventually they recaptured the city and made it capital of New Spain. From here, Spanish power rapidly expanded throughout Mexico and into Central America. Not until Cortés did Spaniards realize the full implications of the conquest. The sight of Aztec treasure—rooms of solid gold and jade carvings—stunned the conquistadors and filled them with wonder. Before long, adventurers were swarming to the Indies in search of riches, often fanciful but sometimes very real.

The conquest of Peru was even more incredible, perhaps the most astonishing military feat in history. Led by Francisco Pizarro, 167 soldiers and a few horses set out to conquer an empire of about six million people, which they accomplished with the loss of just a handful of men. Pizarro was born at Trujillo in Extremadura, about eighty kilometers from the birthplace of Cortés, but was illiterate and quite unlike his polished compatriot. After learning of the Inca's empire, sprawling over present-day Peru, Bolivia and Ecuador, Pizarro set out in 1530 in a single ship with his four brothers and other adventurers.

Finally, after two years of fitful progress, the Spaniards entered the Andean valley of Cajamarca. Here the Inca monarch Atahualpa ruled with the help of an army of forty thousand warriors. For reasons never made clear, the king and his unarmed entourage walked into a trap, and the Spaniards pounced on them in an orgy of bloodletting that left Atahualpa alive but a prisoner. Some historians claim that the king was just incredibly naive to have fallen into Pizarro's net. There were also legends very similar to those of the Aztecs; for the Incas *Viracocha* was a bearded white god who granted the gifts of civilization and then departed by sea. To the *west*, in this version of the legend, with a similar promise to return. According to another story, the Inca ruler somehow understood the Basque spoken by some of Pizarro's men and, believing it to be the "language of the ancients," reckoned that they were gods.

In any case, with their leader imprisoned the Inca army did not attack. Atahualpa filled a room with gold and silver to obtain release, but Pizarro had him baptized and then garroted nonetheless. Spanish troops took the capital of Cuzco without a fight, and in 1535 founded Lima, "city of kings." In a gesture indicative of the times, a royal notary drew up the proper documentation to prove that Spain had legally taken possession.

Pizarro fit or perhaps inspired the harsh stereotype of the cruel and avaricious conquistador. When a priest reminded him of the spiritual mission of Spaniards in America he said, "I have not come here for such reasons. I have come to take away their gold." But he was also a very religious man and embodied that frustrating duality shared by most conquistadors. When rivals finally assassinated Pizarro, he drew a cross on the ground with his own blood and murmured the word "Jesus." Hollywood could not have come up with a better script.

These were heady times. Orellana and his party crossed the Andes from Peru, built a few rafts, and floated five thousand kilometers down the Amazon. In North America, de Soto (also from Trujillo) discovered the Mississippi River, Coronado marched up from Mexico as far north as the Grand Canyon, and Cabeza de Vaca tramped thousands of kilometers around North America, then went to Brazil and walked across the jungle to Paraguay.

The hardships of these men in quilted armor were almost inconceivable: either suffocating in the desert or freezing in the high mountain passes. Hostile natives, wild animals, poisonous reptiles, and swarms of mosquitoes attacked them. Lacking surgery, they dressed their wounds with boiled fat taken from Indian corpses. What made them do it? As one of the men under Cortés explained, "We came here to serve God and the king, and also to get rich." Unfortunately this cut both ways, and many settlers abandoned the settlements if they failed to get rich quickly.

The American lands were divided into two huge "vice-royalties," New Spain and Peru, which formed the basis of government that lasted almost three centuries. They were also two more pieces in Carlos's sprawling domains, each ruled by a viceroy with nearly absolute powers. It should be noted that because of the vast areas involved and small numbers of Spaniards there never really was a "conquest" of the Americas in the strict sense. The stereotype of a powerful colonial regime dominating a defeated people is not viable given the historical evidence. No subjugation or occupation occurred except in very limited areas; in fact not a single Spanish army was ever sent overseas, only smaller contingents of soldiers to accompany explorers and priests. A century after Columbus and even beyond Spaniards were spread so thin they were nearly invisible, their settlements tiny and vulnerable. The frontier in fact was defined more by Indian goodwill than Spanish victories.

During the king's frequent and lengthy absences, Castilla itself was virtually governed by an Andalucían from Úbeda named Francisco de los Cobos, secretary of finance for thirty years. It was a time of domestic peace and prosperity while war raged in the rest of Europe. With money being spent much faster than it came in, Cobos already foresaw trouble and repeatedly warned the king of the situation. Carlos still depended on parliament to finance his wars, and sometimes it refused. Constant demands for more money from the regions tended to entrench his subjects behind their *fueros*. It was clear that the medieval institutions could not cope with the demands of an aggressive, money-squandering empire. Wealth from the Indies helped some, but just like a leaky bucket, the more that came in the more poured out.

The Protestant problem came to a head late in the emperor's reign. In 1547, he won a great victory over the German princes at Mühlberg (pictured in a famous Titian portrait of Carlos), but just five years later Protestant forces drove him out of Germany. Protestantism never had much appeal in Spain itself, largely because the clergy had been reformed and the crown had stood its ground against the pope. Vaguely related to Protestant ideas were those of the Illuminists, a mystical sect notorious for the sexual indulgence of members. The movement was led by a reputed nymphomaniac named Francisca Hernández, of whom "the men spoke with fanatical veneration, and the women with not so much respect," according to one report.

One of those jailed for suspected Illuminist leanings was a man who came to spearhead the Spanish Counter-Reformation—the great Saint Ignatius of Loyola. Several years earlier, this Basque soldier was lying wounded in a hospital when he received a heavenly sign to follow the path of Jesus Christ. He made a pilgrimage to the famous Black Virgin at Montserrat (Cataluña), followed by a confession that lasted three days. Living in a cave, Loyola outlined his great book, *Spiritual Exercises*, which became the cornerstone of the Society of Jesus, the Jesuits. The Jesuits came to be Catholicism's most controversial religious order, especially for their military-style organization and special vow of loyalty to the pope, which did not sit well with Spanish monarchs. With their elitist attitudes about education, they also gained the hostility of regular clergy and other religious orders. But they would become a major force in Spain and stood firm against the rising Protestant tide.

Humanism and other aspects of the Renaissance made some tentative inroads into the Spain of Carlos I. Erasmus of Rotterdam, the leading humanist, actually served as a royal counselor until he became identified with heresy. Humanist scholars were later exiled and their works appeared on the first *Index* of prohibited books. After opening briefly, the window onto Renaissance Europe was beginning to close. Under Carlos's successor it would be slammed shut.

The flowery excesses of Renaissance poetry spilled over into Spanish letters, and Garcilaso de la Vega created an original style with rich imagery.

Spanish Renaissance architects and sculptors produced the regrettable Palace of Carlos V inside the Alhambra and the spectacular tomb of two famous couples—Fernando and Isabel, Philip the Fair and Juana the Mad—inside the royal chapel at Granada's cathedral.

Juana, queen of Castilla, lived on until April of 1555, and her death helped simplify the royal succession. Carlos was prematurely old after a life of intense activity and indulgence in the pleasures of the table. (He belonged to the Order of the Golden Fleece, an aristocratic club whose members took the oath of the Mystic Pheasant and gorged themselves at unending banquets.) In the same year as his mother's death, Carlos shocked all Europe by announcing his abdication of the imperial crown to his brother Ferdinand. A few months later, he handed over the Low Countries and Spain with all its possessions to his son Felipe. Though he had ruled for forty years, Carlos was officially king of Castilla for just nine months. He retired to the monastery of Yuste in Extremadura to live out his final days. With this turn of events the Habsburg Empire was permanently divided into its Austrian and Spanish wings. Along with Carlos went the ideal of a universal order based on one empire and one religion. It was as out of step with the times as the emperor's chivalrous challenge to duel the French king over Italy.

Almost toothless and plagued by gout, Charles settled at Yuste with his cat and parrot to enjoy his art collection and indulge his appetite for anchovies and beer. He spent countless hours trying to synchronize his huge collection of clocks and once exclaimed, "How could I possibly have hoped to unite all my dominions when I cannot make these clocks strike the hour together?"

Two years after his retirement, Carlos insisted on attending a rehearsal of his own funeral. After Mass he caught a chill and soon expired, clutching a crucifix to his breast and with the name "Jesus" on his cold, dead lips. He was fifty-eight.

Sights & Sites

Barcelona: Reproduction of the caravel *Santa María* in which Columbus sailed to America, near Plaza de la Paz; on the square is the sixty-meter-high Columbus Monument (1888).

Cáceres: The old town includes mansions from the period such as the Palacio de los Golfines.

Granada: The Alhambra and Generalife, climax of Moorish architecture; Renaissance Palace of Carlos V inside Moorish structure; Albaicin quarter; Cathedral with reliefs of Moorish surrender, royal chapel and its elaborate tombs.

Huelva: Franciscan monastery of Santa María de la Rábida, which first welcomed Columbus to Spain.

Jarandilla de la Vera (Cáceres): Yuste Monastery, final refuge of Carlos V.

Madrid: Royal Armory at Palacio Real contains pieces spanning Habsburg era; the Prado Museum has early Flemish, Renaissance, Italian schools i.e. Bosch, Durer, Raphael, Titian.

Palencia: Interior of cathedral features Isabeline, Plateresque and Renaissance styles.

Salamanca: Patio de las Escuelas at old university is surrounded by fine examples of plateresque architecture and sculpture; new cathedral completed by 1560.

Segovia: The cathedral was built during the reign of Carlos.

Sevilla: Casa de Pilatos palace is a fine example of Renaissance-*Mudéjar* blending.

Court of Lions at the Alhambra in Granada, final abode of the Spanish Moors

Úbeda: Buildings around Plaza Vazquez de Molina are mostly Renaissance in style.

Valencia: Silk exchange, La Lonja, from late fifteenth century.

Valladolid: National Museum of Sculpture traces evolution of the art from Gothic to Baroque, including works by Juan de Juni and Alonso Berruguete.

Chapter 6

Ecstasy and Agony

Some call the famous El Escorial palace-monastery the "eighth wonder of the world." Others speak in harsher terms: foreboding, frightening, "a granite and slate rectangular monster." Whatever the truth, San Lorenzo del Escorial, forty-eight kilometers from Madrid, can be appreciated on many levels. First, there is the imposing building itself, with its massive gray-granite facade broken only by narrow, prison-like windows and pointed gables. Inside are 134 kilometers of corridors, 16 courtyards, 15 cloisters, 86 staircases, 1,200 doors, and more than 2,000 windows. There is a sumptuous royal crypt, an extremely well-endowed library, and an unbelievable collection of human body parts.

On another level, the Escorial is also the supreme monument of the Counter-Reformation: Spanish Catholicism embodied in solid, unyielding stone. Designed and built by Juan Bautista and Juan de Herrera in a heavy, austere style, it could only have been created in the Spain of the sixteenth century. It is also a near perfect reflection of the man behind it—King Felipe (Philip) II.

Felipe built El Escorial (the name means "slag heap," a reference to nearby mining scoria) to fulfill a vow taken after a Spanish victory on the feast day of

Saint Lawrence. Some claim the gridiron design, complete with handle, was based on the martyred saint's death: he was roasted alive on a grill. The first stone was laid in 1563, and work went on for twenty-one years, a remarkably short period at the time for such an enormous project. Felipe took a deep personal interest in every detail of planning and construction, and signed off on all documents with "*Yo, El Rey*" (I, the King). He sat for hours on a stone bench overlooking the works in order to watch daily progress. (The spot today is called *La Silla de Felipe II*.) El Escorial became a giant metaphor for the empire itself, which the king also tried to control in the minutest detail. The building was completed in 1584, just at the high water mark of Spain's power and influence, a magnificent symbol of imperial grandeur. The royal abode also served as a Hieronymite monastery, reflecting Philip's own intense religious faith. From his Spartan quarters he could look down through a small window to the altar of the main church.

Besides paintings (the nucleus of the Prado collection) and books, the king also snapped up religious relics with characteristic obsession. Among them: a reputed hair of Christ's beard; 103 heads, including that of St. Lawrence; and an extensive collection of arms, legs, fingers, and toes. With later additions, this bizarre assemblage today numbers more than seven thousand pieces. Deep in the bowels of the Escorial, the ornate royal mausoleum contains several rooms of tiered coffins for Spanish rulers, starting with Carlos I, as well as assorted family members and select royal bastards such as Felipe's half brother, Don Juan of Austria. Of course, Felipe himself is there, resting with a calm that eluded him during his lengthy reign.

He began that reign far from Spain and at war with the pope, in league with the French as usual. The exhausted powers were merely going through the motions of warfare, however, and would soon sign a treaty. Felipe inherited his father's hostility to France, but that would soon change, along with many other things. The domain of his father was a vast geographical monstrosity. With the loss of Austria (to his brother Ferdinand), Felipe's inheritance was a streamlined version of the empire, nearly as immense but quite different in character. It became entirely Spanish in orientation after he returned from abroad to rule from the heart of Castilla. Nevertheless, the foreign commitments handed down by his father, especially the Netherlands, would haunt Spain for decades to come.

Encirclement of France was basic Habsburg policy. As part of this strategy, Felipe had married Mary Tudor at Winchester Cathedral in 1554. (His previous wife, María of Portugal, died giving birth to Prince Carlos.) The Spanish sovereign became royal consort of the Tudor queen and was regarded as king of England by everyone but the English. They disliked his personality as much as his Catholicism, even though he tried to restrain Mary's pious persecution of Protestants. The loveless marriage ended with Mary's sudden death, and their failure to produce a child assured that Spain and England would go their separate ways. Although Felipe tried persistently to woo Elizabeth, the new queen, Mary's death meant the end of the brief Anglo-Hispanic alliance. The following year he completely reversed traditional Spanish policy by wedding Elizabeth of Valois, fourteen-year-old daughter of the French king. Thus Spain's new enemy would be England.

Ceaseless conflict under Carlos had left Spain virtually bankrupt upon Felipe's accession. Huge sums were owed to banking houses charging up to fifty percent interest per year. (Genoese bankers were detested as particularly onerous.) Foreigners began taking over Spain's own wealth such as the Almadén mercury mines, which produced a critical element for silver production. Heavy taxation had helped raise some funds, but not enough, and taxes acted to discourage investment. As a result, prosperous merchants abandoned business and joined the ranks of the idle and indolent *hidalgos*. Since so many of the wealthy and privileged were exempt from taxes, the poorer classes paid far more than their fair share. The crown's *quinto real* (royal fifth) of all American treasure was a source of badly needed income, especially after the discovery of a veritable mountain of silver at Potosí (Bolivia) in 1545. In fact, for the next two centuries American mines produced eighty percent of the world's silver, as well as eighty percent of its gold. This fact, more than military prowess, lay at the heart of Spain's imperial power. The flood of new wealth was far from its salvation, however; much of it went directly to paying off debts or was squandered in new European ventures. State finances were so bad that the new king tried to balance the budget by putting his father's jewels up at auction. Moreover, the influx of bullion brought high inflation, with prices doubling between 1510 and 1550. This in turn hurt Spanish

Fray Las Casas, purveyor of the Black Legend

products in the export market. Even at the height of Spain's political power, the economic underpinnings were already rotting away.

Carlos had fancied himself champion of the Catholic religion against Protestants and Muslims alike, and it was a role that Felipe, heir to his father's world-view as well as his crown, played to the hilt. Although a glimmer of Renaissance culture reached Spain under Carlos, his dour son snuffed it out. The best ideas of the Renaissance and Reformation, as well as new scientific methods and economic theories, generally failed to take root and grow. In its self-anointed role as leader of the Counter-Reformation, Spain became the adversary of progress and modernization, distrustful of the outside world and unwilling to change. Purity of faith meant hostility to the ideas and values of contemporary Europe and led to increasing isolation. For example, suspicious foreign books were systematically banned, and Spanish students were forbidden to travel abroad.

Spain and a reactionary breed of Catholicism were continuing to merge, and many Spaniards believed it was their mission to stamp out all heresy and convert the unconverted. Nowhere was this mission more evident than in the Indies, teeming with heathen souls awaiting "salvation." This religious zeal was important in the conquest from the very beginning, as Spaniards found Indian civilizations that they considered backward and inferior. It was the same "superiority complex" of every colonial power throughout history and not completely unfounded. The Incas, for example, did not have a written language, measured years by knots tied in cords, and were not acquainted with the wheel.

With the inevitable exceptions, most priests and monks sincerely believed they were doing the right and good thing for the Indians, even if this sometimes meant their inadvertent destruction, usually by disease. Spaniards conquered the Americas with memories of the Reconquest still fresh. Cortés, for example, reported that Mexican Indians wore clothes similar to the Moors and even had temples that looked like mosques. Before being conquered, Indians were usually given a chance to convert, just as the Muslim infidels had been just decades before. By the end of the sixteenth century about three hundred monasteries existed in the Americas. Clergy saw their mission as divine and taught a pure and mystical version of Catholicism to the Indians.

The cruelty of the conquistadors, though exaggerated by propagandists, was in many cases incontrovertible. It was often used to intimidate vastly larger populations by many individuals (as opposed to state policy), especially when precious metals were at stake. Indians became so resentful of this gold-lust that on one occasion they poured molten gold down the throats of captive con-quistadors. Missionaries scandalized by their compatriots' greed soon became the Indians' protectors, and they could call on the church's considerable power. Their passion for justice can best be seen in the early work of the Franciscans, who founded the first American colleges. And their compassion for their new flocks did much to balance the evil side of the conquest.

On the whole it can be fairly asserted that the Spanish Empire was one of history's most humane, judged by historical standards rather than our own contemporary ideals. The clergy publicly criticized atrocities, and the crown often listened. The New Laws (1542) prohibited enslavement of Indians, lashed out at abuses within the *encomienda* system, and granted wide protection of Indian rights. Carlos even suspended all further conquests until a debate could be held about ethical questions in Spain's new possessions. The common be-lief that Spain's conquest of the Americas was *uniquely* barbarous is simply not borne out by the facts.

Nevertheless, the myths persist for one important reason: Spain's "Black Legend" (*la Leyenda Negra*). Ponder this sixteenth century English descrip-tion of the Spanish: ". . . a craftie fox, a ravenous wolfe, and a raging tygre; theyr filthy, monstrous and abominable luxurie, theyr lustfull and inhumaine deflouring of theyr wives and daughters, matchless and sodomiticall ravishings of young boys . . . a filthie heape of the most lothsome, infected, and slavish people that ever yet lived on earth."

In brief, the Black Legend is the historical and literary tradition of smearing Spain, Spaniards, and anything Hispanic as evil, inferior, and uniquely cruel. This jumble of cliché and error has appeared over time in stereotypes marching through Anglo-Saxon literature and movies. In this "cape and sword" fiction, the Spaniard is the swarthy fellow with black pointed beard and wicked Toledo blade, who is not only cruel and greedy, but treacherous and lecherous to boot. Variations include the sadistic in-quisitor turning the screws, the slippery gigolo, or the cruel viceroy sign-ing death sentences, but the literary dice are always loaded. (One recent Black Legend classic was the film *Elizabeth: The Golden Age*.)

The seeds of the Black Legend were planted during debates over Indian treatment by Bartolomé de las Casas, the first priest ordained in the new world. Prone to wild exaggeration, he began a campaign to prove Spanish crimes with publication of his tract *Brevíssima relación de la destrucción de las Indias*. From this polemic came the still-repeated figure of twenty million

Indians killed by the conquistadors. This included three million on Hispaniola alone, an island that could have supported only a fraction of that population. In truth Las Casas killed more Indians with his pen than all the conquistadors in history.

Indians being burnt alive by conquistadors as depicted by Theodore DeBry in 1598

Chief victim of the Black Legend was Felipe II, who rarely received a kind word from historians until centuries after his death. He is usually pictured stroking his pointed beard with "a thin smile that cut like a sword." He is the "spider of the Escorial," ruling a malevolent empire from the center of his evil web. Behind this simplistic image was a much more complex figure. Son of Carlos I and Isabel of Portugal, this eternal symbol of imperial Spain was only one-quarter Spanish. He was a grave and silent child, and grew up to be a man who terrified even his own ministers with his icy coldness and fixed, emotionless stare. Felipe was modestly handsome, with fair hair, pale blue eyes, and the pronounced Habsburg jaw of his father.

From the dying Carlos he also received one final piece of advice: "Never trust anyone but yourself." Felipe particularly disliked those with strong personalities, such as the Duke of Alba and Don Juan of Austria, and only felt completely safe among stacks of state papers, which he tirelessly read, annotated, and amended. He was forever trying to live up to an idealized version of his father and forever failing, at least in his own mind.

Felipe was a passionate youth and had many leisurely pursuits such as music and chess. His first marriage to his cousin María was reasonably happy, but she left him a widower at age eighteen. Nine years later he married Mary Tudor for reasons of state. He married twice more after becoming king—to Elizabeth of Valois, whom he adored until her tragic death, and to Anne of Austria in a desperate attempt to sire an heir. Felipe spent much of his reign in mourning: seventeen members of his immediate family died during his lifetime. It was enough to extinguish the youthful optimism of any man.

As the king grew older, he became oddly detached and devoted himself to state affairs. No one could guess what he was thinking; whether giving orders for an execution or for a *fiesta* his countenance was the same. It was said that his expression was identical after receiving news of both the stunning victory at Lepanto and the stinging defeat of the Armada. A cool head and cold blood—sinister signs for some observers, but for others clear proof of Felipe's greatness.

Carlos had set up a complicated system of government involving councils and viceroys. These survived more in theory than practice under Felipe, who tried to direct everything personally and to sign every paper with his own hand. Eyes permanently red from overwork, he spent his life shuffling papers as the "world's first crowned bureaucrat." From behind his cramped and cluttered writing desk he guided the destiny of half the world. The overworked king had several lifelike statues of himself made, some with moveable limbs. These would be hauled out whenever a crowd or foreign delegation was deemed unworthy of his attentions and propped up at a safe distance from the throngs, who never suspected that they were cheering a dummy. The transformation from warrior king to ultimate civil servant was complete.

Despite his reputation as a "royal kill-joy," Felipe enjoyed the deep love and respect of his subjects. His outlook was intensely Castilian, and he embodied its espoused ideals—religious faith, personal honor, and heroism. But Felipe also shared the typical Castilian's sometimes-unbearable arrogance and came to regard himself as the source of all wisdom and justice, answerable only to God. Felipe II's reign began with a spectacular *auto de fé* in Valladolid at which several suspected heretics were burned at the stake. The king used the Inquisition to increase his power over the bishops and regions, and this alliance added plenty of juicy material for Black Legend pamphleteers. But how much is "legend" and how much really *was* evil? Felipe was unquestionably a religious fanatic and once remarked, "I would rather reign in a desert than over a country peopled with heretics." He added, "If my son were to oppose the Catholic Church, I myself would carry the faggots to burn him."

As we have seen, the Inquisition's reason for being was to root out suspected "false converts" among Jews, but with the Protestant Reformation it gained a new role and new life. Everything about the Inquisition offends our *modern* concepts of legal justice, particularly its secrecy and slowness. The case of Bartolomé de Carranza, a *converso* and archbishop of Toledo, was one notorious example. Carranza was arrested for admiring the Humanist scholar Erasmus and disappeared into Inquisition dungeons. After eighteen years without a verdict he died, it was said, from despair.

A typical case went something like this: arrest was based on a *denuncia* made by at least two anonymous persons, and the accused was placed in solitary confinement and not told any specifics of the charges. He was assumed to be guilty, and it was the inquisitor's job to obtain a confession. In his own defense, the accused could make a list of his enemies, and if any of the accusers appeared on it, their testimony was discounted and they were punished. The Edict of Grace was a period during which the accused could confess and avoid harsh penalties if he also named all accomplices. Torture was used only as a last resort, possibly because the *threat* of torture was enough to jog most memories. If required, harsher forms of persuasion were the rack, the hoist, the garrote, and the harrowing "water-torture."

A confession was only the beginning of a wild search for accomplices, who might in turn reveal more suspects. Once guilt had been proved, there were a number of punishments geared to the severity of the crime. These ranged from wearing the *sanbenito* (a yellow robe with a red cross) in public to being burned at the stake. Anyone convicted of heresy a second time was usually doomed to the flames, although repentance brought the privilege of being strangled first.

All of this seems abominable to our modern sensibilities. However, by the standards of the time the Spanish Inquisition was not particularly unfair or brutal. Religious intolerance was rife in Europe, and witchcraft and other offenses commonly punished by death. According to experts, the total numbers of persons executed for religious reasons was fewer in Spain than in contemporary England. One eminent English historian even stated that the Inquisition was "the most fair legal system in Europe at the time."

One of Felipe's most enduring decisions was to move the government's administrative center from Toledo to Madrid (1561), then a squalid village of a few thousand souls. (It would not become official capital until the Bourbons arrived more than a century later.) It was selected because of its location at the peninsula's geographical center and the fact that Felipe could mould it to his tastes. Madrid was as Castilian as a roast suckling pig, but had no troublesome regional or aristocratic loyalties as other cities.

Spain's population was overwhelmingly rural, and life seemed strange and primitive to foreign travelers, the dress and customs noticeably medieval. The largest towns were Sevilla, Valladolid, Granada, Toledo, and Barcelona, but none had more than fifty thousand residents. Spain's total population was about nine million at the start of Felipe's reign, compared with sixteen for France and England's four million.

After a few early trips, Felipe remained on the peninsula the rest of his life. He maintained an elaborate court where he could keep an eye on the nobles, many of whom were reduced to the status of official servants—First Gentleman of the Bedchamber or Chief Steward—and they would fight for the honor of handing the king his shirt. Large numbers of new noble positions were created and became dependent on the crown for their existence, but real power gravitated to about a hundred of the top grandees.

Felipe's first domestic crisis involved his son and heir, the infamous Don Carlos. The boy began life with two genetic strikes against him—his mother and father were cousins and both were grandchildren of Juana the Mad. His frail body could barely support his oversized head, and at a young age he displayed a fondness for disgusting acts of cruelty, such as roasting hares alive and flogging horses to death. At seventeen he fell down a flight of stairs and injured his head so badly that doctors had to remove a piece of his skull. Thereafter, his behavior worsened, with uncontrollable fits of fury and wanton violence. Once he flew into a rage at a boot maker and forced him to eat a pair of boots, and he was known to wander Madrid streets shouting obscenities and spitting at respectable women.

All Europe began to take an interest in the fate of the Spanish throne. When Carlos's erratic behavior was compounded with plots against his father, Felipe finally acted, and Carlos was locked up in the old *alcázar* (fortress). When he died under mysterious circumstances a few months later, the king's enemies assumed the worst. The cause of the prince's death was never proved, but historians doubt that Felipe was directly involved. More likely Don Carlos collapsed under confinement from his own physical weakness, compounded by his alternating hunger strikes and gorging and his habit of consuming huge quantities of ice on hot Castilian days. But Felipe was his own worst enemy by refusing to disclose any details the affair. Don Carlos became a hero for hispanophobes, climaxing in Verdi's opera in which his murder is followed by a bloody *auto de fé*.

The year of Prince Carlos' death was a bad one for the king. His French wife also died and a revolt broke out among the Moriscos of Granada. They had been restless for years, suffering under the arrogant and oppressive "old Christians" who settled in the south. For example, one village complained about its parish priest: "All our children's eyes are as blue as his." In 1567, a flurry of restrictive laws cracked down on persistent Muslim customs, and on Christmas Day Moriscos paraded through Granada shouting their loyalty to Mohammed. A revolt spread like brushfire through the wild Alpujarras and Málaga mountains, and Spanish troops under Don Juan of Austria, Felipe's dashing illegitimate half-brother, were called up. Spaniards were especially terrified of Moriscos linking up with fellow Muslims from the Barbary Coast just across the sea. The campaign was unusually brutal, with many thousands killed before the rebels gave up.

The Morisco revolt was only one indication of how precarious Spain's own unity really was, in spite of its imperial successes. Internally, Spain's armed forces were very weak (fifteen thousand men compared with France's half million) and its navy almost non-existent, nearly incapable of defending itself. Almost all armaments were imported from Italy. This hardly fits the image of the mighty empire.

Concern over secret apostates among Muslim and Jewish converts whipped up the Inquisition to even greater frenzy. So-called proofs of traitorous activity multiplied, so that wearing better clothes or failing to light a fire on Saturday (the Jewish Sabbath), washing a corpse in warm water, giving children Hebrew names, and cooking with oil instead of lard were all used as evidence.

An ugly side of Spanish society raised its head with the concept of *limpieza de sangre* (pure blood). No longer was it good enough to be a Christian—one had to be an *old* Christian with documented proof that there was no "tainted" blood in the family. Extensive investigations were conducted to uncover blemishes in family pedigrees, and Spaniards (especially nobles) lived in fear that some suspect ancestor might ruin their lives. Names were changed and ancestries falsified to throw professional snoopers off the trail. (Lineage was normally traced back four generations in search of Jewish or Moorish ancestors.) At first "purity of blood" was required to enter most religious orders and brotherhoods of knights, but the concept spread to the colleges and government as well. Ultimately the testing failed, however, because impurity was found to be too widespread, especially among persons of wealth and power. Untainted blood became a poor man's honor.

Felipe's reign began with a sigh of relief throughout Europe at the breakup of the awesome Habsburg domains, and there was peace for several years. Not one to be denied his taste of glory, the new king turned in a different direction to a deadly serious foe—the Ottoman Empire. The last century had witnessed the decline of powerful city-states such as Venice; inevitably, the vacuum was filled by the rise of sprawling empires, huge leviathans such as Spain and Turkey that controlled the western and eastern Mediterranean respectively. In the areas where the two met, friction and war usually followed.

Turkish power reached its zenith under Suleiman the Magnificent, with a victory at Djerba near Tunis in 1560. Half the allied fleet, led by the Duke of Medinaceli and Genoese magnate Andrea Doria, was destroyed. Ten thousand men, it was said, were paraded through the streets of Constantinople. Five years later, news that the Turks were at Malta hit Europe like a hurricane, but a heroic defense by the Knights of St. John turned back the attack. (Malta's knights were the boldest of the Christian pirates and raided the Levant with impunity.) A year later Suleiman died, and power passed to his weak son Selim, who was fonder of wine than of battle. The tide was turning. An alliance formed between Spain, the Papal States, and Venice to seek out and destroy the Turks while they were down. Twenty-four-year old Don Juan of Austria was named commander of the fleet.

"On that day the insolent pride of the Ottomans was broken forever. It was the greatest occasion the centuries had ever seen." The young Spaniard who penned these words concerning October 7, 1571, thought victory was well worth three wounds and losing the use of one arm. His name: Miguel de Cervantes.

The Spanish and Italian fleet had 208 warships and many smaller vessels carrying an army of 28,000 men. The Turks boasted 230 ships and a nasty reputation. Although each side had been seeking out the other, dawn of October 7 found them unexpectedly face-to-face at the entrance to the Bay of Lepanto in Greece. The day ended with a breathtaking Christian victory from which only thirty-five Ottoman ships escaped. And lest there be doubts about who won, the Turkish commander's head was stuck to a pike. With Lepanto the Ottoman threat was curtailed for decades, and the mystique of their invincible sea power was broken.

Don Juan of Austria was one of the century's great figures, a born leader who was brave, cunning, and ruthless in equal measures. He was also charismatic and hence a threat to his half-brother in Madrid, and when he proposed carrying the fighting on to Constantinople or North Africa, the king refused. Although Don Juan did recapture Tunis a few years later, open warfare between the two empires subsided. Henceforth, threats to Spanish shipping came from pirates based in Algiers.

In addition to sibling rivalry, another concern prevented Felipe from following up after Lepanto. That problem was the Netherlands, Spain's "Fatal Inheritance." With the death of his father, the Low Countries (seventeen separate provinces roughly encompassing modern day Belgium, Luxembourg, and the Netherlands) were no longer one part in an empire of equals. Spain would try to rule them as it did Italy or the Indies. Indeed, Felipe considered Flanders (the southwestern counties) the key to his empire; without it Spain would cease to be a *European* power and shrink back behind the Pyrenees. Unfortunately, events in the Netherlands determined Spain's destiny for the next hundred years. Although the Low Countries were still Catholic in the majority, Lutherans and Calvinists were making much headway in the north. As everywhere, local nobles used Protestantism as a means to assert their waning power and independence. These Dutch nobles were deep in debt and had a vested interest in rebellion and war. Their leader was William of Orange, essentially a corrupt figure mouthing liberal principles to advance his own interests.

The two nationalities were a study in contrast: the Dutch were pleasure-loving businessmen while Spaniards were abstemious and devout. Attempts to transform this urbanized, industrialized country into another Spain—trying to stop students from traveling to Paris, for instance—were futile and foolish. Resistance in the form of riots, church burnings, and other violence began in the mid 1560s and continued for decades. The feared Duke of Alba arrived in Brussels to squelch the bubbling revolt with a hard hand, sending hundreds to their deaths. He remarked, "It is far better to preserve by war for God and the king a kingdom that is impoverished and even ruined than . . . preserve it entire for the benefit of the devil and the heretics, his disciples."

Soon a state of open rebellion existed, and Spain was forced to fight on two fronts: Protestants on land and the Turks at sea. The corresponding financial obligations forced Felipe to suspend all payments (a polite form of declaring bankruptcy). As a result the Spanish army was not paid for months, and in a horrific incident called "the Spanish Fury," soldiers in Antwerp erupted in an orgy of mindless destruction that left thousands of innocent dead (and gave some creedence to the Black Legend). This final humiliation united all seventeen provinces in a common effort to drive out the Spanish.

Amid this background Felipe sent in Don Juan the miracle worker to attempt a solution. Said the departing Alba, "Kings treat men like oranges.

They go for the juice, and once they have sucked them dry, they throw them aside." Don Juan arrived with some farfetched schemes for ending the trouble. Queen Elizabeth I was blatantly aiding the rebels, and the prince concocted a plan to conquer England and wed Mary Stuart. But Don Juan too succumbed to the "fatal inheritance," dying of typhus at the age of thirty-three. His body lies in the Escorial's Pantheon of the Infantes, beneath a lifelike effigy that once moved female visitors to tears, or so it was said.

Ever since the breakup of the Habsburg Empire (and loss of land routes), Spain's control of the Netherlands depended on the neutrality of England and its navy. Thus the Spanish king actively supported Elizabeth against the pope's threats of excommunication and the machinations of Mary of Scots, a French ally. These attempts to cement the Anglo-Spanish alliance belie Felipe's reputation as a rigid religious fanatic. Protestant England counted more than Catholic France when Spain's political interests were at stake.

Inevitably, war and rebellion took their financial toll on Spain's precarious economy, and debt payments were periodically suspended. American silver served as a temporary stopgap, but it was a mere palliative to a fundamentally unsound economy. Castilla exported raw materials such as wool and iron, but suffered a large trade imbalance because it imported far more finished goods. The difference was made up with any American bullion left after paying foreign creditors.

Sevilla became a raffish boomtown at the hub of Spanish-American trade and grew in size to rival Paris and Naples. It was a city of corruption and prevaricating officials, a place in which silver-lust wreaked havoc. To Sevilla came adventurers and thieves, impoverished gentlemen and husbands fleeing shrewish wives—all hoping to slice a piece of the American pie. Foreign merchants soon outwitted locals and gained control of trade.

Disdain for business was but one reason Spaniards failed to seize the moment. There was also a shortage of skilled labor and capital: rather than being used on investment, money was spent to build churches, palaces, and monasteries. (Spaniards discovered the dubious formula for transforming gold and silver into stone, it was said.) Moreover, there was no coherent government planning to infuse American wealth into the economy in some productive way. With a few exceptions agriculture was also a disaster, and much of the country survived on imported wheat. Poor soil, a harsh climate, stifling institutions such as the Mesta and *latifundia*, and too much government regulation combined to produce rural areas that were ill cultivated and under populated. Travelers invariably mentioned the emptiness of the landscape, the solitude of deserted roads. Inns along the way (called *ventas*) served foul-tasting food to guests who ate at a long wooden table with a single carving knife chained to it.

Perhaps the most important factor in Spain's economic plight was the utter lack of commercial values. For a Spaniard with ambition, the road to success meant church, or sea, or royal service. In 1626 there were 9,088 monasteries in Spain. Naturally, this huge group devoted to spiritual matters was unproductive, as was the immense class of nobles and would-be nobles. By the end of Felipe's reign, more than 100,000 persons claimed nobility in Spain, as the cash-strapped crown sold titles like lottery tickets. The payoff was honorable indolence for a lifetime.

Spain's controversial King Philip (Felipe) II, both loved and feared by his people

Commoners were in a state of perpetual restlessness, longing to move up in class through church service or military enterprise. The humblest peasant, "pure of blood" precisely because he was a peasant, sensed that he was somehow a member of the ruling caste. *Hidalguia* (squirearchy) became a state of mind. A true gentleman's income could be as meager as his pride was great; he instinctively abhorred trade and industry and never soiled his hands with manual labor, lest he be associated with Jews or Moriscos. In Madrid, foreign merchants and technicians, mostly French, took over most productive positions, and this community remained vital to the economy for centuries.

Madrid became a town of rich and poor, the latter sleeping in the streets rolled up in their cloaks. In the 1590s, a visiting Italian priest reported that the city was full of squalid mud houses without chimneys or toilets. Vagrants flooding in from the provinces formed their own brotherhood, whose headquarters lay at the Puerta del Sol square in the heart of old Madrid. In the country, the unemployed wandered from one monastery to another in search of free soup. Too often they found it.

In this world of beggars and scoundrels the picaresque novel was born. *La Vida de Lazarillo de Tormes* (1554, authorship disputed) presented a character with just the proper combination of poverty and pride, a poor squire living a life of semi-starvation who scatters a few crumbs of bread on his clothes to prove he has eaten. Lazarillo is a poor boy who must live by his wits amid this world of rogues and hypocritical priests. The picaroon—forever trying to cheat the system and sworn to keep up appearances at all costs— became a Spanish archetype, in life as well as in literature. Another literary light at this dawn of the Golden Century (*Siglo de Oro*) was Fray Luis de León from Salamanca University, who was imprisoned for five years by the Inquisition before being cleared. When he returned to the lecture hall, this poet and scholar began ironically with the words, "As we were saying *yesterday* . . ."

The most essentially Spanish of "literary movements" was the exalted mysticism of St. Theresa (Santa Teresa) of Ávila and St. John of the Cross (Juan de la Cruz). At the age of eighteen Teresa joined a convent, and one day she slipped into an ecstatic trance in which a voice told her to shun further dialogue with mere mortals and converse only with angels. She wrote of the union of her soul with her heavenly bridegroom, "like two candle lights merging," and of her longing for death. Fellow nuns believed she was possessed, but Teresa's visions have long been a subject for art, notably Bernini's statue of her. Teresa founded the secret order of the barefoot Carmelites (they actually wore rope sandals), who slept on straw, ate no meat, and lived a cloistered life of prayer and contemplation. Her practical guide to salvation stressed prayer, self-mortification, and humility. "The Lord walks among the pots and pans," she said. After Teresa died in 1582, it was reported that the fragrance of violets wafted up from her gravesite. Forty years later she was canonized, and a fervent monk cut off one of her hands, which supposedly had the power to perform miracles. (It will turn up again much later in the story.)

Teresa's protégé from Ávila was Juan de la Cruz, a priest who became one of Spain's great mystics and poets. He also helped found the barefoot order and was kidnapped by angry Carmelites and held in solitary confinement for eight months. There, in a gloomy cell, his spiritual ecstasies blossomed, and he wrote a masterpiece called *Dark Night of the Soul*.

Spanish mysticism found its ultimate expression in painting with the work of a man from Crete named Domenico Theotokopoulos, otherwise known as El Greco. After studying in Italy, "the Greek" moved to Toledo and its lively cultural milieu, which included the baroque poet Góngora. El Greco explored the typically Spanish form of brooding, religious realism that pushes its subjects into mystical realms, as in his transcendent *View of Toledo* and

The Burial of Count Orgaz. In the latter he captured the meeting of spiritual and material worlds in the elongated bodies spiraling up to heaven, with their otherworldly expressions and "winged hands." It was a true masterpiece that embodied on canvas the Spanish Counter-Reformation just as the Escorial did in stone.

Felipe's architectural masterpiece was completed in 1584 as the ultimate expression of a peculiarly Spanish style. Ornateness would later return with the Baroque, a grandiose style in keeping with imperial times by its sheer mass and volume. Baroque architecture would dominate tastes until the French launched the classical revival in the eighteenth century.

Felipe settled into the Escorial to run his empire and live his tortured life. The building's fortress-like structure was a perfect metaphor for a sad and introverted man's withdrawal from the world, and within its walls were embodied all his complexities and contradictions. He lived in a modest room overlooking the church, yet kept Bosch's wildly wicked *The Garden of Earthly Delights* above his bed (he also bought many nudes by Titian and Rubens). Book collecting, another of his obsessions, resulted in the stunning royal library, a triumph of both scholarship and architecture. With fourteen thousand priceless volumes, it formed the largest private collection in Europe.

With the passing years the empire's arteries seemed to harden along with Felipe's. He continued to fight a losing battle against all the paperwork the empire could produce, strangely unable to distinguish between the trivial and the important. The details of some religious procession or the bridging of an obscure stream occupied the king's time while crucial issues lay unresolved. He even corrected spelling as part of the routine. Towns in America felt free to write directly to the Escorial about local matters, knowing that an answer would eventually come. As unsettled affairs piled up, Felipe tried to solve them by procrastination; often by the time he made a decision the basics had completely changed. As one Italian minister remarked, "If death came from Spain, we should all live a long time."

Nevertheless, Felipe's empire continued to grow in spectacular fashion, as if by the strength of its own momentum. When the Portuguese king was killed while leading an invasion of Morocco, Felipe claimed the throne through his mother's family. His position was strong, stronger still when backed up by Spanish troops (and the Portuguese parliament), and in 1580 he realized a centuries-old dream of uniting the entire Iberian peninsula under one ruler.

Said Felipe glibly about Portugal, "I inherited it, I bought it, I conquered it. It's mine." The annexation its Iberian neighbor marked the supreme moment for the Spanish monarchy, high tide of its power. For the first and last time a Spanish army entered and took over another country, showing again that Spanish power came largely from dynastic inheritance and metals rather than conquest. This joint Spanish-Portuguese Empire was awesome in size and wealth, taking in most of the western hemisphere and a good deal more, including the Philippines, Guinea, Angola, Mozambique, Cape Verde, and Madeira. In America, the overthrow of native empires was only the first stage of Spanish conquest; they still had to take possession of this vast land and administer it. By 1580, a permanent colony established by Juan de Garay at Buenos Aires completed the founding of cities that now form the capitals of Latin America. At the end of Felipe's reign, 130 Spanish families crossed the Rio Grande and settled in *Nuevo Mexico*, the land that today forms the southwestern corner of the United States.

About 120,000 Spaniards had immigrated to the Americas by 1570. They came with the idea of establishing "new Spains," and soon most of America was dotted with signs of Spanish administration. Towns had municipal institutions like those of Castilla and belonged to vice-royalties, which were on an equal footing with all others in the empire. Spanish America reminded visitors of Spain itself, with fields of vines and cereals, peasants riding burros or tending flocks, sprawling *plazas*, and baroque churches. In the cities colonial architecture was often monumental in size and sumptuous in detail, designed to awe the natives as the Romans had done in Iberia centuries earlier. In the first decades of the colonial era two parallel societies existed, Spanish and native, each with its own culture and ruling elite. Later they converged although skin color and language still counted for much.

If Spaniards conquered the Indies with horses, steel, and gunpowder, their most precious gift was wheat. From America they brought back tobacco, maize, tomatoes, and potatoes (thought to be an aphrodisiac). Spain's initial economic relationship with its colonies was a monopoly that involved supplying products and extracting precious metals. In time, the colonies developed economies dangerously similar to Spain's and became competitive rather than complementary. English and Dutch traders filled the gap, which soon made a shambles of the Spanish monopoly.

Legitimate commerce was not the only foreign threat, as outright attacks on Spanish shipping—both pirate and government sponsored—

multiplied in the late 1500s. To counteract these assaults, scores of vessels would sail in gigantic convoys once or twice a year, often with priceless cargoes in their holds. Despite legend, however, very few Spanish treasure ships fell prey to the likes of Drake and Hawkins. Violent storms sent many more ships to the bottom than pirates, but even these took a relatively small toll. An estimated ninety-five percent of all Spanish treasure ships reached Spain without incident, a remarkable achievement of maritime skill.

Treasure arrived at Sevilla and was registered at the Torre del Oro on the Guadalquivir. Nearby lies the fabulous Archive of the Indies, a vast depository of paperwork covering the entire colonial period: shipping logs, maps, charts—some fifty million documents in all. Many a treasure hunter has uncovered crucial information regarding sunken ships at these archives.

Spanish treatment of Native Americans is a subject of heated controversy. Without question many were enslaved despite the legal ban, though there is also evidence of Indian collaboration. Europe's first great colonial venture led to colossal deeds both good and bad, but indigenous populations were decimated largely by the unintentional introduction of new diseases, not by the sword. But disease and cultural shock were very real and proved overwhelming for the Indians starting with the first pandemic of smallpox in 1518. There is little room for debate regarding the extent of the demographic catastrophe. After two devastating epidemics, the Indian population of Mexico had dwindled from about eleven million in 1520 to two million at the end of the century. Populations fell similarly in Peru and elsewhere, causing an economic catastrophe due to a severe labor shortage.

Among colonial powers the Spanish took their own unique approach to Native Americans, freely interbreeding with them and trying to provide both religious and cultural instruction. The English colonists, on the other hand, stood aloof and rarely intermingled in any way with the Indians; a "half-breed" became the lowest form of human life. For three centuries Spain ruled America without a standing army and without any serious native rebellions. Invariably, revolts started with the Creoles (*criollos*), colonials of Spanish descent who wanted more local control. Today, native cultures are present everywhere in Latin American society, and Indians have served as presidents and leaders in all fields of endeavor. In areas settled by the English or their descendants, the handful of native survivors lived out their

lives—until quite recently—as social outcasts on reservations. This is the ultimate refutation of the Black Legend.

New techniques for refining silver from America produced a startling
increase in bullion imports by the late 1570s. This encouraged Felipe to pursue a more aggressive imperial policy against his northern foes, among them
William of Orange. The Dutch leader had been busy, officially kicking off the
Black Legend with his anti-Spanish tract *Apologia* (1580). His attacks on Felipe
included the charge that he poisoned Don Carlos because he was having an
affair with his stepmother, Elizabeth of Valois. The story would be picked up
by hispanophobes over the next two centuries, each adding grisly details of
the crime.

In 1581, the United Provinces declared their independence while the
south (Belgium) remained loyal. Three years later a fanatical Catholic assassinated William. Shortly after, England and the United Provinces entered into
an accord, prompting Felipe to order the seizure of English ships. Elizabeth
countered by sending Francis Drake to maul Spanish colonies in the Caribbean, and he even swooped into Cádiz and "singed the beard of the Spanish
king." Step by step, outright war was approaching.

In March of 1587, word reach the Escorial that Elizabeth had executed
Mary Queen of Scots, the great Catholic hope. Partly to punish this act and
partly to stop English raids on shipping, Felipe began planning the Great
Armada for the invasion of England. Elizabeth meanwhile pursued an alliance with the Turks, stating that both Muslims and Protestants hated Spanish
"idolatries." The great expedition, in retrospect, seemed doomed from the
outset. Problems started at the top with the king, who typically insisted on
reviewing every detail of planning, and with the Duke of Medina Sidonia,
chosen as commander though he had never been to sea. Felipe viewed the
Armada as a religious mission and commanded sailors to "refrain from swear-
ing and blasphemy." About two hundred priests went along to tend to the
men's spiritual needs, but there were not prayers enough to save the Armada
from disaster.

Trouble started already in Spain at La Coruña, where a sudden summer
storm destroyed about a quarter of the fleet. Due to inept planning,
provisions were already running low, and half the men were ill. Finally, in
July of 1588, about 130 ships and 29,000 men set sail for the English Channel, where the plan called from them to take on more troops in Belgium. The
Spanish fleet went into its feared crescent formation and moved up the

channel with little opposition. But the English under Lord Howard and Drake lay waiting at Plymouth Sound, then slipped out and got windward of the Spanish. (Much credit for the victory goes to the disarming self-confidence of Drake, who played a famous game of bowls as the Armada approached.)

From their superior position, the smaller and faster English ships began snapping at the lurching Spanish galleons like dogs at a sick bull. A fatal strategic flaw sealed the Armada's fate: the Spanish had no port capable of handling their huge ships for re-supplying or boarding their land-based army. They were forced to operate on the high seas, far from home or any hope of aid. In anchorage off Calais, the Armada became a perfect target for fire ships, which caused the Spanish to panic and break formation. It was the beginning of the end, as the retreating fleet headed north into a flurry of storms. Finally, after rounding Scotland and skirting the Irish coast, the remnants of the "Invincible Armada" limped home; sixty-three ships and nine thousand men were not among them.

The decade of the Armada, which began so auspiciously for Felipe, also turned sour at home, culminating in the Antonio Pérez affair and a revolt in Aragón. The shrewd son of a priest, Pérez was the king's trusted secretary, but a bitter rival of Juan de Escobedo, Don Juan's aide in the Netherlands. Pérez raised eyebrows at court when he linked up (in several senses) with the Princess of Eboli, a beautiful widow who wore a black patch over one eye and was famed as an irresistible seductress. She was also skillful at political intrigue, and Escobedo suspected the pair of collusion with the Dutch rebels. When three attempts at poisoning failed, Pérez had him murdered by thugs on a Madrid street.

After waffling for a time, Felipe had his secretary arrested and tortured, and on the eighth twist of the rope Pérez confessed. He languished in jail for years, then escaped (by changing clothes with his visiting wife) and fled to Aragón, where he claimed sanctuary. When the local government refused to arrest the fugitive, officials of the Inquisition grabbed Pérez. This set off aristocratic protest and popular rioting, and Pérez managed to escape to France amid the turmoil. There he peddled state secrets and penned a scurrilous exposé about Felipe, which added more fuel to the Black Legend.

The king replaced Pérez with Cardinal Granville from Belgium, the first non-Spaniard to direct state affairs, because of his expertise in Italy and Flanders. Peeved by the king's increasing demands for money as well as the

Pérez affair, the nobles of Aragón barricaded themselves behind their medieval *fueros*. These were aristocratic privileges rather than popular liberties, but the nobles managed to gain widespread support nonetheless. The brief revolt was crushed, but even Felipe did not dare outlaw the *fueros*, and they would survive to haunt future Spanish rulers.

The impact of Felipe's long, difficult life is revealed in the portrait by Titian when he was twenty and the one done near the end, in which he appears withered and feeble, a mere shadow of a once great king. Among his other concerns, the death of Don Carlos had left Spain without a royal heir. Kingly duty running in his veins, he had married a fourth time back in 1570—to his cousin, Anne of Austria. She bore him five children, but only one survived beyond the age of eight, a feeble son who would become the next king. Said Felipe, "God, who has given me so many kingdoms, has denied me a son capable of ruling them."

In the seventh decade of his life, Felipe was afflicted with a variety of ailments and was carried to the Escorial to die. He held on for fifty-three days, making elaborate funeral preparations and lengthy confessions for "a lifetime of errors." On September 13, 1598, Felipe II finally expired in his little room overlooking the church, clutching the same crucifix his father held on his own deathbed. (On display at the Escorial are the macabre skull-and-crossbones vestments priests wore at his funeral.) Bells began to toll throughout Spain and continued for nine days before an uneasy quiet fell over the land. Felipe was beloved by his people, but his reticent ways made him an enigma to all who knew him. And so he remains. But whatever his mistakes, Felipe had been a great king, and his heir had large shoes to fill.

Felipe's death after almost forty years as king changed everything yet changed nothing. His weak and inexperienced son, crowned Felipe (Philip) III, resembled his father in little but physical appearance and religious convictions. The twenty-year-old king was devoted to hunting, the theater, and religious festivals, but abandoned the role of royal administrator his father had found all consuming. Felipe III inherited an empire that was virtually intact except for the not-yet-official loss of the United Provinces. He also assumed an empty treasury and a hundred-million-ducat debt.

The enormous facade of imperial Spain was like an elaborate setting hiding a great empty stage. From the outside the Spanish Empire still appeared mighty, but Castilla was mired in debt, poverty, pestilence and growing self-doubt. This erosion of morale was already present by the 1590s, with several foiled conquests and a trio of treaties filled with concessions. The monarchy was in retreat. The coming century would be one of political and economic disasters, overseen by a parade of feeble and debauched kings. Yet it was also a time of spectacular cultural brilliance, the culmination of the luminous Golden Century begun under Felipe II. This bitter contrast has haunted Spaniards ever since.

Many historians have tried to explain Spain's precipitous decline in the seventeenth century. Most agree that Castilla became the victim of its own glorious history, trying desperately to re-enact the imperial glories of an earlier age. The crusading zeal born during the Reconquest led Spaniards to commit their attention to both Europe and America, to pursue the medieval dream of Christian universality in a new world of developing nation states. More than an anachronism, this dream became irrelevant.

Miguel de Cervantes, author of *Don Quixote*

The new century began with some unfinished business to settle with an old nemesis—England. Still smarting from the defeat of the Invincible Armada, Spain tried to stir up a rebellion in Catholic Ireland. In 1601, a force of three thousand men landed near Cork to link up with Irish rebels, but the plan was betrayed, for a bottle of whiskey it was said. Nevertheless, the death of Elizabeth and accession of James I (1603) ended Anglo-Hispanic tensions for quite some time. A few years later, Spain gave tacit recognition to the independent United Provinces of the Netherlands and seemed satisfied to hold Flanders along the French border. Encirclement of France returned as the number one priority.

Felipe III began the tradition of rule by select ministers, the "favorites," (*válidos* in Spanish). By pandering to the monarch's weaknesses, the duke of Lerma (Francisco Gómez de Sandoval y Rojas) rose to the position of favorite and became Spain's real ruler. It was an unfortunate turn of events; Spain urgently needed economic reforms, but Lerma often stayed away for days while pressing business lay unattended. Foreign diplomats complained that they could not gain audiences or conduct affairs while in Madrid unless they paid for the privilege. Corruption was endemic at the highest levels during the duke's tenure.

The only act of resolution under Felipe III and Lerma was the expulsion of the Moriscos from Aragón (1609). Spain had struggled for more than a century to assimilate these nominal Christians, stubborn in their Muslim ways and suspected of aiding Barbary pirates. The fact remained that the Catholic religion was the national catalyst, and there was no room for nonconformity. Several hundred thousand Moriscos (estimates range from 150,000 to 500,000) were expelled over a five-year period. Most of the fugitives headed for Morocco where, ironically, they were considered "Spaniards." Many were murdered or sold as slaves. (In Rabat refugees founded their own republic and turned to piracy, the famous Sallee Rovers mentioned in *Robinson Crusoe*). In France, Cardinal Richelieu called the expulsion "the most barbarous stroke in human annals." But there was one notable result: pirate raids along the Spanish coast suddenly ceased.

The affable and easygoing Lerma was mainly concerned with his own wealth and power. Almost any event was greeted with extravagant displays at court, and royal expenditures rocketed. In order to make ends meet, the government decided to debase the coinage with copper, the equivalent of printing more paper currency today. The result was the same—inflation—and huge wagons were soon needed to transport any large sum. (For a century Spanish coins such as gold *escudos* and silver *reales* had been the universal currency in the Mediterranean world and America. From the eight-*real* coin came the expression "pieces of eight.")

The ostentation and immorality of the Spanish capital during the seventeenth century shocked visitors. By mid century there were eight hundred brothels in Madrid, and "public women" moved freely in higher social circles. Laws passed to curb immorality—carriages could not be used with the curtains drawn, for example—proved inadequate. Madrid's population swelled with the influx of beggars and vagabonds, and the gap between rich and poor widened. The middle class was lured by the easy-money of investment and hungered for the titles of their social "betters," the idle aristocracy. Unlike the burgeoning middle classes of other countries, here the young dandies were disinterested in commerce, industry, technology, and science—all the things that were propelling Europe into a new age. Instead, a sense of fatalism and decadence began to creep over the land.

Spanish Possessions in Europe ca. 1600

The key to Spain's imperial power lay more with its continental possessions than the Americas. The Low Countries formed Europe's richest area, with a full-blown capitalist economy centered in Antwerp, so their material worth for Spain was immense. Italy provided men and armaments for the military.

It was amid this setting that *Don Quixote*, Spain's universal masterpiece, sprang from the pen of Miguel de Cervantes de Saavedra. Born at Alcalá de Henares in 1547, Cervantes was a contemporary of Shakespeare. (The two writers both died on the same date, April 23, 1616.) Cervantes led a full life: after fleeing Spain following a duel, he joined the army and fought at the great victory at Lepanto. Later, he was captured by Muslims and held for five years in a fetid Algerian prison to be ransomed at the age of thirty-three. Next Cervantes worked as a tax collector, but was imprisoned in a Sevilla jail (a plaque marks the spot) for malfeasance. Along the way he managed to have affairs with several actresses.

Cervantes struggled as a writer and did not even begin *Don Quixote* until he was fifty-six. His life spanned two ages, the glories of Lepanto and the decline and disillusionment of the early seventeenth century. The book deftly dances between comedy and tragedy, optimism and pessimism, idealism and realism, humor and bitter irony. It is the story of a befuddled knight named Don Quixote on a mission to correct all the world's evils. Taking up a rusty lance, shield, and broken helmet, he mounts Rocinante, his ungainly nag, and marches boldly across the desolate plains of La Mancha in search of adventure. The Don's sidekick is Sancho Panza, an unlettered but perceptive squire, and the novel plays on the contrast between these two characters. It was a brilliant parable for a crusading nation that had found itself tilting at windmills, just like the lovable but pathetic knight-errant.

Felipe III, full of unwarranted contrition for his inconsequential life, died in 1621 at the age of forty-three. His teenaged son was heir to a wasted estate. Although in appearance still Europe's greatest power, Spain was on a collision course with disaster. The new king, Felipe (Philip) IV, became a notorious libertine who entertained an endless procession of mistresses, whom he promptly packed off to convents once he tired of them. He became tormented by guilt and confessed his sins in a series of extraordinary letters to a nun named Sor María de Agreda. Obsessed with death, he spent hours lying in his burial niche at the Escorial. But all this did not stop him from fathering some thirty illegitimate children.

While the king frittered away his time, Spain was governed by a remarkable figure named Gaspar de Guzmán, the Count-Duke of Olivares. This wily statesman, every bit the equal of France's Richelieu (who ruled for Louis XIII), was the son of a Spanish ambassador and led a privileged life befitting a member of the great house of Guzmán. (While a law student in Salamanca, for example, he had nineteen servants.) In Madrid, he insinuated himself in the royal household, then bowed and scraped his way to the top. (He once kissed the prince's chamber pot as a sign of submission.) When the prince became king, Olivares was ready.

The great Count-Duke appears in a magnificent portrait by Velázquez, larger-than-life astride a fine steed, with a swirling moustache and huge floppy hat. For twenty-two years he tried through the strength of his personality to reverse Spain's slide. In a flurry of energy he cut royal extravagance, purged the bloated bureaucracy, and took other measures to transform Spain into a modern nation-state. The manic Olivares could be seen roaming the corridors with state papers bulging in his pockets, surrounded by scurrying secretaries as he dictated correspondence in several languages. He was the grand maestro who moved all the wheels of that great clock called the Spanish Empire.

Olivares believed firmly in the rightness and inevitability of Spanish hegemony in Europe and tried to maintain it at all costs. But times had changed: the Mediterranean was no longer at center stage. The first shots of the Thirty Years War (1618-48) were far away, but the Netherlands were involved and so Spain too would soon become entangled in this sordid struggle. In 1621, Olivares deliberately violated the standing truce with the United Provinces and war followed. Spain was flirting with financial disaster as war broke out with France again and expenditures climbed. The country had grown used to its annual "fix" from the Americas, but in 1628 the Dutch captured the entire treasure fleet. The high costs of war prompted the Count-Duke to seek more revenue from the tight-fisted provinces, but a tax on salt caused riots in Cataluña. For quite some time the crown had been losing its grip on this northeastern region, and the trend worsened. Olivares was facing the fundamental problems of the Spanish monarchy: too much financial burden on Castilla and too many antiquated privileges still used to defend the entrenched social elites.

It is said that in 1640 Olivares lost two kingdoms in one week. In Cataluña, a mob murdered the hated Castilian viceroy, the corpulent count of Santa Coloma, and the Catalans asked for French aid and named King Louis XIII as Count of Barcelona. Later, a combined French-Catalan force defeated the Spanish army on Montjuich hill in Barcelona. Fortunately for the crown, neither Aragón nor Valencia lent a hand to their Catalan "brothers," which might have put an end to the work of Fernando and Isabel. Cataluña returned to the fold with substantial local rights. There was a strong medieval element in the revolt, however, and the price for fighting the "currents of history" is usually very high. Cataluña would discover this cruel fact during the next century under the Bourbons.

The situation in Portugal was analogous. Resentful of the Count-Duke's centralizing policies, the Portuguese turned to the Duke of Braganza. Here things went surprisingly easy for the rebels: four hundred of them rushed a Lisbon palace and proclaimed Braganza as King Joao IV. Although Portugal's independence was not officially recognized for twenty-five years, it was a fact by 1641, just six decades after Felipe II had included Spain's western neighbor in history's greatest empire.

These provincial revolts led to the fall of Count-Duke Olivares in 1643. He retired to his sister's palace in Toro, where he died half-mad a few years later. A man of great plans but inept execution, he himself remarked, "We were trying to achieve miracles and reduce the world to what it cannot be." In a few years most of his policies were in shreds. The 1640s were a terrible decade for Spain. Sicily and Naples also revolted, and there were rumblings of separatism in Andalucía and Galicia. A new offensive against France led to the disastrous battle of Rocroi, which marked the end of Spanish military prestige in Europe. In 1648 the Peace of Westphalia ended the Thirty Years War and recognized what long had been a fact: an independent Netherlands (excluding Flanders). Spain's eighty-year northern nightmare was over.

War with France dragged on until the Treaty of the Pyrenees (1659), the official end of Spain's European power status and the emergence of France under Louis XIV. To drive home the point, the French "Sun-King" married María Teresa, daughter of the Spanish monarch. This marriage turned out to be a crux of history. (One odd remnant of the treaty is Llivia, once capital of Catalan Cerdanya, now an island of Spanish territory north of the Pyrenees completely surrounded by France.)

Historians have drawn a correlation between Spain's declining fortunes on the battlefield and the declining silver cargoes from America. The unfavorable trade balance (raw wool was still the only major export) meant that the little treasure that *did* make it to Sevilla passed on to foreign bankers like water through a sieve. Reform was imperative, but no one seemed willing to face the task. The mines of Potosí and Mexico had always saved the country, so why plan or save? Money would be plentiful again once the fleet arrived, it was reasoned. Many Spaniards held the belief that Spain was richer and more fertile than other countries, hence entirely self-sufficient and without the need for foreign trade. Looms fell silent as industry choked from under-investment and over-taxation. Further crippled by inflation, overpriced Spanish goods could not compete on the world market. Furthermore, by 1650 foreign entrepreneurs controlled almost all the nation's external trade and about eighty percent of its internal trade and industry.

Spain's fossilized social structure and feeble work ethic only worsened matters. Despite a labor shortage, tens of thousands of mendicants disdaining physical work wandered the country looking for free soup. The best men continued to enter the military, church, or government, all honorable but essentially unproductive positions. As one writer lamented, "So many men without posts, so many posts without men."

The church offered the population an unending succession of masses, processions, and religious festivals, which took up about a third of the year. Spain's most important institution also influenced society in other ways. Thus a group of priests summoned to consider a projected canal could flatly declare, "If God had wanted these two rivers to be navigable, he could have affected it simply by a fiat, and it would be an infringement of the rights of providence to improve that which, for reasons not to be understood, it had wished to remain imperfect."

There was an insular and hermetic quality to Spanish life that stifled intellectual progress, a refusal to welcome the culture of other countries. The feeling persisted that the rest of the world could learn from Spain but Spain did not need to learn from anyone else. "All the world serves her, and she serves nobody," proclaimed a Madrid historian in 1658. Spain remained a closed world, divorced from the European mainstream and reluctant to let the world in. For example, two hundred years after the discovery of America, even educated Spaniards displayed an astonishing ignorance about the new continent except for interest in its treasure.

These pervasive attitudes had doomed Spain to future mediocrity, or so it seemed in the year 1700. In just a century, the country had gone from supreme self-confidence to a total loss of confidence. In the midst of all this, however, Spaniards created a cultural golden age with few rivals. Spanish painting in particular exploded with the incredible genius of Zurbarán, Murillo, Ribera, and above all Velázquez. Diego de Silva y Velázquez was both insightful and technically brilliant, and his talents won him a position as court painter. Over several decades the artist produced one superb canvas after another, depicting the homely and troubled king, Prince Baltasar Carlos (who died at seventeen from excessive debauchery), Princess Margarita (who also died young), and other members of the royal family. With the dispassionate mastery of his brush, Velázquez dominated the Habsburg world more completely than even Count-Duke Olivares. A visit to the Velázquez rooms at the Prado is an enlightening journey into the seventeenth century. Here are the riveting portraits of Felipe and Olivares and the painter's undeniable masterpiece, *Las Meninas* (The Maids of Honor), a multi-dimensional look at court life.

Although a royal employee, Velázquez never abused his artistic powers in service of kingly egos. His vision is unnerving at times, and Spain's disillusionment with itself seeps through. Both Cervantes and Velázquez reflected on a country that had climbed to heights and sunk to depths, achieved and lost everything, conquered the world but was vanquished by itself. Scholars still debate the meaning of the painter's treatment of Mars, mythical god of war. In contrast to classical renditions, Mars is an ordinary-looking man seated uncomfortably on the edge of a couch. He is naked except for a blue cape and a helmet that casts his glum face into shadow, looking more dejected than divine. Is Mars the artist's metaphor of Spain's decaying military might?

Spanish painting of the era went far beyond other European schools by infusing a penetrating realism that embraced everything from life's most depressing aspects—dwarfs, drunkards, bearded women—to the most transcendent spiritual realms. Somehow this realism managed to bridge the deep cleavage between the worlds of spirit and flesh. Murillo, for example, painted mostly religious themes, but also delighted in tattered peddlers and street urchins. Francisco Zurbarán's canvases of luminous monks, dressed in stiff white and brown habits, combine stark realism with intense spirituality, capturing the poverty-induced ecstasies of cloistered life.

Spanish sculpture of the Golden Century was likewise realistic, using wood instead of stone or marble as a perfect medium for conveying the violent emotions of grieving Christs and martyrs. Among the masters of polychrome wood sculpture were Becerra and Cano.

Cervantes was but the brightest of many literary lights during Spain's Golden Century. Lope de Vega was an incredibly prolific playwright, with 1,800 known plays of which about 500 survive. Said Lope of his productivity: "More than a hundred of my comedies have taken only twenty-four hours to pass from my brain to the boards of the theater." His observations on war, religion, and love were always entertaining though rarely profound, but he did more than anyone to create Spain's national theater. Drama often revolved around the concept of honor, a gentleman's code that was pushed to ridiculous extremes in seventeenth century Spain. According to the rules of *pundonor*, the true gentleman was willing to risk his life in an instant to defend his good name in a duel or other test.

Other first-class writers included Tirso de Molina, Calderón de la Barca, and Francisco de Quevedo. In *The Deceiver of Sevilla*, Tirso (*nom de plume* of a friar named Gabriel Tellez) created the classic figure of Don Juan the seducer, who embodied Spanish daring and masculinity in the battle of the sexes. The Don Juan character would go on to seduce foreign authors from

Moliere to Bernard Shaw. Calderón appeared as the poet of decline and decadence in the sunset glow of culture during Felipe IV's final years. He epitomized the baroque style, with a love of extremes and marvelous effects, and greatly influenced later Romantic writers.

Quevedo was perhaps the best of all; his style is acerbic and savagely pessimistic about the decay all around him. "I am strong like Spain, for lack of sustenance," he wrote. Quevedo looked back to the days of Spain's greatness, but realized with anguish that his country was slipping into inexorable decline. He was a fervid nationalist and critic of foreign influences. Yet he managed to dissect Spanish life with humor. In *La Vida del Buscon*, the hero goes to school and is served a bit of lamb that "between what stuck under our fingernails and what lodged between our teeth, it was all gone, leaving the belly excommunicated from participation."

The famous painting of Mars by Diego Velazquez

It is ironic that Spain's great cultural flowering would occur at precisely the time when the Inquisition supposedly had a stranglehold on intellectual life. One explanation for this paradox is that few *important* books from Spain or abroad were ever banned, even though the Inquisition had the power to do so. (Many obscure works appeared on its Index.) Nevertheless, the Inquisition continued to meddle in daily life, using spies called *familiares* to keep a sharp eye out for abnormal behavior. Among their special interests were subversive public discussions, usury (lending money at interest), and sexual misconduct. Rooms at Spanish inns could not be bolted from inside so that agents could enter at any time to pounce on any unmarried, hence by definition illicit couples. The Inquisition found its way to the Americas too, but was less influential; only about a hundred persons were executed in 250 years. During the seventeenth century colonial administration was formalized to replicate Spanish models, but the seeds of decay were transplanted to new soil because government in Spain itself was breaking down.

Jealous rivals also continued to pick away at the empire; in 1654 the English took Jamaica, the first permanent loss of Spanish territory. The scourge of piracy swept through the West Indies, climaxing with Henry Morgan and his pirate army. This band of brigands ruthlessly sacked Panama, and the English crown rewarded Morgan with knighthood and the governorship of Jamaica for his deeds. Despite these incidents, however, the Spanish Empire remained vibrant long after Spain itself lay prostrate.

Spain was the first to feel the sting of the printing press in the propaganda wars among rival European powers. Fray Las Casas's *A Brief Relation* proliferated, including one edition subtitled: "The Tears of the Indians: Being an Historical and True Account of the Cruel Massacres and Slaughters of Above Twenty Millions of Innocent People. . . the cry of their blood ceasing at the noise of Your (Majesty's) great transactions, while You arm for their revenge against the Bloudy and Popish nation of the Spaniards."

After about 1660, enemies of Spain plainly saw an enfeebled nation lying south of the Pyrenees. Castilla was dying and hopeful mourners were gathering. Felipe managed to hang on a few more years before succumbing to a skin disease. Mariana, his Austrian niece and second wife, had given him a son and heir, Carlos (Charles), only four when his father died and the final hope for a beleaguered nation. Instead, he became what one historian called "The last stunted sprig of a degenerate line." Carlos II was a tragic victim of royal interbreeding: four generations of predecessors had married cousins or nieces, and their offspring suffered from a variety of physical and mental ailments. Carlos was so weak he had to be presented to the nobles at court held up by strings, which his nurse worked like a puppeteer. Yet he surprised everyone by surviving to reign, if not rule, for the thirty-five years.

Until he "came of age" at fifteen, Spain was ruled by Felipe's widow, the queen mother Mariana, who ushered in a confused period that often took on aspects of a comic opera. Mariana engaged an Austrian Jesuit named Father Nithard as confessor, and he soon became an all-powerful force at court. His archrival was Juan José, bastard son of Felipe and actress María Calderón, who rallied legions of intriguers around him and personally led two coups. One succeeded, and he ruled for two years, albeit no more competently than his predecessors, before dying mysteriously (historians suspect poison).

In view of his feeble physical condition, it was remarkable that Carlos managed to survive to the age of thirty-nine. His huge Habsburg jaw stuck out so far that his teeth did not meet, making it impossible to chew properly and adding indigestion to a long list of ailments, which included fainting spells, fits, rashes, discharges, and eruptions. Exorcists and visionary nuns employed every trick to free him from "the devil." Nevertheless, Carlos "The Bewitched" was not the monster his name implies. His mind was clear if limited and his character kindly. He was conscientious, and his efforts to rule without a "favorite" were well intentioned. But he was weak-willed and became the focus of intrigue and conspiracy. Spain needed a savior, but got poor Carlos instead.

Both the triumphs and disasters of the Golden Century rest on the shoulders of Castilla, and the heartland reached its nadir around the year 1680. Two-thirds of American silver imports were going directly to foreigners, and the economy was in ruins, with wild inflation and worthless currency causing a large-scale return to barter. Adding to the dismal picture was a serious decline in population throughout the century, from about nine million in 1600 to six million a hundred years later. Plagues, emigration, expulsions, high infant-mortality, and a high incidence of celibacy all took their toll.

The final years of the last Habsburg king were a pathetic spectacle of degradation. Said the Venetian envoy: "From the poor to the rich, everyone devours the state of the king, some taking little bites, the nobility large ones, and the greatest enormous portions." All the important posts went to men of rank, who proceeded to do as little as possible. Ministers included the Duke of Medina de las Torres, who spent his life in total idleness, almost exclusively shared between eating and sleeping.

In foreign affairs, all the chickens would come home to roost as Spain became caught up in the last act of the lengthy duel between France and Austria. Carlos was married off to Marie Louise, niece of the French king, but the union soured when no children arrived, apparently because of a mutual ignorance about sexual matters. That or a case of royal impotence. It soon became clear that Carlos would be the last of his regal line, and foreign diplomats and intriguers began gathering.

Rival French and Austrian factions formed under Cardinal Portocarrero and the queen mother respectively. The Austrians convinced Carlos that his fits (probably epileptic) and sexual difficulties were the work of demons and persuaded him to try an exorcist, who then attempted to plead the Habsburg case. When a rival specialist turned out to have French sympathies, both exorcists were driven out of court, and Portocarrero literally camped out in the king's chambers to fend off intruders.

Carlos first named the Prince of Bavaria as heir, but he died suddenly a year later. Numerous other claimants came forth, but the choice boiled down to Leopold of Austria or Philippe, the Duke of Anjou. Finally, on his deathbed in 1700, Carlos signed documents handing over his crown to the French duke and the Bourbon dynasty. The Spanish Habsburgs were no more.

Sights & Sites

Alcázar de San Juan (Ciudad Real):
The supposed site of Don Quixote's battle with the windmills (still extant) lies eight kms. from town.

Alpujarras (Granada): The mountainous region south of Granada retains traces of its history as the final Morisco bastion.

Baeza (Jaén): Superb architectural center includes Lion's Square and Plaza Santa Maria.

Barcelona: Montjuich Castle, built during revolt against Felipe IV in 1640, offers excellent views.

El Escorial (Madrid): Felipe II's masterpiece includes royal apartments, museums, church, library, and royal pantheon.

Granada: Carthusian Monastery features splendid baroque decorative details.

Madrid: Convent of the Descalzas Reales, founded by Joanna of Austria, as religious retreat for women of nobility; the Prado has magnificent collection of all Golden Age artists; El Retiro Park is from the epoch of Felipe IV; Plaza Mayor was heart of old town in seventeenth century.

Sevilla: Fine Arts Museum is one of Spain's best, with outstanding works by Murillo, Velázquez and Zurbarán; Archive of the Indies in La Lonja houses millions of documents from Spanish Empire, including an original letter from Columbus, America's "birth certificate."

El Escorial monastery-palace outside Madrid, built by Felipe II

Toledo: Santo Tome Church contains El Greco's masterpiece "The Burial of the Count of Orgaz"; El Greco House and Museum; Santa Cruz Museum and Talavera Hospital have more than twenty works by the painter.

Valladolid: San Gregorio College now serves as National Museum of Polychrome Sculpture.

Chapter 7

The French Century

Madrid's *Palacio Real* (Royal Palace), home to several generations of Bourbon monarchs, stands regally on high ground overlooking the Manzanares River. From the Plaza de Oriente, you can scan the imposing east facade of granite from the Guadarrama Mountains and white limestone from Colmenar. This palace is Madrid's finest example of neo-classical architecture, a symphony of pilasters, pediments and Corinthian columns, topped by a balustrade lined with statues of Spanish kings. Inside are hundreds of sumptuous rooms decorated with exquisite detail. Visitors enter the palace via a monumental bronze staircase, then proceed through rooms straining to hold the riches—hundreds of tapestries, chandeliers, diamond-studded clocks, lustrous damask work, mosaics, antique furniture, and delicately painted ceilings.

And yet there is something wrong, a piece of the historical puzzle that does not seem to fit. This magnificent architectural creation, a confident statement from a wealthy and powerful monarchy, is not a product of the Golden Century or the glorious heyday of the Spanish Empire. Begun in 1738 by Felipe V, Spain's first Bourbon king, it was built at a time when the nation had supposedly fallen to incredible depths of inertia and poverty. Until a recent flood of scholarly research, the eighteenth century was the "missing" one for Spanish historians. They saw it as an aberration, "the French century," and pushed on impatiently toward the War of Independence and the birth of modern, "genuine" Spain. Many even blamed this period for the "ruination" of their country by a fawning mimicry of foreign ideas and customs. It can be argued, however, that modern Spain really arrived with the first Bourbon. Habsburg glories had withered away. Their last king, feeble in mind and body, had become a pathetic metaphor for a royal line gone sour. The Bourbons brought hope again.

The new century that began in 1701 was far different from the pessimistic, religion-haunted era of decline that preceded it. Spain's far-flung overseas empire remained largely intact, the ballast for a proud nation that would enjoy major power status for another century. The loss of its European possessions in the late 1600s became the silver lining that ushered in an epoch of recovery, reform, and progress. Ironically, despite the losses Spain under the Bourbons became *more* European. "There are no more Pyrenees," proclaimed Louis XIV. France's "Sun King" was grandfather of the new ruler of Spain (still known as *Castilla y Aragón*). Restless, powerful, "modern" France was about to shake static, traditional Spain to its boot heels. This was the century of omnipotent despots, "enlightened" and otherwise, and the Bourbons—armed with new ideas and methods of government—would try to yank Spain into the European mainstream.

Carlos II had made nonsense of the previous thirty years of military struggles by naming Philippe of Anjou, second in line to the French throne, as his heir. (He was one-quarter Spanish Habsburg through his grandmother, María Teresa, and inherited the family's melancholia and odd chin.) Shortly after creating diplomatic havoc with this decision, Carlos expired.

In December of 1700, a mild, docile sixteen-year-old French boy reluctantly departed the gardens and salons of Versailles and rode south on a white mount toward the Pyrenees. After a journey of fifty days, he entered a jubilant Madrid as King Felipe V, the first of a new royal line from a barony south of Paris. Bourbons have remained on the Spanish throne most of the three centuries since Felipe arrived, right down to King Juan Carlos I. (The Spanish Bourbons are distinct from the senior line of French Bourbons, who have not ruled France since 1848. There are also junior lines of Italian Bourbons.)

Louis XIV advised the new king of Spain: "Be a good Spaniard, but remember that you are French by birth . . ." The sentiment was unnecessary; Felipe longed for the French crown and was appalled at the backward Spanish court, where nobles insisted on wearing starched white collars and their own hair (French periwigs had not reached Madrid). Other European powers were gripped with fear that the two monarchies might one day unite, creating a colossus that would straddle the Pyrenees and control most of America.

It is doubtful if Louis ever intended to respect Spanish independence, but all pretenses vanished the moment his grandson arrived at Madrid. Felipe, it soon became clear, was both lazy and moody in addition to being young and inexperienced. Hunting was a passion, and he would throw tantrums or sulk if interrupted for state affairs. Everything about his character encouraged French meddling, and the new king soon found himself with a Paris-approved wife, thirteen-year-old María Luisa of Saxony. Key to Louis' plans to control Spain was the Princess des Ursins, who was named lady-in-waiting to the queen. Attractive, intelligent and wily, the princess was highly skilled at diplomatic intrigue.

Austrian Emperor Leopold, France's archrival, objected to the cozy Bourbon arrangement in Spain. Like Louis, he had married a daughter of Felipe IV and proposed his own son, the Archduke Charles, as legitimate heir to the Spanish throne. By 1701, England and the Netherlands joined Austria in the Grand Alliance to dispute Felipe's inheritance, and within a year Spain would witness the first major fighting on its soil since the Reconquest. The War of Spanish Succession was Europe's first great modern war, whose causes were not religious or even dynastic in the strict sense. The stakes were the balance of power in Europe; neither France nor Austria could tolerate Spain and its empire going over to the other side. England, which held the deciding cards, became the war's chief beneficiary.

In 1703, the Austrian archduke was proclaimed King Carlos III of Spain at a solemn ceremony in Vienna, and shortly after he landed at Lisbon to begin his regal quest. An Anglo-Dutch fleet under Sir George Rooke harassed Cádiz, then took Gibraltar in the name of Queen Anne. The Bourbons responded by assembling a large Spanish-French fleet, but it was badly mauled at the battle of Málaga (off Marbella), the war's largest naval action.

Felipe and his queen had the support of most Spaniards. However, the Bourbons' well-known policy of centralization was feared in the regions, and Aragón and Valencia sided with the Austrian Charles. Using Barcelona as his base, the archduke marched on to Madrid and forced Felipe to flee. Things were going so bad, in fact, that Louis XIV began to secretly deal with the enemy at the expense of his grandson, promising to dismember the Spanish Empire. But Felipe stood firm. The tide was turned at the battle of Almansa, when the Duke of Berwick crushed a coalition

The palace at Aranjuez was only one of several sumptuous retreats for Bourbon monarchs.

of Habsburg supporters. Shortly after, everything suddenly changed: the archduke's elder brother died, leaving Charles as heir to the emperor's throne.

England promptly switched sides; a Spain united with Austria would mean a virtual re-creation of Charles V's sixteenth-century empire, something the English wanted even less than a dual Bourbon monarchy. When Felipe renounced his claims to the French throne, the stage was set for peace. As every schoolboy used to know, the Treaty of Utrecht ended the War of Spanish Succession in 1713. Spain lost Flanders and several Italian territories including Sicily. The treaty is often cited as the death knell of Spanish power, but Spain itself was about the same as before. The war's real significance was the loss of Italy as a bulwark of the empire. On the bright side, the American Empire remained untouched, although Britain forced Spain to concede the slave trade in its colonies. Spaniards were forced to confirm British occupation of Menorca and Gibraltar. The Treaty of Utrecht marked the dawn of Britain's control of the Mediterranean and its rise to world power status. Felipe likened Gibraltar's loss to "thorns in the feet," and so it has remained for Spaniards to this day. Spain and France would spend the next century trying to undo Utrecht.

Meanwhile, Spain had other concerns: namely the rebellious Catalans and Valencians outraged at being stripped of their medieval privileges, among them freedom from wartime levies. In one stroke, the new king abolished the *fueros*, which even Felipe II had not dared attack openly. (Navarra and the Basque lands retained their rights as a reward for their loyalty.) After a heroic defense of Barcelona, the city fell to royal troops in September 1714. In order to keep closer watch on the rebel city, Felipe ordered the building of *La Ciudadela* (the Citadel) overlooking Barcelona. It became for Catalans a much-hated reminder of defeat and a symbol of the new Spain—united at long last as a nation called *España*.

The forty-six-year reign of Felipe V was the longest of modern Spanish history. It was a time of interminable warfare with little or no lasting effects. (As Samuel Johnson remarked, eighteenth-century European politics was much too complicated to understand or bother with.) Although he managed to break the gloomy Habsburg spell, Felipe was a poor symbol for a new age. Even as a young man, he became a hopeless hypochondriac, spending days in bed staring into space and granting midnight audiences to his ministers. Increasingly indolent and melancholic, he often refused to shave or change his stinking clothes for months on end. At other times palace life became the scene of wild and infantile games, with the king and his dwarfs chasing the queen and her ladies in waiting, snatching their wigs, tearing their clothes, and ripping out handfuls of hair in glee.

Maria Luisa died in 1714, worn out by her eccentric and oversexed, albeit totally devoted husband, who had to be stopped from crawling into his wife's bed for his marital rights the night before she died. One cynical minister said that all Felipe needed to keep him happy was "a couch and a woman's thighs." Faced with the king's mercurial moods, the Princess des Ursins immediately sought a successor to María Luisa.

Meanwhile, an Italian priest named Giulio Alberoni turned up at court and managed to worm his way into the inner circle, mostly with the gourmet meals he relished preparing for friends and victims alike. Together with Ursins, he selected as queen-to-be Elizabeth Farnese, niece of an Italian duke. She later remarked, "The Spanish do not like me, but I fully detest them also." Not a healthy attitude for the queen of Spain.

Alberoni, who became the new queen's adviser, soon outmaneuvered Ursins at court. Farnese was a woman of extraordinary energy and willpower, irresistibly attractive it was said, at least to Felipe, who became a docile servant to her political and sexual whims. Foreign policy became the queen's plaything; her main ambition was to provide thrones for her sons, and for the next forty years Italy (still a loose collection of independent states) became the center of Spanish intrigues.

Alberoni busied himself reviving the crippled Spanish army and navy and dreaming up bizarre schemes. Among them was a grandiose plot to persuade Sweden and Russia to invade Scotland in behalf of the Stuart pretender, James III. Although the two countries backed out, Alberoni readied an invasion fleet at Cádiz. James arrived from Rome in March 1719 and was welcomed with honors worthy of a reigning monarch. The hare-brained expedition actually put to sea, but was battered by storms off Cape Finisterre. A counterpart conspiracy in Scotland, known in British history as The Nineteen, also failed. Not long after, Alberoni was deposed.

Yet despite all the antics at court, Bourbon Spain was different—stronger, better governed, more prosperous, more attuned to the rest of Europe. Most important, the centuries-long Castilian push for one unified nation with Madrid supreme became a reality. During this period the red-and-gold national flag was adopted, a national anthem chosen, and a regular army formed. In fact, Spain under the Bourbons was more unified than Britain or even France. The ghost of Count-Duke Olivares had reason to smile.

Under the new order Aragón and Valencia became subject to Castilian laws and language in all official matters. After two centuries of struggle the quasi-independent status of these regions abruptly ended. A military governor reporting directly to the king replaced the old viceroy, and financial officers, mostly French functionaries, made sure that the regions were paying their share of taxes.

The great Louis XIV had proclaimed: "I am the state." His nephew agreed, often using the phrase "for such is my will" in royal decrees. For Bourbons, it was their divine right to rule. Having dealt with the regions, the new regime embarked on its twin goals of centralizing authority in the crown and unifying the morass of antiquated legal statutes and customs. The main power struggle involved the monarch and the high nobility, who traditionally controlled government councils. In place of these, the Bourbons created *departments* run by career bureaucrats who enjoyed privileged and aloof positions and remained loyal to the crown. Resentful nobles had no immediate means of resisting, with the stubborn regional parliaments now defunct and the Castilian Cortes, a feeble body that would convene only three times during the century.

The mass arrival of French and Italians profoundly affected Spain's static insularity, especially after the coming of Farnese and her entourage. Feeling their new home intellectually and culturally backward, the Bourbons brought in foreign technicians and sent young Spaniards abroad. Royal academies based on French models were founded, such as the Academy of Good Taste, which tried to establish neo-classical standards.

This was the century when intellectuals were obsessed with cataloguing, describing, and systematizing, and they produced dictionaries and encyclopedias rather than masterpieces. A history of Spanish literature by Mohedano reached ten volumes and took twenty-five years to write, though it did not get beyond the Roman author Seneca. Nothing could have been further from the transcendent genius of the *Siglo de Oro*. One bright spot for creative literature was the poetry of Juan Meléndez Valdés. For about a century official art became totally French and Italian, until Goya arrived on the scene. Having failed to "hispanicize" Europe the previous century, Spain now experienced a Bourbon campaign to make it European. France's domination of its southern neighbor gave rise to the popular expression, "When France sneezes, Spain rejoins: Bless You!"

The king despised the somber Escorial and decided to create a mini-Versailles at La Granja de San Ildefonso near Segovia. Strolling around the perfectly symmetrical, manicured gardens and through the ornate rooms, visitors today find it hard to believe they are not in France. Felipe succeeded in re-creating the palace of his childhood, right down to the imported chestnut trees. La Granja's twenty-six spring-fed fountains, designed by French sculptors, are among the world's finest.

After Madrid's old *alcázar* was destroyed by fire, work commenced on the Royal Palace, and when finished it amazed European visitors as a worthy rival to Buckingham and Schonbrunn. The magnificent abode at Aranjuez south of Madrid was also completed to please Bourbon tastes, and the court moved between the various palaces with the regularity of a traveling circus.

Nevertheless, with the passing years Felipe grew more despondent and homesick for France. Even La Granja was not good enough. During several lengthy periods he refused to leave his room, and though rarely violent toward others, he would bite and scratch himself viciously. Elizabeth tried to frustrate his attempts to abdicate, but during one spell of black melancholy in 1724, the forty-year-old king stepped aside for his son, then sixteen. He became the little-known King Luis I of Spain. Unfortunately, Luis died of smallpox just seven months later, and Felipe resumed his royal duties for another two decades. Largely through his wife's efforts, the king's depression was kept under control. She sent for the greatest singer of the day, the Neapolitan *castrato* Farinelli, whose job it was to entertain the king and soothe his nervous tension. Felipe was so enchanted by the singer's ethereal voice that Farinelli stayed on at court, singing the same four arias nightly for the next ten years.

By the end of Felipe's reign, Spain's prestige and military might were almost as great as in its days of glory. French and Spanish Bourbons signed the Family Pact, and Britain re-emerged as Spain's chief enemy for the entire century, largely due to English commercial ambitions in the Mediterranean and Americas. One curious conflict occurred in 1739: the War of Jenkins' Ear. By previous treaty, Britain enjoyed a monopoly of the American slave trade, and its ships were exempt from examination or duty. Naturally, this produced a lively contraband trade and piracy in the Caribbean, mostly out of Jamaica. Weary of incessant infractions since the days of Henry Morgan, Spain began searching British vessels.

In the midst of this tension, a Mr. Jenkins turned up in London with a box containing his severed ear, claiming that it had been lopped off years earlier by a Spaniard. Both Parliament and the public were outraged and made Jenkins' ear the symbol of Spanish "harassment." All this poppycock led to war, but Spanish victories soon proved that Bourbon reforms were working, at least in rebuilding the military. After a year, the conflict merged with the War of Austrian Succession and became an odd footnote to a confused era. Yet it did in fact mark a turning point: after 1750 Britain replaced Austria as Spain's major enemy.

This was the century of the Enlightenment, when ideals such as rationalism, natural law, and scientific progress became the rage in intellectual circles. Writers such as Voltaire pointed an accusing finger at Catholic, traditional Spain as the epitome of backwardness and intolerance. Their invective did much to carry the Black Legend into modern times. Voltaire even concocted a false decree from the Spanish king ordering the exterminatation of the American Indians.

By mid century, the new ideas were trickling into the peninsula, brought in part by French families living in Spain. A few Spanish adherents came forth to promote the new ideas (*luces*) through local societies called Friends of the Country. These were designed to promote innovations in agriculture, commerce, industry and science, among them the Economic Society of Madrid. (Under its auspices a minister named Jovellanos later produced a brilliant report on agrarian reform.) One notable spokesman for the new ideas was a Benedictine monk named Feijóo, who attacked astrology, magic, false miracles and other forms of popular superstition. Wrote one admirer: "Thanks to the immortal Feijóo, spirits no longer trouble our houses, witches have fled our towns, the evil eye does not plague the tender child, and an eclipse does not dismay us."

Standing squarely in opposition to "enlightened" progress was the Catholic Church and its dreaded Inquisition, living symbol of how far out of step Spain remained. The church, especially the Jesuits, fought with all its considerable powers, not only banning and burning books, but also hauling up suspects to face the grand inquisitor. Wrote one critic, "The frightful caverns of the Inquisition open up to swallow the poor wretch who has incurred the indignation of the priests and hypocrites. Spain is a thousand leagues from Europe and ten centuries from the eighteenth."

Yet Enlightenment thought did make some inroads in Spain, and the seeds of ideas planted during this era would grow and bear fruit in the next

century with liberalism, revolution, and other concepts born during the Enlightenment. However, the intellectual ferment affected only a tiny minority. Devotion to the Catholic religion remained the strongest social force in Spain, especially among superstitious commoners. There was no shortage of miracle workers, such as the Beata of Cuenca, who claimed her flesh had been transformed

A matador incites a bull in a Spanish *plaza de toros*. Bullfighting became a national passion.

into the body and blood of Christ. A fierce intellectual struggle broke out between those wanting to share in European progress and those afraid that Spain was losing its unique identity to the onslaught of Francophiles. Conservatives blasted the Masonic lodges, known for spreading Enlightenment ideas, and appealed for the return to true "Spanishness."

Many customs today regarded as typically Spanish sprang from the widespread hostility to France at this time. In spite of (or because of) several royal bans, the bullfight became popular and evolved into its modern form: aristocrats on horseback were replaced by matadors on foot working with short sword and cape. (The aristocratic version survives with the *rejoneo* style.)

Likewise, religious festivals and processions such as *Semana Santa* (Holy Week) took on new fervor, and young people adopted the folkloric style of dress and manners seen in Goya's paintings of the *majos y majas*. These lower-class idols were intensely anti-French young bullies who wore long capes and broad-brimmed hats. The fashion spread, and it was said that "a Spaniard might be willing to go around without shoes, but without a cape, never. They are even buried in them."

Another reason the new ideas met resistance was that Spain really *was* different. The census of 1797 put the unproductive classes, from grandees down to vagrants, at 30 percent of the male population. Mendicants subsisted on a free pittance from the church and spent their lives in idleness and rags. Even worse, two classes—the nobility and the church—held about two-thirds of the land, most of which lay fallow. About half-a-million Spaniards claimed noble birth (more than in France, which had twice the population), and they shared contempt for farming and the "vile trades."

The grandees derived their power from their *señoríos*, rights dating back to the Reconquest. The dukes of Alba, for instance, were *señores* of one-quarter of Salamanca province, 168 towns and villages in all, as well as vast tracts of Andalucía. Beneath them came the *hidalgos*. Their mansions can be seen throughout Spain, especially in Andalucían towns such as Ronda and Baeza, where social life centered on horse breeding and other gentlemanly pursuits. Carlos III had abolished the ban on *hidalgos* doing manual labor, but such enlightened bourgeois values threatened the very concept of an unproductive nobility and met staunch resistance. In Spain, the minor gentry still preferred beggary to work, and a royal proclamation that trade and manual labor were *not* incompatible with honor had little impact. Much of the nation's essential work was not getting done.

As a prop of the old order and its ways of thinking, the church's influence was pervasive, percolating down to every level of life. The numbers were staggering—about 250,000 Spaniards were priests or members of religious orders. The power of the parish priest went unchallenged, especially in the stable peasant societies of the north, where Catholicism was not just a faith but like a second skin. Educational institutions also resisted the Enlightenment for a simple reason: the Jesuits controlled Spanish schools, where the guiding principle was still the quite unenlightened *la letra con sangre entra*, "it takes a little blood to let learning in."

Spanish scientific progress has never kept pace with the rest of Europe, a fact which some blame on Spaniards' extreme individualism, unsuited to "teamwork" and methodical research. While other countries excelled in mathematics and science, Spain produced theologians and painters. In the age of Bacon and Descartes, the study of science languished and theological problems were endlessly debated at the clergy-riddled universities. While the rest of Europe advanced in technology, Spaniards were discussing which language the angels spoke and whether the sky was made of bell metal or a wine-like liquid. On the positive side, the second half of the century witnessed some progress in the biological and natural sciences. A botanical garden was founded in Madrid and scientific expeditions sent to America.

Fernando (Ferdinand) VI, Felipe's eldest surviving son by María Luisa, succeeded his anguished but long-lived father in 1746. Everyone was eager for peace—and to be rid of Elizabeth Farnese. The new consort was Barbara of Braganza, a homely but strong-willed Portuguese princess who shared her husband's desire for neutrality and reform. Fernando replaced French advisors with Spanish, and under the sure hand of ministers such as Ensenada, finances were reorganized, the navy expanded, and the Inquisition's feared *autos de fé* stopped. (The Inquisition's last victim, an old crone accused of "having carnal converse with the Devil and laying eggs that had prophecies written on them," was burned at the stake in Sevilla in 1780.) Under Fernando, a concordat was signed with the pope placing the Spanish church largely under the king's authority, which capped a long struggle.

These were years of tranquility and recuperation. The royal couple was devoted to each other and to enlightened prosperity and good music (their "royal master" was Domenico Scarlatti). For diversion, they enjoyed sailing in the "toy fleet" of barges that cruised the Tajo River at Aranjuez. Unfortunately, this dream world began to crumble after just a few years. Devastating earthquakes rocked the peninsula in 1755 and 1756, and several cities (including Lisbon) were destroyed. After Barbara died two years later, Fernando lapsed into the typical family melancholia. At times he sat motionless on a stool for hours; at others he lay in bed screaming and throwing dishes at the servants. Fernando died a year after his wife.

And yet, despite troubles within the monarchy, Spain was once more a prosperous nation with a powerful fleet and modern army for the first time. By mid century the Spanish economy was undergoing a remarkable transformation as Basque shipyards bustled and Catalonian looms hummed. By the end of the 1700s Cataluña was second in textile production only to England; once again Barcelona became a great Mediterranean port and Spain's leader in commerce and industry. Ironically, the Bourbons' destruction of Cataluña's medieval rights may have helped push the region toward the economic modernization that became its great strength.

In Castilla there was reason for concern: the peninsula's coastal areas were outstripping the center in population, economic growth, and standard of living. While Bourbon centralization was trying to pull everything to the capital, economic realities were doing just the opposite. Something had to give. Two vastly different Spains were emerging: the center and south—arid, sparsely populated, with large landholdings—and the coastal areas of the north and east with small farms, growing industries, and open ports. A line drawn between the two areas roughly corresponds (except for Madrid) with the front lines during the first year of the Spanish Civil War almost two centuries later. That is not mere coincidence.

Spain's crucial economic problem was land, its distribution and use in a staunchly conservative society trying meekly to reform. There was corresponding agricultural diversity, from the poorest type of dry cereal farming on the *meseta* to the verdant gardens of Valencia, from the handkerchief plots of Galicia to the sprawling untilled estates of the south. Perhaps the most important impediment to progress was the land itself, with its poor soil and erratic rainfall. For these reasons, Spain did not achieve the dramatic rise in agricultural production seen elsewhere in Europe, a rise that helped lead to the Industrial Revolution.

There was another essential split developing in Spanish society between the cities and countryside (and its villages). Spain was still overwhelmingly rural, with only a few cities of more than 100,000 inhabitants. Generally, the great unwashed and untitled masses lived in isolated, backwater towns and shunned anything that smacked of novelty. Everything revolved around the *pueblo* (village), whose very name in Spanish also means "the people." The typical Spaniard saw himself belonging first to his village or town, then to his province or region, and finally to his nation. Castilian was not even universally understood much less spoken at this time. The language is full of contemptuous references to other regions, such as "rather be a slut than a Gallegan." The persistence of the *pueblo* phenomenon sprang from poor roads and communications in a countryside often sparsely populated and dangerous. Early travelers, such as a British major touring Spain in 1774, reported that Andalucía was a land of smugglers and bandits chased by the *migueletes*, predecessors of the civil guard.

Most cities were squalid. Madrid was the worst of all, with about 150,000 residents living on narrow, dark streets where slop was hurled from the windows onto unsuspecting passers-by. People fled to the cafés where (believe it or not) laws prohibited smoking, reading newspapers, talking politics, or playing cards. The capital's medieval panorama began to change with the Bourbons (especially Carlos III) who sprinkled Madrid with new buildings, the first sewage system, and street lighting. Order improved after neighborhood watchmen called *serenos* were introduced. With the wider, more pleasant streets, the *paseo* (stroll) became a mandatory evening social activity. For literary types, the *tertulia* was a conversational gathering in a bar or café, where the drink of choice was chocolate, considered one of life's necessities. The state lottery was also introduced in this era and became a fixture in Spanish life.

For the upper crust, elaborate carriages became the rage. This aristocratic means of transport reached a remarkable level of sumptuousness, with gilded panels, monograms, and decorative shells to dazzle humble observers. The Carriage Museum next to the Royal Palace in Madrid contains an impressive display of these delightful vehicles from another era.

When Fernando died childless in 1759, his half-brother (son of Farnese and Felipe V) succeeded him as Carlos (Charles) III. The new king came well prepared, having served twenty-four years as king of Naples, and he is considered a bright star in the dark sky of the Spanish monarchy. Carlos was one of Europe's new "enlightened despots," whose attitude might be described as "Everything for the people, but nothing by the people." Indeed, with all his good intentions, Carlos governed more despotically than even Felipe II would have dared. He once remarked, "My subjects are like children; they cry when they are washed."

Goya's portrait of Carlos hanging in the Prado is sympathetic if not flattering: a narrow face creased with wrinkles, piercing blue eyes, a prominent nose and drooping mouth. (It was said that Princess Adelaide of France refused to marry him after one look at his portrait.) Carlos was not a brilliant man and comes off as something of a yokel in Goya's work—in a simple hunter's costume, musket in hand. His main diversion was deer hunting, and he lived an untypically modest life as a widower.

Carlos ruled through a series of astute ministers, often Italians or Spanish Francophiles. For example, his trusted aide from Naples, the marquis of Esquilache, became minister of finance and war. Together they unleashed an offensive to crush the foot-dragging church and sheath the sword of the Inquisition. Even though Carlos was a pious Catholic, he targeted the Jesuits in particular for royal discipline, mainly because of their fanatical loyalty to the pope. Moreover, they were generally nuisances in a society trying painfully to make intellectual headway. For example, Jesuits claimed that events such as the great Lisbon earthquake were "punishment from God" and opposed any relief efforts.

An odd series of events led to the expulsion from Spain of this "fighting order" of priests. (The unpopular Jesuits had already been booted out of France and Portugal.) First, the government tried to outlaw the traditional cape and brimmed-hat on the grounds that criminals used them to hide weapons. Troops patrolled the streets of Madrid, accompanied by tailors brandishing shears to cut the offending capes and pins to fold back hat brims into the acceptable French tricorn. Matters were made worse by the high price of bread at the time, and serious riots ensued, which were blamed on the Jesuits. The Count of Aranda, friend of Voltaire and member of the Freemasons, ordered several thousand priests and novices rounded up and shipped off to Rome. Ironically, the pope himself did not allow the Jesuits to land, and when their boats arrived in Italy, papal troops threatened to open fire. Most of the fugitives went to Corsica, but were later allowed into Italy. A few years later the pope abolished the Society of Jesus altogether.

The three decades of Carlos III's rule were much more positive in tone, however. For the first time in memory, Spain entered the European mainstream. Madrid was transformed with the royal palace, the future home of the Prado Museum, the Alcalá arch and Cibeles fountain, and grand avenues such as Madrid's Paseo del Prado and Las Ramblas in Barcelona, all in the neoclassical style. Spanish-baroque architecture also continued to flourish in the 1700s, as many older churches and mansions received new facades or interiors. The exuberance of the age outdid itself with the gushingly ornate Churrigueresque style, named for three architects: brothers José, Joaquin, and Alberto Churriguera.

"Enlightened" public works took precedence over church building for the first time. Spanish roads had outraged travelers for years, but a new corps of road engineers began a highway network shooting out from Madrid like the spokes of a wheel. The great Canal of Aragón (begun two centuries earlier) was finally completed, and, true to the times, the king even built a model port near the mouth of the Ebro.

Carlos thought big and acted decisively, usually with success. He called for Spain's first census in 1768 (Britain's first was in 1801), which counted 10.2 million residents, a healthy increase after the decimation of the final Habsburg years. To deal with sparse population in the bandit-riddled Sierra Morena, the king arranged for about six thousand Bavarian immigrants to settle in thirteen new villages. To bolster the army, one man in five was drafted for eight year-stints. In another decisive measure, the king ended the ancient privileges of the Mesta. One area in which even Carlos had to struggle was agrarian reform; here he met with virulent opposition from landed interests.

Foreign policy under Carlos got off on the wrong foot. Spain's late entry into the Seven Years War between Britain and France led to humiliating defeats in Cuba and the Philippines, although the Treaty of Paris largely confirmed Spain's American territories. The tension heated up under the Anglophobic Carlos. Sources of hostility lay in Gibraltar and Menorca, which Spain claimed, and in Britain's lust for the Spanish Empire. And there was already friction over the Falkland Islands (Las Malvinas) after the arrival of some English "settlers" in the 1770s.

The American Revolution gave both France and Spain a chance for revenge, and both nations aided the Americans. A combined Spanish-French fleet took control of the English Channel and prevented Britain from sending reinforcements to the beleaguered Lord Cornwallis, who was forced to surrender to the Americans in 1781. There is a story that money intended to finish the second tower of Málaga's cathedral was diverted to help the American colonists. The church, known as *la manquita* (the one-armed) still has only one tower.

For Spain the war's most notable event was the Great Siege of Gibraltar. Lord Elliot and his men defended "the Rock", and today you can get a real glimpse of the siege by visiting the Upper Galleries in Gibraltar. Here, men using hand tools and explosives cut gun positions into solid rock and installed the heavy cannons that decided the battle. The attackers used enormous, heavily armed floating batteries in Gibraltar Bay, but were driven back by cannonballs raining down from above. After three years of unsuccessful attack, Gibraltar had proved impregnable to the armies of that day.

Nevertheless, when all the smoke had cleared and all the deals were done at the Treaty of Versailles (1783), Spain tasted the sweet grapes of revenge, winning back Menorca and a good deal of pride. Spain's power was its greatest in nearly two centuries, especially in the New World, where the empire still took in all of South and Central America (except for Brazil and Guiana), as well as Mexico, Florida, and the vast Louisiana territory. (Spain's share of lands that became the United States was far larger than England's.) Soldiers and priests were taming the American southwest (the future Texas, New Mexico, and Arizona), and a humble fray from Mallorca, Junipero Serra, was finishing a string of missions in a faraway land called California. Spain, the fallen giant, was still a world power.

One interesting footnote: the name *California* derived from a Spanish novel published in 1510 called *Las Sergas de Esplandian*. For several generations after the first landfall, Spaniards believed that California was an island, and the book described it as such. "I wish you now to learn of the strangest thing ever written or recorded by man. To the west of the Indies there was an island, called California, very close to the earthly Paradise, inhabited by black women with no men among them, and who lived as the Amazons did."

In this third century of empire, America seemed oblivious to the chronic crises of Europe. Nevertheless, Spain's loose-knit control could not successfully resist aggressive interlopers forever. British merchants backed by the royal fleet rallied round the Black Legend by supporting the "end of despotism" in order to carve a slice of the American market. And they succeeded. As the popular saying went, "Where Spain keeps the cow, the rest of Europe drinks the milk." The opening up of trade to Spain's non-Castilian cities (1778) helped some, but by then much of America had become an economic fief of foreigners. Moreover,

The formidable and much-disputed Rock of Gibraltar, British territory since 1713

administrative reforms from the enlightened monarchs, the first major changes in two centuries, actually served to undermine Spain's control. Reformers suffered from the delusion that good government would solve colonial problems. But their policies backfired. Under corrupt and inefficient viceroys, Creoles had grown wealthy and independent, and the new laws merely underscored the inconvenience of the Spanish connection.

Following the American Revolution isolated rumblings of discontent stirred in Spain's colonies. In Peru, Tupac Amaru, supposedly a descendent of the Inca kings, led an uprising of sixty thousand Indians that was severely crushed—Amaru's body was mutilated and pulled apart by teams of wild horses—proving that behind every legend (even black ones) is some fact. Rebellions would become commonplace after 1800.

The French Revolution had even greater impact than the American, upsetting the precarious union (achieved by Carlos III) between crown and enlightened Spaniards. In truth, the great reforms of the past few decades sprang from enlightened despots and shrewd ministers who permitted no opposition or debate. Now Spain found itself at odds with the spirit of the times, what might loosely be called "democracy." The French Revolution terrified Spaniards generally, especially after moderation boiled over into the Reign of Terror. Minister Floridablanca threw up an unsuccessful *cordon sanitaire* along the border to keep out the revolutionary virus, and every foreigner entering Spain was forced to swear an oath of allegiance to the throne and Catholic Church.

Carlos III died in 1788 of a cold caught while hunting. His second son, Carlos (Charles) IV, was a simple fellow of forty with a taste for clocks and fine embroidery. His mushy will and fuzzy intellect did not bode well for dealing with two decades of challenge, though some historians claim he has been judged too harshly. Nevertheless, he soon came under the domination of María Luisa of Parma, his Italian wife. Goya's portraits show her as strong-willed and modestly attractive, with auburn hair, hypnotic eyes, and a sensuous mouth. According to reports Carlos himself was dissolute, but the queen was downright abandoned to sensuality. Their advanced state of physical and moral decay comes through well in Goya's dazzling and disturbing masterpiece, *The Family of Carlos IV*.

Francisco José de Goya y Lucientes was born near Zaragoza and became the official court painter for thirty years. In that position he moved in the highest circles and had a stormy affair with the Duchess of Alba, Spain's richest woman. She was *not* the model for the famous *majas* (naked and clothed), but a portrait of her does exist in which she points to words in the sand at her feet that read *"Solo Goya."*

It is from Goya that we enjoy a remarkably clear picture of the era. In addition to royal portraits, he created scenes of typical Spanish life in paintings and hundreds of tapestries, today on display at Madrid's Royal Tapestry Factory. We see common people working or at *fiestas* and high society living the idyllic life. Later, after a serious illness left him deaf, his art became darker and more biting. A series of 80 satiric etchings called the *caprichos* depicts foppish gallants, pompous priests, and ladies of easy virtue. And there was much more to come as the old world crumbled in the following decades.

Carlos IV was a first cousin of Louis XVI, and after the French king met the guillotine (1793), Spain found itself at war with revolutionary France, which vowed "to help all peoples who desire to recover their liberty." Waves of anti-French and anti-Revolutionary sentiment swept across Spain, including a popular belief that a mortal struggle for control was taking place between Freemasons and Jesuits. In time, liberals and progressives of any stripe came to be seen as traitors to Spain and its traditional values, the origin of the profound split into the "two Spains" so often blamed for the nation's ills.

Carlos appointed a royal guard named Manuel Godoy, twenty-five at the time, to serve as chief minister, and he proved to be a loyal servant for two decades. According to the popular version of the story, this handsome young man from Extremadura had caught the queen's eye, and many believed he became her lover. It was a common practice among aristocratic women of the time, and Carlos seemed willing to play the cuckold. No one was really sure how much the king knew, but the queen herself referred to the strange relationship as "the earthly trinity." Naturally the common people were outraged at rumors of such scandalous behavior.

Godoy was an adventurer with more ambition than brains, and he could be vain, tactless, and opinionated. But he was far from the buffoon of legend; many of his "enlightened" ideas and programs continued the best work of Carlos III. In any case, the royal couple showered him with honors and gifts, naming him Prince of Peace (which outraged the grandees) and giving him a carriage with his own monogram. In time María Luisa, about twice Godoy's age, treated him more as a spoiled son than a lover, but she also regarded him as a political genius. The aristocracy and commoners reacted with disgust, and crown prince Fernando (Ferdinand) strongly resented his mother's brazen affair. The idea that a cuckold king, a lascivious queen, and an empty-headed paramour were governing Spain broke the regal spell Carlos III had cast over Spaniards. The monarchy would never again be quite the same.

In 1795, with the relatively moderate Directory running the show in Paris, Godoy struck a treaty with France that pledged military cooperation against Britain. Sporadic war raged for the next few years. With Napoleon Bonaparte's coup d'etat in 1799, royalist Spain slept easier, viewing his rise as the first step toward Bourbon restoration. The Spanish king launched a fierce crackdown on liberal ministers, and even Godoy fell under the scrutiny of a revived Inquisition for "atheism and immorality." (He was absolved.)

Carlos feared French ambitions in Italy, but Bonaparte wanted Spanish support and flattered the royal couple with presents. His cynical intentions soon became clear, however, when Spain found itself taking part in an invasion of Portugal, England's ally. This "War of the Oranges" inspired Goya's painting of a swaggering Godoy on a mock battlefield with the bombastic title *Generalissimo of the Armies*. As usual, Godoy's "crimes" were really his vulgarity and ostentation.

War with England ceased briefly in 1804, the same year Napoleon declared himself emperor, then resumed. Like the proverbial lamb, Spain went willingly to the slaughter as France's ally, the executioner none other than Lord Nelson. The British fleet met a French-Spanish navy off Cape Trafalgar (between Algeciras and Cádiz) on October 21, 1805, in one of history's most decisive battles. In Gibraltar, you can visit Trafalgar cemetery, where many of the fallen lie, and see the beach where the fatally wounded Nelson was carried ashore. (Later his body was pickled in rum and shipped back to England, according to legend.)

This great British triumph destroyed the Spanish fleet, so painstakingly built up during the 1700s, and was the *real* end of Spain's sea power, 217 years after the defeat of the Invincible Armada. It also signaled the end of Spain's ability to protect its empire, either from revolutionaries within or from foreign navies. France too had been badly hurt at Trafalgar, but Napoleon was still in firm control on land, and many great victories lay ahead.

Two years after Trafalgar, a treaty between France and Spain arranged for the partition of Portugal, with Godoy receiving the southern section as

"Hereditary Prince of Algarves." Bonaparte's troops poured into the peninsula, but what had been agreed as "safe passage" through Spain to Portugal soon became outright occupation. By March of 1808, a hundred thousand French soldiers were on Spanish soil, and they controlled Madrid itself. Rumors began to spread that Godoy was conspiring with Napoleon to deprive Prince Fernando of his rightful inheritance.

The two men had clashed before, as much for the queen's affection as the rights of succession. Fernando had in fact secretly approached Bonaparte with a scheme to overthrow the "earthly trinity" and praised him as the "savior of Europe." Someone (one of those great "someones" of history) left a note on the king's dressing table informing him of the plot, and Fernando, caught trying to conceal papers, was arrested for high treason. After three days of interrogation he made a humiliating confession: "I crave Your Majesty's pardon for having deceived you, and beg, as a grateful son, to kiss your royal feet." He was promptly pardoned, but his own mother called him "a spiked vine of cowardice."

In the popular mind Godoy rather than Fernando had come to represent collusion with the French, but even he had begun to suspect Napoleon's real motives. Sensing trouble, Godoy and the royal couple left Madrid hurriedly, heading south to the palace at Aranjuez. To the hysterical populace it seemed that the "earthly trinity" were trying to escape. In just a few hours, the scene at Aranjuez was uncomfortably similar to Versailles just before the French Revolution, as gangs of malcontents from Madrid descended on the palace demanding justice.

The following events marked the end of the Old Regime in Spain. On March 18 violent riots broke out, and Godoy only managed to save his skin by hiding for two days in a rolled-up carpet. When he emerged it was too late: Carlos had abdicated to his son, proclaimed as King Fernando (Ferdinand) VII. Godoy was roughed up by the rabble and made to grovel at his rival's feet. The masses had entered Spanish politics with a vengeance. A thrill of expectation swept across Spain at the prospect of a new monarch who, ironically, came to symbolize staunch opposition to the French after his spineless father. In reality, the knave had succeeded the fool: Fernando VII, the most contemptible king in Spanish history.

Sights & Sites

Aranjuez (Madrid): Neo-classical Royal Palace dates from the reign of Felipe V; Carlos IV signed abdication in throne room.

Cádiz: Model of town during reign of Carlos III in Historical Museum; Cathedral, built 1720-1838, has outstanding silver collection.

Fuendetodos (Zaragoza): Goya's House (birthplace)

Gibraltar: Upper Galleries and Trafalgar Cemetery date from Napoleonic wars.

Madrid: National Library founded in 1711 by Felipe V has one of Europe's largest collections, including eight hundred editions of *Don Quixote*; much of city is a neo-classical showcase of Carlos III: Royal Palace, Cibeles Fountain, Alcalá Arch, etc.; Chapel of San Antonio de la Florida has fresco by Goya; Prado Museum's Goya rooms are superb; Royal Tapestry Factory has display of Goya originals; Basilica of San Francisco el Grande has imposing facade by Sabatini.

Petra (Mallorca): House-Museum of native son Junipero Serra, famous missionary of California.

Puerto de la Cruz (Canary Islands): Botanical Gardens dating from reign of Carlos III are outstanding.

Ronda (Málaga): Beautiful bullring built in 1785; scene of annual Goyesque Fair devoted to eighteenth-century-style bullfighting.

Salamanca: The Plaza Mayor, built for the city by Felipe V, is among most beautiful in Spain; designed by the Churriguera brothers.

La Granja Palace near Segovia was a perfect re-creation of a French palace for the royal elite.

Santa Cruz de Tenerife (Canary Islands): Attacking Paso Alto Castle in 1797, Lord Nelson lost his arm.

Santiago de Compostela (La Coruña): Baroque facade (1750) of earlier cathedral is a masterpiece by Fernando Casas.

Segovia: La Granja de San Ildefonso and Riofrio palaces built by Philip V and Elizabeth Farnese, eleven kms. from town.

Sevilla: Gaudy baroque specimens are Chapel of San José and San Telmo Palace.

Toledo: Transparente by Narciso Tome is a controversial baroque island in the famous Gothic Cathedral.

Vic (Barcelona): Neo-Classical Cathedral (1781-1803) and Episcopal Museum.

Zaragoza: Seo Cathedral has a fine baroque facade.

Chapter 8

Liberal Spain

Hanging in Madrid's Prado Museum are two of Goya's most powerful canvases, titled simply *The Second of May* and *The Third of May*. Together they depict the most important forty-eight hours in Spanish history, essentially the birth of modern Spain. For the story of Spain and its empire, the year 1808 was the most important since 1492. Events shook the nation from centuries of ingrained attitudes, astounded a continent on the verge of collapse before Napoleon, and set ablaze the whole of Spanish America.

On May 2, 1808, a Madrid mob rose with incredible fury against the French army and its Mameluke cavalry. Men and women from the poor neighborhoods grabbed any weapon they could find—knives, shovels, sticks, axes—and descended on the intruders. Balconies and windows vomited a shower of tiles, bricks, stones, boiling water, washtubs, and furniture. In *Dos de Mayo* Goya painted knife-wielding women pulling the terrified Mamelukes from their horses. Dozens of these Egyptian mercenaries were bludgeoned to death before French regulars regained control. Throughout the uproar wealthy *madrileños* locked their doors, and the Spanish garrison stayed meekly in its quarters. This was a new type of popular street rising that would come again. Those suspected of the massacre were rounded up and executed the following day, a scene Goya witnessed from a nearby window while he sketched feverishly. More than its companion oil, the painting *Tres de Mayo* is considered a landmark of modern art, both in its impassioned theme and innovative technique. Goya captured all the emotion of the scene—the ominous firing squad, the terrified but defiant victims with their outstretched arms, the blood-drenched corpses rapidly filling the square. He also preserved for eternity those few frenzied moments that marked the start of Spain's War of Independence (also known as the Peninsular War).

Goya himself viewed that war with the same mixed emotions felt by many Spaniards. As any good patriot he detested the invader, but he greatly admired many French accomplishments championed by Napoleon, which seemed to herald a new world capable of replacing Spain's inert society. In the end Goya came to detest war regardless of its outcome; his series of searing etchings, *Disasters of War* (also in the Prado), contain no marching armies or glorious deeds, only the horror and destruction of warfare. To Goya we owe our visual perceptions of these frightful times. His macabre vision took Spanish realism into realms never imagined by Velázquez or Ribera.

After his father's forced abdication at Aranjuez in March, a triumphant Fernando had returned to Madrid. Here, the new king by acclamation discovered that a French army under Murat had occupied his capital the day before. Napoleon, refusing to recognize Fernando's claims, summoned the royal family and Godoy. Appearing before the emperor at Bayonne, they put on a degrading spectacle that shocked even the cynical Frenchman, shouting scandalous insults at each other and groveling for his favor. When Fernando brashly accused his mother of repeated adultery, Napoleon quickly pointed out that if this were true it might create doubts about his own lineage and compromise his claims to the throne. The French ruler later wrote that Carlos was "a nice man" but his son "very stupid and very wicked" and the queen "has her past and her character written on her face, which is all I need say. It surpasses anything one dare imagine."

Fernando was forced to abdicate to his father, then Carlos in turn to Napoleon's brother, Joseph Bonaparte. Fernando was detained at the emperor's pleasure and would not see Spain again for six years. Word spread among Spaniards that their "prince charming" was urging resistance, and they dubbed him *el deseado* ("the desired one"). Carlos, his queen, and Godoy were packed off to early retirement and a lifetime of exile in France. Even after their scandalous world came tumbling down, however, they remained loyal and devoted to one other. (The ex-king and his queen died within the same month in 1819, while Godoy managed to survive another three decades, finally dying in obscurity in Paris.) Deposing the Spanish Bourbons was one of Napoleon's most high-handed actions and later, in exile on St. Helena, he traced his own downfall to that one day's events at Bayonne.

As Napoleon conducted his four-ring circus in France, the events leading to May Second were unfolding back in Madrid. Crowds gathered outside the palace, and rumors spread that the royal family had been lured away to be murdered. For all their scorn for the "earthly trinity," people were outraged; and their love for Fernando grew more passionate. After some minor incidents the mob grew unruly, and French soldiers fired into the crowd, setting off the citywide melee. In a matter of days, word of the Madrid revolt hurtled though the nation, and men from all corners of the peninsula began to take up arms. Napoleon was livid when he heard the news, but predicted a quick end to the affair.

Placed on the throne by his brother, Joseph Bonaparte found few supporters in Spain.

"Spaniards, after a long agony your nation is perishing. I have seen your ills and I shall remedy them." Thus read Napoleon's proclamation to the Spanish nation, unfurled by his brother as he launched his brief reign as King José I. It was Joseph's mission to replace Spain's medieval remnants with modern French ideas and systems, to complete the work begun by the great reformer-king, Carlos III. But the emperor had misjudged his brother, who has been described as amiable, placid, and soft-spoken—decidedly un-Napoleonic traits. He also misjudged the Spanish temperament. Within months the "intruder king" would write: "My position is unique in history. I have not a single supporter here."

Joseph was exaggerating to make his point. Most Spaniards still listened to fire-breathing conservative friars for political guidance, but the "new order" appealed to many intellectuals weary of Bourbon incompetence and sloth. Many young men had welcomed the French Revolution and its ideals and belonged to republican clubs and Masonic lodges. These Spanish supporters faced a profound crisis in having to choose between revolutionary France and reactionary Spain, between head and heart as it were. Those who served Joseph would one day regret their choice, and hidebound traditionalists could henceforth equate liberal thinking with treason.

The outburst of Spanish resistance was spontaneous and reckless, challenging Europe's finest army to combat without a thought of its own strengths or those of the enemy. Napoleon's fatal mistake was to underestimate these ill-trained, ill-equipped bands of patriots fighting for their homeland, and by summer his army had suffered setbacks at Valencia and Bailén (Jaén). Although regular units fought these battles, Spaniards soon became famed for their devastating hit-and-run tactics, guerrilla warfare in the long-standing Iberian tradition. This often-romanticized style of fighting was perfectly suited to the tough Spanish terrain and to the character of its residents.

Napoleon was so upset by Spanish victories that in November (1808) he arrived with 135,000 men to take personal command. In a month of brilliant soldiering he completely reversed the tide and marched into Madrid unopposed. French troops fanned out across the peninsula, taking control of the important towns despite some fierce resistance. At Zaragoza, for example, starving but defiant citizens (in the manner of ancient Iberians) threw back loaves of bread tossed over the city walls by French soldiers.

By the fall of 1810, the nucleus of Spain's loyalist government was cooped up in the seaport of Cádiz, surrounded by French troops. Adding insult to injury, Joseph made a triumphal march through Andalucía. But the French occupation was illusory, in spite of several hundred thousand troops under a gaggle of illustrious commanders. The peninsula was just too big to control. Communications lines were easily cut, and sizable armed escorts were required for simple things like delivering the mail. *Guerrilleros* struck at will, then retreated to their mountain strongholds.

Britain soon realized the importance of Spain's resistance and dispatched General Arthur Wellesley, the future Duke of Wellington, to Portugal. By the fall of 1810, he commanded about twenty-five thousand British troops and about the same number of Portuguese, compared with a French force at least five times that number. Yet Spaniards have never given the Iron Duke his proper due for helping to win their War of Independence. Madrid boasts no statue or street in his honor, even though he liberated the capital from French occupation. Nevertheless, victory was achieved in a two-pronged effort. Spanish guerrillas numbering about thirty thousand worked in perfect complement to British regulars in creating Napoleon's "Spanish ulcer." These savvy, ruthless fighters could tie up and harass huge numbers of French troops while Wellington and his aides carefully engineered one triumph after another.

The breakdown of the Bourbon government led to the creation of local and regional authorities called *juntas*, which tended to act with alarming independence and lack of cooperation. (Galicia sent its own emissary to London "as nation to nation," and Sevilla and Granada nearly went to war at one point.) As regionalism approached anarchy, a Central Junta formed at Aranjuez to rule in the name of Fernando. Among its members were Jovellanos and the venerable Count of Floridablanca. Later the group was forced to flee first to Sevilla, then Cádiz.

The famous Cortes (Parliament) of Cádiz convened at the Church of San Felipe Nero. Here, they produced the Constitution of 1812, the birth certificate of Liberal Spain. The men at Cádiz claimed to represent the nation in its darkest hour, but in reality they were far from typical Spaniards. The city itself boasted Spain's most bourgeois, liberal society, in which business acumen and commercial wealth counted more than aristocratic privilege. For obvious reasons, representatives from the different areas of Spain, especially the conservative interior, could not readily attend. Instead, Cádiz residents from those cities or regions (and the colonies), invariably more progressive than their compatriots back home, sat at the Cortes to decide the nation's future. They voiced the interests of a tiny minority.

The meeting of a single *national* parliament (as opposed to the traditional regional bodies) was a profound event, but it arrived long after the decline of Spain's medieval political institutions. Hence, there was no real tradition of a unified representative power strong enough to stand up to the monarchy. The celebrated Constitution of 1812 was an even more daring step than one might imagine. Echoing the recent American and French documents, it contained most of the liberal menu: sovereignty of the people; the sanctity of individual property rights; curtailment of aristocratic and church power; uniform laws; centralized government. The policies of enlightened despots such as Carlos III were pushed to their logical conclusion.

Unfortunately, the Cádiz "liberals" (the word itself is of Spanish origin) were building castles in the sand. The admirable but totally impractical constitution humbled Spain's two strongest institutions, the crown and the church, without creating anything strong enough to replace them. The monarchy was treated as a necessary evil; the Catholic Church, although acknowledged as the only "official" religion, had to accept the closing of its monasteries and other galling measures. Inevitably, both monarchs and bishops became instinctive enemies of the Cádiz liberals and their work.

Napoleon's downfall had begun on the peninsula, but the year 1812 brought even more serious problems with his sputtering Russian campaign. In Spain, the allies took advantage of large French troop withdrawals to score a string of victories at Ciudad Rodrigo, Badajoz, and Salamanca, followed by Wellington's triumphant entry into Madrid, an event painted by Goya. (The artist supposedly had to be restrained from shooting the outspoken general when he criticized Goya's work.)

The final victory came a year later at Vitoria in the Basque region, when an army of seventy thousand French was routed. (Beethoven composed *Wellington's Victory* to commemorate the battle.) King Joseph himself was present at the debacle and escaped capture by a whisker, losing his carriage and silver chamber pot in the confusion. Every June 21, in what must be the British army's strangest tradition, the men of the Tenth Hussars unit drink champagne from a replica of the pot. (The original sits in a Manchester museum.) And there *is* a monument to the victory in Vitoria's main square.

For all intents and purposes, the War of Independence was over. The struggle had cost the French about 180,000 casualties and sealed Napoleon's eventual fate. Spain "the giant killer" had dished out its revenge for centuries of French interference. Mild-mannered Joseph fled, and in the spring of 1814 Fernando, "the desired one," returned to the ecstatic adulation of his people. But Spain's troubles were only just beginning.

Except for the brief Spanish-American War (1898) and some colonial strife in Morocco, the War of Independence was Spain's last foreign conflict. But the war—and the French Revolution itself—unleashed most of the internal conflicts that would haunt Spain for generations, the source of countless political crises and several civil wars. Spanish nationalism was indeed born in this patriotic war against the French, but it was a highly reactionary variety that rallied to the defense of religion and king as well as country. Moreover, the national unity was hollow. Beneath the seeming solidarity, Spain was breaking up into unyielding factions of conservatives and liberals, traditionalists and reformers. From the return of Fernando to the last days of General

Franco the "two Spains" would grapple with the problem of the country's role in modern Europe.

The war also meant the final demise of Spain as a major European power. Much of the country's influence during the last century derived from its French alliance, but with this shattered Spain was relegated to a second-rate status. When the European powers met at the Congress of Vienna (1815) to decide the continent's fate, Spain was not invited to attend.

What really toppled Spain from its pedestal was the humiliating loss of most of its American empire during the war and its aftermath. Spain's occupation by Napoleon and the collapse of Spanish colonial authority provided the Creoles, an American-born economic and social elite of pure Spanish blood, with their chance to declare independence. Exploiting the myth of Spanish oppression, they convinced the normally passive natives to fight for their goals. Yet just a few decades later the beast they let loose would come back to devour them.

The new spirit of independence was led by Venezuelan Francisco de Miranda, whom Napoleon compared with Don Quixote "except that he is not mad." He called for the creation of a vast, enlightened country uniting all of South America to be called Columbia. Another prominent Creole and man of the Enlightenment (he studied in Paris) was Simon Bolívar, called "the George Washington of South America" for his key role in the liberation of five future countries: Bolivia, Peru, Ecuador, Venezuela, and Colombia.

Strong independence movements formed in Mexico, Venezuela, and Argentina around 1810. Two rabble-rousing priests led the Mexican insurgents, and their attempts to foster a social revolution scared off the Creoles and brought a loyalist triumph. Everywhere else the revolts met with success, but by the end of the Napoleonic Wars (1814) Spain's position was still salvageable. A year later a force of fourteen thousand royal troops under General Morillo arrived to fight the rebels. But force alone would not suffice, and Spain—itself exhausted and divided—utterly failed to offer any constructive solutions to the American problem.

"A Bourbon never learns anything, and never forgets anything" according to a traditional Spanish saying. Champion of Spain's proud and obstinate stance was *el deseado* himself, King Fernando VII. Born in 1785, he was only twenty-nine when he returned as conquering hero, yet he already possessed a markedly debauched look—bloated and bleary-eyed, with a huge lip and drooping nose. Even his own mother called him ugly, and his mother-in-law said that he was "hideous" and "utterly dull." Writer Gerald Brenan remarked that Fernando had all the defects of his people and none of their virtues. Nevertheless, the vast majority of Spaniards believed him a savior who had successfully defied Napoleon in captivity while he planned Spain's liberation. No one knew that he had spent these years living in vice and indolence on Talleyrand's splendid estate, forever trying to marry Napoleon's niece. Fernando's return coincided with the comeback of French king Louis XVIII as a wave of conservative reaction swept across Europe. In Spain, jubilant crowds shouted: "Long live our chains!" and "Viva despotism!" as Fernando marched toward Madrid.

Although some naive liberals pinned their hopes on the new king, it soon became clear that he intended to turn the clock back. His first decree declared the constitution null and void, and liberals who had fought the French while the king groveled before Napoleon were jailed or exiled. About twelve thousand reputed French sympathizers were banished, and the Jesuits returned and resumed their vise-grip on education.

To support this naked power play Fernando relied on his army of mass supporters throughout Spain. In Cádiz, an angry mob sacked the Cortes building, and in pulpits across the land liberal-bashing clergy thundered out their approval of the king's draconian methods. But in appealing to the masses, the church and crown released a genie that would never go back into the bottle again. Throughout the previous century, "the people" had been politically apathetic; reforms came from the top or didn't happen. But the French Revolution, the events at Aranjuez, and the War of Independence changed all that. No longer were the common people mere cannon fodder and tillers of the fields. After all, they had dethroned two kings and made another.

In the minds of many Spaniards, the monarchy's prestige had suffered tremendously and would never again enjoy its lofty status. For six years Spain had proved it could live without a king, and the new liberal ideas slowly began to spread. One place they took root was in the Spanish army, where freethinking officers resented such customs as having to say the rosary in formation. They flocked to Masonic lodges and other liberal clubs to discuss change. (The Freemasons became the perennial bogeyman for Spanish reactionaries, long after they were considered a harmless social fraternity in most other countries.)

In 1820, an army of reinforcements was sitting in Cádiz awaiting transport to the Americas. Bored with their condition, eager for advancement, and hostile at having to fight—and quite possibly die—in the colonies, the troops revolted in the name of liberalism under the leadership of Colonel Rafael de Riego. This was the first army *pronunciamiento* (a "pronouncement" of rebellion), but definitely not the last. From 1820 to 1874 there was one every twenty months on the average. The liberals had let loose a lion onto the Spanish political scene.

Garrisons throughout Spain rose to support Riego, and the king's "people's army" failed to react. A few months later, a thoroughly humiliated Fernando pledged to reform. Riego and his band called for the return of the constitution and other changes, including an end to the Inquisition. Time had already done its damage to this once almighty body. When a mob broke into one of the Inquisition's few remaining prisons, they found just one French priest, comfortably housed in the attic and reluctant to leave. All Europe was astonished at Riego's daring coup d'etat, the first crack in its post-war conservative monolith.

The revolt also assured the independence of the American colonies. The year 1819 had been a pivotal one for the rebel cause, as Bolívar led his ragtag army through high mountain passes to win the battle of Boyaca in Columbia. In the south, José de San Martín conducted a brilliant campaign that involved crossing the Andes from Argentina into Chile (where Bernard O'Higgins had already declared independence), then pressing north to Lima, the center of loyalist strength. Venezuela fell when Riego's army, the expeditionary force that was supposed to relieve Morillo, failed to arrive.

Mexico declared its independence in 1821, and soon almost every other colony had jumped on the freedom wagon. In December 1824, two armies clashed at 2,700 meters in the Peruvian mountains at the battle of Ayacucho. It marked the end of Spanish power on the mainland. Only the islands of Cuba and Puerto Rico remained of the once-sprawling American empire.

When the smoke cleared, there was not one vast country as Miranda had envisaged, but seventeen separate, squabbling republics. And there was no social revolution to accompany independence. Instead, power passed directly to the local Creole oligarchies. A tradition of alternating despotism and anarchy would plague Latin America from that day forward. Having destroyed Spanish authority and institutions, the rebels did not replace them with

Spanish Possessions in America in 1800

Entering its fourth century of existence, the empire had rarely produced serious signs of unhappiness with Spanish rule. Yet an American-born economic and social elite of pure Spanish blood, the Creoles (*los criollos*), clamored for more power. Lower classes included the *mestizos* of mixed blood and the large majority of pure Indians.

anything but the rule of self-interest. Said a bitter Bolívar, "America is ungovernable. He who serves a revolution ploughs the sea."

Back in Spain, the liberals brought to power by Riego were splitting into conservative (*moderado*) and radical (*exaltado*) wings, the classic division between those who wanted slow, orderly change (men of property and position) and those preaching social revolution (the urban radicals). Civil disorder was driving the radicals to despotic measures that alienated the little popular support they enjoyed. Liberal Spain was a hollow facade; when Fernando appealed to other monarchs of the Holy Alliance for help, only a handful of Spaniards objected. Said one liberal officer, "The Constitution was made entirely for the people, but they hated it."

The French king sent an army to aid a fellow despot in 1823, the "Hundred Thousand Sons of St. Louis," which was more like a military promenade than an invasion. Although he promised amnesty, Fernando immediately unleashed a reign of terror against liberals that shocked even the French. Riego was taken to the center of Madrid in a coal cart, there to be hanged, drawn, and quartered for public display. The mere possession of his picture carried the death penalty, and hundreds went to the gallows.

The remaining decade of Fernando's reign was an era of knee-jerk reactionism and bureaucratic bungling. The king's ministers were mediocre sycophants, each kept in ignorance of his colleagues' policies. After the war the nation was devastated, its trade and industry in shambles and the countryside depopulated and infested with bandits. Visitors commented on the squalid poverty, appalling roads, and wretched inns. This was the golden age of the *bandoleros*, often guerrillas reluctant to abandon their arms and lives of freedom. Most famous of all was Hinojosa Cobacho, better known as *El Tempranillo*, who controlled much of Andalucía for a decade. "In Spain the king rules, but in the Sierra I do," he declared.

All this fed Spain's picturesque image, the popular impression that maybe Africa began at the Pyrenees after all. In truth, the Iberian Peninsula retained much of the medieval panorama fast disappearing in the rest of Europe. One curious component of this scene was Carlism, the most hopeless of lost causes in that its principal enemy was time itself. The ultra-conservative Carlists took their name from Don Carlos, King Fernando's younger brother, who stood to inherit the throne. They were extreme monarchists who believed even the intransigent Fernando was too soft on liberals, having left a handful of them in office after his purges. Carlists called for the dissolution of the liberal-infested army, exile of all progressives, abolition of public education, and restoration of the Inquisition. One Carlist bishop founded "The Society of the Exterminating Angel" to oppose the constitution.

By 1829, Fernando's three marriages had failed to produce children, and everyone assumed that Carlos would inherit the throne from his gout-ridden brother. But a year later Fernando wed María Cristina, his Italian niece, who soon became pregnant. The Carlists were outraged, but felt at least partially protected by the law. During the War of Spanish Succession Felipe V had declared the Salic Law, which stated that no woman could rule Spain. Hence Carlos would still become king unless the queen gave birth to a son. But things were not that simple; in 1789 a secret session of the Cortes had repealed the Salic Law, thus opening the door to a female monarch.

In 1830 Princess Isabel was born, and clouds began to form. Three years later, as Fernando lay dying at La Granja, he added to the debate by repudiating his daughter's rights. This caused an uproar in María Cristina's faction that led to insults, at least one face slapped, and the king's ultimate reversal of his recent repudiation. Before finally expiring he remarked, "Spain is a bottle of beer and I am the cork. When that comes out, all the liquid inside will escape, God knows in what direction."

Upon the king's death, María Cristina was named regent for Isabel. The Pretender Don Carlos, living in exile in Portugal, simply stated, "Now I am king." The nation braced itself for its first civil war since the Revolt of the Comuneros more than three centuries earlier. Yet the First Carlist War was no mere dynastic struggle. This breach in the royal family can be blamed for many of Spain's subsequent political ills.

The backbone of Carlist support came from the ranks of traditional Spain—clergy, ultra-conservative monarchists, and foot-dragging peasants—especially in northern areas with long histories of local rights, the persistent *fueros*. These troublesome regions included the strongly Catholic Basque country, Navarra, and mountainous parts of Aragón and Cataluña. Don Carlos swore to honor the *fueros* beneath the famous oak tree of Guernica, symbol of Basque freedom. But more than the champion of regional rights, Carlism was a reaction to the modern world. Hence, the predominately rural supporters shared a strong hatred for cities and their "liberal" ways. These masses who answered to the call of "*Viva* Christ the King" were the same peasants who would form the ranks of Franco's army in 1936.

Pious and severe, Don Carlos was a man of some backbone; among the royal family he alone had stood up to Napoleon's badgering. But from the outset his cause was futile, an absurdly romantic and tragic attempt to return to the days of Felipe II. Among other quixotic gestures, he named Our Lady of the Sorrows as *generalisimo* of his armies. Indeed, the Duke of Wellington called him "one of the silliest devils I ever knew."

Spain's political history in the nineteenth century was a comic opera in which every act ended in tragedy. The war fought over the next six years (1833-39) cost Spain 140,000 lives. The Carlists' ferocity was legendary, with soldier-priests of the "Exterminating Angel" leading their troops in appalling barbarities. The red-bereted warriors seemed to attract the best and worst types, and their campaigns often became mere excuses for brigandage. One of the more "romantic" heroes was Tomás Zumalacarregui, who gained worldwide fame among schoolboys in the popular illustrated journals of the day, shown wearing his goatskin cloak and red beret.

Almost the entire army remained loyal to Isabel and the regency. But the Carlists were guerrilla fighters, and government forces had problems winning decisive victories without resorting to the same kind of outrages committed by the opposition. In addition, anti-clerical mobs sacked convents and murdered monks to destroy the perceived enemy of the liberal state, the Catholic Church. An outbreak of cholera was blamed on priests poisoning the wells, and mobs killed about seventy clerics. Said one writer of the war: "Here lies half Spain, done to death by the other half." The First Carlist War witnessed the birth of popular anti-clericalism in Spain, which reached ghastly proportions in the next century. Whether as victim or instigator, the church (and one's attitude toward it) lay at the heart of most of Spain's social questions. As a popular expression put it, "Everyone in Spain follows the church: half with a candle, the other half with a club."

Much like the civil war of the 1930s, the Carlist War captured the attention of all Europe, which saw it as a mortal struggle between liberalism and reaction. Idealists, adventurers, and journalists descended on Spain to "fight the good fight." This produced its share of bizarre incidents, such as the young Irish aristocrat who used his yacht to seize Málaga briefly in the name of Don Carlos. (Later he was named bishop of Dublin.)

The war reached a stalemate in 1834. Meanwhile, Spain under the Regency of María Cristina was undergoing profound changes. Liberals returned from exile in droves to re-light the torch extinguished by Fernando VII. A new constitution granted limited suffrage, centralized government, and bourgeois property rights, and was supported by both radicals (by then known as progressives or *progresistas*) and the more conservative *moderados*. Although there would be other constitutions and countless crises and military coups over the next decades, these two liberal political groupings divided power and patronage between them for almost a century.

The conservatives usually held the upper hand. They were the bourgeois landowners and aristocrats who championed property rights, the high-placed civil servants and army officers who wished order above all, the lawyers who defended the status quo for handsome fees. Their task was to defend the "ruling class" without resorting to the threadbare arguments of the Carlists. The progressives counted among their supporters a few generals and most of the junior officers, merchants, needy journalists, and the aspiring urban lower middle class.

During the height of the Carlist War and anti-clerical frenzy, the regent called on a Basque financial wizard named Juan Mendizabal to head the government. A decree in 1835 closed all religious orders; in Madrid alone forty-four churches and monasteries were shut down. Then, in an act of vast impact, this *progresista* banker launched a program of land reform that confiscated church property and offered it for sale. About one-quarter of all church lands went on the block in the first two years. More than any other single action, this action created a permanent breach between progressive liberalism and the Catholic Church.

Naturally, poor peasants did not have the money to buy the land they worked, and wealthy landlords and speculators snapped up most of the bonanza. Thus the largest transfer of property since the Reconquest brought no agrarian reform. In one case lands farmed by six thousand families suddenly supported only four hundred. Indeed, the Andalucían *latifundia* system of huge estates worked by landless peasants became worse—all in the name of "Liberalism." Even more important, the reformers put an end to land entailment (hereditary line of inheritance), which drove a huge wedge between the two liberal factions. The reforms also pushed vast numbers of landless peasants, who regarded collective land-use a God-given right, into the arms of the Carlists and, much later, to the Anarchists.

The centralized state in Madrid became the sworn enemy of both the extreme right and the extreme left, which shared much more in political philosophy than is commonly realized. Other legislation based on the French model created the forty-nine provinces of modern Spain, often disrupting long traditions of local or regional rule. Thus well-meaning reformers sowed the seeds of modern regional upheavals in Cataluña and the Basque lands.

In 1837, the Carlists gambled everything on a disastrous march on Madrid. They lost the war because, as one historian put it, "They were even madder and more foolish than their adversaries." At Vergara (1839), two opposing generals embraced theatrically, then signed an agreement that recognized Isabel as Spain's legitimate queen. The pact also achieved a truce between the church and the middle-class values of the *moderado* order. Don Carlos retired to France with several thousand followers, and there were many suicides in Carlist ranks, including two fanatics who simultaneously skewered each other with their bayonets. But after the peace of Vergara, Carlism became largely confined to the province of Navarra.

The army emerged from the war as Spain's most solid institution, happy with its new role as arbiter of the country's destiny. Having stood by the constitutional monarchy against the Carlists, the generals would demand their pound of flesh. In essence, the war and its aftermath allowed them to take command of Spanish politics, which became its peculiar feature. As all sides began to accept the new rules, the main question revolved around who would control the army. Liberals of both persuasions were equally high-handed in forcing their programs on the nation, and *políticos* had no qualms about using military sedition to achieve their ends.

The age of "romantic militarism" began in 1840 with a coup by General Espartero that ousted María Cristina. She had slowly lost support, especially among the generals, after secretly marrying Augustín Munoz, ex-corporal of the guard and son of a shopkeeper. Critics started calling him "Ferdinand VIII" behind his back when they noticed he was wearing the deceased king's tiepins, and they thundered about the "royal whore" when she failed to conceal a series of pregnancies.

Baldomero Espartero was a flamboyant figure with a blustery voice who enjoyed the total devotion of his men, but he was politically naive. His famous taste for the ladies prompted one British lord to remark, "He wore out more sheets than shoe leather." Espartero's coup represented progressive interests, which defended local power in the face of *moderado* centralization. It was during a crisis over this issue that the general forced the resignation of

María Cristina, who had appealed to him for support at one point. Espartero became new head of state, and the departing regent remarked, "I have made you a count and a duke, but I could not make you a gentleman."

With Espartero's coup the militarization of Spanish politics entered a new phase, as governments were made and unmade by the "sword arm" of each political party. The progressives had surrendered their leadership to a general, and the conservatives would soon find one of their own. Espartero's regency lasted two troubled years, during which more church land was nationalized and sold, driving the clergy further rightward. In 1843, another coup led by *moderado* generals Serrano and Narváez forced Espartero from power. The pattern had been firmly established.

During the 116 years between Riego's *pronunciamiento* and General Franco's Putsch, there were more than a hundred military rumblings of varying types: foiled café-conspiracies; sergeants' uprisings; barracks plots; colonels' coups. Almost like classical drama, *pronunciamientos* followed well-defined stages: first came the preliminary plotting—the *trabajos* to win over supporters—often in a mineral spa or café; the *compromisos* followed, by which the accomplices were bound to action; finally, at the preordained moment, came the *grito*, the "cry" of insurrection by the leader (*el jefe*) to his assembled troops, explaining his reasons for wanting to overthrow the government.

As the army grew to see itself as a legitimate option to quarrelling factions, there emerged the prototype of the conservative soldier-politician. By definition he was authoritarian, monarchist, rigidly Catholic, and often from a humble background (many generals rose from the ranks) and therefore hostile to aristocrats and intellectuals. In the tradition of St. James the Moor Slayer, he identified his opponents as godless rebels. Narváez once wrote to General Zurbano, who was planning a coup: "By violating the law, as I once violated it, you are moving straight towards a bottomless pit." He then threatened to shoot him.

The fall of Espartero brought the declaration of the new queen, Isabel II, at the premature age of thirteen. She was a poor successor to her namesake, prompting one eminent Spanish historian to write, "Her coming of age (to rule) was a pure constitutional fiction. Queen Isabel was never of age, though she died a grandmother."

Isabel was plump, comely, easy going without pretensions, generous and good-hearted, and above all passionate. Shortly after her accession she lent

herself to a hare-brained plot involving a dashing cavalry officer that brought down the government. Indeed, like a reckless teenager who
never grew up, Isabel let her passions rule, and
she rivals Catherine the Great of Russia as
history's most lascivious queen.

Royal councilors began to worry that an
heir might arrive on the scene before a husband,
so an exhaustive search commenced among
Europe's elite. The unfortunate choice for the
hot-blooded, sixteen-year-old queen was her
Bourbon cousin Francisco de Asis, who had a

The Spanish parliament
(Cortes) building in Madrid,
site of several coup attempts

high, squeaky voice and was soon dubbed "*Paquita*" (roughly translated as
"Fanny"). Later, Isabel described their honeymoon: "What can I say of a man
who on his wedding night wore more lace than I." To everyone's amazement
children began to arrive like clockwork. Said one observer, "The queen
has plenty of faithful subjects who can replace Francisco in case of need."

The history of Isabel II's reign was largely consumed with power struggles
between three rival generals: Espartero, Narváez, and a Spaniard with an Irish
surname, Leopoldo O'Donnell. It was a gray period of revolving governments
(forty different ministries, eighteen coup attempts) dominated by General
Narváez, who based his dictatorial powers on obscure passages of the constitution and pure chutzpah. On one occasion he appeared at the council of
ministers and announced, "Gentlemen, by royal order you have all been relieved of your functions."

Ramón Narváez was an Andalucían squire who loved power for its rewards: a fine coach, a palace, inside financial tips. He had a violent temper
and would tolerate no contradiction, once calling his political opponents "filthy
mutineers." He led the *moderados* and served as prime minister five times over
two decades. During this period electoral fraud became a regular practice,
and with the voting machinery in the hands of the governing party, revolution became the only hope for change. Excluded by a corrupt political system,
the *progresistas* usually resorted to coups to gain power. The conservatives
accepted the change until they decided to return to power by means of their
own general.

Narváez reconciled the formerly anti-clerical landowners with the church,
who formed an alliance against the lower middle class championed by

Espartero. Narváez maintained power by keeping the army contented, and he used it often to quell dissent and sedition, from progressives to diehard Carlists, who rose up again briefly in 1848. He employed any means necessary to defend the monarchy of Isabel from its many opponents. When asked on his deathbed if he had forgiven his enemies, Narváez replied, "I have no enemies, father. I have had them all shot."

The era of Narváez was, despite the ongoing political carnival, one of peace and prosperity. To bring the bandit-infested countryside under control, a rural police called the *guardia civil* (civil guard) was set up on the French model. One rule was that *guardias* could not be natives of the districts they served. This reduced the chances for corruption, but alienated the civil guards from the people they served. This rural police force was also created to stifle local influences objectionable to Madrid, and it served *all* governments against *all* forms of sedition from left or right. *Guardias* made the roads safe for travelers, but also made things "safe" for landlords by crushing any glimmer of social revolution. Hence they became the sworn enemies of regionalism and working-class movements.

Foreign travelers wrote of rural banditry and many other aspects of Spanish life during Isabel's reign. Literary apostles of Romanticism, then the rage throughout Europe, found in Spain the picturesque and exotic life—peasants tilling with ancient ploughs or beating laundry along a stream bed—that was fast vanishing elsewhere. They attributed this to some intangible "Spanishness" which they hoped would stem the tide of modern "progress." Among the writers to produce a cluster of classic Romantic travel accounts were Henry Inglis, Washington Irving, Richard Ford, and Theophile Gautier. Ford called Spain "Roman, African or, in a word, un-European" and lamented that ". . . *mantillas* are going, alas!" George Borrow's eccentric book *The Bible In Spain*, describing his adventures as a bible salesman, became an instant best seller (1842). Offshoots of this fascination with Spain were a series of gothic novels, complete with dim dungeons and rattling chains, and wild exposés of life in Spanish monasteries and nunneries. The Black Legend had gone Romantic.

Spanish liberals returned from abroad with the literary Romanticism of Walter Scott in their cultural baggage. This gave rise to the *costumbrista* school of writers, recording strange types and regional oddities with relish. One of the better products of this phenomenon was *La Gaviota* (*The Seagull*) by Fernán Caballero, considered Spanish literature's first modern novel. Writers could either revel in Spain's uniqueness or see it as symbolic of *retraso* (backwardness).

Among those who blasted the mimicking of foreign literary trends was Mariano José de Larra, who described Spain as the country of *casi* (which means "almost" or "not quite"). Something was always missing, from institutions recognized by "not quite" the whole nation to canals "not quite" finished and museums "not quite" arranged. What was picturesque for foreign romantics finally drove Larra to suicide.

S panish Romanticism got mixed up with revived Catalan "national" pride in a movement called the *renaixenca* (renaissance). As a cultural vehicle the Catalán language virtually died in the sixteenth century. But when a bank clerk published a poem in Catalán in a Barcelona newspaper (1833) it marked the beginning of a revival. The cultural rebirth had its underpinnings in Cataluña's remarkable industrial development (mainly textiles) in the first half of the century, which gave Barcelona the moniker "The Manchester of Spain." Favoring high tariffs to keep out English goods, Catalans developed a new hostility to meddling from Madrid that went far beyond the old rivalry with Castilla. Catalan businessmen allied with the equally industrious Basques, more by trade policies than by authentic regional spirit. They also shared a "reverence for money," which Castilians scorned. Most of the important banks seemed to spring from Barcelona or Bilbao and were housed in massive neoclassical buildings typical of the age. Although Basque wealth was founded on iron deposits in Vizcaya, scattered homesteads gave the countryside the appearance of one vast, prosperous village.

There were still many Spains. Galicia was desperately poor, its peasants futilely trying to eke out a living on their "handkerchief plots." Like the Irish, countless Galicians fled their land of gorse and granite to better lives elsewhere. Equally impoverished, but for entirely different reasons, were the landless *braceros* of Andalucía, working sporadically during the grape and olive harvests, then suffering in squalid misery the rest of the year.

Dry cereal farming occupied the farmers of Castilla and Extremadura, a barren land of rock fences with "hardly a branch on which a bird might light." (The destruction of Spanish forests continued unabated throughout the century.) In a complete turnaround from the days of the Mesta, livestock was woefully inadequate to supply Spain's needs for meat, wool, and fertilizer. Scattered across this bleak tableland were depressing villages whose streets were alternately dusty in summer and mud-choked in winter. The intense dry cold of the heartland spawned a saying about the air of Madrid, "so keen and subtle that it will not extinguish a candle, but can put out a man's life."

Spain's strong regional identities and differences translated into economic fragmentation. Indeed, much of Spanish society's chronic instability stems from very unequal rates of economic growth during modern times. There was no real national economy with common concerns and policies. Railroads, for example, came late and never really developed as in other countries. Even the tracks were a different width than in the rest of Europe. Railroads were largely financed by foreign (mostly French) capital, the Rothschilds and Pereires. British investors chose minerals such as Almadén mercury and the copper mines of Rio Tinto, and English capital flooded into the Jerez area and its burgeoning sherry trade.

Economic historians have proposed a myriad of reasons for Spain's failure to create a modern economy. Poor agricultural production kept farmers bound to the land, which meant fewer workers for industry. The weak domestic market (no one had money to spend) meant little demand for Spanish products at home, and foreigners were not beating down the doors either. The Bank of Spain spent most of its energy furnishing loans to the government rather than on productive investment. Finally, there was the nation's work ethic, still suffering from tradition. In 1830, Henry Inglis described Madrid's Puerta del Sol, with "hundreds of gentlemen standing there with no other occupation than shaking the dust from their cigars."

"There are but two families in the world," said Sancho Panza. "The haves and the have-nots." Foreign visitors were struck by the presence of beggars in every Spanish town, and in Madrid alone convents were dishing out thirty thousand bowls of soup daily. Moreover, as in much of Europe the urban poverty of *les miserables* was creeping into Spain, and this new alienated working class would grow into a major force.

Although Spain's middle class remained weak in numbers at mid century, this was the "age of the bourgeoisie." Middle-class tastes determined styles from the royal palace on down—a prosperous merchant might use the same silver tea service as the queen. The aristocracy clung to its titles and court offices (the Duke of Osuna had over 50 titles), but some nobles realized that the road to survival meant adoption of bourgeois goals. The two classes began to merge, and the high bourgeoisie allied with the nobility rather than becoming its rival and watchdog, as in other countries. Successful soldiers, politicians, financiers, and industrialists were granted titles of nobility to accompany their wealth. These *poderosos* (powerful ones) often ran things at the local level and became staunch pillars of the status quo.

The thirty-eight-year reign of Isabel II was punctuated by bizarre behavior at court that spilled over into the political arena. Wrote the American ambassador: "A safe word whispered by a crawling confessor, an attack of nerves on a cloudy day, the appearance of a well-made soldier at a levee, have often sufficed to make and break administrations." Behind the throne stood Father Claret, Isabel's confessor, and Sor Patrocino, "the bleeding nun," whose hands and feet supposedly bore the wounds of Christ. The queen's love life continued to outrage her subjects and husband alike, with a parade of paramours passing through the royal palace. Among them were General Serrano and an American dentist named McKeon, who may have fathered Alfonso, the first Prince of Asturias born in the century and future king. Said the *London Times* glibly: "Isabel is guilty of high treason against the cause of virtue and morality."

Compounding the public outrage were reports of massive corruption in the royal family, especially the shady dealings of the queen mother in railway construction and the Cuban slave trade. Popularly labeled *la ladrona* (the thief), she was even caught trying to switch the palace's silver service for pewter imitations. Eventually, "the impossible lady" alienated even her few remaining supporters. When the increasingly obese queen took a new lover named Carlos Malfori, son of an Italian pastry cook, it was the last straw. The progressive liberals, excluded from government by the queen, formed a coalition with discontented generals to plot her overthrow. When both generals O'Donnell and Narváez died, it removed the queen's main props for the past thirty years. Progressive General Prim "pronounced" in 1868 for a "Spain with honor," and Queen Isabel, by then thirty-eight, fled to France. It appeared that the Bourbons were finished in Spain after 168 memorable years.

Prim was a strong-willed Catalan who admired Abraham Lincoln. Together with Serrano, the queen's former lover, he formed a provisional government that granted a liberal constitution. It seemed to offer Spain a true representative system for the first time since the constitution of 1812. Nevertheless, most Spaniards remained monarchists at heart and started looking for a new king rather than considering other options. The honor of obtaining the Spanish throne, once the envy of all Europe, was politely turned down by several candidates before Leopold of Hohenzollern accepted briefly, then backed down. (The affair sparked the Franco-Prussian War of 1870.) Prim remarked that finding a king to rule a constitutional monarchy was "like looking for an atheist in heaven." The name of General Espartero was even mentioned, but somehow the idea of a King Baldomero I never caught on.

Finally, the *políticos* settled on the somewhat reluctant Amadeus of Savoy, second son of Italy's King Victor Emmanuel, who was known for his liberal views. When parliament approved the choice of Amadeo I by a vote of 191 to 63, he became known as "king of the 191." Amadeo's reign had an inauspicious start: on the day he arrived in Spain, General Prim—his main supporter—was assassinated on a dark Madrid street. The shaky coalition that had made the revolution of '68 was already splintering over the issue of religion, perennial prism of Spanish politics. The church had regained much of its power over the past two decades, and the clergy were outraged by the choice of a liberal, hence in their minds "Godless" monarch.

Moreover, the new king was considered a foreign interloper and treated with outright disrespect at every level. For example, on Amadeo's first day at the royal palace he asked for breakfast at eight, but was curtly informed that he would get nothing until eleven, as was customary. (He went out to a café for breakfast.) He and his wife were insulted at the theater and given the cold shoulder by the aristocracy, which began to split between supporters of the Carlist candidate and Isabel's son Alfonso. Realizing their opportunity, the supporters of Carlos VII (grandson of the original Don Carlos) began the Second Carlist War in April 1872. This conflict and his less-than-cordial treatment convinced Amadeo to abdicate the following February. He thanked Spain "for the great honor it had bestowed on him" and promptly left for Portugal.

Spain's First Republic could not have been born at a worse time. General Prim once said, "If it was not easy to make a king, it will be even more difficult to make a republic in a country where there are no republicans." The situation was approaching chaos in many parts of the land, with most of the north acknowledging Don Carlos, Barcelona virtually autonomous, and anarchist agitators whipping up the peasants in Andalucía.

Amid all this parliament proclaimed a republic, with Catalan Pi y Margall as national president despite the fact that he was a firm believer in local self-government. A few months later, a federal republic of seventeen states in a decentralized nation was declared. The Republic lasted just eleven months and had four presidents, all lawyers or professors. Politicians seemed incapable of putting aside their differences to form a strong government, and parliament could not even agree on simple matters of form and procedure.

The federal idea soon degenerated into "cantonalism," a curious theory based on extreme localism in an already centrifugal state. By the summer of 1873 Valencia, Málaga, Granada, and other cities and regions had declared their independence from Madrid. The Spanish navy defected to the Canton of Cartagena. Sensing the time was right for Spaniards to choose between monarchy and anarchy, Carlists stepped up their military campaign. Soon they controlled most of Spain north of the Ebro River and seemed poised to topple the defenseless Republic. But the Carlists, champions of a Spain that was passing away, could not follow through.

Meanwhile, the "Alfonsists" plotted. Isabel's sixteen-year-old son was enrolled at Sandhurst, England's royal military college. Military in education and interests (he knew army regulations by heart), Alfonso seemed an ideal choice to lead Spain out of the mire of republicanism. The inevitable *pronunciamiento* came in 1874 at Sagunto (the old Iberian village made famous during the Second Punic War) with the *grito* delivered by General Martínez de Campos. In Madrid General Pavía rode his horse up the steps of the Cortes building, where his men shot a few rounds into the air that scattered the delegates. Pavía declared support for the new king, Alfonso XII, and delirious crowds received him in the capital on January 12, 1875. The army had knocked the Bourbons off the throne seven years earlier, and now it was bringing them back again. It did not bode well for Spanish politics.

By the time of the Restoration, liberalism in the army had shriveled to insignificance. Most officers accepted the *moderado* coalition of monarchy, church, and landowners as the natural order. That was the *real* significance of Alfonso's return. The new soldier-king showed signs of becoming a good ruler, and the future looked relatively bright. The Carlists, having missed their golden opportunity, were soon crushed but would be heard from again decades later.

The Constitution of 1876 was a solid document that recognized the joint rule of king and parliament and became the first great "liberal" success in erecting a stable political system. Key player in the new system was Antonio Cánovas del Castillo, a squint-eyed schoolmaster from Málaga who looked like an unmade bed. His opponents called him "the monster," but he was a hard worker and electrifying speaker. His goal was to bring stability to the political scene by injecting common sense instead of ideology. He explained:

"The constitution should be formed on principles as liberal as the condition of the country will allow."

Common sense for Cánovas also meant excluding groups on the fringe, such as republicans, Carlists, and regionalists. His system also put an end to military meddling, now that the army was a reliable pillar of the system. Crucial to maintaining the new order was the concept of the *turno*, a periodic rotation of power between the two accepted political groupings, the conservatives and liberals, represented by Cánovas and Sagasta. After decades of mock battles, little of substance separated the two parties, and the system was a cynical perversion of true parliamentary democracy. But it worked.

The orderly "changing of the guard" depended on a corrupt electoral process. Election-fraud started at the top and filtered down to the smallest village, where political bosses called *caciques* (from an Indian word for chieftain) controlled voting and handed out patronage. The average person was politically indifferent in any case and disinterested in what happened in faraway Madrid. The rigging of elections became a fine art. Lists of voters were drawn up locally, and on one occasion the occupants of an entire cemetery, seven hundred names in all, were called on to vote. During the 1886 general election that brought Sagasta to power, the results appeared in an official newspaper the day before voting took place. This corrupt system increasingly came to depend on the backward regions of Andalucía and Galicia, where the votes of an illiterate, apathetic electorate could be easily falsified.

The Cánovas system worked because the king, unlike his mercurial mother, let it work. Alfonso attended to routine matters and rarely meddled in real politics. After his first wife died, he married María Cristina, daughter of an Austrian duke. She was fated to rule Spain for seventeen years. In 1885, severe earthquakes in eastern Andalucía destroyed thousands of buildings and left hundreds dead, and a severe cholera outbreak followed. Alfonso, whose health was never strong, insisted on visiting the stricken areas and died a few weeks later of a lung infection. He was not yet twenty-eight.

Maria Cristina became Regent of Spain, just like another foreign consort of the same name who ended life in exile. But this time it would be different, and the Regency ushered in an optimistic era. When Alfonso died the queen was pregnant, and the nation yearned for an heir to head off another dynastic crisis. According to tradition, the royal artillery in Madrid would launch a twenty-one-gun salute if a boy were born, but fire only fifteen times for a baby girl. On May 17, 1886, normal life ground to a halt in the capital as crowds gathered outside the royal palace to await news. Suddenly the cannons started to thunder, and on the sixteenth salvo the city went wild. There would be a new king, after all.

The 1890s were good years economically for Spain as they were for most of Europe and America. On the surface everything looked fine: Cánovas hobnobbed with the aristocracy and handed out thousands of new titles. Queen Victoria even managed a visit during the fading glow of the "liberal century" (she found the tea undrinkable). Underneath, social and political tensions in the working class and regions were beginning to boil. In the next decade—the next century— they would erupt.

Citizens of Madrid reading news of the Spanish-American crisis

The best way to gain a feeling for the life and times of late nineteenth-century Spain is by reading the novels of Benito Pérez Galdós (1843-1920). In the opinion of many critics, he was on a par with Zola, Balzac, Dickens, and Tolstoi with books such as *Dona Perfecta* and *Fortunata and Jacinta*. Pérez Galdós wrote of indolent bureaucrats and decayed aristocrats, and of small Castilian towns that embodied the stagnant, fanatical side of Spain. He championed the new literary theory of "realism" and captured the attention of critics on both sides of the Atlantic.

So long as the two elder statesmen lived, the illusion of Spain's stability and strength could continue. Then, in 1897, an Italian anarchist assassinated Cánovas, and Sagasta died of natural causes a few years later. The "powerful ones" had built a house of cards that was about to come crashing down. Spaniards would discover how corrupt and inept their leaders had become, how far Spain had fallen behind, with the disaster of 1898—the Spanish-American War.

Spain had been fighting a simmering revolt in Cuba for many years without much success, and tens of thousands of Spaniards had perished in Cuba, mostly from disease. The Spanish repeatedly refused to reform the corrupt colonial administration or allow more autonomy, choosing instead to send in a get-tough general named Weyler to turn things around. His use of prison camps and other harsh measures, although exaggerated by the

American press, earned him the hatred of Cubans and nickname "Butcher Weyler." When Spain offered limited autonomy it was too late.

Key to Cuban independence was the posture of the United States, where Congress passed a resolution demanding Spain's withdrawal. American newspapers, led by W. R. Hearst's *New York Journal*, unleashed blistering attacks on Spanish rule: "Weyler the brute, the devastator of *haciendas*, the destroyer of families, and the outrager of women . . ." proclaimed one editorial.

In order to "protect American life and property," the battleship *Maine* was dispatched to Havana harbor. There, on the night of February 15, 1898, an explosion ripped open the ship's hull and killed 260 men. Americans blamed the disaster on a mine, but Spaniards denied any involvement. Hearst offered a $50,000 reward for the culprits and banner headlines called for war. Future U.S. president Theodore "Teddy" Roosevelt bellowed: "The *Maine* was sunk by an act of dirty treachery on the part of Spain." In this atmosphere, it was not surprising that war was soon declared to the cry of "Remember the *Maine*!"

In 1898, Spain's military forces accounted for about half the national budget, but of the fifty thousand men on active duty, five hundred were generals and twenty four thousand lower officers. The navy was a shore-based bureaucracy rather than a fighting force, with over a hundred admirals and few sea-worthy ships. The Pacific Squadron based in the Philippines existed mostly on paper, but it was here that action commenced in May. In a one-hour battle, the American navy led by Dewey blasted the Spanish ships out of Manila Bay as if they were practice targets.

The Spanish-American War itself lasted just three months. At a naval encounter at Santiago de Cuba, the entire Spanish squadron was destroyed with just one American casualty, completing the matched pair of modern history's two worst naval disasters. An expeditionary force including Roosevelt's "Rough Riders" landed in Cuba and stormed up San Juan Hill to victory. "It was a splendid little war," exclaimed Teddy.

By July peace negotiations were underway, and the Treaty of Paris was signed by year's end. Spain was forced to abandon the last crumbs of its once vast overseas possessions: Cuba, Puerto Rico, the Philippines, and Guam. The historical cycle that started one October day in 1492 had finally ended. The mighty Spanish Empire was no more.

Sights & Sites

Alicante: The Castle of San Fernando, constructed during the War of Independence, is now a park with a good view of the town.

Bilbao (Vizcaya): Town Hall built in 1892 on the site of a monastery.

Cádiz: Church of San Felipe Neri, site of the historic Cortes and Constitution of 1812; seafront promenades such as Parque Genovés reflect nineteenth century styles.

Irún (Guipuzcoa): The San Marcial Hermitage lies on the site of a great Spanish victory over the French in 1813; excellent panorama of the province.

Madrid: The Prado Museum's Goya rooms contain his *Disasters of War* series and the huge oils *May 2nd* and *May 3rd.* ; the Casón del Buen Retiro features a major section of lesser-known nineteenth-century Spanish artists; the Romantic Museum contains period furniture and paintings left by the Marquis of Vega-Inclán; the massive neo-classical Palace of the Cortes, inaugurated in 1850 by Isabel II, is a monument to the *moderado* order; the Plaza de Oriente next to the royal palace dates from the time of Joseph Bonaparte and is adorned with statues of Spanish kings; the Military Museum was founded in 1803 by Godoy.

Mallorca (Balearic Islands): At the Valldemosa Carthusian Monastery, George Sand and Frederick Chopin passed a few months in 1838-39; Sand wrote her book *A Winter In Majorca* from the experience.

Montserrat Monastery near Barcelona is home to the Black Virgin image.

Montserrat (Barcelona): The French sacked the original monastery in 1812, and existing buildings date mostly from the nineteenth century. Symbol of Catalan culture.

Nerja (Málaga): While on his tour of earthquake-ravaged Andalucía, Alfonso XII strolled out on the promenade and dubbed it *El Balcon de Europa.*

San Sebastián (Guipúzcoa): Neo-classical buildings include the Town Hall and Diputación; Miramar Palace was the summer residence of the royal family, dating from the era of María Cristina.

Villanueva y Geltru (Barcelona): The Casa Papiol house presents a perfect picture of bourgeois life in the early 1800s.

Vitoria (Alava): Plaza de la Virgen Blanca contains a massive monument to Wellington's crucial 1813 victory.

Chapter 9

Best of Times, Worst of Times

Antoni Gaudí's Sagrada Familia Church is to Barcelona what the Eiffel Tower is to Paris. Standing in front of this unfinished architectural treasure, visitors to Spain's "second city" encounter one man's transcendent vision cast in stone and mortar. Gaudí worked nine years on the swirling chaos of the Nativity façade, imbedding statues, sculpted stone, and leering gargoyles into the fluffy surface. On the portal he carved trees, shells, animals, and the mountains and seascapes of his beloved Cataluña. Here as well is a strange dragon-demon handing a bomb to an anarchist, an appropriate touch for turn-of-the-century Barcelona. The architect's later years were spent on four amazing towers that look like stone-and-mortar space-ships with nosecones of colored glass-and-tile mosaics. There is an almost reptilian quality about these hundred-meter spires, huge stones coating them like protective scales. You can climb one tower and look out on Gaudí's other works in Barcelona, buildings that appear molded from lumps of clay.

Born at Reus in 1852, Antonio Gaudí Cornet was a founding father of *art nouveau*, a highly decorative style that fused medieval and modern elements and used exotic and sometimes erotic symbols for ornamentation. (Salvador Dalí called the Sagrada Familia "a gigantic erogenous zone.") But

Gaudí cannot be pigeon-holed as part of a movement. His cosmic creations are highly personal, his unique church a religious poem written in "living" stone. Gaudí's talents were not overlooked in the vibrant, freewheeling Barcelona of 1900, and he became the favored architect of several wealthy patrons. Among his commissions were the Pedrera building, a fantasy of wave-like facades, astounding chimneys, and twisted wrought-iron balconies.

Gaudí was just one figure in a head-spinning cultural revival in Spain, especially Cataluña, during the first years of the new century. In 1900 a young, unknown painter named Pablo Ruiz Picasso held his first exhibition at a small Barcelona café called "The Four Cats." Born in Málaga in 1881, Picasso moved to the throbbing Catalonian capital at the age of fourteen. Here he attended art school and spent several formative years before moving to Paris. His *Les Demoiselles d'Avignon* (1907), depicting a group of Barcelona prostitutes, is cited as the first important Cubist painting, a major milestone for modern art. Picasso, of course, went on to become the century's most famous artist, a citizen of the world but always a Spaniard.

Another crucial figure in modern art was Juan Gris, co-founder of Cubism. After studying in Madrid, he also moved to Paris, but his austere still-lifes stretch back to the pure color and line of Zurbarán. Other great Spanish artists of the era include Valencian Joaquin Sorolla, who painted dramatic landscapes splashed in color and sunlight, and Ignacio Zuloaga, with his vivid renderings of bullfighters and Basque peasants.

There was a parallel explosion in music, particularly in Barcelona under the influence of master Felipe Pedrell. Enrique Granados is remembered for his piano works, *Spanish Dances* and *Goyescas*, and the music of Isaac Albéniz, especially *Iberia*, combined Spanish folk material with brilliant pianistic idiom. Better known is Manuel de Falla, whose music is rooted in Andalucian folk songs (he was a Catalan born in Cádiz). Among his many masterpieces is *Nights in the Gardens of Spain* (1916). Yet another Catalan was Pablo Casals, a prodigy who began his concert career in 1891 and became the greatest cello virtuoso of modern times (he died in 1973). Indeed, there is truth to the adage that if you pinch a Catalan he or she will always cry out in perfect pitch.

After the turn of the century, Spanish literary figures were also breaking down cultural barriers. José Echegaray became the first Spaniard to win the Nobel Prize (1904) for his skillful if now dated melodramas, and Vicente Blasco Ibáñez gained worldwide fame for his superb novels of simple life in Valencia. North American literary critics championed Blasco and other

Spanish realists, and Hollywood later discovered his potboilers *Blood and Sand* and *The Four Horsemen of the Apocalypse*. In 1904, the Hispanic Society of America was founded in New York; Spain's cultural revival was crossing the Atlantic as well as the Pyrenees.

The most important phenomenon of all was a loose-knit collection of writers who came of age around the time of the Spanish-American War and continued producing through the early 1930s. Although sharing no common creed or interests except Spain itself, they came to be called "The Generation of '98." Confronted with national humiliation and Spain's failure to keep pace with Western Europe, writers of widely varying talent and point of view took to dissecting their country. The fundamental question: Where had Spain gone wrong?

Forerunner of the movement was Francisco Giner de los Ríos, who founded the Free Institute for Education in 1875. Seeing a kind of intellectual malaise around him—few people read books and science lurched forward under a cloud of suspicion—Giner de los Ríos tried to create a school where Spain's future leaders could receive the type of modern education they would need to guide the nation into the next century. The school's point of view was liberal, secular, and European—all the things that traditional Spain was not. "There is a generation or two of intelligent people," Giner de los Rios wrote. "Then comes a political catastrophe, and we have to begin all over again. We are so deeply divided between Catholics and liberals, right wing and left, that one-half can never profit by the knowledge and achievements of the other."

Just prior to the debacle of 1898, Angel Ganivet wrote an essay on the nature of "Spanishness" and Spain's place in the world, stressing the positive side of the national character. This search for "the soul of Spain" continued with Joaquin Costa, who urged Spaniards to mend their ways and become more European, that is, more "modern." It would not be easy for a nation that had always looked to the rest of Europe with admiration, but also with a fear of losing its own personality.

The main themes of this national soul-searching were just coming into focus when the military disaster in America hit like a Yankee broadside. The realization that the empire was gone was particularly devastating because it had created the very idea of Spain four centuries earlier. To the pessimists, the entire nineteenth century seemed a dismal spiral of dwindling empire and declining national prestige. Preoccupied with religion and political intrigue,

Spain lagged in scientific thought and invention, while most of its people lived in a kind of intellectual fog. As the poet Antonio Machado wrote:

Wretched Castile, yesterday the ruler
wrapped in rags and scorning all it does not know.

The empire was gone and good riddance, said most of the "Generation." America had been a mixed blessing at best, the cause of all Spain's troubles, said many. It was high time to "lock the sepulcher of El Cid," to swap glory for progress and battleships for schools. Spain did not need heroes and martyrs but intelligence, restraint, and enough food on the table.

"In Spain, there is a good deal to see but not much to eat," observed José Ortega y Gasset, one of the giants of the movement. This philosopher-writer studied in Germany and sought to bring Spain closer to Europe in order to solve its problems. In *Invertebrate Spain* he wrote, "Spain today, rather than a nation, is a cloud of dust remaining after a great people have galloped down the highway of history." Another key figure was Basque writer Miguel de Unamuno, a solitary and arrogant figure best known for his book *The Tragic Sense of Life*. Unamuno saw Spain's salvation in its own unique qualities. He held that the words "Spanish" and "European" were incompatible and disliked all schemes for the regeneration of his country, an attitude Ortega called Africanism. "Our defects, or what others call our defects, are usually the root of our excellencies," wrote Unamuno. "The qualities that are censured as our vices are the foundation of our virtues." He was far from being a reactionary, but he wanted the world to know that if Africa did not begin at the Pyrenees, a unique place called Spain most certainly did.

The first quarter of the twentieth century witnessed the highest cultural level in Spain since the 1600s. Among many other writers normally included in the Generation of '98 were the Sevillian Machado, Nobel-Prize winner Juan Ramón Jiménez (*Platero y Yo*) and Pío Baroja (*The Tree of Knowledge*), whom Hemingway idolized. One writer of notable success (a Nobel Prize, 1922) *not* part of the group was Jacinto Benavente, who rescued Spanish theater from its overwrought melodramatic style.

Besides providing fodder for intellectuals, the Spanish-American War took a heavy toll on the political system of the Restoration, and on the facile optimism and national pride of an essentially corrupt government. In the soul-searching aftermath inept politicians, rather than the military, were blamed for Spain's disastrous performance against the upstart "nation of sausage eaters." Spaniards wanted change.

Spain's political history from 1898 to 1923 was a prolonged attempt—in the face of regionalism, violent labor strife, assassinations, and more foreign fiascos—to redeem the dying parliamentary system of Cánovas. For two decades it tottered on the brink, hopelessly out of step with the changing times. In simpler days, the progressive and conservative factions had represented most of the country's economic interests. But the Spain of 1900 was changing, and many new voices strained to be heard among the old elitist chorus. A fistful of new problems would combine to break down the Restoration consensus.

For a start, Spain's economic growth was very uneven. On one hand, the first two decades of the new century witnessed sudden vitality in industry, commerce, mining, banking, and transportation. Spain made progress in light industries like cement and chemicals, producing such marvels as a concrete boat and the highest cement chimney in Europe. For the first time there were more industrial workers than artisans. On the other hand, virtually all the economic strides occurred in Cataluña and the Basque provinces, followed later by Madrid. (By 1920 Cataluña was using half the national power output.) Spain as a whole was still a rural country with half its workers employed in agriculture, the highest percentage in Western Europe. And its farms were the least productive, with millions of acres lying fallow while much of the nation went hungry. Part of the problem was Spain's harsh climate and poor soil, but it was also a question of attitudes. In 1907, some peasants destroyed the local meteorological station and killed its director because they believed it caused drought.

Modern Spanish cities took shape with the new economic realities, bursting out of their almost medieval confinements. Squares were opened up and wide streets—such as Madrid's Gran Via and Barcelona's Via Layetana—built through congested areas. Opulent neo-classical banks testified to the power and wealth of the new business class. Madrid in 1900 was Spain's administrative and educational capital, and over the next three decades it would also become a city of bankers, businessmen, and factory workers. The last group formed seventy percent of Madrid's population by 1930, and the capital could no longer be considered merely a paradise for bureaucratic parasites.

With its sumptuous buildings and middle-class trappings, Barcelona seemed respectable and prosperous. The city was staging modern plays, producing architects like Gaudí, and attracting a lively bohemian world to its old Gothic quarter. But all this was on the surface. Underneath lay another dimension, a seething world of wild-eyed anarchists and common hoodlums. Occasionally it boiled over, as in the 1893 bombing of the Liceo Theater. There was indeed another Barcelona, described by the Czech writer Karel Capek: a city with a dirty, noisy harbor, a murky red-light district (the *barrio chino*), and a famous street called Las Ramblas, "designed to ogle the girls and to start a revolution." For Capek, working-class districts were full of "men with clenched fists in their pockets and rabid, defiant eyes."

Industrialization in Spain meant the same things Great Britain experienced half-a-century earlier: large-scale peasant migration from country to city to escape rural poverty, only to find that in the city their poverty was no longer picturesque. Barcelona in particular gained ill repute for its squalid slums of workers' shacks, occupied by poor Catalans and starving peasants from Murcia and Almería provinces, the social pariahs of Spain. These desperate men would form the armies of working-class agitators that seemed so out of place in bourgeois Barcelona.

Between 1900 and 1913, 1.5 million Spaniards (from a population of 18.6 million) moved to cities or immigrated to Latin America. Many more yearned to go, including all three hundred inhabitants of the village of Boado, who offered their services in a letter to the president of Argentina (he declined). Emigration abroad was an important safety valve, especially in poor regions like Galicia and Andalucía, and it peaked in the years prior to the First World War.

Amid these profound changes, the Catholic Church remained Spain's most important social institution. since the Restoration of 1875 it had regained much of the power, prestige, and wealth lost during its struggles with the liberals. For the most part, the Spanish church abandoned its historic role as a positive force for the common man and embraced the wealthy and reactionary classes. The Jesuits in particular succeeded in joining the elite, and by 1912 they controlled an estimated one-third of Spain's capital wealth. They also had an iron-grip on secondary education. ("The Jesuits do not educate, they domesticate," it was said.)

Aligned with the forces of reaction, the church took up a rabidly anti-liberal posture. Clericalism in Spain was not just a matter of religion; the church's insidious presence was felt in every realm of thought and action.

Students were taught that if they associated with liberals or Freemasons they would go to hell. A Catholic catechism (1927) featured a series of questions and answers for young pupils such as: "Q: What kind of sin is Liberalism? A: It is a most grievous sin against faith. Q: What sin is committed by him who votes for a liberal candidate? A: Generally a mortal sin."

And yet by 1900 many Spaniards had lost their faith and, as former believers tend to be, many ex-Catholics were strongly anti-clerical. Less than five percent of the men of New Castilla and Andalucía attended Mass, although the figures were much higher in the north, especially among the staunchly Catholic Basques. The most significant trend was the large-scale rejection of religion by the new urban working class, who viewed it as one more pillar of a system that oppressed them. There were also strong feelings about religion among the middle class; for example, an anti-clerical play, Pérez Galdós' *Electra* (1901), sold ten thousand copies in two days.

In fairness, not all church leaders were knee-jerk reactionaries. A Catholic reformist wing, gathering round the teachings of Pope Leo XIII, tried with some success to create workingmen's associations and promote social justice. But there were new creeds preached by more persuasive "miracle workers," which vied for workers' allegiance: namely anarchism and Marxian socialism.

The astounding growth of anarchism is modern Spain's most distinctive political feature. In no other European country did it have such an impact. The Russian Mikhail Bakunin, who broke with Marxists and called for the end to all government, created anarchism as a political philosophy. He proclaimed: "The new world will be won only after the last king has been strangled in the guts of the last priest." Anarchism first entered Spain in 1868, and within five years there were an estimated fifty thousand Spanish followers. Part and parcel of the creed was the mystique it attached to revolutionary violence, called "propaganda by deed." In 1883, a conspiracy called The Black Hand, which supposedly planned to murder the entire upper class of Andalucía, was uncovered and fourteen anarchists were garroted in Cádiz. A few years later, thousands of peasants armed with sickles marched into Jerez de la Frontera and attacked anyone wearing good clothes. Political bombings began in the 1890s and included the famous attack on the Liceo that killed dozens. In the next few years, anarchists killed three prime ministers and wounded another and made two nearly successful attacks on the king.

Anarchism may have appealed to the Spaniard's famed independent spirit, the natural inclination to imagine himself an "absolute monarch" of his own destiny. But there was more to the story. In the south anarchism was more a state of mind than an organized movement and fit nicely with the village mentality of complete self-reliance and distrust of outsiders. In a region of grating poverty and huge, under-worked estates, anarchist ideas became almost a religion with promises of "salvation" by distributing land—the semi-mystical *reparto* that would usher in a utopian society called "libertarian communism." Every *pueblo* had its village anarchist, often-austere preachers of vegetarianism, sexual abstinence, and atheism as well as hatred of government. "Converted" workers suddenly gave up smoking, drinking, gambling, and whoring. They never married, but lived openly with a *compañera* and refused to baptize any children that might arrive. There was something strikingly backward about the rural anarchists' vision, as if they were trying to recover a lost medieval bliss, when there were common lands and every man enjoyed equality and dignity. In their resistance to modern economic conditions, anarchists shared much with Carlists. Hence, the new "political religion" also appealed in rural Cataluña and Aragón, once Carlist strongholds.

Anarchism also took root in Barcelona, usually known for its *seny* (Catalan common sense), but with a restless new working class to deal with. Here developed the anarcho-syndicalist strain that appealed to factory workers by using trade-union tactics (the CNT). The general strike was the ultimate weapon to bring down the system, and with it would come one final outburst of violence "to end all violence." Many of these true believers were fanatical teetotalers and vegetarians, as interested in closing *barrio chino* brothels as in economic progress.

Spanish Socialists (the PSOE, founded in 1879) despised the sentimental brand of revolution preached by these so-called left-wing Carlists. The UGT was the party's moderate and disciplined trade union, Marxist in theory but cast in the European social-democratic mould and led by the son of a poor washerwoman. Its numbers rose sharply: from 115 branches in 1906 to double that four years later. The UGT was strongest in Madrid and Bilbao and came to represent Castilian centralism as opposed to the separatism of Barcelona. Yet party membership lagged behind the anarchists; a miraculous *reparto* was more appealing than tedious Marxist doctrines about slow economic transformation.

Growing regionalism further complicated the Spanish political landscape around 1900, dominated by the "Catalan Question." Catalans disliked centralizing Madrid, but Catalanism was more a product of new economic realities than traditional rivalry with Castilla. The movement always had its radical-left side, which often overlapped with anarchism, but around 1900 conservatives took charge. Businessmen had enjoyed a virtual monopoly of Cuban trade, and the disaster of 1898 hit hard. Over the next two decades, the main goal of the *Lliga Regionalista* party became trade tariffs and other protection for industry. Later, Catalans would demand much more.

The Basque movement was quite different, springing from a kind of primitive peasant nationalism based on fuzzy conceptions of the Basque race that advocated isolation to preserve "racial purity." Make no mistake, Basques *are* different (they have been called the Scots of Spain) and their language is unique. But unlike Catalans, Basques lacked a truly distinctive culture other than their quaint folk festivals of wood-chopping, stone-lifting, and other "manly sports." Basque writers such as Baroja and Unamuno invariably wrote in Castilian.

Basque nationalism became a force in the 1890s through the ideas of Luis and Sabino Arana, who realized that Carlism was a hopeless cause but shared the movement's archaic values. They considered Basques superior to other Spaniards and invented the term *Euskadi* to describe the seven provinces (four in Spain, three in France) that should comprise a new Basque nation. Sabino also designed a Basque flag, worked to produce a standardized language, called *euskera*, and founded the Basque Nationalist Party (PNV).

Basques have always been Spain's most fervid Catholics (remember St. Ignatius), and there was a large degree of ultra-conservative Catholicism in their philosophy. Extremists muttered about lost *fueros* and isolating the Basque lands from the outside world in order to recover the old pre-liberal way of life. Indeed, all that liberalism seemed to bring were higher taxes and military conscription. By contrast, *Euskadi* would be a theocratic state that excluded non-Catholics. In addition to its rural roots, Basque nationalism also sprang from very real social-economic changes after 1900. The population of Vizcaya province, for example, had doubled since 1850, largely from the massive immigration of Castilian workers to Bilbao and other industrial centers. Moreover, Basque businessmen—among Spain's most successful—had their own commercial needs that often clashed with policy from Madrid and also became "nationalists."

Spain's new king, Alfonso XIII, found out how much things were changing on his wedding day in 1906. A crazed anarchist hurled a bomb at the
royal carriage that killed twenty-four and barely missed the king and his bride.
Alfonso had come of age four years earlier, assuming power from his doting
mother, the regent. He was taller than
average, robustly healthy, affable, and
fairly good looking. Alfonso was also
the king of Spain and, in short,
Europe's most eligible bachelor. While
a guest of Edward VII in London, he
fell madly in love with Victoria
Eugenia, the king's niece and grandchild of Queen Victoria. (Her father
was Prince Henry of Battenberg, great-
grandfather of England's Prince Philip.)
Once back in Spain, Alfonso bom-

Basques speak a language unrelated to
any other

barded "Ena" with affectionate postcards, and the couple was married in
Madrid's San Jerónimo church a year later. And so the British and Spanish
royal families became inextricably linked.

Alfonso seemed a decent fellow at first: he was self-confident, but with a
good sense of humor, even at his own expense. He practiced a methodical
routine, rising precisely at seven to begin his day, and lived in Spartan surroundings. (You can see his bedroom exactly as it was in Madrid's Royal Palace.) Most important, the king swore to observe the constitution. There were
troubling signs, however, that Alfonso did not intend to reign in the detached
style of a constitutional monarch. With his constant meddling in the government, he became merely another politician, and many ministers resigned an-
grily or were sacked. Sixty-six (including eight prime ministers) came and
went during the first four years of Alfonso's reign, and there would be thirty-
three different governments in all from 1902 to 1923, the year he turned to a
dictator to save the monarchy.

Like his brother-in-law, Kaiser Wilhelm II, Alfonso adored military pa-
rades and uniforms, and he changed clothes four or five times a day. Since
boyhood his closest contacts were military attachés, and the army came to
represent all that was manly and admirable for him, his "right arm" emotion-
ally if not yet politically. Whenever parliament became critical of military
blundering, the crown stood behind "its" officers.

Even after its pasting in 1898, the army proved remarkably resilient. The military budget, for example, was considered something beyond question, even though it ate up half the government's revenue. Most of the money went to salaries of the swollen officer corps (one for every ten men, compared with one for twenty in France). But when reformers tried to deal with this problem, a panel of generals suggested ending the imbalance by calling up more men for service. In truth an army of bureaucrats more than soldiers, the military became a state within the state. The war minister was a general, and there were no civilian watchdogs against corruption or waste. The army's main concern became "defending its honor against insults," that is, press criticism and objectionable newspaper cartoons. In 1905, it won a major victory by gaining the power to try civilian critics in military courts.

After the loss of America, the army's main interest shifted to Morocco. Many Spaniards brought up on Reconquest lore held a vague belief in their historic destiny to control North Africa, and Spain already boasted two tiny colonies on the Mediterranean coast, Melilla and Ceuta. In the 1880s the desolate Rio de Oro outpost on the Atlantic side was added. Then, at the Algeciras Conference (1906) France and Spain were entrusted with the "supervision" of Morocco. Eventually Spain's protectorate would include the entire northern coastal strip excluding Tangier, which was under international control. (French Morocco was much larger.)

Spain received poor compensation for accepting the French land-grab. Its zone was poor, nearly without roads, and filled with restless Berber tribes that not even the sultan could control. Anyone who dared entering the mountainous interior was either castrated or murdered and sent back lashed to a donkey. In 1909 a handful of natives wiped out a Spanish column, which led to a serious crisis when the government tried to call up reserves in Cataluña to serve in Morocco.

The "Tragic Week" in Barcelona began with a general strike and became much more. Street barricades were thrown up, bombs tossed (many by government agitators), some fifty churches and convents destroyed or damaged, nuns "liberated" from their virtue, tombs desecrated. The frenzy led to some macabre scenes—drunken workers dancing in the streets with corpses of disinterred nuns and other shocking outrages. Government reaction to the violence was swift and merciless: 175 workers were shot in the streets and many more executed in the aftermath. In some cases, simultaneous hanging and shooting satisfied both civil and military justice. Naturally, all this led workers and police alike to swear more oaths of hatred and revenge for "the next time."

The Tragic Week also saw the emergence of a new political force with an interesting future—the Radical Republicans of Alejandro Lerroux, a strange group even in the weird world of Barcelona politics. Lerroux was a young journalist with an outrageous streak who relished his role as "Emperor of the Paralelo," referring to a vice-ridden slum quarter where he drew support. His inflammatory speeches and articles attacking the middle class and clergy became legendary: "Young barbarians of today, enter and sack the decadent civilization of this unhappy country; destroy its temples; finish off its gods; tear the veil from its [religious] novices and raise them up to be mothers to propagate the species." Many of Lerroux's "young barbarians" manned the barricades during the revolt and vied with anarchists for worker loyalty.

The troubles in Cataluña ruined the conservative coalition of the prime minister, Antonio Maura. The liberal party was hardly in better shape, with its promising leader, José Canalejas, killed by an anarchist's bullet in 1912. By the arrival of the World War (1914-1918) the parliamentary system was in its final throes, but the economy of neutral Spain—Catalan cloth and Basque coal—was booming and helped delay the imminent collapse. Public opinion split over the war, and the king carefully walked the tightrope of neutrality; his mother was Austrian and his wife English, enough to seal the lips of any man.

As in most of Europe, the post-war years brought more troubled times for Spain, a deadly cocktail of working-class strife, regionalism, wild price fluctuations, revolving-door government ministries (about one every six months), and a new twist—a labor union of some army officers, the *juntas de defensa*. In 1917, various elements converged on the government to demand "renovation." Trouble started in the spring with the army unions, when the champions of law-and-order turned against the state with the very power entrusted to them. However, when labor organized a general strike that summer, the army returned to the fold and ruthlessly crushed unrest. It had "saved" the nation once again.

These were heady times for revolutionaries, who could reflect on recent events in Russia that toppled an old order in some ways similar to Spain's. The anarchist labor union (CNT) surged from fourteen thousand members in 1914 to *seven hundred thousand* only five years later. The Socialists—who regarded anarchists as gun-toting cranks—also gained ground. In the following years political violence grew worse, especially in Barcelona, which became a refuge for every type of sordid character—spies, gangsters, hired gunmen called *pistoleros*, professional agitators—all offering their services to police, employers, and unions alike. Virtual gang-warfare broke out between the CNT and the owner-backed Free Syndicates. In five years about a thousand people were gunned down in Barcelona, including twenty-one assassinations in thirty-six hours in January of 1921. After the government responded with force, Prime Minister Eduardo Dato met with a hail of bullets from a passing car as he walked across Madrid's Plaza de Independencia.

Spain's constitutional monarchy was deeply wounded by 1920. What finished it off, however, was not revolutionary violence but the war in Morocco. Local tribes under the leadership of the charismatic Abd-el-Krim were stirring up trouble, and an impatient Alfonso ignored the head of the war office (whom he called "an imbecile") to direct the campaign personally. The king's choice as commander was the brash and daring General Silvestre, who proceeded to lead his men into the greatest military blunder since the "charge of the light brigade." In July of 1921, at a place called Anual, a small force of Berbers ambushed a meandering Spanish column and slaughtered about ten thousand men. (Silvestre promptly killed himself.)

The news of the Anual disaster staggered a nation just starting to forget the army's previous failures. It arrived only two days before Alfonso planned to announce a great Moroccan victory during a speech at the grave of El Cid in Burgos, on the feast day of Santiago, St. James the Moor Slayer. Needless to say, the event was spoiled. Parliament called for an investigation and, in addition to Alfonso's meddling, other troubling questions emerged. Such as why there was not a single armored vehicle in Melilla when half the national budget went to the military.

After two years, on September 17, 1923, the report was finally scheduled for presentation to parliament. But on September 13 General Primo de Rivera led an army uprising and offered his services to the king. It was the first *pronunciamiento* in almost 50 years, and the final nail in the coffin of parliamentary Spain, the end of Spanish liberalism. Primo commanded the important Barcelona garrison, but few of his colleagues around Spain rallied to his *grito* before hearing the king's reaction. According to one story, when the general called in the middle of the night, Alfonso muttered, "Am I awake? Am I dreaming? Am I mad?"

Others claimed he had prior knowledge of the coup. In any case, the king did nothing to stop it. The next day Alfonso's ministers resigned en masse, and he asked Primo to form a government. Many never forgave the king for naming an upstart general as prime minister while the coup's fate was still in doubt. Even worse was his refusal to abide by the constitution and reconvene parliament within three months. The supposedly provisional government lasted six years. When Alfonso broke his oath, he undermined the foundations of the Bourbon Restoration. If the constitution was dead, eventually the king too must go.

Miguel Primo de Rivera y Orbaneja, the Marquis of Estella, was born at Jerez de la Frontera in 1870. He came from an old Andalucian family of landowners with a taste for military service (his uncle was also a general). Primo was in many ways a prototype of the old-style Andalucian aristocrat: hard drinking, horse loving, skirt chasing, garrulous and outspoken, hugely generous and disarmingly sincere. Primo thought he represented a new order, but he belonged more to the same breed of nineteenth-century conspirators as Riego and Pavía. Primo de Rivera believed he was saving the country from ruin, that he was the "iron surgeon" writer Joaquin Costa had prayed for. But cynics called this misguided knight-errant a kind of glorified café politician, with a vague dream of righting all wrongs by making himself ruler. The great historian Salvador de Madariaga wrote that this was in fact the ambition of every Spanish general, if not every Spaniard.

Primo's coup was welcomed with a wave of popular approval and good will. The masses could identify with this sincere Andalucían squire, and Primo played on the paternalistic image by speaking frankly to his fellow citizens on a new contraption called the radio. To the politically naive, Primo seemed the kind of benevolent dictator who could produce the miracles Spain needed, the way a winning lottery ticket can create a rich man in an instant. During a visit to Rome, Alfonso introduced Primo to the Italian king with the words "This is my Mussolini." But Primo was no Mussolini. Although sometimes ruthless, he was too easy-going and optimistic about his fellow man to be a good modern dictator. Censorship was rigid, but he never executed a single political opponent—remarkable for Spain.

The virtue of military rule, said Primo, was that it saved on salaries by replacing civilians with soldiers. It was this kind of irrefutable illogic that gained mass support and caused others to tear out their hair. He had a genius for doing the unexpected. Once, when he learned that the budget deficit had vanished, he announced that the government would redeem all the mattresses the poor had pawned. He loved sitting up till the wee hours discussing politics over a brandy in some dingy café. Later that night he would pen a decree to be issued the next day, only to be cancelled the following. Worn out from these late nights and hard work, he took old-fashioned *siestas*, donning nightcap and nightdress before retiring for several hours. There was always the Primo touch: one night at the theater he lit a cigar but was told that smoking was prohibited. Spain's ruler jumped up and announced, "Tonight everyone may smoke."

Primo was respectful to the king, but never let him have much to do with government. Alfonso seemed content to live the life of a royal playboy, dominating the social pages with his "horsy" wife and flitting between Madrid and aristocratic gathering spots like San Sebastián and Biarritz. The 1920s were a relatively prosperous, carefree decade, and Alfonso enjoyed the sporting life—he was a crack shot—and the frivolity of social affairs. The spirit seemed contagious among Spain's swollen aristocracy. Even Don Jaime, the Carlist pretender, was more interested in nightclubs than in pressing his claims.

Despite his eccentricities, Primo de Rivera brought Spain more than belly laughs. While everyone had their own plan for "regeneration," Primo put his faith in industrialization and public works: roads, harbors, dams, power plants. He left Spain with an improved road system and encouraged tourism by establishing the network of government hotels called *paradores*. Some claim he even made the trains run on time. In other words, he achieved all the goals of a benevolent dictator. Primo's problem was that his dreams were far too grandiose for Spain to pay for. Lacking all but a superficial understanding of a situation, he would issue wildly optimistic proclamations, then discover there was no money in the treasury. Economic planning bogged down in committees that frittered away time and resources on half-baked projects. Moreover, his creation of state monopolies, such as the CAMPSA petroleum company, outraged foreign investors. Unamuno said of Primo: "Spain needed an iron surgeon and got a quack dentist instead."

Primo nonetheless achieved many of his goals. Like all Spanish generals he was anti-regional and especially disliked the Catalan movement. (He even forbade innocuous cultural aspects such as the *sardana* folk dance.) Catalanism had grown more demanding by the early 1920s, moving from autonomy to outright separatism as preached by the nationalist party *Estat Catala*. When the socially conservative *Lliga* supported Primo, Catalanism split in two, and the radical wing slowly gained the upper hand.

Primo also drove a wedge between Socialists and anarchists by embracing the UGT. The union's president was Francisco Largo Caballero, a plasterer who learned to read at age twenty-four and favored cooperation with Primo's paternalistic notions. Driven underground by Primo, the anarchist union grew more revolutionary, creating a terrorist wing called the FAI. One of the leaders was Buenaventura Durruti, who shot the bishop of Zaragoza in revenge for the killing of a CNT official.

The dictator's greatest success came in Morocco. Here, the Berber tribes of the Rif Mountains had unified under Krim and an aristocratic cattle-thief named El Raisuli, whose capital was the holy city of Chechaouen. Primo's decision to negotiate a treaty of withdrawal was bitterly opposed by the "warrior party" in the army (the *africanistas*). Especially indignant were the crusty leaders of the new Foreign Legion—generals Sanjurjo and Millán Astray and a young major named Francisco Franco. Just when things were becoming tense within the military itself (General Weyler of Cuban fame was caught plotting a conspiracy at the ripe old age of eighty-six), the over-confident Moroccans attacked French territory. The two colonial armies crushed the revolt, and the campaign was crowned by Sanjurjo's victory at Alhucemas Bay (1927). The army had redeemed itself and created a new legend.

As might be expected, Primo had trouble with Spanish intellectuals and students. His mildly authoritarian state gave new ammunition to writers of the Generation of '98 such as Unamuno, who called Primo "a coward, a robber, a felon." It had to be admitted by the disillusioned prophets of renovation that parliamentary institutions did not seem to take root in Spain. Nevertheless, a new generation of Spaniards, reaching maturity in the 1920s, gave impetus to a burgeoning avant-garde culture.

A trio of gifted *enfants terribles*—Federico García Lorca, Luis Buñuel, and Salvador Dalí—met as students in Madrid and blazed new cultural trails over the next few years. Born near Granada in 1898, Lorca is undoubtedly the best-known writer of twentieth-century Spain. His many masterpieces of drama and verse explore the themes of death, violence, and sex in a hostile world. The "mad Catalan" Dalí eventually became a self-promoting showman, but his best work—from his Surrealist period of the 1920s and 30s—remains essential to the history of modern art. Paintings such as "The Great

Masturbator" and "Sodomy of a Skull with a Piano" assaulted conventional taboos with an almost anarchistic contempt for bourgeois values. Buñuel was a brilliant filmmaker who collaborated with Dalí in projects such as *An Andalucian Dog*. A more solitary genius was Joan Miró, who studied in Barcelona and moved to Paris (1919), where he encountered Surrealism and Cubism. Here he explored the role of the subconscious in art and developed a remarkably personal style of pure, brilliant color and the playful juxtaposition of lines and abstract shapes. Miró later returned to Spain and spent many years creating astonishing masterpieces at his retreat on Mallorca.

It has been said that nowhere else are heroes so quickly built up and torn down as in Spain. No one can survive long in a country where half the population sits for hours in cafés criticizing the government. So it was with Primo de Rivera, whose own inabilities helped in the demolition process. The dictator's swansong came in 1929 with magnificent international expositions in Sevilla and Barcelona (much of which remain standing). Then came the crash on Wall Street and a disastrous fall in the *peseta*'s value that shattered Spain's temporary prosperity. The end was near.

Although Primo had many enemies, his downfall came after he crossed swords with the army's artillery corps over the subject of promotions. This broke rule number one in Spain: do not disturb the harmony of the "military family." A conspiracy was soon uncovered and its leaders rounded up, but when an army court declared them innocent the message was clear: Primo had lost the support of the one institution that kept him in power.

The international exposition held in Sevilla in 1929, Primo de Rivera's last hurrah

True to his unpredictable form, Primo conducted his own popularity poll among army brass and learned the truth. This breach of royal prerogative was enough grounds for Alfonso to dismiss the old warhorse in 1930.

Primo moved to Paris, where he divided his time between the local church and brothel, and died within a few months. The king believed that by sacking the dictator he could somehow erase his part in the coup of 1923, that his questionable actions would not come back to haunt him. But with Primo gone, public attention focused on the king himself, who had alienated just about everyone. Calmly assuming that things would soon return to normal, he appointed General Berenguer to head the government until elections could be held.

Proponents of a republic were weak in 1930. There was Lerroux and his Radical Republicans; the "Emperor of the Paralelo" had toned down his shrill rhetoric somewhat, but his brand of republicanism failed to gain middle-class support. Many liberal monarchists, Socialists, and Catalans leaned towards a republic, but there was no concerted plan to that end. Then, in August of 1930, the leaders of various anti-Alfonso factions created the Pact of San Sebastián, the "birth certificate" of Spain's Second Republic. Everyone agreed they were against the monarchy, but there were few positive ideas yet. Significantly, they felt that the monarchists would rig popular elections and that a coup was therefore a legitimate means to achieve power.

A revolt was planned for December 15, spearheaded by pro-Republican army officers. But as sometimes happens with Spanish coups, plans went haywire and a certain Captain Galán rose up three days early at Jaca (Aragón). In Madrid, Republican leaders were unable to rally support for the premature uprising, except for the playing of "The Marseillaise" in a few bars. On December 16, Major Ramón Franco (an aviation hero and Francisco's brother) flew over the capital scattering leaflets threatening to bomb Madrid if the garrison did not rise. (Alfonso watched the performance from the roof of his palace.) Nevertheless, within a few days all the rebels were captured and Galán executed. The Republicans had botched the rising but had their first martyr.

Alfonso finally called for municipal elections on April 12, 1931. The results were startling: forty-six of fifty provincial capitals went Republican. It was said that even conservative Madrid police officers, worn out by strikes and student riots, voted Republican in order to get a good night's sleep. Although suspect votes from the corrupt rural areas in the end gave a majority to the monarchists, the popular will was clear. As Alfonso himself remarked, "I had the impression of calling on an old friend and finding him dead."

Events followed rapidly: a republic was declared in Cataluña; in Madrid unruly crowds gathered to demand the king's abdication; General Sanjurjo, by then commander of the civil guard, informed Alfonso that he could not guarantee the loyalty of his men; most important, the army did nothing—a kind of negative *pronunciamiento*. Outside the royal palace the hooting, cursing crowd grew larger, and the king's chief minister, Count Romanones, advised him to leave for his own safety. On the evening of April 14 Alfonso declared, "Sunday's elections have shown me that I no longer enjoy the love of my people." With that he scurried off to Cartagena and boarded a ship bound for France and exile. After 231 years the great Bourbon dynasty had succumbed with but a whimper.

There are numerous myths and misconceptions about the Second Republic. Many believe it brought five years of uninterrupted progress toward a democratic Spain, which was then smashed by a military uprising in 1936. In fact, the Republican experiment can be divided into three periods: roughly two years of radical social change under the left-center; another two years controlled by the right-center during which much of the previous legislation was overturned; and finally, about six months of Popular Front rule before the civil war. Each of the three periods had to contend with a serious armed rebellion. Another myth is that the largely progressive government was destroyed *solely* by a reactionary right. In reality, the moderate parties that launched the great experiment were assaulted mercilessly by both political extremes. Because of the need for coalition governments, the center was never really stable. In the end no middle ground remained, and the course of moderation and compromise—pragmatic politics—was totally abandoned.

Supporters called the Second Republic *la niña bonita*, the pretty girl. It was the last great hope for the "regeneration" of Spain and began with a wave of hopeful optimism. Left-wing Republicans wanted to finish the aborted liberal revolution of the nineteenth century, and the masses of "have-nots" were wildly enthusiastic that a great social revolution had arrived to end their misery. Meanwhile, conservatives watched warily. The key to the Republic's success hinged on the attitude of the middle class, relatively small by European standards but still a pivotal force.

Soon after the king's departure, a provisional government was formed from the same coalition that made the Pact of San Sebastián: Republicans, Socialists, and regionalists. Much of the unfolding story involved the gradual disintegration of this coalition. A moderate Andalucian lawyer named Niceto Alcalá Zamora was elected prime minister to reassure the middle class, already nervous about recent events.

The Republic's honeymoon lasted about a month. During this time the royal flag of red and gold was replaced by the tricolor banner, the royalist national anthem changed to "The Hymn of Riego," and streets and squares around Spain renamed. But by the end of April, the Carlist pretender Don Jaime had already called on anti-Republicans to rally round his cause, and peasants in Navarra started oiling their rifles. By May a wave of church-burnings and lootings around the country (mostly the work of anarchists) had shattered the wild optimism of April. The all-pervasive religious problem was raising its head again, ready to divide Spanish society down the middle. One story tells it all; upon hearing of the monarchy's fall, the mayor of one town telegraphed the new government to ask: "We have declared for the Republic. What shall we do with the priest?"

In the June elections the Socialists emerged from a pack of twenty-six others as the leading party, followed by the Radicals and the Republican Action Party led by newcomer Manuel Azaña. The first Cortes (parliament) opened on July 14, Bastille Day in France, and boasted 123 lawyers, 41 doctors, 65 professors, and 24 workingmen. The socialists were led by Largo Caballero and Prieto and the radicals by Lerroux, a rather misplaced cynic among all the idealists.

The most intriguing figure was Azaña, fat and ugly but a strong-willed intellectual who had been president of Madrid's Ateneo, a literary-political club closed down by Primo for its Republican sympathies. The chain-smoking Azaña was a believer in the "European solution" of the Generation of '98 and a writer of some merit, if not success. This led Unamuno to write: "Beware of Azaña. He is an author without readers. He would be capable of starting a revolution in order to be read." Azaña was named minister of war and promptly embarked on a daring policy of trimming back the military behemoth. He disbanded ten divisions and offered retirement to all officers with *full pay*. Nearly half accepted the plan, but many would soon join the ranks of café politicians, each with his own plan for saving the nation. Azaña made more enemies by closing down the new military academy at Zaragoza, eliciting a bitter speech from its director, General Franco.

Conspicuous by their absence from the Republican coalition were the powerful anarchists of the CNT. Philosophically, they rejected the very idea of government, believing that a "workers' state" was as evil as a bourgeois one. Organization was considered a socialist vice; with over a million members in 1936, the CNT had only one paid secretary. Their idea of politics involved strikes and random violence, anything to weaken the government and bring on the revolution. In response to this threat, the new Republic created its own police force, not called "peace officers" or "constables," but *guardias de asalto*—the assault guard.

The Republic's first order of business was a new constitution, and its drafting created serious rifts from the outset. Rather than a broad statement of principles, it became a controversial political document, full of emotive language and threatening statutes. Spain was defined, with certain illogic, as "a republic of workers of all classes." It would have a president with carefully limited powers and a one-house parliament chosen in free elections.

The democratic consensus unraveled abruptly, however, with the infamous Article 26 dealing with religion. Rather than merely ending the cozy arrangement between church and state and establishing religious freedom, anti-clericals such as Azaña seemed eager to grind the clergy into the mud. Spain, he declared, had ceased to be a Catholic country as of April 12, 1931, and he intended to prove it. Curiously, most members of parliament had received their education at Catholic schools. Azaña himself was a student at the Augustinian college of the Escorial, and much has been made of his own personal motives—rebelling against his former teachers by denying that Spain was Catholic. Article 26 removed Catholicism as the official religion, forbade religious orders from teaching, abolished clerical salaries, legalized divorce, and paved the way to disbanding the Jesuits. Later laws banned Catholic burials unless requested in the deceased's will and prohibited such things as religious processions and ringing church bells. Many provisions were wildly unrealistic; for example, the state lacked the means to replace the church's secondary schools, where most Spanish youths were educated. (Ironically, since the Jesuits in theory no longer existed, many continued to teach as laymen.) Many Catholics in parliament vigorously protested Article 26, and Prime Minister Alcalá resigned. It was happening again—half of Spain was beating up on the other half.

Part of the problem was Azaña himself, a lonely and arrogant man with an acid tongue, who refused to admit mistakes and took every opportunity to pour scorn on opponents. Politics as "the art of the possible" was not Azaña's style; he equated intransigence with integrity and compromise with weakness. (There is no word in Spanish that really equates with the English "to compromise.") The Republic's anti-clerical legislation threw down the gauntlet to Catholic Spain, still a formidable force. In the 1930s the church had thousands of religious communities with more than fifty thousand priests, monks, and nuns. While it is true that two-thirds of Spaniards did not practice their faith, many resented the slap at their collective heritage—something essentially Spanish since the Reconquest. As Unamuno said, "Here in Spain we are all Catholics, even the atheists." Even so, there was a strong anticlerical current supporting the legislation. Catholic workers' federations claimed hundreds of thousands of members, mostly in the countryside, but the church had come to represent the entrenched ruling class to most workingmen. Anarchists in particular equated the church with everything evil and attacked it with their own "religious" passion.

The new constitution also promised a Catalan autonomy statute, agrarian reform, and other measures. Among the most important was granting the franchise to women, who in Spain at the time could be expected to vote more conservatively than men. After much wrangling, the document became law in December of 1931; in a spirit of consensus Alcalá Zamora agreed to become president and then named Azaña as prime minister. The preliminary stage was over; now it was time to get down to business. However, it soon became clear that the "new Spain" created by the constitution was *too* new for half of the country and not new *enough* for the other half. Attempts at land reform were typical of Republican laws in being threatening in principle but weak in practice. The constitution included a vague clause that made property of all kinds "the object of expropriation for social utility." This and later laws affected not only the large landowners but also middling farmers. Hence, aside from the pitiful landless class of Andalucía, the peasants of rural Spain never really supported the Republic.

Agrarian reform was probably the most serious issue facing the new government because Spain in the 1930s remained a predominately rural country. Farm owners tended to have either very large estates or tiny plots; the middle sector was small. In Andalucía, one percent of the owners controlled forty-two percent of the land, much of which was not tilled. For example, near Jerez de los Caballeros, fifty six thousand acres served as a shooting estate. Agricultural methods were backward and produced poor harvests on large estates and *minifundia* alike. The landless workers of the south (*los braceros*) formed Spain's most wretched class; well over half were illiterate and chronically unemployed or under-employed. They worked part of the year on the wheat or olive harvest, then subsisted in idleness and semi-starvation in their whitewashed *pueblos* (not yet considered picturesque) until the next harvest came along. They were potentially the most revolutionary group in the country if they could shed an ingrained sense of resignation to their fate. These workers were soon flooding the ranks of the socialist union or were confirmed anarchists awaiting the revolution. Their sworn enemies were the hated civil guard, often men of their own class who ruthlessly protected the property owners. Organized as part of the army and led by a general, the *guardias*—with their green uniforms, tri-cornered hats, and Mauser rifles—numbered about thirty thousand at the time.

Reformers pointed to statistics and advocated land re-distribution, but they were torn between handing out small parcels and creating large, more efficient collective farms. What was most needed—investment in irrigation and other measures to improve production—was given short shrift. The only real solution to the agrarian problem was to reduce the rural population by encouraging industry, a long-term project. And hungry workers were not thinking in the long term. Agrarian reform was therefore a disappointing muddle. Any farm over fifty-six acres not being worked could be confiscated at its appraised value, and in two years about twelve thousand families received land. But the total area under cultivation had actually dropped by 750,000 acres. Largo Caballero called the reforms "an aspirin to cure an appendicitis."

Cataluña's autonomy statute gave the region a powerful government called the *Generalitat* with its own president, parliament, tax system, and flag, but it stopped short of outright independence. Both Socialists and the right wing attacked Catalan autonomy as a threat to national unity, but it made Cataluña a stronghold of the Republic. Legislators began working on another statute for the Basques, who were likewise eager for local rule.

With all the changes right-wing reaction was sure to come eventually, and it cropped up first with an ineptly planned coup in the summer of 1932 led by General Sanjurjo. This haphazard plot was discussed in Madrid cafés for weeks, and the government apparently learned details through a chatty prostitute. When Sanjurjo finally "pronounced" in Sevilla it was a fiasco, and he was promptly arrested. The bungled coup was merely the comical side of a host of threats to the Republic. Opposition to reforms from both left *and* right grew steadily stronger during those first two years, while few seemed satisfied. Azaña's religious policy had virtually forced every practicing Catholic to oppose the Republic, splitting the middle class. The working class too was wary. The success or failure of the Republican experiment depended on its ability to please the workers without triggering violent reaction. But was this possible?

The anarchists dismissed the Republic as a bourgeois façade and sponsored ceaseless strikes and disruption. The extremist wing in particular (the FAI) wanted to get on with the business of class revolution. The southern anarchists—angry at the slow pace of *reparto*—were likewise becoming more restive. Villages were striking at will, but usually at the least effective times— when there were no crops to harvest. In January 1932, four civil guards were murdered during a riot in the town of Castilblanco (Extremadura). Their bodies were hacked to pieces while village women danced round them in glee.

Another less dramatic but no less deadly enemy of the Second Republic was the sluggish Spanish economy, just starting to feel the effects of the Great Depression. By mid-decade exports were about one-quarter the 1930 level, and the ranks of the unemployed swelled to 600,000 by the end of 1933. And men without jobs are usually unhappy with whoever is in power. Although Spain did not suffer the same collapse as more industrialized nations, it was not an auspicious time to initiate a political experiment.

The powers of high finance and big business also detested the egalitarian Republic. Among them was a swashbuckling capitalist named Juan March, whose life became the stuff of legend. March was a farmer's son from Mallorca who became Spain's richest man by intelligence, daring, and ruthlessness served up in equal portions. In 1916, he founded the Transmediterranea shipping company, controlling maritime traffic between mainland Spain and the islands. Later he snared the tobacco monopoly in Spanish Morocco and created a thriving smuggling empire. After being elected to the Republican parliament by admiring Mallorcans, March was charged with fraud and hauled off to jail. He escaped, and then proceeded to sabotage the Spanish currency from abroad. A confirmed enemy of the Republic, March would reappear later in the story.

Sadly, the Republicans themselves helped undermine the "beautiful girl." Of the three major parties, the Socialists and the misnamed Radicals (Lerroux's group was now quite conservative) were bitter rivals, leaving Azaña's weak left-Republicans holding the balance of power. In that role, the party's coldly detached leader succumbed to petty squabbles and personality conflicts with Lerroux and others. He therefore allied with the fickle Socialists, who were ready to abandon the Republic at the slightest provocation. As the two extremes loomed menacingly in the wings, the center grew steadily weaker. Spain needed statesmen or, at the very least, pragmatists to solve problems, not ideologues passing quixotic resolutions. It seemed that Azaña had read but not digested the message of the Generation of '98: bring reason to Spanish society or perish.

Contrary to conservative claims, however, the Azaña government was far from weak toward social upheaval. There were more police in uniform than under Primo, and large numbers of suspects were held in prison without trial or banished, as in the case of one Azaña opponent sent to a remote village and forced to live in a stable. A serious blow to the Republic's prestige was the affair of Casas Viejas, a poor village in Cádiz province that proclaimed itself independent under *comunismo libertario* in January of 1933. When the *guardia civil* and assault guards besieged a group of ringleaders, about twenty villagers died under questionable circumstances. Outrage among the left ensued when the commander swore that Azaña had ordered a take-no-prisoners policy.

A swing to the right began with the elections of 1933, in which six million women voted for the first time. Chief beneficiary was a union of conservative Catholic factions called CEDA, under the leadership of José María Gil Robles. This loose coalition included monarchists, Carlists, and anyone else appalled by Azaña's religious policies and by anti-clericalism generally. (In the Republic's five years about two hundred clerics were killed and five hundred churches damaged or destroyed.) Gil Robles had been an attorney for the Jesuits and the Sanjurjo conspirators and was rather slippery in his politics, refusing to confirm or deny his support of the Republic. CEDA's own propaganda implied that it sought to impose an authoritarian government by gaining a parliamentary majority. One reason for the rightward turn was that left-Republicans and Socialists had refused to cooperate in the elections. Nevertheless, they were outraged by the prospects of a CEDA government, and President Alcalá named Lerroux as a compromise prime minister. Naturally, this new center cabinet was inherently unstable.

Thus opened a period dubbed *el bienio negro*, the two black years, during which much of the previous legislation was overturned or ignored. Particularly galling was the release of Sanjurjo and his cohorts, a virtual green light for future military meddlers. Soon the left began to look at new options, and Socialist leader Largo Caballero declared that revolution was the "workers' only hope." When one clerical newspaper called for peace and harmony amid the growing tension, *El Socialista* replied: "Harmony? No! Class war! Hatred to the death for the criminal bourgeoisie!" The anarchists in turn were outraged by Largo's attempt to steal their revolutionary thunder and stepped up agitation of their own.

Meanwhile, another force had emerged on the left: the Spanish Communist Party (PCE). Since splitting with the Socialists over the course of the Russian Revolution, the Communists had been the odd-man-out in Spanish politics, with only about a thousand party members in 1930. But three years later they numbered twenty five thousand and received four hundred thousand votes. The first Communist was sitting in Spain's new parliament.

Jose Antonio Prima de Rivera, leader of Spain's fascist movement, the Falange

Another newcomer to the Cortes was the leader of the Falange, an extremist group not unlike others sprouting up across Europe. And like the Italian Fascists, German Nazis, and Belgian Rexists, Falangists forged an odd blend of working-class sentiment, blatant nationalism (in this case calls for a new Spanish Empire), and plain hooliganism. The group's name, which meant "phalanx," was taken from the Macedonian army unit that overthrew the republic of Athens in the fourth century BC.

The Falange's leader was the charismatic José Antonio Primo de Rivera, thirty-year-old son of the fallen dictator, whose tarnished honor he swore to defend. José Antonio was a complex figure, born to the life of a *señorito* (a wealthy Andalucian playboy), but in reality much more—charming, daring, and passionately concerned with the fate of Spain and the average Spaniard. Falangism as a political creed owed much to the soul-searching of the Generation of '98, and José Antonio mesmerized throngs with brilliant oratory about the "new Spain." He called for land reform and socialization of the banks and railways, which angered conservatives. Despite its lip service to the working class, most Falangists were students, disgruntled anarchists, and offbeat intellectuals. Besides Madrid, Spanish fascism drew support in the Sevilla-Cádiz area, precisely where the Communists were most active. In 1933, José Antonio merged his band with kindred spirits, and they adopted fascist trappings such as blue shirts and the raised-arm salute. For their flag they chose red and black, the same colors as the anarchists. Their symbol was the yoke and arrows of Fernando and Isabel, and the maudlin tune "Face to the Sun" became their anthem. All this sentimentality could not disguise their use of hard-core street violence to achieve their goals.

Alongside the Falange, the red-bereted Carlists seemed positively antiquated, but their ranks grew steadily with ultra-conservatives, especially in Catholic Navarra. In splitting with the Basques, Carlists had chosen the monarchy and nation over the old issue of local rights. And they now had an efficient organization under Fal Conde, a pretender in Alfonso Carlos, and hidden stockpiles of arms in remote corners of Navarra. There were also reports of four hundred Carlist officers, disguised as Peruvians, training in Italy.

The Republic had banished Alfonso XIII for "high treason," and he lived out his life in Italian exile, occasionally traveling abroad as the Count of Covadonga. Monarchists grouped around the *Renovación Española* of José Calvo Sotelo, former finance minister under Primo. They gained forty-four seats in the November 1933 elections.

As the year 1934 began, therefore, the Spanish political scene was splitting into two hostile camps. Each side became convinced that the other was on the verge of seizing power and planned the appropriate countermeasures. That summer in Madrid a young Falangist was beaten to death at the Casa del Campo by a group of socialist thugs; his eyes were gouged out and a girl in the mob urinated into the empty sockets. When news of the outrage spread, a falangist posse drove to a working-class district and began shooting randomly at suspected Socialists. Somehow they managed to kill the squatting girl. It was but one more incident of hundreds in a spiraling cycle of violence gripping the country.

In the purely political sphere, it was growing evident that the exclusion of CEDA from the cabinet could not continue. When parliament adjourned in July, everyone assumed that October would bring a crisis. It came on schedule with the inclusion of three CEDA members in the Lerroux cabinet, which sparked a full-scale Socialist revolt against the "fascist conquest of the Republic." (The far left was convinced that Gil Robles was a secret fascist.) The UGT called for a general strike, and from the balcony of the Generalitat, Luis Companys proclaimed an independent Catalan state *within* a federal republic. But the trouble soon died out or was crushed throughout Spain—

everywhere except in Asturias. This rugged mining region in the north had strong Communist unions and a reckless tradition of direct labor confrontation. One local Communist heroine was Dolores Ibarruri, dubbed *La Pasionaria* (the Passion Flower), who always wore black and was regarded as a kind of revolutionary saint. The right spread rumors that she had once slit a priest's throat with her teeth.

Upon learning of the general strike, rebels in isolated mining towns south of Oviedo rose up and attacked police and army posts by hurling sticks of dynamite "liberated" from the mines. For about a week workers' committees controlled Asturias without opposition as the government waited, fearing that regular troops might not fire on the miners if a showdown came. Finally, as reports of murdered priests and other atrocities spread, Madrid decided to send in the Foreign Legion. With them were mercenaries called *regulares*, actually Moroccans under Spanish command. The irony was profound—Muslims being called in by Catholic Spain to crush the one region never conquered by the Moors. Based on the French model, the Spanish Foreign Legion was created in the twenties as a crack unit to fight Moroccan mountain tribes. The legionnaires, mostly Spaniards, were a tough, harshly disciplined force trained to cry *"Viva la muerte!"* ("Hooray for death!") as they rushed into battle. They were led by one-eyed, one-armed General Millán Astray and an eager understudy who had designed the legion's uniform and written its history: Francisco Franco.

Franco's army of legionnaires and Moroccans moved through Asturias with bloody precision, village by village, house by house. There were many reports of murder, torture, rape, and other crimes against the population, especially by the Moors. When the smoke cleared about two thousand were dead and thousands more wounded or in jail. It was like a dress rehearsal for the civil war to come, as the split between right and left widened into a gaping chasm: no one could sit on the political fence after Asturias.

About thirty thousand Spaniards were in jail, among them opposition leaders Azaña and Largo Caballero. The aging Socialist remained behind bars more than a year, giving him the chance to read Marx for the first time and ponder the coming revolution he felt destined to lead. (*Pravda* deemed him "the Spanish Lenin," and Largo was intoxicated with the image.) The recent revolt had failed, but there could be another and still another if necessary.

In the months of right-coalition government that followed October 1934, the Catalan Statute was suspended and much of the agrarian reform repealed.

The country remained in an official "state of alarm," but the right, significantly, did not try to take over, even when the appointment of Gil Robles as prime minister became long overdue. The reason, perhaps, is that reactionaries did not yet have the full support of the ultimate arbiter of Spanish politics—the army. In the years following Sanjurjo's failed coup, a hidden but heated debate simmered within the ranks. An officer's first duty was loyalty, said some, whether to a monarchy or republic. Yes, replied others, but what if obedience conflicted with "dignity"? In 1933, a secret society of disgruntled junior officers (the UME) formed and began plotting. Everyone in the army continued to watch and wait, including the tight-lipped Franco, named chief-of-staff in May of 1935.

While the political world seethed, there was a final radiant glow from the fire of Spanish culture lit earlier in the century. García Lorca published three new plays in 1935, and the poets Alberti, Aleixandre, and Guillen contributed to the ongoing literary flowering. The same year, Buñuel produced his documentary masterpiece *Land Without Bread* about the squalid Las Hurdes area in Extremadura. And in Barcelona, Pablo Casals created a symphony orchestra and choral society. This exuberant cultural scene stood in stark contrast with the political disintegration all around.

Corruption finally brought down the Lerroux government, the twenty-eighth cabinet in five years, and Alcalá decided to call elections for February, believing that the nation was ready to elect a moderate government. He could not have been more wrong. Remembering the last electoral debacle, leftist parties merged into the Popular Front, a Communist-inspired tactic already used in France to defeat "fascism." (The Popular Front per se was not Communist.) Previously aloof (they called Socialists "social fascists" and anarchists "petit-bourgeois pseudo-revolutionaries"), the Communists now championed the spirit of working-class cooperation. In response, conservative groups united in the so-called National Front, lumping together parties from conservative Republicans to fascists and appealing to the Catholic middle class and peasants of northern Spain. The center was growing smaller, but could count on the Basque nationalists, still going their own myopic way.

Fierce campaign rhetoric swirled around the issue of the October 1934 revolt. Leaders of the major parties all stated publicly that they would only respect the election results if they won, *never* if they lost. Largo declared that if the right won, he would "proceed to declare civil war," and Calvo Sotelo told Spaniards that "a red flag would fly over Spain" if they did not vote for the National Front. Voting took place on February 16, 1936, Carnival Sunday just before Lent, and about 70 percent of the electorate went to the polls. Although the popular vote was extremely close—4.6 million (PF) and 4.5 million (NF)—Popular Front candidates won 263 seats in parliament to the right's 133. The center captured only Vizcaya, Guipuzcoa, and Soria provinces, but held a good deal of power with 77 seats. Conservative Spain was shocked at the results, and General Franco promised support if the interim prime minister chose to declare a "state of war" rather than hand over power. But he declined the offer.

Thus Spain's last elected government for forty years was born amid general panic—the left fearing an army coup and the right a social revolution. Azaña (having been freed earlier) was named prime minister of the Popular Front government, and he moved quickly to grant amnesty to political prisoners, restore Catalan autonomy, and move generals of questionable loyalty to remote posts. Franco was sent to the Canary Islands. José Antonio of the Falange was arrested in March on a weapons charge and languished in an Alicante jail. The new government was doomed to failure from the outset, however, by Largo's refusal to cooperate. Socialist post-election victory marches featured huge portraits of Stalin and Lenin, as thousands of slogan-chanting workers with clenched fists carried banners that read, "Long live the red army." All the while an increasingly horrified middle class looked on. With the Socialists' refusal to join the government, Spain began its final dance of disintegration. There was no turning back.

B y spring the countryside was on the verge of social revolution. Early one morning in March, sixty thousand peasants in Extremadura occupied the large farms, cried "*Viva La Republica!*" and started to plough. In just over two months there were 196 peasant strikes in Andalucía alone. In Madrid, vendors of the Communist journal fought pitched battles with newsboys hawking conservative papers. Cars full of Falangists, armed with machine guns, cruised the main avenues looking for "lefties" to mow down. Often the resulting funeral turned into a political rally that ended with a pitched battle between rival factions right in the cemetery.

In this violent atmosphere, enrollment in extremist factions swelled. The moderate right began to abandon Gil Robles' CEDA for the more inflammatory Calvo Sotelo, who openly longed for the nation's missing "spinal column." But the army itself was divided; a pro-Republican group (the UMRA) was picking up support and began trading random assassinations with the UME. Despite it all, Azaña scoffed that rumors of army coups were "as plentiful as the acacia trees on the Castellana."

In mid-June, Gil Robles stood up in parliament and indicted the government for its failure to maintain order. In four months, he said, there had been 269 murders and 1,287 injuries in political attacks, 341 strikes, and almost 400 churches destroyed or damaged. He went on: "A country can live under a monarchy or a republic, with a parliamentary or a presidential system, under communism or fascism. But it cannot live in anarchy."

Gil's figures were exaggerated, but the point was clear nonetheless. On July 11, Calvo Sotelo delivered another bitter attack on the government. When he sat down, Ibarruri (*La Pasionaria*) reportedly shouted, "That was your last speech." (Some sources dispute this incident.) Four days later, an officer in the assault guard (and UMRA member) was cut down by falangist gunmen. Vowing revenge, several of his comrades, led by a Communist civil-guard captain, went to the home of Calvo Sotelo. The politician was suspicious, but he agreed to accompany them to an undisclosed destination. He left home promising to telephone his family soon, "unless these gentlemen are going to blow out my brains." A few hours later, his battered body—with a bullet in the back of the neck—was dumped at the gates of the local cemetery.

The murder of Calvo Sotelo by a squad of off-duty police sent a shudder throughout Spain. Many believed the government was responsible, proving that the Republic was unfit to rule and that Spain itself was spinning out of control. On Friday, July 17, 1936, the army garrison at Melilla in North Africa revolted, and the next day other commanders around Spain rose up against the Republic. The Spanish Civil War had begun.

Sights & Sites

Algeciras (Cádiz): Hotel Reina Cristina, named for the queen regent, welcomed diplomats and spies alike; the Casa Consistorial (town hall) was scene of the 1906 conference that led to Spanish Morocco.

Astorga (León): Episcopal Palace by Gaudí blends Gothic, Moorish, and Art Nouveau.

Barcelona: Spanish Village (Pueblo Español), erected for Primo's 1929 exhibition in Montjuich Park, re-creates the nation's architectural heritage; Joan Miró Foundation contains a vast selection of the artist's work; Pedralbes Palace, erected for Alfonso XIII in Italian Renaissance style; Gaudí's Barcelona includes Sagrada Familia Church, Güell Park, Casa Mila, and the Pedrera building; Picasso Museum contains collection of early works; the Art Nouveau Palacio de la Musica ; Four Cats Café in Barrio Gótico.

Madrid: Royal Palace features the private apartments of last occupants, Alfonso XIII and Queen Victoria Eugenia; main post office on the Plaza de Cibeles designed by Palacios; Sorolla Museum was formerly artist's studio; Banco de España facing the Paseo del Prado built at turn of century by new commercial wealth.

Málaga: Picasso Museum in the Palacio de Buenavista has a large collection acquired from the family; artist's birthplace on Plaza de la Merced is now a museum.

Sevilla: María Luisa Park was re-designed in 1929 for the Ibero-American Exhibition, and several buildings remain.

Vic (Barcelona): Paintings by Catalan artist José María Sert cover the walls of cathedral.

Civil War era painting by Miró from the Joan Miró Foundation in Barcelona: *Aidez L' Espagne* (Help Spain!) The poster asked for a one *franc* donation.

Chapter 10

The Spanish War

Perhaps the most famous painting of the twentieth century hangs in Madrid's Reina Sofia Museum near the Prado. In addition to its aesthetic qualities, Picasso's masterpiece *Guernica* has a remarkable history behind it. In January 1937, the Republic invited the artist to paint a mural for the Spanish Pavilion at the Paris World's Fair coming in June. Picasso began doing preliminary drawings, but the project had not really come into focus.

Then, on April 26, a swarm of German planes strafed and bombed a defenseless Basque village. Guernica was nearly leveled and hundreds of civilians were killed during a three-hour rain of explosives and incendiary bombs. This was not just any village, but the traditional home of Basque liberty, which was guaranteed by Spanish kings in an oath sworn beneath a famous oak tree. On hearing the news, Picasso decided to make this brutal attack the subject of his painting.

More than fifty preparatory studies on display at the Reina Sofia preview the kind of powerful images—a mother gripping her dead child, a screaming horse, a soldier's fingers clutching a broken sword—which the artist would employ in *Guernica*. Many were motifs from earlier works such as the *Minotauromachy*. The huge painting itself does not convey its message by using blood and gore, or even the passionate colors of Goya's *Third of May*. It is surprisingly cool in tone, its baffling images rendered in black, white, shades of gray, and a faint, rinsed-out blue. Even so, the painting's distorted, agonized human and animal figures perfectly transmit the brute force and sheer terror unleashed at Guernica. Whereas Goya's masterpiece did not quite escape from the "history genre" of painting, Picasso soared above it, using one small incident in a much larger conflict to give the world something truly universal: a profound protest against war and violence.

For two generations of Spaniards *Guernica* was much more than a painting, and smuggled prints were snapped up and hung in quiet, secret defiance. Unwanted in Francoist Spain, Picasso's masterpiece lived an exile's life for forty-four years, residing most of the time at New York's Museum of Modern Art until "coming home" in 1981 (it had never actually resided in Spain). The work became a symbol of all the shattered dreams and mindless brutality of the Spanish Civil War.

Calvo Sotelo's murder did not cause the military revolt of 1936—there had been plotting for months—but it may have been the last straw for one reluctant rebel who would rise to supreme power in Spain. Serious planning had started soon after the February elections and the decision to transfer grumblers such as Franco to distant posts. The conspiracy's nominal head was old General Sanjurjo, exiled in Portugal, but the real leaders early on were generals Goded and Mola. Franco straddled the fence, doubting the chances for success and fearing a rupture within the army.

In March, several high-ranking officers met at the home of a Madrid financier. They agreed to support a *golpe* (military rising) if Largo was named prime minister, if the civil guard was disbanded, or if anarchy overwhelmed the country. By a stroke of luck or foolishness, Mola was deemed trustworthy by the government and transferred from Morocco to Pamplona, heart of Carlist country, where a pretender to the throne was waiting in the wings. General Emilio Mola was a stone-faced puritanical type who wore wire-rimmed spectacles and looked like a stern schoolmaster. Soon he took over the plotting in earnest.

By late spring everyone, including the government, knew something was up. Calvo Sotelo and José Antonio were not made privy to details, but pledged their support. Mola's plan called for a classic rising of army garrisons around Spain to form a national government under military command. But the sympathies of regional commanders were by no means clear, and Mola was eager for the highly respected Franco to commit to the cause. In an act that may redeem Franco in history, the reticent general wrote to the prime minister in June and warned—in carefully vague terms—of the dangers of anarchy and its effect on "the discipline of the army." The letter fell somewhere between an ultimatum and a final attempt at conciliation. Ill at the time, the prime minister did not respond, and sometime shortly after Franco joined the plot. Another recent convert was a flamboyant loudmouth named Queipo de Llano, a former Republican who switched sides after the sacking of President Alcalá (Queipo's son was married to Alcalá's daughter).

By July 1 it was only a question of fixing a date. Plans calling for the revolt to start during San Fermines (the running of the bulls) at Pamplona were scrapped when word leaked out. Finally, Mola sent out telegrams reading "On the fifteenth last, at four a.m., Helen gave birth to a beautiful child." This meant that the revolt would start in Morocco on July 18 at five a.m., followed by garrisons throughout Spain. Plotters hoped that their *pronunciamiento* would come off, as so many others, quickly and with relatively little bloodshed. But this time it would be different. Due to a last minute change, the Melilla garrison rose up a day early, and a certain colonel arrested and shot the loyal commander, General Romerales, and any others who resisted. Martial law was immediately declared. The insurgents had lists of all members of suspect groups—trade unions, left-wing parties, Masonic lodges— and quickly made arrests and some executions. It was a pattern soon to follow throughout Spain.

After hearing of events in Morocco, Franco proclaimed the reasons for the coup in his Manifesto of Las Palmas, which ended on an incredible note by appealing to "Fraternity, Liberty, and Equality." In slightly different order, these were the ideals of the French Revolution, everything Franco professed to despise. On July 11, the *Dragon Rapide*, an aircraft chartered by Mallorcan tycoon Juan March, had departed from Croydon Airport near London. It followed a circuitous and secret route destined for the Canary Islands and the eagerly waiting Franco. On the nineteenth he boarded the chartered aircraft bound for Tetuan and his expectant legionnaires, a trip that would culminate in supreme power over Spain for four decades.

Who was this remarkable creature? Forty-three at the time, Franco had a distinguished army career behind him, but only a psychic would have predicted his breathtaking rise. Francisco Franco Bahamonde was born in 1892 at the naval base of El Ferrol in rainy Galicia, whose residents are known for their thriftiness and unnerving patience. Franco came from a family of navy men (his philandering father was a paymaster) and yearned to enroll in the naval cadet school. And yet, in one more reverberation from the disaster of 1898, enrollment was cut back and Francisco forced to enlist instead in the infantry academy at Toledo. He was to be a soldier instead of a sailor, and Franco always blamed politicians who had "lost the war" for his fate.

Francisco was just fifteen years old when he entered the academy, and his small stature and high-pitched voice made him the butt of pranks. His academic performance was mediocre (ranking 251st out of 312 graduates), hardly indicative of a career that would make him the youngest general in Europe since Napoleon Bonaparte. After graduation he volunteered for Moroccan service and rose rapidly, winning thirteen medals and other honors for leadership, discipline, and bravery. The Moroccans claimed he had *baraka*, a phenomenal luck, and entering a battle on his white charger he incarnated the ideal of a dashing commander. First with the regular army and later with the Legion, he became (in succession) the youngest captain, major, colonel, and general—the last at thirty-three.

Franco was army to the marrow. Unlike most officers he did not smoke, drink, or hang out in seedy Moroccan brothels, preferring to spend evenings poring over maps or supply lists. Shy around women, he apparently remained aloof from worldly temptation prior to his marriage to Carmen Polo in 1923. But though self-righteous by nature, he was not especially religious until later, when the influence of his pious wife began to seep in.

His values were military ones: patriotism; belief in the unity of Spain; hostility to politicians; and exaggerated concepts of honor, integrity, order, and discipline. Above all discipline. Franco was known as the scourge of slackers, especially Catalans. One time while he was inspecting the troops, a legionnaire unhappy with the quality of the food threw the contents of his mess kit into Franco's face. He betrayed no emotion, calmly wiped his face and continued the review. After dismissing the men, he had the offending soldier arrested and shot. Then he gave orders that the food be improved.

The Spanish Civil War (1936-1939) is one of the most written about military conflicts in history. For many observers it was the dress rehearsal for the larger European conflict to come (it ended just five months before the invasion of Poland). It was "the good fight," the battle to stop Fascism, a death struggle between the forces of light and darkness. Wrote George Orwell in *Homage to Catalonia*: "The question is very simple. Shall the common man be pushed back in the mud, or shall he not? That was the real issue of the Spanish war . . ."

Nevertheless, though the war had its universal qualities, it was essentially a Spanish struggle, springing from the army's peculiar political role since the last century. When news of the rising first came, many people shrugged it off as just another café conspiracy, especially after hearing that Sanjurjo was involved. Madrid radio announced "No one, absolutely no one on the Spanish mainland, has taken part in this absurd plot."

After Spaniards called in foreign aid (which they grew to detest), the struggle took on its much-discussed European implications. But Franco was not the "fascist" of enemy propaganda, nor was he doing battle with "reds" (at least in the beginning) as his supporters claimed. It was a Spanish affair, a rebellion that started no better or worse than scores of others since 1820, but which grew into something incredibly ugly and frightful. It was almost as if the old anarchist dream of one final outburst of violence "to end all violence" had finally arrived—but in a way no anarchist imagined.

News of the impending war was greeted with wild enthusiasm by extremists on both sides, who viewed it as a battle between good and evil. Yet it was in fact a complex struggle between classes (peasants vs. landlords, workers vs. factory owners, anti-clericals vs. the clergy), between ideologies (at least a dozen political parties and two monarchist factions as well as fascists and Communists), and between regions (roughly western vs. eastern Spain, a division that dates back to the days of Celts and Iberians). And yet for all its myriad aspects, the war itself transformed complex issues and tensions into one simple choice—to attack the Republic or defend it.

A man's loyalty sometimes depended on where he happened to be at the time of the rising. The rebels quickly captured Spanish Morocco, the Canaries, Galicia, Navarra, and most of Old Castilla and Aragón. In Sevilla Queipo de Llano bluffed the entire city into surrender with just 150 men. First he rounded up all the loyal officers and shouted at the top of his lungs "You are all my prisoners!" (They meekly complied.) Next he captured the radio station and bombarded the city with news that a huge army from Africa was advancing, and that anyone resisting would be "shot like dogs." His handful of men darkened their faces with walnut juice (to look more like the dreaded Moors), jumped into trucks, and drove round the city repeatedly to create the impression of overwhelming strength. The ruse worked, and Sevilla fell with hardly a shot fired.

Spain in the First Months of the Civil War

By August of 1939 the Nationalists held most of southwestern Andalucía, as well as Córdoba and Granada, and the bulk of northwestern Spain, except for the Asturian and Basque coasts. Franco then chose to press on to Madrid.

Wherever the populace and security forces supported the government, or where the military was divided or hesitant, the rising failed. In Madrid rebel General Fanjul dallied too long, and a crowd stormed the Montana Barracks and overwhelmed the insurgents, killing many. (A group of officers committed collective suicide.) In Barcelona, armed workers and loyal *guardias* and *asaltos* took to the streets and defeated the rising even before its leader, General Goded, had arrived from Mallorca. Goded was soon shot, and Sanjurjo died in Portugal when his plane crashed on takeoff (he had insisted on bringing two heavy trunks loaded with dress uniforms). That left Franco, Mola, and Queipo in charge, each acting as a kind of independent warlord. The revolt had not failed, but it had not succeeded either, which meant only one thing: civil war. A week after the rising, the rebels' situation looked hopeless; they had failed in five of Spain's six largest cities and held less than a third of the mainland. The Republic also controlled about seventy-five percent of Spain's industry and commerce. Contrary to myth, at least *half* of the army and security forces remained loyal to the Republic. This included most of the generals (many recently appointed) and half the lower officers. Mola's and Queipo's forces were weak, so Franco's Army of Africa seemed to be the decisive factor, but it was stuck in Morocco. Most of the navy and air force had remained loyal, dashing rebel plans for transporting troops to Spain, something essential to any hope of success.

From the outset the Republic enjoyed a wave of popular support. In Madrid, a delegation of drivers offered three thousand taxis "to fight fascism," and there were other similar gestures. But Azaña's government seemed to slip into paralysis by refusing to hand out arms to the workers. Weak leadership in Madrid in these early days meant that soon there were not just two Spains but two hundred, each acting in a vacuum. Local power fell to the strongest political party or union; in Cataluña the mantle was shared between the Generalitat and the CNT. The Basque provinces were bitterly divided over the rising, but Vizcaya and Guipuzcoa went with the Republic

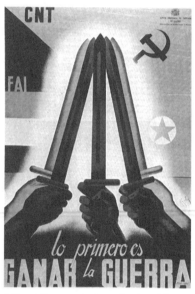

A Republican poster from the Spanish Civil War

upon being promised an autonomy statute. From that point the Basques governed as an almost independent state.

The first days and weeks after July 18 unleashed a fury of popular violence seldom seen or imagined before the twentieth century. Wild stories circulated throughout the panic-stricken middle class and foreign community, like the one about reds crushing naked nuns with steamrollers in the streets of Málaga. But each case of hyperbole was matched with cold fact. Barcelona's bourgeoisie virtually vanished as a class overnight, many killed and the rest suddenly converted into workers. To wear a coat and tie or carry a briefcase was to invite physical attack. In the Andalucian town of Ronda, about five hundred members of the middle class were herded to the Tajo gorge and hurled hundreds of meters to their deaths. (Hemingway adapted the scene in his novel *For Whom The Bell Tolls*.)

The clergy stood out as the most-hated symbol for the "uncontrollables" of the so-called Red Terror. Several thousand priests, monks, and nuns (as well as twelve bishops) perished in the bloodbath. In one case, rosary beads were forced into a monk's ears until the drums were perforated; another monk was thrown into a ring of fighting bulls and gored into a bloody pulp. In Barcelona, a crowd set fire to the Carmelite church and machine-gunned priests as they ran out. Hundreds of churches were destroyed during the summer outburst, but much valuable gasoline was wasted trying to burn Gaudí's Sagrada Familia, made of stone and mortar.

Estimates of political murders behind Republican lines vary widely, from twenty thousand to more than fifty thousand, with most coming during the first three months. Body counts on the Nationalist side—as the insurgents came to be called—were even higher, and the executions lasted far longer. Having little popular support in most areas, the desperate rebels knew they must terrorize residents into submission. This was especially true in regions that had voted for the Popular Front such as Andalucía. From Sevilla Queipo conducted wicked nightly radio broadcasts, threatening the terrified populace with brutal murder and rape by Franco's Moroccan soldiers. Sure candidates for Nationalist death-lists were loyal officers, labor union or party leaders, Popular Front deputies, and anyone else suspected of belonging to "anti-Spain." Sometimes there were summary trials lasting a few minutes; others were executed without pretense. Among them was Spain's literary genius García Lorca, shot gangland-style near Granada, a town in precarious rebel control. In a seldom-remembered counter-crime, Loyalists—as supporters of the Second Republic were known—killed right-wing intellectual Ramiro de Maetzu, a member of the Generation of '98.

As in most civil wars, family loyalties came second to political ones as brother fought brother and father battled son. Even Franco had his own cousin shot when he arrived at Tetuan. At least fifty thousand died at the hands of Nationalist death-squads during the first six months, perhaps twice that number before the war ended. Most were shot or hanged, although there were more imaginative techniques: some prisoners were beaten to death with crucifixes (a tradition from the Carlist wars) or buried alive with mocking final eulogies about agrarian reform. ("Here is your piece of ground, you son of a whore!")Captured Loyalist militiamen were shot en masse, with little exchange of prisoners. When approached with the idea a startled General Mola replied, "How can you expect us to exchange a Spanish gentleman for a red dog?"

The revolt's success hinged almost entirely on Franco's getting his crack troops—about thirty thousand strong, chiefly legionnaires and Moroccan mercenaries—across the strait and into Spain. He decided to seek foreign help, and by July 25 his agents were in Rome negotiating with Mussolini for planes. Things were speeded along by the presence in Italy of Juan March, who arranged credit, and a call from a foreign resident of note, none other than Alfonso XIII. About the same time, Hitler agreed to send aircraft: twenty JU-52 transport planes and six Heinkel-51 fighters to support them. In the first major airlift of troops in history, thousands of men crossed over to Algeciras (in the shadow of Gibraltar) on several hundred flights during August and September. (Said Hitler: "Franco ought to erect a monument to the glory of the Junkers-52.") More men were ferried across later, after two German battleships in Spanish waters prompted the Loyalist navy to retire to port. Franco flew to Sevilla on August 6 to take charge of the Nationalist campaign.

This was not to be a fumbled coup d'etat, after all, and Loyalists immediately had to think about creating a fighting force to meet the threat. The Republic still had thousands of loyal officers, but they were regarded with suspicion by some and not used effectively. Instead, militia units began forming under control of the anarchist or Socialist parties and often acted independent of the war ministry. One of the first Republican counterattacks involved militia from Barcelona (led by the famous terrorist Durruti), which tried to retake Zaragoza without any artillery or battle plan. The quality of the militias started to improve after Largo Caballero was named prime minister in September to rally worker support. Even the CNT abandoned anarchist principles of non-involvement and joined the coalition.

Generally speaking, it was a "pauper's war" for both sides, with a shocking lack of modern weapons and equipment. When the war started the army did not have a single tank or modern airplane. Even the Legion had to use old machine-guns with defective firing pins. On the other hand, the war was the first to make effective use of inventions like the radio and telephone and, with foreign involvement, such military innovations as rapid tank deployment and aerial bombing of cities.

Lacking the proper means to fight a war, both sides immediately turned to other nations, whose response did much to decide the final outcome. French president Leon Blum at first seemed enthusiastic about the Republic's appeals, but a trip to London made him aware of Britain's cool attitude. Foreign secretary Anthony Eden warned that if French involvement south of the Pyrenees (in what he called "the war of the Spanish obsession") led to conflict with Germany, Britain would step aside.

By July 31, Britain introduced a unilateral ban on arms shipments, and Blum followed suit and closed the French border in August. Thus the Republic was denied the internationally accepted right of a government to purchase arms to defend itself from rebellion. But this was the age of non-intervention and appeasement; two years later, the infamous Munich Pact would extinguish the Republic's last hope of receiving help from the western democracies. Nevertheless, France unofficially provided more aid than is generally recognized. About twenty thousand of its citizens fought in Spain, and the Nationalists brought down more than a hundred French aircraft. Far more important was military assistance from the Soviet Union, especially critical during the first few months. This included planes, tanks, and artillery, as well as hundreds of trained advisers. These "commissars" would later help whip the chaotic militias into a real army.

In one of the war's most-debated incidents, Largo and his finance minister, Juan Negrín, decided to move most of Spain's huge gold supply (the world's fourth largest) to Russia. Their reasons were twofold: fear that it might fall into rebel hands and the need to pay for arms purchases. In October 7,800 boxes of gold bars, valued at about five-hundred million U.S. dollars, were loaded onto four Soviet steamers bound for Odessa. There is a story that when the shipment arrived, Stalin held a banquet and announced: "The Spanish will never see their gold again, just as one cannot see one's own ears." (When Spain tried to reclaim the gold in 1956, the Russians said there was none left, and claimed an additional $50 million owed by the Republic.)

Although Russian aid was substantial, it already began to dry up by mid-1937. More important in tipping the scale for the Nationalists was aid from Germany and Italy. Like the Soviet Union, they had accepted a non-intervention pact, but all blatantly ignored it and offered only feeble excuses. Mussolini claimed that the seventy thousand Italian troops in Spain were "volunteers" without government sanction and tried to deny that Mallorca was virtually an Italian base throughout the war. (Palma's main street was renamed Via Roma.) The Germans were eager to test new equipment and strategy in the field. Spain also provided "a convenient sideshow" (as Hitler put it) to distract Britain and France from Germany's skullduggery in central Europe. Although their numbers were far fewer (about five thousand maximum) than the Italians, Germans provided technical advisers and the best air unit in Spain, the renowned Condor Legion. Consisting of about one hundred planes and pilots and commanded by a General Von Sperrle, the legion helped transform Salamanca into "a German military camp," according to the American ambassador at the time.

Speaking of the Americans, president Roosevelt and his government, despite some sympathies for the Republic, toed the non-intervention line. The policy was nearly reversed in 1938, but a last-ditch effort by Joseph Kennedy, American ambassador at the Court of St. James (and father of the famous Kennedy brothers), convinced Roosevelt to back down. There were just too many Catholic voters in America.

Franco decided to push north through Extremadura and link up with Mola's army, then attack Madrid to end the war quickly. In the first such raids in history, German bombers were already softening up the capital. Staying close to the Portuguese frontier, the African Army sliced through resistance and soon reached the border town of Badajoz in Extremadura. Here transpired one of the war's most disgusting spectacles, which shocked world opinion and gained great popular sympathy for the Republic. Legionnaires singing "I am the fiancé of death" and Moroccan *regulares* entered the town, and vicious hand-to-hand fighting soon degenerated into a bloodbath. Among the dead were two defenders slain on the steps of the cathedral's high altar and about two thousand Republicans rounded up and shot in the bullring. As was Moroccan custom, the corpses were castrated and strewn throughout Badajoz that night.

The next objective was Madrid, but first another drama waited to be played out in Toledo. There the revolt had fizzled, and about 1,300 conspirators and 700 non-combatants retreated to the old Alcázar fortress under the command of a Colonel Moscardó. The Loyalists tried every means to dislodge them, including tunneling under and dynamiting one tower, but the defenders held out like true Iberians. One day someone phoned Moscardó and announced that he had ten minutes to surrender or his son would be shot. When the captive son came on the line, the colonel (much like Guzmán El Bueno centuries earlier) responded: "My son, commend your soul to God, shout *Viva España!* and die like a hero." The son was shot, but not until a month later, and the incident was endlessly recalled by Nationalist supporters for the next forty years. Franco saw the Alcázar's propaganda value and decided to divert his attack from Madrid to relieve the defenders from the two-month siege. The Nationalist army under General Varela reached Toledo on September 27, captured the historic town, and began a reign of bloody reprisals. Realizing their fate, a group of about forty anarchists got roaring drunk on anisette and set fire to the building they were occupying. All perished in the flames.

The war saw many such incidents. A lesser-known last stand took place near Jaén at Santa María de la Cabeza, where about 350 insurgents and their families held out for nine months before being overwhelmed. During the siege all supplies—including delicate medical instruments and bottles of wine—were airdropped by a most ingenious form of parachute: live turkeys, which landed gently after a largely vertical flight. There was also the ultimate statement made during the war's first month at Gijón, where a group of 180 desperate rebels faced certain defeat. Finally, a message was sent to a Nationalist ship lying offshore: "Defense is impossible. The barracks are burning and the enemy is starting to enter. Fire on us!" The request was honored and all were killed by artillery fire.

The crucial delay caused by the siege of Toledo allowed *madrileños* time to shore up defenses, a task made more difficult by the widespread refusal to dig trenches, a tactic viewed as cowardly. Four Nationalist columns were marching on the city, and Mola coined a phrase now used in every language by stating that a "fifth column" (of Nationalist supporters) was already in Madrid. He remembered that almost half the residents had voted for the National Front a few months before. The city was surrounded, but Franco left a wide corridor open to the southeast, believing (as Madariaga wrote) in the Spanish saying that "a fleeing enemy should have a bridge of silver." Indeed, Largo and his government soon moved to Valencia, and defense planning fell to General Miaja and a Colonel Rojo, considered the Republic's finest military mind.

The ten-day battle of Madrid became the civil war's central epic, as the world's attention suddenly riveted on Spain. Women and children threw up barricades and shouted *No pasarán!* (They shall not pass!) and "Madrid will be the tomb of fascism!" La Pasionaria toured the streets with a loudspeaker, urging wives to prepare boiling oil for the invaders. And just as the attack began, another heroic element was added with the dramatic arrival of the first men of the famed International Brigades. Although the initial group of 1,900 was mostly French and German, delirious crowds greeted them with cries of "*Viva Rusia!*"

This was because—despite the presence of many idealists and adventurers—the International Brigades were conceived, organized, and manned by Communists. The whole concept sprang from a Comintern meeting a few days after July 18, and even Largo viewed the brigades as a potential tool of Stalin. Recruiting of these "armed tourists" remained in Communist hands, and no one of questionable political background was supposed to be admitted. Of the thirty thousand or so who reached Spain, most came from working-class backgrounds and were either party members or sympathizers. The British Batallion contained mostly unemployed industrial workers plus 174 Welsh miners experienced at fighting police. The American Abraham Lincoln Battalion, on the other hand, consisted mainly of students and sailors and was not as politically motivated as others. Many were bitterly disillusioned upon realizing they were pawns in a planned Communist takeover. Casualties were also extremely high among the brigades, as much as half in some units.

Nevertheless, the brigades' presence at the battle of Madrid was not only inspirational, but also decisive in holding back the assault. Fighting took place west of the city in the Casa del Campo and university campus (the pride of Alfonso XIII). Here the Nationalists attacked in force, but Madrid's defenders had captured a battle plan the day before and were ready. After fierce fighting the lines were drawn and would not move more than one hundred meters in either direction for more than two years. One final note on the battle of Madrid: for some reason the attackers never thought of cutting off the city's water supply, which would have ended the siege in short order.

After the "victory" of November 1936, Madrid took on the appearance of a Communist city, with red flags and pictures of Lenin everywhere. Cinemas played films about the Russian Revolution instead of more popular MGM musicals. Workers with clenched fists roared around in lorries shouting "*No pasarán!*" and La Pasionaria's "Better to die on your feet than to live on your knees." Communist Party membership in Spain rose dramatically in the weeks after the battle to a million by mid-1937. It seemed as if Franco's wild rhetoric about fighting "the reds" had become self-fulfilling.

The civil war unleashed a spontaneous yet profound social revolution in much of Spain during the second half of 1936. Labor unions seized seventy percent of Catalonian factories, the CNT controlled all public services, and in the country farms were collectivized or parceled out and property records destroyed. Debts and even money were abolished with the stroke of a pen, and luxury hotels and private residences were converted into schools or hospitals. Writer George Orwell arrived in December to join a Trotskyist militia unit (not the International Brigades) and later described Barcelona: "Even the bootblacks had been collectivized and their boxes painted [anarchist] red and black. Waiters and shop-walkers looked you in the face and treated you as an equal . . ."

Barcelona became much more proletarian than Madrid and displayed a passion for equality. Everyone said *tu* (you) rather than the more formal *usted*, and *Salud* (good health) replaced *Adios* (go with God) when people parted in this classless, godless world. Women in particular experienced tremendous liberation under anarchist "rule" by taking jobs and responsibilities previously denied them. Righteous reformers opened "anti-brothels" where repentant prostitutes could learn to cook and sew. Bars were closed, and coffee and alcohol outlawed. There were no private cars or well-dressed people any more; even judges and doctors wore blue overalls, and a Russian diplomat was denounced for wearing a hat. The obsession with rejecting the "class tyranny" of clothing reached comic extremes with the Mangada Column of militia, organized by the eccentric vegetarian and nudist, Colonel Mangada. Troop transport vehicles filled with his naked followers could be seen roaring aimlessly around Barcelona as bewildered spectators gaped.

The policy of the well-disciplined Communists was to create a strong central government and army and to concentrate on winning the war. However, the anarchists of Barcelona and Valencia had other ideas—to launch the long-awaited social revolution that would smash the old order. To extremists, the Republic was "not worth a single drop of a worker's blood." Many anarchists joined Catalan Nationalists in calling for a complete break with Madrid and washing their hands of Spain once and for all. After Luis Companys declared himself "president of Cataluña" a power struggle was sure to come.

The splintering of the Republic must have bemused General Franco, who had successfully consolidated his own power and that of the Nationalists at Salamanca in October. With the sullen consent of Mola and Queipo, the insurgent officers agreed to a single command under Franco, the *generalisimo* (highest of all generals). Soon after, he also claimed to be head of state and began using the title *caudillo* (an awkward translation of *duce* or *führer*). Much like Julius Caesar two millennia before, Franco was making himself dictator. Some protested, but when a colonel Yagüe, "the hyena of Asturias" and one of Franco's strongest supporters, threatened to launch a coup within a coup, the muttering abruptly ceased. In August, Franco had stated that Spain would remain a republic, but one based on law and order, and the bombastic Queipo ended his broadcasts on a confusing note with "*Viva la república!*" Later such references vanished, and Nationalist posters read "One state, one country, one chief."

Generally speaking the insurgents won the war because they united to create a more efficient, better-trained and equipped military force than the Republicans. From their new headquarters at Burgos, Nationalist generals began to build a huge army around a nucleus of veterans. Middle-class youths became temporary second lieutenants, but casualty rates were so high that a popular saying soon went: "temporary second lieutenant, permanent corpse." The rank-and-file came from the tradition-bound peasantry of northern and central Spain, pious and city hating. At some point the Nationalists began to view their struggle as a holy crusade like those that had expelled the Moors and baptized millions of Native Americans. Said one new crusader: "We fight for love and honor, for the paintings of Velázquez, the plays of Lope de Vega, for Don *Quixote* and the Escorial." The previously indifferent Franco began attending mass regularly, and the clergy thundered from their pulpits about a "war of extermination."

After a winter lull, fighting resumed in the spring of 1937. Black-shirted Italian troops spearheaded the ignominious defeat of Málaga, which was followed by gruesome Nationalist reprisals and pillage. Among the booty was the reputed hand of St. Teresa of Ávila, a treasured relic that Franco kept at his bedside for the rest of his life. The battle of Jarama near Madrid, at which the Lincoln Battalion saw its first action, ended in a stalemate. But near Guadalajara, the Republican army gained a rare victory by routing a largely Italian force, the first of many mishaps for *Il Duce*'s "volunteers."

Later that spring, the action shifted north to the isolated coastal strip still under Loyalist control. From the war's outset the Catholic and conservative Basques had been going their own way, deeply suspicious of the revolutionary, anti-clerical bent of their "allies" elsewhere. Generally, Basque units refused to fight outside *Euskadi*, and when they did would often withdraw from battle at critical moments.

Perhaps the war's best-known event occurred during the Nationalists' big push north. Monday, April 26, was market day in the quiet town of Guernica, historic home of Basque liberties but with no strategic value. Suddenly and without warning, a swarm of German aircraft descended on the town with wave after wave of bombs and machine-gun fire. Flying with the Condor Legion that day was a Colonel Von Richthofen, cousin of the legendary Red Baron. Most of the town was leveled and about a thousand civilians killed during the three-hour nightmare, and Guernica became a worldwide symbol of fascist terror and the horrors of modern warfare. Reacting to the international outcry, Nationalist leaders claimed they had no prior knowledge of the attack and revised the death count to twelve. Later they explained that it never occurred, and that Guernica was destroyed by retreating Basques. But there were too many witnesses who knew better.

Flanked by Nationalist army officers, a group of Spanish bishops give the Fascist salute.

Summer brought more bad news for the Republic, with the fall of Bilbao, Santander, and Asturias, the last collapsing "like meringue dipped in water," according to the Nationalist commander. The short-lived Basque republic was soon just a memory, and firing squads were kept busy dealing with Catholic "traitors," among them many priests. Franco's Catholic supporters worldwide suddenly became very confused about the Crusade. The capture of Basque iron ore and industry was vital for the Nationalist effort. Their "alternate" economy was in good shape, with enough food, a steady supply of armaments, and the backing of most Spanish and European financiers. The ubiquitous Juan March alone chipped in fifteen million pounds sterling. By 1937, the Nationalist *peseta* had a higher rate of exchange than Republican money.

Another important event of the northern campaign was the death of General Mola, Franco's only serious rival, in a plane crash. All evidence points to an accident, but for many years a man in Valladolid kept two loaded pistols with him at all times, ready for the man who killed his son, the pilot. Said

Hitler: "The real tragedy for Spain was the death of Mola. There was the real brain, the real leader . . ."

Loyalist counterattacks near Madrid (Brunete) and on the Aragón front failed to halt Franco's war machine. Adding to the Republic's woes was an internal crisis that had been simmering for months; the multi-headed revolutionary hydra was about to devour itself. The Spanish Communist Party, by then taking direct orders from Moscow, was determined to seize control of the war effort by crushing troublesome anarchists and a new player, an anti-Stalinist (Trotskyist) group of Marxists called the POUM. The Communists were also determined to dump the dour and incompetent Largo, who had outlived his usefulness.

The crisis came in May over control of Barcelona's *Telefónica*, the main telephone exchange, held by the CNT and POUM. On May 2, an operator interrupted a conversation between two important Republican leaders, stating that the lines should be used for more important things. It was just one of many incidents that prompted the government to take control, and some unidentified gunfire coming from the building unleashed a furious battle that spread through the city. About five hundred persons were killed, and Largo was bitterly discredited by this shadow civil war and resigned. The Revolution was over; the Communists had won.

Looking around for a new puppet, the party of Stalin found Dr. Juan Negrín and managed to convince Azaña—by then a mere whisper of his former self—to name him prime minister. Negrín was a respected scientist with many admirable qualities, but his earlier decision to export half of Spain's assets left him tied to Moscow with a "golden chain," as he would soon find out. Negrín inherited a disastrous state of military affairs and vowed to put all effort into winning the war, the not unreasonable Communist policy. With the help of Russian advisers, the ragtag Loyalist army began to shape up. But something seemed to go out of the Republic after the events of May. Workers' collectives were disbanded, and dreams of independence shoved aside in favor of unity. The last flicker of Catalan separatism was snuffed out by November, when Negrín moved his government from Valencia to Barcelona.

A darker side of the Negrín regime soon emerged. These were precisely the months of Stalin's infamous show-trials in Moscow, at which political opponents confessed to crimes as "fascist spies" and promptly disappeared. Stalin's paranoia spilled over into Spain through his agent Colonel Orlov and a dreaded new security force intent on rooting out Communist rivals. This particular reign of terror climaxed with the brutal murder of POUM head Andreu Nin, who was former secretary of Stalin's arch-foe, Leon Trotsky. Nin was tortured mercilessly in a secret Communist prison in Madrid, but refused to "confess" and was killed. Negrín did nothing to stop or condemn the outrage and lost his last shred of respectability. Wrote a bitterly disillusioned Orwell: "This war, in which I played so ineffectual a part, has left me with memories that are mostly evil."

Meanwhile Franco grew stronger. One possible rival had been José Antonio, but the falangist leader was executed in November 1936. (Largo's son was shot in revenge.) The young fascist had actually despised Franco as an unreformed "reactionary," but agreed to support the rising nonetheless. The Falange's so-called Socialist wing, which hated capitalism as much as *international* communism, survived with the "old shirts" of Manuel Hedilla. But a phenomenal increase in "new shirts" (a million by 1937) threatened to swamp the Falange's original ideals. Inevitably, power struggles and anti-Franco plots began to brew in Falange circles, and the *generalisimo* used one violent incident as an excuse to arrest Hedilla. He spent the next four years in solitary confinement. At the insistence of his brother-in-law, Serrano Suñer, Franco used the trouble to cement his position as Spain's once-and-future *caudillo*. In yet another "coup," he created a single political umbrella called the *Falange Española Tradicionalista* (FET) that embraced *all* groups on the right and neutralized their often-contradictory philosophies.

The original Falange, for example, was socially revolutionary, anti-monarchist, and merely tolerant of religion. Carlists and Alfonsists each had a would-be king and were intensely Catholic. Franco needed to rein them in if he was to survive as dictator after the war. His decision to retain the name *Falange* for the movement, along with important symbols such as blue shirts and the fascist salute, did much to foster the myth that he himself was a fascist. But Franco was never more nor less than one thing—a Francoist. His tactic of unite-and-conquer toward the feuding Nationalist factions laid the foundation of his forty years in power, and the base was rock solid because all army officers were obliged to join FET.

The new coalition (later called "the Movement") issued twenty-six points, mostly lifted from the Falange, defining the future state. Spain would be totalitarian, unitary, anti-capitalist, anti-Marxist, and fervidly Catholic. There was one important omission: no mention of the monarchy. This obvious slight upset supporters of Alfonso, who had settled into a life of polo and bridge in Rome, and his heir Don Juan. But the army had not lifted a finger to save Alfonso in 1931 and was not about to have him back. When Don Juan showed up in Spain during the war, Mola sent him packing.

Meanwhile Don Carlos, the Carlist pretender and last of the original line, had died, leaving a distant relative named Francis Xavier as heir to the great lost cause. Aside from their red berets (now worn with falangist blue shirts) as part of the Movement's uniform, very little of Carlism survived in the FET. And despite all the fascist claptrap, members of the old Falange had to settle for mostly ceremonial rewards, like the officially sanctioned cult of José Antonio, henceforth called "the absent one" at all party functions.

Franco's power play really marked the victory of ultra-conservative Spain, its principles more akin to Fernando and Isabel than to anything in the twentieth century. (In one of the regime's more curious propaganda feats, one ideologue of the Movement tried to claim that the Spain of the Catholic Monarchs was "fascist," the genuine precursor of Mussolini's Italy.) Franco and his followers yearned for the days of Spain's glory and tried to root out foreign influences of the past two centuries. Much of the attitude was dangerous (calls for a new empire) and much merely silly (the banning of Russian salad and French omelettes). But the Movement now had its own myths to fight for—the glories of a Spain long gone—that seemed as powerful of any modern "ism."

In December of 1937, the Republicans tried to derail the Nationalist juggernaut with a bold offensive at Teruel. Caught off guard, Franco dropped his own plans and managed a successful counterattack by February. Not a tactician of great imagination, Franco was held in contempt as a hopelessly hesitant plodder by his German advisers. Gaining ground and holding it seemed Franco's style, rather than the swift mechanized warfare of the Third *Reich*. Franco's approach—in military strategy as well as politics—was to wait cautiously for the right moment to attack, to wear down the enemy by attrition, above all to *endure* longer than his opponents.

In the spring of 1938 Franco's army, with about 100,000 men, 1,000 planes, and 150 tanks, broke through the Aragón front and swept east to the Mediterranean, cutting the Republican zone in two. Confounding his advisers again, Franco then turned south toward Valencia rather than marching on Barcelona. Cataluña's capital was weak, having recently suffered heavy bombardment by the Mallorca-based Italians, which drew more international protest. Mussolini boasted, "I am delighted to see Italians horrifying the world for a change instead of charming it with their guitar-playing skills."

But Franco stubbornly turned south, and soon his army was bogged down along the coast. Using this turn of events, the Loyalist army enjoyed its last hurrah by launching a daring offensive in July along the Ebro River aimed at Franco's rear. Wedged between the Pyrenees and Iberian ranges, the Ebro Valley is one of Spain's two great geographical depressions (the Guadalquivir Valley is the other), and summer temperatures are brutal. Here the two armies massed for a bloody artillery duel and war of attrition that cost more than fifty thousand casualties, including twenty thousand dead. In its last action of the war, the British Battalion suffered staggering losses, with more than half killed. After three months Nationalist air superiority decided the battle, and the Republican army collapsed. "You could break our front with bicycles," observed Negrín.

Even before the battle's conclusion, the International Brigades were being disbanded and sent home, their ranks decimated and their propaganda value nil. Even the Lincoln Battalion had a majority of Spaniards by 1938. Yet their farewell parade in Barcelona equaled their inspiring entrance into Madrid. All stood while La Pasionaria gave her famous speech. "You gave us everything: your youth or your maturity; your science or your experience; your blood or your lives; your hopes and aspirations. You are history. You are part of our land. When the olive trees blossom again, come back." (In 1988 about three hundred original members *did* return to Barcelona on the fiftieth anniversary of their departure.)

In late December Franco finally attacked Cataluña, and a month later Nationalist troops, led by Carlist *requetés* and Moroccans, poured into Barcelona unopposed. It was more of a victory parade than a battle. In early February, Azaña, Negrín, and other leaders crossed the French border on foot, two days ahead of Nationalist troops. Hundreds of thousands of refugees were herded into France and told not to return. Many never did. On February 27, Britain and France recognized the Franco government, and Azaña resigned as president the next day. Negrín, who remained as prime minister, pinned defeat on the western democracies for failing to help the Republic. Among the exiles, ideological feuds continued to flourish, old scores were settled (one security officer was buried alive), and everyone argued about who was to blame for the disaster.

The Loyalists still had half-a-million men under arms and held Madrid and Valencia. But the war was effectively over, and only Negrín and the Communists wanted to fight on. The prime minister, who had returned to Spain, wanted to gain time to bargain with Franco over surrender terms. Others were taking the "Numantian posture," vowing to fight to the last man in the manner of ancient Iberians.

This was the stage setting for the war's bizarre finale in Madrid. While Nationalist forces gathered on the outskirts and waited, Republicans conducted their own mini-civil war to decide how to end the larger war. It began when a Colonel Casado staged a coup against the Communist-run government, hoping to stop the fighting and elicit better terms from Franco. Claiming that *the army* rather than by politicians like Negrín represented the legitimate government and popular will, he "pronounced" in the name of the so-called National Council. To complete the irony, Casado claimed to be saving Spain from communism. Six days of fighting broke out and left about 250 dead, but the Communists were broken. After Franco's promise of pardon for "all who are not criminals," the Loyalist army seemed to melt away. On March 28, 1939, Franco's troops entered Madrid through the rubble of University City, where they had been thrown back two years—and half a million lifetimes—before. Crowds of Nationalist sympathizers, many sheet-white from years of hiding, gave the fascist salute and shouted "*Han pasado!*" (They have passed!). On April 1 Franco announced that the war was over.

Supporters of the Republic around the world were stunned. Wrote the French philosopher Camus: "It was in Spain that men learned that we can be right and yet be beaten, that force can vanquish spirit, that there are times when courage is not its own reward. It is this, doubtless, which explains why so many men, the world over, regarded the Spanish drama as a personal tragedy."

The Spanish Civil War was Spain's share of the general breakdown of Europe and much of the world during the 1930's and 1940's. Yet it was distinctly Spanish. Rather than a return to the sixteenth-century empire as Francoist propaganda would pretend, the victory of "traditional" Spain brought back the old *moderado* order. With greater power than ever before, the unholy trinity of church, army, and landowners made one final, desperate attempt to halt the forces of liberalism and modernization unleashed in the nineteenth century. And for another three decades they succeeded, largely through the efforts of one man and the state he created.

Sights & Sites

Belchite (Zaragoza): Nearly razed during civil war, the town was left intact as a monument to Nationalist dead.

Guernica (Vizcaya): Town that came to symbolize the horrors of civil war after being bombed by Germans; famous oak tree remains a symbol of Basque liberty.

Madrid: Picasso's masterpiece *Guernica* hangs in the Reina Sofia Museum; the Casa del Campo and University City were sites of fierce fighting during civil war.

Mount Teide (Santa Cruz de Tenerife): This superb vantage point has an obelisk called *Las Raíces* marking the start of Franco's rising.

Pamplona (Navarra): Monumento de los Muertos is a memorial church dedicated to civil war dead.

Toledo: The Alcázar, destroyed and rebuilt many times since the thirteenth century; in 1936 it withheld eight-week Republican siege in epic fashion; today a military museum.

The Alcazar in Toledo, site of Colonel Moscardo's defiant gesture

Chapter 11

The Age of Franco

few kilometers north of Felipe II's El Escorial sits another man's grandiose statement on his life and times. Inaugurated on the twentieth anniversary of the end of the Spanish Civil War, the colossal Valley of the Fallen monument took many years to complete and involved thousands of men toiling as virtual slaves. Most workers were war prisoners, although in theory the monument honored the dead of both sides. Like Felipe, Franco supervised the plans and often visited the site. The design reflected the overblown style favored by all totalitarian governments, in this case "victorious" Spain's pretensions of a holy crusade and an imperial past. Since 1975 it has served as the tomb of Francisco Franco and his era. Yet in its sheer pomposity, the Valley of the Fallen also expresses the ultimate folly of the Spanish Civil War.

This neo-Valhalla was carved and blasted from the innards of a huge granite mountain in the Sierra de Guadarrama. The first thing visitors see is a gigantic stone cross, 150 meters high and weighing thousands of tons, clutching the rock like some freak bird-of-prey. You enter the monument via a long, cave-like tunnel lined with chapels whose walls conceal the tombs of thousands of civil war dead. At the far end is a massive basilica with marble floors, tapestries, and intricate mosaics of Christ and the saints. Like Franco's Spain itself, the setting is the perfect blending of religion and military pomp.

For the grand opening in 1959, the remains of José Antonio Primo de Rivera were transferred here from the Escorial (where he had been buried many years earlier). Blue-shirted members of the Falange were out in force that day to hear Franco proclaim: "The struggle between good and evil never ends no matter how great the victory. Anti-Spain was routed, but it is not dead." This same sentiment dominated nearly forty years of Spanish history.

The figure of one million war-related deaths has been refuted, but the eminent authority Hugh Thomas considers half that number to be a reasonable estimate. This includes about 200,000 killed in combat, some 150,000 murdered or executed behind the lines by both sides, and at least another 100,000 executed or dying in prison in the years immediately after the war. Another 300,000 fled their country, never to return, pushing the figure of "lost" Spaniards close to 800,000. This does not count the injured and maimed. Post-war Spain swarmed with armless, legless or otherwise crippled soldiers in search of work. Only the lucky ones got jobs selling lottery tickets.

Without any doubt, the war's crowning tragedy and Francisco Franco's greatest failing was his utter lack of mercy and compassion toward the defeated, millions of his fellow Spaniards. For Franco the vanquished represented "anti-Spain," and those not slaughtered on the battlefield should be exterminated or severely punished. There was no program of national recovery and reconciliation to bind the nation's wounds, as President Lincoln proposed "with malice toward none" at the end of the American Civil War. But then Franco was no Lincoln.

In fact, the diminutive dictator never admitted that a civil war between Spaniards had been fought; instead Truth had triumphed over international Evil. The ultimate irony came when courts of rebel army-officers sentenced Loyalists to death for the crime of "rebellion." The Law of Political Responsibilities (1939) tarred nearly everyone connected with Popular Front parties or government as guilty of something, and about a quarter of a million arrests were made in the first months (well over a million by 1942).

The summer of 1939 was an orgy of informing, private vendettas, and sanctioned executions. Tens of thousands died in the mass bloodletting; Mussolini's son-in-law reported 250 executions a day in Madrid alone, mostly by firing squad. It got so bad that many of Franco's supporters protested the bloody reprisals. But they did not subside. (Franco gave orders that a maximum of one in five suspects could be acquitted.) When France fell to the Germans in 1940, many republican leaders were sent back to their death in Spain, among them Catalan president Luis Companys. Facing the firing squad, he took off his shoes and socks so that he could die touching the soil of Cataluña.

Another side of the tragic story was Spain's loss of virtually an entire generation of artists and intellectuals, either killed like Lorca or in exile. Machado died in France. Jiménez and many others went to live and write in Latin America. Other exiles were writers Américo Castro, Madariaga, Ramón Sender, and Rafael Alberti, the cellist Casals, and filmmaker Buñuel. Spain did not begin to make cultural progress again for many, many years.

Wrote Hugh Thomas: "Upon the heaped skulls of all these ideals, in the dust of the memory of so much rhetoric, one more cold-hearted, dispassionate, duller, and grayer man survived triumphant . . ." The man named Franco who had risen to supreme power remained an enigma. "A less straightforward man I never met," said one American journalist. He was short, increasingly stout, and had a shrill voice "like that of muezzin," according to one observer. Moreover, he had an ordinary manner and was a poor speaker—hardly the charismatic traits of a modern dictator—yet it was said that those in his presence grew frightened and submissive.

Franco had proved his military skills and personal bravery. Yet he had a nasty vindictive streak that spoke volumes about the man. One time he strongly reprimanded Yagüe, a fervid supporter, when he praised the bravery of Republican troops. Thirty years after the war, when someone suggested that Loyalist veterans receive pensions, Franco was outraged: "You can't combine a glorious army with the scum of the Spanish population."

Spain's conservative powers clearly dominated the post-war landscape. The army had proved it had the last word in Spanish politics and was showered with special privileges. And yet, even though cabinet members during the first twenty years were nearly half military men, Franco's Spain was not literally "governed" by the army. With Franco in charge, the military slipped back to a state of political indifference, concerned more with promotions and getting new hardware. Many veterans joined the ranks of the civil guard.

In April 1939, Pope Pius XII congratulated those who "rose in defense of the ideals of faith and Christian civilization." The Catholic Church, acting as a catalyst among all elements of the Nationalist coalition, was another clear winner. The loyal church would receive its rewards, as bishops sat in parliament and on the Council of the Realm, and laws had to conform to Catholic dogma. Once again classrooms had crucifixes and pictures of the Virgin Mary, along with that of the *caudillo*. The Jesuits were allowed back and given charge of most secondary schools, proving again the old adage that "Night and the Jesuits always return."

The clergy also assumed the role of guardians against "moral lapses" such as holding hands in public, wearing sleeveless shirts, or being seen conversing with Protestants. In short, it was a hidebound brand of Catholicism going back to the age of Felipe II. The church and military often linked arms in defending the new regime.

General Franco, who never forgave his enemies, remained an enigma.

One naval training handbook read: "Other nations struggle to gain more territory, more food, more petroleum. Spain has battled and will continue to do battle so that there are more Catholics and honorable men in the world."

Initially at odds, the church and Falange began to cozy up, and blue shirts and fascist salutes became common at mass. Even bishops and nuns thrust out a raised arm at every opportunity. And the church had a new "saint" in José Antonio; his disinterred body was carried on the shoulders of Falangists all the way from Alicante to the Escorial for reburial—a trip lasting ten days and nights. (His burial at the royal site stirred monarchist ire.) Franco had crushed the Falange's radical wing, and post-war attempts to create a fascist state were thwarted by conservatives. One exception was the Spanish labor movement, awarded as a kind of booby prize to the Falange, which created "vertical syndicates" combining both management and labor of each economic sector into individual unions. The idea was to replace class struggle with cooperation in a kind of a state-run paternalistic world. The Falange also controlled the press and government propaganda machine, the bark if not the bite of power.

The monarchists must also be considered winners in post-Republic Spain, but it was a hollow victory without the return of the king or his heir. Alfonso XIII was reasonably content with life in exile, though he complained that with each passing year he was seated one row farther back at polo matches. He died in Rome in 1941, shortly after he renounced his rights to his son,

Don Juan, who began to drum up support and issue manifestos calling for a return to the monarchy. This merely served to annoy Franco, who had no intention of relinquishing *any* of his power. Noting the presence of anti-monarchists among his supporters, Franco claimed his rule was "that which divides us least." Many of the more realistic political exiles came to realize that a constitutional monarchy was the only hope for a return to some semblance of liberty. It was a great irony indeed when these republicans looked to the Bourbon pretender to deliver them from Franco. On the subject of pretenders, Francis Xavier pressed his claims; later the Carlist torch was passed to his son Hugo Carlos. (This odd bird made nonsense of the entire movement by becoming a Socialist in the 1960s.)

Just a few months after the surrender of Madrid, the Second World War broke out with the joint German-Soviet invasion of Poland, a cynical act of collusion that shocked Franco. Although indebted to the Axis powers, Franco steered an evasive course that kept him out of the war. Especially after Hitler's pact with Stalin, Franco had reason to suspect the Germans, who could care less about Spain except for its vital strategic importance in the Mediterranean.

After the fall of France, Spain became distinctly less neutral, and there was talk about inheriting French North Africa as part of the "New Order." In October 1940 Hitler and Franco had their famous meeting at Hendaye in France. After keeping the *führer* waiting an hour, the Spaniard proceeded to drive Hitler to distraction with a masterly display of his strongest quality— the ability to promise everything but give nothing. Franco willingly agreed to become an ally, but would not commit to any timetable for Spain's entry into the war. Every request by the German leader was met with a counter-request in Spain's interest, such as sovereignty over Morocco, to stall a firm commitment. Finally Hitler gave up and later remarked, "I would rather have three or four teeth pulled than meet that man again."

German diplomats continued to press for safe passage of troops through Spain for an attack on Gibraltar, a plan called Operation Felix. But Franco would not budge, and even stated that any attempt to cross the Spanish border would be resisted. Finally Hitler wearied of the debate and turned his attentions to the invasion of Russia. The German failure to gain passage proved to be a major turning point. In October 1941, an Anglo-American force massed at Gibraltar for the crucial invasion of North Africa, the beginning of the end for the Axis. Even Churchill praised Franco's role—however selfish—in turning the tide. (Franco was also credited with allowing many Jewish refugees from France to seek haven in Spain.)

Yet Franco regained much of his pro-fascist ardor with Hitler's invasion of Russia. Nearly twenty thousand Spanish "volunteers," the famed Blue Division led by General Muñoz Grandes, set off for the eastern front to help fight communism. They saw some of the war's bitterest fighting, including the battle of Stalingrad, and suffered heavy losses. In a 1942 speech Franco offered a million Spanish volunteers to defend Berlin.

By 1943 the war's outcome was uncertain, and Franco began to backtrack by recalling the Blue Division and affirming Spain's neutrality. Spanish pyrites and tungsten for munitions were sold to the highest bidder at unheard-of prices. After the Normandy invasion, the American ambassador noticed that the photos of Hitler and Mussolini in Franco's office—previously flanking another of the pope—had suddenly vanished. The defeat of Germany marked the end of Spain's so-called fascist period; even the infamous raised-arm salute was banned. Realizing his country's weak position, Franco began to work on his image abroad.

With the defeat of the Axis, much of Europe and most exiled Spaniards expected Allied armies to cross the Pyrenees and oust the "last fascist dictator." But this was not to be, largely due to growing concern about Soviet intentions in Europe. Nevertheless, in 1945 the new United Nations voted to formally exclude Spain from the same community of nations that included the likes of Stalinist Russia. The next year France closed its border, and most governments withdrew their recognition of Franco's regime. With consummate skill, Franco used this diplomatic isolation to rally Spanish patriotism and consolidate his own power.

Francoism came to be, in the words of its wily architect, "a novel solution." After so many rigid ideologues, Franco was the supreme pragmatist, who sought to achieve a perpetual balance of power among the loyal but sometimes rival "clans" that formed his power base: church, army, Falange, monarchists, bankers. To all he gave something, to each never enough. And no one was really sure how Franco would act or react. Most of the political history of his thirty-six-year reign traced the fate of each "family member."

Franco's attitudes about government were simple: politicians were corrupt and should be eliminated; the press was biased and should be controlled. In politics as in war, procrastination was his main policy; he always preferred to delay action rather than act unsuccessfully. The secret of Franco's power lay in his right to name and dismiss ministers at will. (Over almost four decades there were nineteen major shakeups and 120 different ministers sitting on the council.) These ministers ran the government under a fairly loose rein, but were replaced whenever squabbling grew too vocal or their power too great. Quite unlike a ranting Hitler or Mussolini, Franco would preside over council meetings with a detached serenity, rarely making a comment. Said one monarchist: "A lot of the time he didn't have anything to say. He was a sphinx without a secret."

The Spanish Cortes was a rubber-stamp parliament of appointees. Of the thousands of laws passed during the Franco era, only two actually originated in parliament. The courts were likewise mouthpieces for official policy: all power resided in the executive branch and ultimately with Franco himself. One critic shrewdly observed that he was really "the supreme Spanish anarchist," answering to no law but his own.

In 1945, as part of his window-dressing campaign to improve Spain's image abroad, Franco gave the nation its Charter of Rights. But the new clothes were threadbare, denying such basic liberties as freedom of expression and political association. Many of the rights granted were routinely trampled on, and with the courts part of the monolith, the average citizen had no place to protest government or police abuse. The press was totally controlled, and the string of state-sponsored provincial dailies of abysmal quality. Reading them became an art in itself; if headlines pronounced "No Strike in Cataluña," it meant something big was happening.

Franco's social philosophy was likewise simple; "For the good of Spain, I should like there to be rather fewer rich people and rather fewer poor," he once remarked. Labor laws used a clever blend of carrot and stick to bring the traditionally unruly working class to heel. Reflecting falangist influence, both capitalism and socialism were rejected in favor of government paternalism. Workers gained a plethora of benefits like social security, numerous paid holidays and bonuses, and job security so sacred that only the most heinous offense warranted dismissal. On the other hand, strikes were considered acts of sedition punishable by long prison terms. The policies of long-time Labor Minister José Antonio Girón (1941-56) were very popular with workers and won much good will for the regime from the common man.

When peace came to Spain the economy was in shambles: fields lying fallow, factories smashed, cities bombed. Rebuilding would not be easy, especially when Franco maintained that things would "right themselves" in time.

New labor laws defined Spain's economy as "totalitarian." Its principles were self-sufficiency (the end of "exotic products"), government regulation, and vertical syndicates. This nationalistic and authoritarian version of economics (called "autarky") meant inefficiency and corruption, a clumsy bureaucratic machine, and thriving black markets to deal with people's real needs. Spain's economy had numerous fundamental weaknesses. It was still based on a system of agriculture mired in backward techniques and the unresolved land problem (e.g. in Málaga province less than two percent of the landowners still controlled fifty-five percent of the land). Transportation was also backward; until 1947 there was no railroad between Madrid and Valencia, Spain's third largest city. Goods to and from the provinces were forced to take the most roundabout routes, always via the capital. Additionally, worker productivity was low.

In Franco's Spain, Madrid bureaucrats were free at last to carry out the centralization begun by Felipe V. Direct state investments into the economy were funneled through an unwieldy agency called the INI, whose name became a byword for ineptitude. Grandiose schemes were launched with little or no planning, then became bogged down in a sea of regulations, many self-imposed. The average businessman was required to fight a losing battle against paperwork from Madrid.

The first decade after the war were the "years of hunger" for most of Spain, and economic life was primitive and often picturesque. Private cars practically disappeared due to a gasoline shortage, and strange contraptions burning charcoal or almond shells were seen rumbling through the potholed streets. Mechanical wizards kept the most dubious wrecks rolling. It was an utter contrast with a consumer society: toothbrushes were reconditioned rather than replaced and fountain pens sold on the installment plan. Electricity and water could be cut at any moment, and telephone service was sporadic at best. State control left enormous loopholes for corruption, and favoritism and influence peddling became part of the system. The only way to get things done—finding an apartment, getting a telephone, making a business deal—-was through a friend or an *enchufe* (a contact, literally a "plug"). The idea of conflict-of-interest between government and business did not exist. Anyone who did not line his pockets when given the chance was considered deranged. Juan March was probably the ultimate product of the system; his smuggled cigarettes almost broke the government monopoly, and it was said he had forty thousand Spaniards on his payroll from customs officials to ministers. When he died in 1962 (his Cadillac collided with another car) he was reputedly the world's seventh richest man.

Franco was personally honest, but turned a blind eye to those around him. His brother Nicolás, for example, got involved in many shady deals. Economics was not Franco's strong suit, and there are indications that he never grasped how bad things really were in those first years. Like the Bourbon kings, he went hunting several times a week and spent little time on the nation's business.

Part of Francoism was a self-orchestrated personality cult that eventually reached the absurd with such titles as "minister of God" and "the sword of the most high." Every Spanish town had its *plaza* or *avenida* named in his honor; his photo was in every office. Franco lived at El Pardo Palace outside Madrid, but played king in grandiose style at lavish receptions given at the Bourbon's Palacio Real in the capital. Imperial touches included a personal bodyguard of turbaned Moroccans. Franco was king in all but name, and he may have considered taking that final title if he had sired a son (he and Carmen Polo had one daughter). One man who urged him to do so was his fanatically loyal aide, Admiral Luis Carrero Blanco. For thirty years he was the dictator's right arm, his alter ego, and he came close to succeeding his mentor. Carrero was an interesting breed of archconservative; he detested the Falange, yet regularly made harangues about the usual liberal vices. Among them he counted Judaism, "the origin of all other evils from the Enlightenment to Marxism."

Over the years Franco's search for legitimacy and popular approval developed into a complex structure of institutions he hoped would outlive him. The Law of Succession (1947) defined Spain as a monarchy; Franco was regent with the right to name the successor to the throne. The new monarch had to meet specific criteria: he should be male, Spanish-born, Catholic, over thirty, and must swear loyalty to the Movement's principles. A national plebiscite of questionable validity confirmed the law. Don Juan, the legitimate heir, protested Franco's manipulations from his Portuguese exile. He correctly suspected that Franco the temporary guardian would become Franco the permanent dictator. The two rivals finally met in 1948 aboard a yacht off San Sebastián and disliked each other instantly. They agreed only that Juan's son, Juan Carlos, would be educated in Spain.

Under the stifling cloud of Francoism cultural achievements were meager. One best seller on the civil war theme was *The Cypresses Believe in God* by

José María Gironella. Of more literary merit, perhaps, were works by Camilo José Cela, *The Family of Pascual Duarte* and *The Hive*, the latter about the miserable life in post-war Madrid. Art made a tentative comeback in the late forties with Antoni Tapies, called "the black knight of modern painting." Miró continued to paint and to champion Catalonian culture, "like a carob tree, deep-rooted and evergreen." Dalí remained in Franco's Spain, opening a museum in his native Figueres once called a "temple of kitsch." Public architecture reverted to the "Escorial style" seen in massive buildings like the air ministry in Madrid and the ultimate travesty—the Valley of the Fallen.

In music Joaquin Rodrigo penned his brilliant musical masterpiece, the *Concierto de Aranjuez*. With Buñuel in exile and censorship severe, the promising Spanish cinema took a sharp nosedive. All film scripts had to be submitted for approval, and the dubbing of foreign films was compulsory. Audiences tried to fathom the mind-boggling plots created by the censor's scissors in which, at the risk of implying incest, mistresses were converted into sisters and lovers into uncles. One amusing film in 1952 was *Bienvenido, Mr. Marshall*, a comedy by Berlanga about the new connection between the wealthy, powerful United States and impoverished but proud Spain.

With the start of the Cold War in the late forties, Franco could play his anti-Communist card with the Americans, well aware of Spain's strategic location. The ice was broken in 1950 with an American ambassador to Madrid and a loan. President Truman disliked Franco—especially after discovering Protestants had to be buried at night—but his successor was a general and had fewer misgivings. In 1953, President Eisenhower and Franco signed an agreement permitting four American bases on Spanish soil in return for substantial aid ($1.8 billion by 1965). "It was like water to the desert," said one minister. The treaty helped launch Spain's economic recovery and indirectly its later political reform, but at the time its most important result was to legitimize the Franco regime. Upon signing the accord he remarked, "At last I have won the Spanish war." In 1955, Spain was admitted to the United Nations. Franco also played his Catholic card by concluding a concordat with the Vatican (1954). Priests were put on the state payroll, and in return Franco won the right to approve bishops. The Vatican even bestowed its highest honor on Franco: Knight of the Order of Christ.

Spain's only other diplomatic successes were in fostering cultural and economic ties with Latin America, and in its friendship with several Arab nations. In the middle of his Arab overtures, Franco seemed caught off guard when France announced its withdrawal from Morocco (1956). But he too had to face the inevitable and abandoned Spanish Morocco. Spain retained the ports of Ceuta and Melilla, and (until 1975) the phosphate-rich Spanish Sahara (Rio de Oro), the last crumb of Franco's neo-colonial delusions.

In 1964, colorful posters began appearing all over Spain announcing the completion of twenty-five years of peace. The Francoist press claimed it was the longest period without domestic or foreign war since the Pax Romana, and many believed that the time for reconciliation had come. By 1964, forty-three percent of the population had been born since the war, and Franco was the only leader they had known. Unfortunately, the propaganda machine continued to dwell on the fear and hatred of the civil war, and a film about the new Cid, called *This Man Franco*, played to packed theaters around Spain.

The old man had settled into a comfortable life of fishing and hunting. He also took up painting, favoring seascapes and game-animals, and even did a self-portrait in an admiral's uniform, the one denied him by his exclusion from the naval academy. He still dabbled in politics, especially if it involved sacking a minister who had grown too independent. His style spoke volumes: In 1966, Muñoz Grandes of the Blue Division, considered a possible successor, discovered he had been relieved as vice-president of the government by reading about it in the official gazette.

Franco registered in the Society of Spanish Authors under the pen name Jaime de Andrade for his history of the foreign legion and a 1940 screenplay called *Raza* (Race). Using the pseudonym Jakim Boor, he also penned an astonishing treatise on Freemasonry called simply *Masoneria*. In it he claimed that modern history resulted from their conspiracy to rule the world, and that all Spain's modern ills sprang from Masonic intrigue.

Order was the undeniable achievement of Franco, but the price was high. By the 1960s Spain was still an authoritarian state with a rubber-stamp parliament, shackled press, and jails filled with political prisoners. Passing out pamphlets or "spreading false news" were considered acts of "military rebellion," and army courts tried student pranksters. Large garrisons were located just outside the major cities, and the civil guard had its fortress-like *cuarteles* in every small town, from which they patrolled the countryside. In the larger towns and cities a new force called the *policia armada* (nicknamed "the grays" for their uniforms) struck fear in potential criminals and dissidents alike. There was also a plain-clothes secret police based in the *gobernación* building on

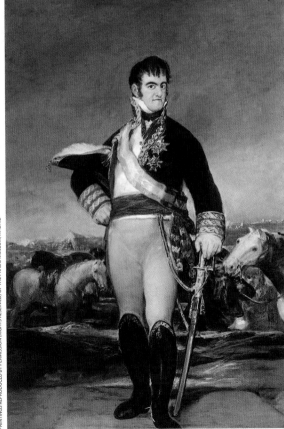

The neoclassical palace (above) at Aranjuez south of Madrid, painted by Francesco Battaglioli, was one of several royal residences used by Spain's Bourbon monarchs in the eighteenth century. A revealing portrait by Goya captures King Fernando VII (left), who had all the defects of his people and none of their virtues.

Goya's paintings "Second of May" (right) and "Third of May" (above) depict crucial events in Madrid in 1808, when the populace rose up against Napoleon and suffered bloody reprisals. Gaudí's Sagrada Familia church (facing page) captures the exuberance of Barcelona around 1900.

The bombing of Guernica during the Spanish Civil War inspired Picasso's famous painting (above). General Franco (right) and other brass in Burgos, Nationalist capital during the war. The ruins of Belchite (far right) near Zaragoza were left untouched as a reminder of the horrific conflict.

Portrait of General Franco in 1942 (facing page) is by Luis Mosquera. Said one critic about the dictator: "He was a sphinx without a riddle." Franco presided over the investiture of Prince Juan Carlos (above) as successor to the throne. In 1981, a civil guard colonel (right) held hundreds of parliament members hostage during an aborted coup. Following page: Spain's popular King Juan Carlos takes part in a Barcelona regatta.

Madrid's Puerta del Sol. A strong hand was often not necessary, however. Crime rates were low, and most of the populace had slipped into political apathy and sports mania. With rare exceptions—like Manolete (killed in the ring in 1947) and El Cordobés (a sixties mop-top)—soccer had replaced bull-fighting as the national passion. Franco himself was an avid fan, and the nation went berserk with its victories over England (1950) and the Soviet Union (1964).

Feeling a new prosperity along with the twenty-five years of peace, Span-iards of all classes began to appreciate the accomplishments of Francoism. Given a kick-start with foreign loans and freed from many government con-straints, the economy was definitely improving. Facing ongoing disasters through the decade, economic ministers from a new school had convinced Franco of the need for fundamental changes. His reluctant approval led to the Stabilization Plan (1959), the death knell of twenty years of state planning and its pitiful results. Price controls, import quotas, limits on foreign invest-ment, and other economic remnants of autarky were finally dropped in favor of a relatively free market.

Among the new ministerial voices were members of Opus Dei ("God's Work"), a lay-Christian group of hazy origins and purposes (critics called it Octopus Dei). Founded by an Aragonese priest in 1929, Opus Dei strived to increase Catholic influence in all realms of society, especially among the intellectual elite. Its handbook, called *The Way*, read like a Spanish version of the Protestant work ethic, and group members' talent and effort (plus Carrero Blanco's support) propelled them into key positions in the government.

One vital element of the economic miracle was tourism. Numbers of foreign visitors rocketed from four million in 1960 to fourteen million by 1965 and would go through the roof in the next decade. Tourism provided jobs and badly needed foreign exchange for purchasing imports such as petro-leum. More foreign currency poured in from Spanish workers abroad, more than half a million by 1970. With the influx of tourists, Spain seemed to go mad with building projects along its coast, and even Falangists such as Girón made fortunes on the Costa del Sol and elsewhere.

Construction also boomed in the cities, where industries were suddenly humming like never before. During the decade Spain's overall growth rate was second only to Japan's, and in the fifteen years after 1960, industry's share of exports rose from twenty-one to seventy-eight percent. By 1965 Spain ranked sixth worldwide in shipbuilding, *ahead* of the United States. When the first SEAT factory was built in 1952, managers worried that the market could not absorb a hundred cars a month; by the 1970s SEAT employed 20,000 workers, and Spanish automakers churned out 750,000 cars a year.

Manning these new factories required a huge population shift from country to city. In 1960 agriculture still employed forty-two percent of the labor force, but this had shrunk to twenty-five percent a decade later. By 1970 1.6 million Andalusians had left their region, and about half of them were living in Barcelona. Emigration from Extremadura and the bleak Castilian plain also reached tidal-wave proportions. Except for the elderly who stayed behind, village after hopeless village was abandoned for the baubles of Bilbao or Barcelona. The old ways—pack animals lumbering along cobbled streets, plowing with mules, oil lamps and charcoal fires—were retreating to the remote *pueblos* for a last stand before finally succumbing to the onslaught of motorbikes and slot-machines.

Franco's speeches during the 1960s dropped falangist rhetoric and hammered on the theme of prosperity, glossing over problems like inflation and labor strife. Yet 1962 witnessed the most industrial unrest since the Republic, as well as rumblings at the universities. The central drama of the Franco era was how to modernize the economy yet keep Spaniards content with the old social-political order. In the end it was *not* possible; changing realities made Franco-style rule obsolete. The ultimate irony for Francoism, therefore, was that the progress it had spawned would come back to bring it down.

Consider the changes wrought by tourism. In the 1950s tourists were arrested for wearing bikinis or kissing in public. A Spanish cardinal stated, "Public bathing . . . constitutes a special danger for morality. Mixed bathing must be avoided because it almost always gives rise to sin and scandal." By 1970 this world had completely changed as Spaniards were bombarded with foreign ideas like democracy and socialism, not to mention consumerism and free-spirited *rubias* (blondes) from the north. In a survey of non-congenital mental illness in Málaga province, ninety percent of the afflicted were teenaged males who had gone to work on the coast and could not adapt to the new ways. By 1975, more than forty million tourists were coming to Spain every year, outnumbering the entire Spanish population. Spain also became a consumer society, less interested in religion and political rhetoric than in "the good life." Television sets jumped from fifty thousand in 1960 to 1.75 million by 1965, and there were more than a million private cars by the same year.

Spain's economic miracle and its social effects were felt most strongly in the old regional bastions of Cataluña and the Basque lands. There the native residents continued to regard themselves as more productive and culturally advanced, more "modern" than fellow Spaniards, especially the droves of immigrant *catetos* (hicks) flooding in from rural provinces. By 1970 for example, only twenty-five percent of the residents of the Basque provinces could speak the native language.

Torremolinos in the 1970s, mass tourism on the Costa del Sol

Not surprisingly, regionalism began to raise its head again. The evolution of Basque nationalism defied all logic—from its ultra-conservative Carlist roots to reluctant support of the Republic, from crude racialism to an odd breed of revolutionary Marxism. In 1959 by a few pseudo-intellectuals tired of the old Basque party founded the now-infamous group called ETA (*euskadi ta askatasuna*), but by 1967 extremists dedicated to violence had taken control. Of nine "states of emergency" called by the government from 1962 to 1975, six were in the Basque country. And when the police over-reacted, moderate Basques started to sympathize with ETA.

Faced with a host of new realities, the political world started to divide in the 1960s between those who wanted to "open up" Spain to modern influences and those who steadfastly resisted. The former included a new civil service based on a college-educated middle class, best represented by Manuel Fraga Iribarne, who became Minister of Information and Tourism in 1962. Opus Dei members favored economic opening, but shied away from politics. The forces of reaction were called "the immobile ones" and later "The Bunker."

By the late 1960s the question on everyone's lips was *Despues de Franco, que?* (What happens after Franco?) The aging dictator tried to head off an impending crisis by serving up the final course of political institutions, leaving things "tied up and well tied down" in his own words. The Organic Law of 1966 allowed the "contrast of opinions" but not political parties, and the election of one-fifth of parliament by "heads of families." These and other curious features comprised something called "organic democracy."

Many of the reforms were comical. According to the liberalized press law, there was no more "prior censorship," but copies of periodicals had to be in the government's hands half-an-hour before publication. If there was a problem, the issue was confiscated—often ripped from readers' hands right on the street. Thus the burden of complying with Francoist principles shifted from the censors to editors and reporters. One paper was fined for printing a critical article in which Franco was referred to as "De Gaulle." Another was closed for four months, then dynamited, after its editor criticized the regime in a *French* daily. When the Organic Law was put to a vote in 1967, Spaniards said "yes" by a ninety-five percent majority. (A "no" vote meant leaving things as they were.) Franco had staged another triumph without granting more than a wisp of reform.

The same year as the plebiscite, Carrero Blanco was named vice-president and became the heir apparent. His views on reform were simple: "To offer change to a Spaniard was like offering a drink to a confirmed alcoholic." Carrero was a strong supporter of Don Juan's son, Juan Carlos, to fill the vacant throne, and in 1969 Franco made the long-expected announcement. Little was known about the thirty-one-year old prince or his views, but nearly everyone was suspicious. He was born in Rome in 1938, baptized by the future pope, and brought to Spain for his education at the age of ten. This included stints at the three military academies and the University of Madrid, where he was a capable if not brilliant student.

While still in school, Juan Carlos was invited by Queen Frederika to Greece, where he met princess Sofia (sister of future-king Constantine). The attractive young couple was married in 1962 at a spectacular double-ceremony using both Roman Catholic and Orthodox rites. Their first-born son was Felipe (the future Prince of Asturias), and his baptism in Madrid was a veritable Bourbon reunion, with the exiled queen, Victoria Eugenia, making her first appearance in Spain since 1931.

Over the years it became evident that Franco had no intention of bringing back the legitimate heir, the feisty Don Juan. In 1962 he told Juan Carlos, "Your highness has a better chance of becoming king than your father." Two years later, the young prince was asked to join Franco on the podium at the annual victory parade. By 1968, Juan Carlos had decided to "leapfrog" over his father to the throne, a decision that outraged many monarchists to whom the line of succession is sacred. Their displeasure grew after his investiture, at which he knelt and swore loyalty to Franco and the Movement. Thereafter

Juan Carlos was usually present at all state affairs, stone-faced and towering awkwardly over the Lilliputian dictator forty-six years his senior.

Supporters of Don Juan grumbled, but within the Movement only a few old Falangists and Carlists opposed the choice of Juan Carlos. The Carlist pretenders Francis Xavier and Hugo Carlos had already been expelled from Spain and were not a threat; the latter became a favorite of the society pages after marrying Princess Irene of the Netherlands. A more serious challenge was Alfonso, son of *Don* Jaime. (Jaime, Juan's elder brother, had renounced his rights in 1932, but tried to reclaim them in 1964.) Young Alfonso—actually Alfonso XIII and Eugenia's first grandchild—did not press his claims, but tongues wagged furiously when, in 1972, he married one of Franco's granddaughters. Juan Carlos was on notice not to deviate from his passive role. According to one story, after he was seen dining with a leading liberal, Franco remarked, "The choice belongs to your highness; you can either be a prince or a private individual."

Francoism began to seriously unravel after 1969, with a major cabinet crisis, serious student unrest, wildcat strikes, and ETA terrorism. At a *pelota* match attended by Franco, one zealous Basque doused himself with gasoline, lit a match, and jumped in front of the astonished crowd (he miraculously survived). There were even rumblings within the two pillars of Francoism, the church and army. A group of young officers with democratic sympathies was discovered and punished, but a new generation of soldiers looked to the future.

Far more serious and especially galling to Franco were changes within the church during the 1960s. Basque and Catalan priests had traditionally supported more political and cultural freedom for their regions. Then, with the winds of change blowing from the Vatican under liberal Pope John XXIII, the foot-dragging Spanish church began to loosen its grip. The younger clergy and even some bishops became more radical and supported worker and student groups, and the most radical even offered their churches as refuges for ETA fugitives. The regime reacted by creating a special prison in Zamora where about two hundred liberal priests served time, more than in all of Europe's communist countries combined.

One key figure in the struggle was Cardinal Enrique y Tarancón, archbishop of Madrid. In 1971, an open letter from the Spanish bishops asked forgiveness of the church for taking sides in the civil war. Three years later, the

Bishop of Bilbao was placed under house arrest for writing a defense of the Basque language, and Tarancón warned Franco against interference in church matters. It was said that the pope even had a decree of excommunication for the general awaiting signature should the Basque bishop be expelled. Franco was livid; in his mind the circle had been squared.

In June 1973, Franco resigned as president of the government (retaining his other titles) and appointed Carrero, then seventy-one, as the chief guarantor of Francoism after Franco. In December, a group of ETA commandoes tunneled beneath the street where Carrero passed daily on his way to mass and deposited a cache of explosives. When it passed the spot the morning of the twentieth, the president's special armor-plated Dodge was blown five stories into the air, over the top of the church, and into a courtyard on the other side. It was the first major assassination since the civil war. (Cynics called him "Spain's first astronaut.")

The nation and above all Franco were severely shocked, and the hardcore right wing began bracing for battle. At Carrero's funeral, Cardinal Tarancón was jostled and insulted by thugs, who yelled "to the firing squad!" Franco appointed a rigid conservative named Arias Navarro as president, indicating that he would not consider backing down. But when even Arias showed signs of "opening up" small groups of extremists like "The Warriors of Christ the King" began to appear, beating up "red" priests and slashing Picasso paintings. The year 1975 was the most violent since the 1940s, with terrorist groups mushrooming on both extremes. ETA and new bands like FRAP continued a rampage of random violence in which many innocent people were slaughtered. Spain seemed to be lurching toward disintegration once again, and cynics began referring to the king-to-be as Juan Carlos, *El Breve* ("the Brief").

King Hassan of Morocco chose this moment to launch his "Green March" of unarmed civilians against the phosphate-rich Spanish territory of Western Sahara, in order to press claims of sovereignty over the region. Spain tactfully withdrew, and Morocco inherited a colonial war against the area's independence movement, supported largely by neighboring Algeria.

The nation's seeming decay was matched by that of Franco himself, suffering from several ailments in addition to old age. In September 1975, the trial and execution of several terrorists created an international scene, with the temporary withdrawal of ambassadors and other measures. Soon after, Franco had his last hurrah at a huge rally in Madrid's Plaza de Oriente. The old dictator, his hands shaking and his voice shrill, rallied the sea of supporters by blaming the uproar on a conspiracy of freemasons, Communists, and other enemies of order. It was his final speech.

For the next five weeks all Spain—and half the world—watched Franco's inevitable decline. In a desperate effort to keep him alive, doctors (led by Franco's son-in-law) connected him to every life-support device imaginable, and he was heard to mutter "Why is it so difficult to die?" Like a true soldier, he bore the pain and endless operations with famed Spanish stoicism, the mantle of the Virgin of Pilar and St. Teresa's severed hand by his bedside. Finally, the pattern of brain waves recorded on a bedside graph flickered and stopped. The age of Franco was history.

Sights & Sites

Benidorm (Alicante): Classic example of the tourist boom that transformed Spain in the 1960s.

Cuenca: Museum of Abstract Art in one of famous hanging-houses includes work by Chillida, Tapies and Saura.

El Pardo (Madrid): Franco lived for thirty-five years at this palace, now open to visitors; King Juan Carlos and his family reside five kms. away at Zarzuela Palace.

Figueres (Gerona): Salvador Dalí Museum in the town of artist's birth in 1904.

Madrid: The Reina Sofia Art Center has Picasso's masterpiece *Guernica* and dozens of other important paintings; Spanish Museum of Contemporary Art has works by Fortuny, Rosales, Miró, and others; the Plaza de Oriente next to the Royal Palace witnessed countless mass-rallies for the *caudillo*.

Valle de los Caidos (Valley of the Fallen) monument to civil war dead

Torremolinos (Málaga): The good, bad, and ugly of mass tourism in contemporary Spain.

Valle de los Caidos (Madrid): The Valley of the Fallen lies a few kilometers from El Escorial; gigantic cross and a basilica containing remains of Franco and José Antonio Primo de Rivera.

Chapter 12

Contemporary Spain

Thursday, November 20, 1975: The day began like any other for most Spaniards, until they turned on their radios and heard somber requiem music on every station. Newspapers soon hit the streets with a headline long-since set in type: *Franco Ha Muerto*. Details were finalized for Franco's funeral, and for the investiture of Juan Carlos de Borbón y Borbón as king of Spain.

The *caudillo's* body, dressed in a captain-general's uniform with a red sash, was first taken from La Paz Hospital in Madrid to El Pardo for a private service, attended by family members, ministers, and a few old cronies. One of them was José Antonio Girón, who defiantly dressed in a falangist blue shirt rather than mourning clothes. Mass was celebrated by a vocal Franco critic, Cardinal Enrique y Tarancón, who gave a restrained eulogy. Before the public funeral and burial, Franco's body lay in state at the Palacio de Oriente, and for two days hundreds of thousands of Spaniards passed before the open coffin. Many wept, prayed, or spoke aloud, like one crippled veteran who knelt and cried out, "*Adios*, my general. . . at your orders always!" Some mourners grew hysterical and had to be dragged away; others gave the fascist salute or silently clutched five red roses, a falangist symbol. (Elsewhere in Spain, it was said, countless bottles of champagne were consumed.)

Held at the Plaza de Oriente, the state funeral service was attended by a handful of foreign dignitaries and half of Madrid. Afterwards, the red-bereted *guardia del generalisimo* escorted Franco's coffin to the Arch of Victory near the university. From there his body was transferred from a horse-drawn carriage to a hearse for the forty-five kilometer drive north to the Valley of the Fallen. Later, as the body was lowered into the grave, artillery outside thundered a final twenty-one-gun salute.

But throughout these days of pomp and ceremony, the question on everyone's mind remained: After Franco, what? Two days after the general's death, Cardinal Enrique y Tarancón called on Juan Carlos to become "king of all Spaniards," and his meaning was clear. At the ceremony of investiture the thirty-seven-year-old prince, dressed in the uniform of an army general, stood up before parliament. On a nearby table were a golden crown and a jewel-encrusted scepter, symbols of the monarchy absent from Spain for forty-four years. Placing his hand on a bible, Juan Carlos swore an oath to uphold the laws of the state and the Movement. At long last Spain had its king, but what would the future bring?

Everything seemed to hinge on Juan Carlos. Would he be "king of all Spaniards" or merely a puppet for the old guard? He was still a political enigma, though he maintained close personal contacts with many military leaders. His statements had been vague, and few people seemed to like or trust him. Privately, however, the king was known as a man of considerable warmth and charm who entertained many liberal ideas. Wanting to keep a low profile, Juan Carlos chose to live at the relatively modest Zarzuela Palace with his family: Queen Sofia and their children, including Felipe, Prince of Asturias and future king.

The new monarchy was untainted by the civil war, giving Spaniards hope that at long last they could turn the page on that sad event. Ironically, the new king was not really succeeding General Franco but his own father, Juan de Borbón, the son and legitimate heir of Alfonso XIII. In strictly monarchist terms Juan Carlos had committed the ultimate *faux pas* by jumping the royal queue at Franco's behest, and rumors were rife of bad feelings between father and son. Yet in May of 1977 Don Juan showed his mettle by renouncing his claims to the throne, allowing Juan Carlos to carry on without a disruptive dynastic struggle.

The achievements of Spain's young leaders and the entire nation during the decade after Franco were nothing short of remarkable, especially in the context of Spain's modern history. The formidable challenge at hand was to transform Spain into a European-style democracy in a peaceful and civilized manner, despite vehement opposition from the bastions of right-wing power. In the king's first decisive action, he replaced Arias Navarro as president with a virtual unknown named Adolfo Suárez, a move that surprised and dismayed many observers.

Both Juan Carlos, as Franco's wooden mannequin, and Suárez, a high official of the Movement, had poor credentials for leading a nation to reform. In hindsight, the king risked everything by giving the top job to Suárez, on the surface a political hack with staunchly *franquista* credentials. But together the unlikely pair embraced the complex task with vigor and managed to dismantle most Francoist institutions in several rapid, orderly stages. For his pivotal role in the process, King Juan Carlos was dubbed "the motor of change" as the monarchy and reform became inextricably linked. Critics of all stripes were mystified, then delighted or infuriated, but the king held one essential trump card—the unswerving loyalty of most Spanish generals.

Franco had predicted a smooth transition through the institutions he created, but history would prove him right in ways he could never have imagined. It was the ultimate paradox: a liberal constitutional regime that evolved from the shell of a dictatorship as Franco's ironclad institutions dissolved themselves. The king used his immense powers to implement reform, divest himself of power, and ultimately assume a largely ceremonial role as a constitutional monarch.

The year 1976 was critical because champions of the old guard remained strongly entrenched in power, and there were some dicey moments as police—the much feared and hated *grises*—continued to crack the heads of dissenters. Yet the tide of change ran even stronger, and Franco's old rubber-stamp parliament passed the Law for Political Reform, which included its own dissolution. A year later the Francoist Movement itself was abolished, and Spain conducted its first general elections in forty-one years. A centrist coalition (UCD) led by Suárez emerged victorious, but the Socialists (PSOE) made a strong showing. The new parliament's task was to draft a constitution suitable for a monarchy, essentially a return to the system destroyed by Primo de Rivera's *coup* in the 1920s.

The next year saw the legalization of trade unions and the Communist Party (PCE), unthinkable just two years earlier, and the return of Dolores Ibarruri, "*La Pasionaria*" (after thirty-eight years in Russia) and Josép Tarradellas, former president of Cataluña's *Generalitat*. The pace of change was breathtaking, and army saber rattling noticeable only by its absence. In an exemplary show of innate sense, a genuine spirit of consensus and cooperation reigned across the political spectrum. Republicans accepted the monarchy (and its flag), Socialists abandoned Marxism, Communists disowned Moscow, labor strikes were infrequent, and through it all the steady hands of the king, Suárez, and Socialist Party leader Felipe González carefully guided the rhythm of reform. In the end these exceptional men *did* play all the right cards; there was no Francoism after Franco.

The key to a successful transition was to align the new political system with the social and economic realities of Spanish society. So much had changed since the civil war that Spain was almost a different country. Among other things, massive foreign investment over two decades had transformed it from an agricultural backwater to the world's tenth or eleventh industrial power. The old *moderado* order of large landowners, army, and church was based on a society of ignorant peasants who voted per *cacique* instructions. By 1975, most Spaniards lived in cities and had different expectations; if they never got their plot of land, at least they had an apartment with a bathroom and television set. The "two Spains" of city and country, which had produced so many clashes throughout history, had evolved almost beyond recognition.

If the landed class could no longer rely on servile country folk, it had also lost much economic clout to a new elite—industrialists and bankers, financiers and businessmen. Moreover, there was a vastly larger middle class concerned with order and prosperity as well as political rights. The old-fashioned "Liberal revolution" of Western Europe, largely a nineteenth century phenomenon, had finally happened in Spain. Other historic areas of tension had also subsided. Significantly, the clergy no longer battled liberals as champions of the status quo, thereby healing one of Spain's most bitter cleavages. And working-class parties were no longer hotbeds of anarchism and revolutionary ferment, having become much like other social democrats throughout Europe.

Coming eighteen months after the general elections, the Constitution of 1978 established the basic political structures of post-Franco Spain. A bicameral parliament was set up and protected by certain built-in mechanisms to prevent governments from falling too easily, which was the scourge of the 1930s. The leader of the largest party became prime minister or premier (called "president of the government" in Spanish) if he could muster a majority with his own party or in coalition with others. The Catholic Church lost its dominant role as state religion, being mentioned in only one article, but otherwise the document did not attack the bastions of economic, social, and military power. Moreover, unlike the Republic's political "manifesto," the new constitution had the passionate support of Spaniards, as demonstrated in a landslide of approval in a special national referendum.

One historic trouble spot that would not vanish with the stroke of a pen was regionalism. At times Spain has seemed a nation of nations, a Balkan-like patchwork of feuding ethnic groups and local interests. According to the Constitution of 1978, Spain was a federal state made up of seventeen different regions, and the new government proposed autonomy statutes strikingly similar to those of the Second Republic. Everyone knew they must tread lightly, however, because any hint of outright separatism would be a sure way to ruffle military feathers.

Some generals were already fidgeting. Despite all the political progress since 1975, the Basque provinces remained in turmoil as armed terrorists cranked up the heat. (During 1968-75 ETA killed 43; in 1976-83, 380 died.) Born in the darkest years of the Franco era, ETA regarded itself as a band of patriots fighting for liberty against an occupying army. What frightened Madrid more was the widespread sympathy they enjoyed among ordinary Basques with ETA's political mouthpiece, the Herri Batasuna party, winning up to twenty percent in elections. Even the mainstream Basque Nationalist Party (PNV) seemed to tolerate the carnage, using it as leverage for promoting its own agenda. Clearly ETA's bloody campaign posed the greatest single threat to the new democracy, and parliament passed the harshest anti-terrorist law to date. Madrid declared war by sending in an elite police force called the GEO's and pressuring France to turn over suspects in hiding. Yet the problem grew worse, and the government seemed powerless to end the slaughter. Meanwhile, security forces brooded over the failings of democracy.

With all its rhetoric about national identity, Cataluña took a less radical path to autonomy. Ruling the political roost was Convergencia I Unió (Convergence and Union), a center-right party favored by business, whose pragmatic leader Jordi Pujól was arguably Spain's wiliest politician. He believed that Cataluña, as the country's most productive region, deserved special concessions across the board, including maximum autonomy just short of independence. On the national stage Pujól became a master at using his large Catalan minority in parliament to swing votes on important issues, collecting favors for his *patria chica* in the bargain. This tactic became more effective as UCD's slim majority shrank after the 1979 elections.

The hope among moderates was to diffuse the more pugnacious Basques and Catalans by granting various degrees of autonomy to all seventeen regions—each with its own president, legislature and court system. This plan produced a complicated mosaic of regional governments whose effectiveness was yet to be proven, each burdened with overlapping authority and loyalty. Among other things several regional languages were recognized as co-official with Castilian, and in recognition of ancient *fueros*, the Basque provinces and Navarre even gained control over tax revenues previously sent to Madrid.

By 1980 the post-Franco euphoria began to sour as people realized that "democracy" would not solve all of Spain's problems overnight. Although Sancho Panza's two families—the haves and have-nots—might grow closer, they would always exist. Poor farm-workers in Andalucía still clamored for *pan y tierra*, but their cries fell on the same deaf ears. (About 200,000 landless laborers lived in Andalucía.) It was clear that the country's *real* strongholds of power and wealth were not about to surrender their privileges. Many of the same faces remained in high positions ("old dogs with new collars" it was said), and people began to suspect that the political changes were more cosmetic than real. Streets and plazas were no longer named after civil war generals, but who held the *real* power in Spain? It was curious, for example, that Franco's security forces remained intact and unpunished, despite clear proof of police misconduct.

Democracy also seemed to bring a plateful of social problems—crime, drugs, pornography—that did not exist before or were swept under the rug. There was widespread grumbling among police as crime rates rocketed after thousands of common criminals were released along with political prisoners. By 1978 there were thirty muggings a day in tourist mecca Torremolinos, and robberies of Spanish pharmacies went from zero in 1974 to nearly two-thousand only five years later. The drug problem exploded and by 1980 Spain had an estimated eighty thousand heroin addicts. Some sixty percent of South America's cocaine now came into Europe through Madrid's Barajas Airport.

What was happening? According to some observers, many Spaniards hold a uniquely anarchistic definition of democracy that boils down to "everyone can do whatever they want," or, in short, "anything goes." Suddenly bewildered tourists could see and do things in Spain—from watching oral sex on stage to sitting topless at a beach-bar—that were unthinkable in far-older and relatively permissive democracies. Barcelona became the Hamburg of southern Europe, and one outrageous sex show was only broken up through the intervention of the Society for the Prevention of Cruelty to Animals. Spain was still managing to be "different."

Social change would bring a profound improvement in the status of Spanish women. For decades they had cowered under Article 57 of the civil code, which stated that a husband's approval (*permiso marital*) was required for virtually every decision or activity. This law was repealed, and divorce, contraception, and limited abortion became legal. Women began working at jobs that would have been out of reach twenty years earlier and *without* their husbands' permission. Slowly, the infamous Spanish *machismo* seemed to be retreating in the face of women's rights, but even in Spain centuries of tradition are not erased overnight. And the Catholic Church, despite its waning political clout, maintained a powerful social presence by opposing the new liberal laws. Conservative clergy added to a swelling chorus of discontent over the flurry of changes.

President Suárez, though brilliant during the early transition, proved a weak leader in the backbiting world of petty politics, and he watched helplessly as his cherished consensus eroded. Making matters worse, the economy was in dire straits with rising inflation and high unemployment rates. The year 1981 began with a political impasse and the resignation of Suárez. Then, during squabbling over a new government, the perennial question "After Franco, what?" received a perverse response.

On the evening of February 23, a band of gun-wielding civil guards, led by the mustachioed Colonel Antonio Tejero, invaded parliament and held deputies hostage for many tense hours. It was a complicated affair involving a handful of army brass, including the king's close advisor, General Armada. A former Blue Division commander named Jaime Milans del Bosch managed to lead tank units through the streets of Valencia, and certain civilian extremists such as Girón and the neo-fascist Fuerza Nueva also took part. It was the boldest *golpe* since General Pavía rode his horse up the steps of the Cortes building a century earlier.

Yet this was no laughing matter. For five years the generals had stood by sullenly as profound changes occurred in society. Many were unhappy over regional autonomy and legalization of the Communist Party, and by ETA's murderous campaign, which had recently claimed a top army commander. Now the military and *guardia civil*—albeit a tiny part of it—and the archconservative "Bunker" had finally spoken. That night Spain's fragile democracy hung in the balance. Fortunately the plot fizzled without bloodshed after Juan Carlos calmly rallied loyal generals and gave a stirring televised speech in which he told the rebels they would "only succeed over my dead body." The king's deep ties with the military had paid off, but privately he was warned that Spain was approaching the brink. The message was clear: Don't let democracy become anarchy.

In the coup's aftermath the ranks of *"juancarlistas"* swelled considerably as the nation finally realized its good fortune, and millions took to the streets in support of democracy. In Madrid, leaders of the four major parties led a parade with arms linked in solidarity.

Yet many Spaniards were profoundly embarrassed by the comic-opera spectacle played out on a worldwide stage (including the cover of *Time*). Perhaps the fatalistic view of Spanish history was right after all, as Salvador Madariaga claimed; that when it came to good government Spaniards suffered from a collective psychological failing. (It was curious as well that later many people accused Juan Carlos of secret complicity in the plot.)

After his heroic actions during the crisis of February 1981, King Juan Carlos became a hero to the Spanish people.

In the days following the coup, a stodgy and aloof centrist named Leopoldo Calvo Sotelo was elected prime minister. Political consensus returned amid fears of further right-wing plots, yet little of great consequence was accomplished during the next two years. A prolonged trial of Tejero and his cohorts riveted the nation's attention, while the press also focused on various scandals and a public health disaster (in which hundreds died) caused by the sale of tainted cooking oil.

Regional autonomy proceeded at a reduced pace, but Josép Tarradellas, who had signed the 1932 Catalan Statute, lived to put his name to a new one exactly fifty years later.

Everyone knew that the process of democratization would only be complete with the peaceful transition from one government to another, so the elections of 1982 were clearly a watershed. The 164 political parties of the first national election had boiled down to a handful of coalitions. In a vigorous national campaign Felipe González promised modernization and a *real* change ("*el cambio*") in Spain after several years of throat-clearing. His Socialists were favored to win, but for the seething right wing this would be the final betrayal of those who died to keep Spain from "going red." As the votes poured in on election night, the PSOE took 201 of 350 seats in parliament with twice the total votes as the nearest rival, the conservative Popular Alliance. The triumph included a complete sweep of Andalucía, whose huge block of delegates (twenty percent of the seats in parliament) held the key to political power in Spain. Suárez's UCD, the centrist coalition that carried democracy through its troubled honeymoon period, essentially collapsed. By the time Juan Carlos opened the new legislature, it was clear that the change from dictatorship to parliamentary monarchy had taken root.

When Felipe González moved into Moncloa Palace in December of 1982, he capped a stunning political rise. Yet he had pulled it off in seemingly effortless fashion, as if believing that fate had touched him on the shoulder. He was charismatic, but exuded a calmness that inspired confidence. He seemed a hardworking, straight-talking family man with a sense of duty and honor. Breaking with the elitist tradition in Spanish politics, Felipe was a man of the people, with an unassuming boyish quality that endeared him with friend and foe alike. He came from a humble background—his father herded livestock at a dairy farm—and grew up a working-class lad in Sevilla. There he earned a law degree and became a Socialist while a student during the 1960s. He was arrested on several occasions and used the code name "Isidoro" in his political activities.

By the early seventies González, barely more than thirty, was elected secretary general of the outlawed Socialist workers Party (PSOE) at a conference near Paris. Soon several top "Eurosocialists" befriended him. By all accounts a shrewd politician, Felipe struggled to nudge the party into the European social-democratic mainstream by ousting its radical Marxist wing. He wanted to jettison party dogma to win elections, and he succeeded in remarkably rapid fashion. In 1976 "Isidoro" was still dodging Spanish police, and only surfaced a year later when political parties were legalized. By 1982 the forty-year-old with mussed hair and rumpled suits was going by a different name: *señor presidente*.

The victory of Felipe González represented the triumph of a generation that came of age during the waning years of an obsolete political system. They witnessed the enormous gap between it and the realities and expectations of Spanish society. Virtually every member of the new ruling elite (with hardly a "worker" among them) belonged to this new generation and embodied the same spirit of *cambio*. Among them was González's colleague since law school, Alfonso Guerra, said to be the real political mastermind and Felipe's alter ego. While the president cultivated his statesmanlike image, his aide was sharpening the knives for political opponents. "Guerra's in the kitchen cooking up the meal and González is out front serving it to the public," remarked one observer in the press.

The Socialists had gained victory by rallying behind the banner of change, but ruling successfully might prove to be another matter. The "wonder kids" faced formidable problems: a sinking economy and foot-dragging bureaucracy; strong opposition from conservative Spain and the military establishment, wary of any threats to national sovereignty. Said noted historian Gabriel Jackson: "As González began it seemed almost like Azaña's challenge in 1931: the resistance of power centers; autonomy statutes; modernization of the military and bureaucracy; budget deficits and corruption in government. I think the Socialists found that everything was worse than they thought."

During these early years González walked a tightrope between competing interests with consummate skill, soothing the fears of the old guard and foreign investors while mollifying Socialist radicals eager for reform. He knew that social programs cost money and made creation of wealth—building up the floundering economy—the top priority. Bankers and businessmen could relax with the new regime. Indeed, nearly everyone seemed willing to give the likeable González a chance to make good.

After the botched coup of February 1981, it was clear that Spain's "spinal column" was still a factor in the equation. Therefore González's main challenge became clipping the military's wings in the political arena while keeping the top brass content in other ways. Franco's army had always looked inward—stationed outside Madrid and the provincial capitals—and slowly these units were moved away. González stressed that the PSOE was a *national* party as opposed to regional ones, which played well in the barracks. In fact, after the electoral landslide of 1982, which ended a period of divisiveness, there was a noticeable pause in army grumbling.

In truth, Franco's government had not been a *military* dictatorship; the generals did not hold power as such and the defense budget was small. It was said that Franco did not really trust other generals and that tanks were always short of fuel. By the seventies the army had grown desk bound and lethargic, with an aging and bloated officer corps; two-thirds of the military budget was spent on personnel, even though most career men were grossly underpaid. All this began to change under the Socialists, with hefty budget increases that stroked the army's pride with salary increases and modern equipment. Slowly the Spanish army began to resemble its European counterparts.

After some hesitation, González came to support Spain's entry into NATO as a step toward European integration. In doing so he was bucking a long-standing Spanish isolationism, which had kept the country sitting on the sidelines during Europe's wars for almost two centuries. Ironically, the president played the anti-American card to gain support for a national referendum on NATO (he sold it as a *European* alliance), and the long-time special relationship with Washington ended as American bases (with the exception of Rota) were shut down.

Spain hoped that NATO membership might even provide a solution for the nagging problem of Gibraltar, Britain's once-great colonial fortress. This was one issue on which 99 percent of Spaniards agreed. In 1969 Franco had sealed the border between the Rock and Spain, and the gates remained tightly locked for sixteen years. But it made little sense to have barbed wire between two NATO allies, and the border finally reopened in 1985 amid new talks. Over the next few years Gibraltar's economy boomed, and Spain remained adamant in its claims to sovereignty, charging that the Rock was a hotbed for money laundering and drug smuggling. Meanwhile Britain found itself awkwardly retaining a place that no longer served its interests.

Spain's curious role on the world stage began to change during the 1980s. Franco's "special relationship" with the Arabs shifted noticeably when Spain finally recognized Israel in 1986. Relations with Morocco remained cordial, largely due to a personal friendship between Juan Carlos and King Hassan, although some predicted future problems if Muslim fundamentalists ever gained power. (Hassan died in 1999 after several decades on the throne.) The

Spanish colonies of Ceuta and Melilla on the north Moroccan coast seemed a crisis waiting to happen. Yet optimists could note that talks continued about an underwater tunnel across the strait that would link Tangier and Tarifa and two historic enemies.

The English writer W.H. Auden had described Spain as "crudely soldered on to Europe," and clearly much work remained before the two would bond. González and the PSOE firmly believed that Spain's future success lay in its role in a democratic, prosperous Europe. Sounding like one-half of the Generation of '98, he pointed to Spain's historic isolationism as the source of its political and economic catastrophes. "If Spain is the problem, Europe is the solution," he remarked. In the beginning membership in the European Community (EC) had more political importance than economic. It was a long road to Brussels, beginning with the old Common Market's refusal to consider Franco's Spain in 1962. But just a few years later, a trade agreement with the EC proved crucial to Spain's economic recovery. With Franco gone and Spain politically in step with Western Europe, economic integration was nearly assured. Despite some opposition from French farmers, approval was gained for a phased-in entry beginning in 1986 with full membership by 1992.

Louis XIV of France once proposed a simple plan: "Let us sell merchandise to the Spanish and obtain from them gold and silver." Foreign investment largely built Spain's economic miracle, which laid the foundations of post-Franco society. But Spain was still an economic island, and the end of trade protectionism and other government handholding also meant more competition. Spaniards needed to restructure industry and improve productivity if they hoped to compete successfully with the likes of Germany and France and avoid the fate envisioned by the French king.

As Spain struggled to define itself in Europe, González had a plateful of challenges at home, not the least being hotheads of his own party who felt the workers were being betrayed. Indeed, Spanish Socialists had undergone such changes that Pablo Iglesias would no longer recognize the party he founded. Nicolás Redondo, leader of the Socialist labor unions (UGT), chided González for his bourgeois inclinations and threatened strikes and other action (he eventually quit in frustration). As other Eurosocialists, the PSOE had become a southern version of a modern welfare state. In response to critics the Socialists passed an ill-advised Worker's Statute in 1984 that laid down paternalistic and highly restrictive labor policies, which virtually guaranteed lifetime job security to employees. This acted as a disincentive to employers and investors alike, who feared rocketing labor costs. As a result, many companies simply stopped hiring and unemployment climbed well above twenty percent, far and away Europe's highest. By 1987 only twenty-seven of every one hundred Spaniards were officially working. However, some claimed the figures were misleading, and that many were working in an underground economy while collecting government benefits. Yet Spain's costly and rigid labor market, together with a weak entrepreneurial class and inefficient government bureaucracy, did not bode well for Spain's competitiveness. Clearly the economy had some painful adjustments to come.

Conservative critics still complained that things were "better" under Franco and bemoaned the explosion of drugs and common street crime, especially in Sevilla and tourist areas. ETA stepped up its campaign, including bombings in Madrid and the Costa del Sol in the summer of 1986. The government responded with tougher laws and more support for the special-forces, yet murders and kidnappings continued. It appeared that the government was losing the fight against terrorism when groups from the Middle East, the Islamic Jihad and Abu Nidal, began making Spain their operations base for attacks throughout the region. In one troubling turn, groups of off-duty police and military men formed anti-terrorist squads that made forays into France to root out ETA commandos in hiding.

As complaints of police abuse grew, some voices cried out for dissolution of the historic *guardia civil*, passionately hated by ETA but still revered by many Spaniards. Instead González chose to modernize the sixty-thousand-man paramilitary force. He named a civilian head for the first time in its history, an appointment that would cost the president dearly down the road. In a related matter, the plotters (mostly civil guards) of February 1981 were convicted by civilian courts and received stiff sentences. Many within the military, however, pressured throughout the decade for early release. (Colonel Tejero, the last of the men released, finally got out after fifteen years in jail.)

Yet by 1986 it was clear that things were generally working in the new Spain, despite some bumps in the road. The economy was showing good signs as inflation fell, productivity rose, and the huge budget deficit became a surplus. Under the Socialists democracy was firmly consolidated and the military modernized and removed from the shadows, a profound change in the larger historical context. Spain had proved to be a model of peaceful democratic reform and at long-last part of the European mainstream.

The year 1986 also marked the fiftieth anniversary of the Spanish Civil War and saw a mountain of new books and documentaries. There were calls for a final reconciliation, yet Spaniards on the whole appeared less interested than foreigners in remembering the past. The new generation seemed bored with the civil war and Franco as though only the present and future mattered. Surveys shows that young Spaniards rarely if ever read any printed medium (books, magazines, newspapers). Television, movies and later the internet occupied most of their time.

In response to these good times, voters gave the PSOE another landslide victory that summer. Running a distant second was the right-wing Coalición Populár, led by a former Franco minister, the temperamental and dogmatic Manuel Fraga. Once considered "liberal" among a gaggle of hardliners, he now seemed hopelessly out of date in preaching the virtues of a bygone era. Support for the PSOE was so great that some worried about Spain developing a one-party system akin to Mexico's ruling PRI, essentially a giant bureaucracy and election machine.

To be forty and a Socialist during the 1980s meant having Spain at your feet, as PSOE membership became a passport to advancement. Andalucía was a Socialist fiefdom with Sevilla its capital, and Spain itself was now run by *sevillanos*. It has been said that Spaniards tend to put off immediate action, believing that "everything will work out." This procrastination is followed by sudden bursts of impatience in which they try to accomplish everything at once. Such were the eighties.

The pragmatic and easy-going González (with his ruthless lieutenant Guerra) used charm and some arm-twisting to take on the bloated bureaucracy, the key to power since Felipe II. They launched major development programs in agriculture and tourism and rebuilt the infrastructure, especially the nation's crumbling road system. With the economy improving steadily, money began pouring into government coffers, and it seemed as if a new "golden age" had arrived. Many began looking ahead to the year 1992, when the eyes of the world would be on Spain.

Entry into the EC helped create these heady boom days as foreign money poured into the Spanish economy, which enjoyed the fastest growth rate in Europe. The end of trade barriers and government controls was like a breath of fresh air, and for several years Madrid's stock market was the most active and profitable in the world. But there was a down side. Imports flooded into the country and exports dropped, a textbook example of what happens to a protected economy when it enters the free market. By the decade's end international interests owned all six of Spain's car manufacturers; foreigners soon controlled eight of the top ten chemical companies; and multinationals moved in on a grand scale. Among other sectors, they swarmed into Cataluña and bought forty percent of the food and drink production, everything from biscuits to beer. The Spanish wine industry had over expanded and was ripe for takeover as well. Even the landed gentry of Jerez were giving way to a new world ruled by marketing men and "bean counters," epitomized by the sale of the famous Domecq sherry *bodegas* to a French conglomerate.

Spain's trade balance was partially saved by its huge currency reserves, largely due to foreign investors drawn by high interest rates and to tourism (in 1987 foreign tourists topped the fifty million figure and spent about $12 billion). But the government began facing deficits due to high unemployment and its free-spending social programs. Already a year after entry, Spaniards were grumbling about more taxation and higher prices on the basics of life—such as wine and cigarettes—clear signals that the European Community would not be a panacea.

Throughout the decade Spain's production system, faced with real foreign competition for the first time, underwent a crash "get-fit" course. In particular the Basque region, formerly the nation's economic powerhouse, was burdened with outdated "smokestack" industries—coal, steel, shipbuilding—that had fallen on hard times. Factories were in dire need of modernization if they hoped to remain competitive, yet foreign investors were wary of the region and its ongoing political problems. In 1975 Vizcaya was Spain's richest province per capita, while ten years later it had slipped to fourteenth position. On the other hand Cataluña, well placed to serve the huge European market, was reaping great benefits from EC membership. Some Catalans began speaking of a Europe of "regions" rather than nations and had their own lobby in Brussels. Indeed, all Spain was delighted with the huge amounts of cash available for roads, airports, and other public projects. The Fund for Regional Development dovetailed nicely with the country's new federal system, and many of the seventeen regions began to negotiate directly for their own pet projects.

No other nation seemed more enthusiastic over the idea of a united Europe than Spain. The nation's acceptance of foreign leadership reflected an intrinsic mistrust of Madrid and Spanish politicians generally; even the Cortes seemed willing to abrogate much responsibility to the EC. This romance with Europeanism was a complex affair revealing deeply ingrained national traits. For many Spaniards, including the influential prime minister, a united Europe seemed more important than Spain itself. González even proposed European citizenship, by which one could live, vote, or do military service in any member country. This concept would be unthinkable to most French, British or Germans. Yet González, perhaps with some of his Marxist instincts still intact, spoke of the "rhythms of history" as if nothing else mattered. With breathless optimism he predicted that EC membership, the final stamp of modernity, would produce such a leap forward that Spain would be unrecognizable by the year 2000.

That prophecy would prove an exaggeration, but Spanish society was in fact greatly transformed during the first two decades of democracy. The stampede from countryside to cities continued and gave Spain the highest percentage of apartment dwellers in Europe, who often lived in intensely urban surroundings. Conversely, rural areas became markedly under populated, with villages of the mountains and *meseta* literally deserted or left to aging *pensionistas*. In 1960, forty-one percent of the population was employed in agriculture, but by 1990 only fifteen percent remained. Those who lived in rural areas were still largely poor and illiterate, as if castoffs from society's mainstream. Even today travel through the Spanish countryside, with its abandoned towns and crumbling castles, harkens back to another age like nowhere else in Europe.

The new urbanized Spaniards seem delighted to wallow in the temptations of modern consumer society, from cell phones to Mercedes sedans (the dream of every Spaniard, it was said), as if trying to hoard those things denied them under the old regime. By 1990 Spaniards enjoyed a place among the world's highest disposable incomes and enjoyed longer life expectancies than Americans and Britons. Truly times had changed.

Spain has often been called a nation of extremes, and this seemed the case with the sexual revolution of the 1980s, described by Spaniards themselves as a "binge" or "debauch" (the Spanish word *desmadre*). Curbside vending machines sold condoms anonymously, and prostitutes named their specialty and price in the classified ad sections of the mainstream press. Gays and lesbians proclaimed their proclivities openly for the first time. Though contraception was widely available, abortion rates rocketed—one for every two live births, highest in the western world. The nation that once led Europe in birthrates now had just 1.5 children per family. Quite different from the glum and intolerant figures of history and lore, many Spaniards were "free spirits" whom Felipe II and Franco would have found incomprehensible.

Through it all Spain has remained nominally a religious country, with about eighty percent of the population identifying themselves as Catholic. Only one in five Spaniards attends church more than once or twice a year, but this figure was still higher than most countries, and forty percent of Spanish children attended church-affiliated schools. Even so, the Catholic Church had suffered a huge decline in size and influence since its heyday under General Franco. For example 78,000 priests resided in Spain in 1952 but fifty years later the number had fallen to only 18,500.

Something like London of the "swinging sixties" happened in Madrid around mid-decade, a social and cultural explosion deemed *la movida* (the happening). Suddenly the Spanish capital was the "in-spot" for hip cognoscenti worldwide, and *la movida* became the buzzword for a generation of *madrileños*. The phenomenon built on Madrid's traditional ebullience with a frenzy of new activities, from quasi-punk rock bands and flamenco-inspired *sevillanas* clubs to a public interest in the visual arts (contemporary painting and sculpture) that became—with an endless series of exhibitions—a kind of frenzy. A few Spanish contemporary artists such as Miguel Barceló and Antonio López gained international fame and approval.

As Spain opened up, high-achieving Spaniards in other fields, from golfers and motorcyclists to skiers and tennis players, gained worldwide recognition for the first time. The provincial quality of Spanish pop music, with its melodramatic ballads and aging stars, was transformed with the success of crooner Julio Iglesias, who recorded the first non-English record to sell a million copies internationally. During the 1980s flamenco guitarist Paco de Lucia collaborated successfully with top American musicians, and the next decade saw dancer Joaquin Cortés score success with an inventive fusion of flamenco and modern styles. Opera stars Plácido Domingo, José Carreras, and Monserrat Caballé became famous in Europe and America.

Yet on the whole critics noted a surprisingly sparse cultural flowering in the post-Franco years, and Spain was likened to a former athlete whose muscles had turned to flab after so many years of inactivity. Nevertheless, there were positive signs of an awakening. In 1977, a Spanish National Ballet Company was formed at long last, and a few years later a national theater created for staging Spain's abundance of classics. Unfortunately, nothing written in Spanish during the last fifty years was considered worth staging, and the biggest theatrical successes were productions of *Hair, Jesus Christ Superstar, Cats* and other foreign imports.

Spanish cinema showed greater promise with the emergence of several fine directors, such as Carlos Saura (*Deprisa, Deprisa* and *Carmen*) and José Luis Garci, who one an Oscar from Hollywood for best foreign language film, *Volver a Empezar* (1983). A younger generation included Pedro Almodovár and Fernando Trueba, who picked up an Oscar for *Belle Epoque* in 1992. In the 1990s Spain could even claim its first real international movie star in Antonio Banderas, a Málaga lad who stepped onto the world stage in *The Mambo Kings* and later performed alongside Hollywood's biggest stars with films such as *The Mask of Zorro*.

During the same years a literary tradition that defined itself by its opposition to Franco was struggling for a new identity. In the Hispanic literary world, Spanish poets (a movement called the *novismos*) were regarded as more important than the country's prose writers, but this began to change. Authors abandoned the social realism of the gray decades for new directions, as seen in works of novelists Juan Benet and Juan Marsé. By the 1990s writers Manuel Vazquez Montalban and Arturo Pérez Reverte were having their works translated into English. Camilo José Cela, previously little known outside Spain (even Graham Greene never heard of him), won the Nobel Prize for Literature in 1989. Although the honor recognized much earlier works (*The Family of Pascual Duarte* and *The Hive*) it elicited surprise and delight to those following Spain's burgeoning cultural rebirth.

By the late 1980s the nation as a whole continued to celebrate its success and prosperity, though troubling reports surfaced about corruption in high places, "the traffic of influences." In Spanish politics the concept of conflict of interest is something of a contradiction because public office and private business are not considered mutually exclusive. Many of the same PSOE officials who had promised an end to corruption eagerly engaged in stock market speculation, real estate deals, and even the sale of state property for private gain. This transformation from Marxist ideologues to high-rolling capitalists was embodied in the figure of Miguel Boyer, who preached austerity as economics minister, then resigned to hobnob with jetsetters and celebrities. Alfonso Guerra, who had made many enemies with his acerbic tongue, was tarnished by a scandal involving his brother and forced to resign.

The magic spell was broken. Though González himself did not appear involved, he showed a disturbing tolerance for corruption around him. Appearing in public dressed in impeccable suits and gold cufflinks, he was called power hungry and egocentric by the press (and in a best-selling book *The Ambition of Caesar*). Said Nicolás Redondo: "Power changed Felipe González completely." As the decade ended, the UGT led a national strike to protest government insensitivity and corruption.

There was an arrogance and complacency about the Socialist politicians that was especially unsettling coming from the party of *cambio*. The old Spanish practice of "favoritism" meant that loyalists to the PSOE were installed at all levels in a blatant attempt to monopolize power. The right *"enchufe"* would still make or break a career as it had always done in Spain. Nothing had really changed, it seemed, and already by 1990 it was clear that the ruling party had been in power too long. Yet the only opposition, the cen-

Felipe Gonzalez, socialist premier of the "new Spain" for fourteen years

ter-right Partido Popular (People's Party) led by young José María Aznar, was not yet strong enough to challenge the PSOE.

Spain's role in world affairs continued to change radically under the new democracy, as did its image abroad. Even the hispanophobic British press eased off a bit (though the Black Legend lived on in countless Fleet Street headlines). No longer would Spain to sit on its hands and watch world affairs as it had for so long. Despite strong domestic opposition, the government allowed former U.S. bases to be used as critical staging areas for the Gulf War of 1990, undoubtedly because it was waged under United Nations—rather than American—auspices. (Spain is among the ten largest contributors to the U.N.) Even Spanish naval forces, last used in the debacle of 1898, were deployed to the Gulf to assist in an international embargo. Then in 1991 Madrid served as site of important Middle East peace talks.

Spain re-emerged as an important diplomatic force in the Americas through its advisory and peacekeeping efforts in Nicaragua, El Salvador and Guatemala. It also played a role in the Balkan conflicts of the decade (NATO's leader during the Kosovo crisis was Spaniard Javier Solana). Now a stable and united Spain could lend a hand as Yugoslavia disintegrated into civil wars not unlike its own nightmare decades earlier. And a nation traditionally located on the fringes had clearly forsaken isolationism and taken its place in the new order. (Although a high percentage of the population rejected foreign involvement of any kind and were increasingly anti-American.) Spain's prestige abroad was at its highest level in hundreds of years as the magic year of 1992 began.

Clearly the nation was obsessed with showing its best face. Large-scale public works transformed highways and airports, and a new "bullet-train" between Sevilla and Madrid was launched. To commemorate the quincentennial of America's discovery, the city of Sevilla played host to a colossal international exposition built around the old Cartuja Monastery. After top-level bickering and dire predictions, Expo-92 was a hit. The same year Barcelona served as site of a highly successful Summer Olympic Games and used the occasion for extensive urban renewal. Not to be outdone, Madrid presented a non-stop series of events as self-proclaimed "Cultural Capital" of Europe.

At the end of 1992 Europe's single market would be in place—the Pyrenees breached forever. The year brought an end to the seven-year transitional phase into full EC membership, and Spain eagerly ratified the historic Maastricht Treaty, which took steps toward Europe's political as well as economic unification, including a security force to eventually replace NATO. With a common currency and central bank linking the economies, the next step would be transfer of sovereign powers to faceless EC bureaucrats. These developments would come as a shock to many. In 1995, for example, mandated reforms to Europe's wine industry, designed to slash production, included ripping up 340,000 hectares of Spanish vineyards. Some feared that one day these same "super bureaucrats" in Brussels could become more powerful than national leaders and parliaments.

In return for his staunch support for EC membership, González insisted on "cohesion," a vague word that meant the richer nations would help develop the poorer ones (including Spain). At the same time he demanded that Spain be considered among the top tier of members, a senior partner like

France and Germany rather than be lumped together with the likes of Portugal and Greece. This was problematic given Spain's basic economic weaknesses (inflation, unemployment, deficits), and the rest of the decade was spent trying to meet strict EC guidelines for joining its monetary union. As Eastern Europe opened up, Spain felt its influence begin to wane. Foreign investment moved on to sow virgin fields, and some Spaniards began to wonder if the country was wrong to bet everything on EC membership. Indeed, it almost seemed as if Spain was receding to the periphery again; that the balance of power was shifting from the Mediterranean to Eastern Europe.

As many times before calls rang out for renewed ties with Latin America based on common language and culture, and Spain seemed ideally placed to become a bridge with Europe. Investment grew significantly in the banking, telecommunications and electricity sectors, and as the new century arrived Spain had overtaken the United States as largest investor in the region. It was a special relationship that would cut both ways.

Among its other structural weaknesses Spain had a low level of ecological awareness. About one-quarter of the land suffered from serious erosion, yet an estimated five hundred million trees were cut down during the 1980s alone. The following decade brought a devastating series of droughts, forest fires, and torrential downpours that exacerbated the erosion problem. Industrial toxins were largely unchecked and flowed mainly to the sea. In a best-selling book, *The Silent Death*, author Joaquin Araujo estimated that two hundred thousand animals were being poisoned each year by pollutants.

The year 1992 marked a decade in power for González and the Socialists, far longer than any previous elected government in Spain. Though sullied by corruption and criticized for pandering to big business, the "boys from Sevilla" were still riding high. Indeed, there was good reason to celebrate. During the Socialists' tenure Spain shook off decades of isolation from the rest of Europe, a change of monumental importance. The demons of Spanish history had been laid to rest: obscurantist clerics and coup-happy generals were gone from the stage; fratricidal regionalism gave way to rational autonomy; even terrorism was on the wane as ETA failed to disrupt the year's widely covered public activities. In an historical context, all these developments in such a short time were truly astounding.

Some pundits predicted there would be a Spain *before* and a Spain *after* 1992, but as the year wound down some wondered if it would mark a beginning or and end. If the political and social transition had changed things forever, or if the nation would return to its slow-moving ways. Curiously, rather than presenting a new face, Spain's own pavilion at the Sevilla Expo contained a collection of old master paintings—hardly a future-looking gesture.

By 1992 a world economic crisis was having serious effects on the Spanish economy, and the miracle machine landed with a bump. There were clear signs that the long national *fiesta* was over at last: the Madrid stock market declined thirty percent in a year and foreign investment plummeted. The trade deficit ballooned to $30 billion as imports flooded in to fill the void left by stagnant domestic production. Ominously, this widening gap indicated just how much money the other EC countries were making out of Spain, not unlike the fate envisaged by Louis XIV. Economists glumly warned that the nation was living beyond its means and could no longer consume far more than it produced.

Spain needed desperately to create wealth, yet unemployment remained high with huge segments of the population standing by idly. Instead of the free soup of centuries past, many were receiving regular welfare checks. The government itself was going broke with plummeting revenues and burdensome social programs, a vast cradle-to-grave system modeled after its wealthier neighbors. In 1994, when public spending peaked at close to fifty percent of the GDP, about twelve million persons were employed and more than nine million received relief benefits. Attempts to rein in the public deficit by a freeze on spending met with stiff resistance, and the Socialists split into two feuding factions.

Facing the problem head on, the government focused on a key competitive weakness: the high cost of labor. Over the years the labor unions and paternalistic laws from the Franco era had priced Spain out of the market, and the Socialists decided to dismantle their own creation (the Workers Statute of 1984) before it was too late. Like two pugilists in a ring, slowly and warily the government and the unions were preparing for outright war. Nicolás Redondo described PSOE 's backing of anti-labor legislation as "a profound social counter revolution."

Realizing that a key base of support was slipping away, González promised real social change to pacify the working class. The master-politician from

Sevilla, with his chameleon-like instinct to adapt, proved he still had the right stuff by narrowly winning a fourth term in 1993. The Partido Popular (PP) came a close second and made important regional gains, and it was clear that Spain was developing a healthy two-party system. There would be an alternative to the Socialists after all.

In order to rule effectively, González was forced to rely on minority support from the Catalans and Basques, and he became involved in controversial horse-trading to pass legislation. This weakness underscored the Socialists' failure to resolve Spain's regional problems over the past decade. Inspired by political events in the Soviet Union and Eastern Europe, in which several new nations were born, nationalism resurfaced in Cataluña (six times richer than Lithuania) and the Basque provinces. This became mixed up with a kind of romantic idealism involving language and culture. Cataluña passed draconian laws to assure the dominance of its native tongue, and Catalán became the standard language used in all regional schools. Even Pujól's conservatives got involved in the rhetoric, but stopped short of calls for outright independence.

Regional autonomy had greatly swollen the ranks of Spanish bureaucracy. In just ten years (1982-1991) the number of civil servants working in the seventeen regional governments increased by twelve times to more than half a million. The Generalitat of Cataluña was almost a state within a state with tens of thousands of employees. Yet there was little decline in the national bureaucracy entrenched in these same areas; government employees and the public expenditure had merely doubled. This duplication of services could be mind-boggling: in some areas as many as four or five different police forces were operating, and at times they were even known to arrest each other.

Part of the endemic labor problem stemmed for society's attitudes toward work itself, still

Barcelona played host to the 1992 Summer Olympics and remained vibrant throughout the decade. The *sardana* is a traditional Catalan folk dance.

rooted in the days of imperial glory. It seemed that too many Spaniards dreamed of having a safe, paper-shuffling job in a government office—part of a huge army of unproductive civil servants. This affinity for cushy office jobs, according to surveys, reflected deep-seated attitudes of Spaniards, who regarded work as a necessary evil at best. (Thirty percent of Spaniards said they would not work if they didn't have to and only thirty-nine percent reported some job satisfaction.) This prevailing work ethic, together with lagging standards in education and research, compounded the problem of Spain's uncompetitive labor force. In order to compete in Europe of the next century these things needed to change.

Yet the European Community seemed part of the problem as it dished out millions in "structural funds" to ecstatic Spaniards. Since Brussels was now building Spain's highways and other projects, the Madrid government could afford to lavish its citizens with social benefits. Under the "Rural Employment Plan" entire villages were receiving some form of state aid, yet there was no corresponding economic growth. Andalucians were not getting any less poor relative to other Spaniards or Europeans generally. Said one critic of the Euro-bonanza: "Life involves a Goethean pact in which you take your benefits, twiddle your thumbs and spit at the sun. You certainly don't work in Europe. You just live off it."

With his narrow victory González was given one last shot at power. Through intelligence and dedication he had accomplished most of his goals over the past decade; Spain was no longer a fragile young democracy. Yet the youthful leader now seemed distant and prematurely old. Corruption was rampant everywhere, and the promise of "one hundred years of honesty" now seemed a cruel mockery. Both the opposition party and the press, particularly the daily *El Mundo*, were delighted by the spectacle and pounced on every chance to belittle the Socialists. Never elevated, the level of political debate continued to sink.

Cronyism and corruption were rampant in high places. The government reached a nadir when Luis Roldan, the first civilian head of the *guardia civil*, was caught stealing from secret funds used to pay informants and the widows of slain policemen. Roldan went into hiding as the nation jeered (he was eventually convicted and jailed). The glamorous director of the Bank of Spain (subject of countless fawning press articles) was locked up for financial malfeasance. Yet few offenders from the power elite were ever punished for corruption, and Spaniards became increasingly cynical.

In a nation with such a large underground economy, tax evasion and fraud became a national sport.

In some ways Spain after 1992 sank into a kind of post-party stupor, spent and exhausted for a few years after so much hoopla. And incapable of cleaning house; overall the courts and jury system were ineffective and little respected. Most politicians were viewed as a necessary evil, and one had to wonder if democracy itself was similarly regarded. As merely the fashionable form of government for a "modern" nation, but installed on shifting ground rather than firm bedrock. And if the "new" Spain had any true belief in its democratic institutions. The great Hispanicist Americo Castro once remarked that Spain was the only nation capable of verbally maintaining one idea while practicing entirely the opposite.

A few years earlier Spaniards had shown contempt for the political process by sending a disgraced tycoon named Ruiz Mateos to the European Parliament. The flamboyant tycoon had lost his huge company (RUMASA) to government expropriation in 1983 and was forced to flee Spain by hiding in the trunk of a car. A member of Herri Batasuna, ETA's political wing, was also elected to the same body. Though now officially part of Europe, Spain continued to be a distinctly idiosyncratic society.

One more scandal that nearly toppled the government involved the running sore called ETA. Suspicious links were shown between the interior ministry and a group of off-duty policemen thought responsible for numerous deaths of suspected terrorists. The former interior minister went to jail, but a narrow supreme court vote spared González—who had been implicated in the scandal—from direct interrogation. Felipe's famous luck held again.

By mid-decade it was clear that Spain needed a change, a passing of power through the ballot box. Leader of the opposition party was José María Aznar—small of stature, mild mannered, and rather colorless. He was a former tax collector from Valladolid and had played no role in the post-Franco transition. Thus he became the first national figure to come of age in post-Franco Spain. Above all he wanted the Partido Popular to finally shed lingering right-wing stigmas and capture the middle of the political spectrum. Slowly gaining supporters, Aznar's popularity soared after he survived an ETA bomb attack.

In 1995 Jordi Pujól declared that the Socialist government "lacked credibility" and formally withdrew vital Catalan support. Parliament returned a no-confidence vote, and González called early elections for March 1996. It was seventh time he would lead the PSOE in the general elections, but a last-ditch effort that included dire predictions about a return to "Fascism," fell just short. Aznar barely snatched a victory by winning a plurality just twenty seats short of a ruling majority; once again the prime minister needed regional parties to form a government. After two tortuous months of backroom dealing, Aznar was sworn in as premier. Twenty years after the *caudillo*'s death, conservatives were finally accepted as a legitimate political force. Now the transition was *really* over.

The new prime minister promised an austere program of spending cuts and financial reforms, "two years of sacrifice" to meet strict EC guidelines for joining the monetary union. Aznar's agenda included major reductions in the civil service and mass privatization of state-run companies. It was not the exciting fare served up by the boys from Sevilla, but the nation seemed ready for Aznar's honest, business-like style. It was time for a pause.

In 1997 the murder of a Basque official caused enormous national outrage, and it seemed that lingering support for ETA among Basques was finally fading. In the fall of 1998 a peace treaty was signed between the government and terrorist group, but a few months later one of ETA's top leaders was captured in Paris. Just fourteen months after the ceasefire, ETA returned to terrorism with the murders of police and politicians. Aznar refused to flinch and responded with even tougher measures that eventually led to the banning of the Herri Batasuna party, ETA's not-so-secret political front. Nor would he permit a referendum on "self-determination" as proposed by the Basque National Party (PNV), which had run the region since 1980. Clearly there was the danger of a victory for the independence vote, which would violate the constitution and possibly invoke military intervention, the last thing Spaniards wanted.

One prominent opponent of ETA terror, a crusading judge named Baltasar Garzón, emerged during the decade as Spain's most famous citizen. He was involved in several high-profile investigations involving drug cartels, terrorists, and police hit squads, then became an international celebrity by ordering the arrest of former Chilean dictator Agusto Pinochet.

Fortunately for the Aznar regime, Spain's economy bounced back and remained vibrant into the new century. Unemployment plummeted and productivity soared. Spaniards remained slightly poorer per capita than most of Western Europe, but they were making headway. Aznar and the PP won an absolute majority in the general elections of March 2000, ending the need for making side deals with the Catalans to pass legislation. (The old warhorse Jordi Pujól finally retired in 2003.) The Socialists seemed in disarray, and Aznar used the momentum to launch further economic reforms, including changes in the labor laws that sparked a general strike.

With its economic strides during the decade Spain formed part of the core group to launch the European Monetary Union and its multinational currency, the Euro. (On January 1, 2002, the Spanish *peseta* and other currencies ceased to exist.) Skirmishes with the EC invariably involved Spain's insistence on belonging to the top tier of powerful European nations, the same old dilemma that never seemed to go away.

The Gibraltar question continued to embitter relations with Great Britain. In 2002 the British foreign ministry revealed plans for joint sovereignty with Spain. Outraged Gibraltarians organized a referendum in which ninety-nine percent of voters opposed such a move. Henceforth, the British swore to abide by the principle of self-determination in Gibraltar's constitution and seemed to remove the possibility of ever abandoning the colony. However, in politics and history nothing lasts forever, and Gib's eventual fate remains uncertain.

The fragility of the environment was painfully reinforced with a horrific disaster in November of 2002, when an oil tanker broke up and sank off the coast of Galicia. The government was savagely criticized for its ponderous and inept reaction to the crisis, and the overly confident Aznar finally had to back peddle. Critics detected a growing arrogance and authoritarian streak in the Spanish premier.

At no time was this more evident than when Aznar ignored strong antiwar opinion (up to ninety percent in some polls) to join the United States and Britain in supporting a war with Iraq in 2003. Spain sent only about 1,500 troops and modest monetary support, but its posture shook up opinion throughout the Hispanic world. It seemed to some that Aznar had grandiose pretensions of making Spain an important player on the world stage once again.

Then the worst nightmare happened, as terrorists struck hard at Madrid's train system with several bombs, killing two hundred and injuring more than a thousand. The event occurred on March 11, 2004, just three days before the general election, and an angry electorate voted the Socialists into power for the first time in eight years. The new prime minister would be Jose Luis Rodriguez Zapatero. Authorities first suspected ETA, then arrested (and eventually convicted) several Moroccans as members of a Muslim terror network. However, in the minds of most Spaniards the train bombings were clearly a payback for Spain's role in the Iraq war.

With the new century Spain faced a number of challenges that continued to linger in that peculiarly Spanish way. Just when the Civil War seemed to have become the stuff of history books, the Law of Historical Memory mandated that local governments fund efforts to unearth mass graves (where tens of thousands of bodies supposedly lay) and make war era archives more accessible. The law formally condemned Franco's coup and dictatorship and demanded the removal of any remaining monuments, street signs or other reminders of the era. Clearly much bitterness remained below the surface.

The Socialists brought in a broad and aggressive agenda for liberal social reform, including nearly unrestricted abortion rights and same sex marriage. Naturally this outraged traditional Spain, and the powerful bishops conference called on Catholic voters to defend traditional values. Zapatero was livid at "church interference in politics," which became a divisive theme during the spring 2008 elections, as was the faltering economy (perhaps the weakest in Western Europe). Amid much political rancor Zapatero's party just managed to hold onto power and looked with some trepidation into the future.

Yet one can surely ask if Spain has really changed as much as the optimists contend. In truth, history unfolds over generations and centuries rather than a few years of frenzied activity. What would happen if the monarchy produced another Carlos II or Fernando VII? Or if a severe political or economic crisis created the emergence of another "savior" from the nation's "spinal column"? Recalling Santayana's words that "Those who cannot remember the past are condemned to repeat it," only time will tell if Spaniards have truly learned the lessons of their turbulent history. And if the Story of Spain will have a happy ending.

They Reigned in Spain

(Beginning with national unification)

Aragón and Castilla

Isabel I (of Castilla) and
Fernando V (of Aragón)
1479-1504

Philip I (the Fair)
and Juana (the Mad)
1504-1506

Regencies of Fernando
and Cardinal Cisneros
1506-1517

House of Habsburg

Carlos I (Emperor Charles V)
1517-1555

Felipe II
1555-1598

Felipe III
1598-1621

Felipe IV
1621-1665

Carlos II
1665-1700

House of Bourbon

Felipe V
1700-1746

Fernando VI
1746-1759

Carlos III
1759-1788

Carlos IV
1788-1808

(Pretender) Joseph Bonaparte
1808-1814

Fernando VII
1814-1833

Regency of Queen María Cristina
1833-1843

Isabel II
1843-1868

Revolutionary Period

Provisional Government
1868-1871

Amadeo I (of Savoy)
1871-1873

First Republic
1873-1874

House of Bourbon (restored)

Alfonso XII
1874-1885

Regency of Queen María Cristina
1885-1902

Alfonso XIII
1902-1931

Second Republic

1931-1939

General Francisco Franco

1939-1975

House of Bourbon (restored)

Juan Carlos I
1975-

Suggested Reading

General

The History of Spain, Louis Bertrand and Charles Petrie; MacMillan (1971)

Spain: The Root and the Flower, J. A. Crow; University of California Press (1985)

Spaniards In Their History, R. Menéndez-Pidal; W.W. Norton & Co. (1966)

Tree of Hate, Philip Powell; Basic Books (1971)

The Buried Mirror: Reflections on Spain and the New World, Carlos Fuentes, Houghton-Mifflin (1999)

Spain: A History, edited by Raymond Carr, Oxford University Press (2000)

Ancient & Medieval

Spain at the Dawn of History: Iberians, Phoenicians and Greeks, Richard Harrison; Thames & Hudson (1988)

The Romans in Spain, J.S. Richardson; Blackwell Publishers (2002)

The Making of Medieval Spain, G. Jackson; Harcourt, Brace, Jovanovich (1972)

A Short History of Islamic Spain, W. Watt and P. Cachia; Edinburgh University Press (1979)

Moorish Spain, Richard Fletcher; University of California Press (1993)

The Quest For El Cid, Richard Fletcher; Oxford University Press (1991)

Spain in the Middle Ages: From Frontier to Empire, 1000-1500, Angus MacKay, St. Martins Press (1977)

Early Modern

Isabel the Queen: Life and Times, Peggy K. Liss; Oxford University Press (1992)

The Golden Century of Spain, 1501-1621, R. Trevor-Davies; Harper Collins Publishers (2000)

The Mediterranean and the Mediterranean World in the Age of Philip II, Fernand Braudel; University of California Press (1996)

The Golden Age of Spain, 1516-1659, A. Domínguez Ortiz; Basic Books (1971)

Imperial Spain, 1469-1716, J.H. Elliot; Penguin USA (2003)

Empire: How Spain Became A World Power, Henry Kamen; Harper Collins Publishers (2003)

The Spanish Inquisition: A Historical Revision, Henry A. Kamen; Yale University Press (1998)

Seven Myths of the Spanish Conquest, Matthew Restall; Oxford University Press (2003)

Modern

The Eighteenth Century Revolution in Spain, Richard Herr, Princeton University Press (1958)

Bourbon Spain, 1700-1808, John Lynch, Blackwell Publishers (1994)

Spain, A Modern History, Salvador de Madariaga; Vintage/Ebury (1961)

The Spanish Bourbons, John Bergamini; G.P. Putnam's Sons (1974)

Goya, Robert Hughes; Knopf (2003)

Spain, 1808-1975, Raymond Carr; Oxford University Press (1982)

The Spanish Labyrinth, Gerald Brenan; Cambridge University Press (1990)

Homage To Catalonia, George Orwell; Harvest Books (1969)

The Spanish Republic and the Civil War, Gabriel Jackson; Princeton University Press (1987)

The Spanish Civil War, Hugh Thomas; Modern Library (2001)

Franco: A Biography, Paul Preston; Basic Books (1996)

Contemporary

Spain: Dictatorship To Democracy, R. Carr and J. P. Fusi; Unwin Hyman (1993)

The Transformation of Spain, David Gilmour; Quartet Books (1985)

The New Spaniards, John Hooper; Penguin USA (1995)

The New Spain, from Isolation to Influence, Kenneth Maxwell and Steven Spiegel; Council on Foreign Relations Press (1994)

Index

W

X-Y-Z

Sights & Sites Index

The Great Mosque at Córdoba

The famous Tajo at Ronda

Vera Cruz Chapel at Segovia, erected in
the 13th century by medieval knights.

Granada continues to celebrate the
Festival of the Reconquest by Isabel and
Fernando, each year on January 2.